The Prehistory of Egypt

From the First Egyptians to the First Pharaohs

Béatrix Midant-Reynes

Translated by Ian Shaw

Preface by Jean Leclant

Blackwell
Publishing

BLACKWELL PUBLISHING
350 Main Street, Malden, MA 02148-5020, USA
9600 Garsington Road, Oxford OX4 2DQ, UK
550 Swanston Street, Carlton, Victoria 3053, Australia

First published in French by Armand Colin Éditeur, Paris,
as *Préhistoire de L'Égypte* in 1992
First published in English by Blackwell Publishing Ltd in 2000

5   2006

Library of Congress Cataloging-in-Publication Data

Midant-Reynes, Béatrix.
    [Préhistoire de l'Égypte. English]
    The prehistory of Egypt from the first Egyptians to the first pharoahs / Béatrix
Midant-Reynes ; translated by Ian Shaw ; preface by Jean Leclant.
        p. cm.
    Includes bibliographical references and index.
    ISBN 0-631-20169-6 (hb) — ISBN 0-631-21787-8 (pb)
        1. Prehistoric peoples—Egypt. 2. Prehistoric peoples—Nile River Valley. 3.
    Pharoahs—History. 4. Egypt—Antiquities. 5. Nile River Valley—Antiquities. I.
    Title.
    GN855 .E3M53   2000
    932' .011—dc21   99-33594
                                                                          CIP

ISBN-13: 978-0-631-20169-4 (hb) — ISBN-13: 978-0-631-21787-9 (pb)

A catalogue record for this title is available from the British Library.

Set in 10½ on 12 pt Sabon
by Ace Filmsetting Ltd, Frome, Somerset

For further information on
Blackwell Publishing, visit our website:
www.blackwellpublishing.com

THE PREHISTORY OF EGYPT

This book is dedicated to all those whose affection and friendship have enabled it to be written.

Contents

Illustrations

CHARTS

MAPS

Preface

In the Nile valley, with all its monuments and great diversity of archaeological remains, the interest of prehistorians was somewhat slow to emerge.
The pharaonic period is so rich in antiquities of all kinds that for a long
time it may have seemed pointless – even sacrilegious – to seek out their
antecedents. Although it is difficult to work in the field of Egyptology
without taking into account the evidence from the Coptic period (i.e. the
Christian period, which followed more than three thousand years of
pharaonic civilization), it is far less common to encounter anything more
than a brief summary of the long millennia during which one of the first
great civilizations was emerging. Around the year 3000 BC, the Egyptian
state appears to have emerged – in an extremely rapid fashion and via a
series of sudden 'mutations' – complete with its pharaoh, its hieroglyphs,
and its distinctive social and economic system, all of which were subsequently to remain relatively unchanged.

As this book makes clear from the outset, there were still major doubts
being expressed concerning Egyptian prehistory when the first worked
flints were collected in the Theban high desert in 1869, half a century
after the impressive discoveries made by Jean-François Champollion.
These doubts continued to surface sporadically until as recently as the
1950s. We should therefore be grateful to Béatrix Midant-Reynes that
she has joined those pioneers who are developing a whole new area of
research: Egyptian prehistory. In order to cope with the special demands
of her chosen field, she has had to acquire the necessary knowledge and
technical ability to enable her to work both in prehistory and Egyptology. Having received her doctorate from the University of Paris, where
she studied various specialized courses and actively participated in
Egyptological and prehistoric research groups, she has also benefited from
her knowledge of German. She was at first invited to participate in the
excavations of the Belgian Mission of Louvain, and more recently was
invited to direct archaeological excavations at the Predynastic site of

Adaïma in Upper Egypt. I am also happy to say that she has lent her support to my research team at the Collège de France, thus extending our coverage back to the earliest periods of chronology.

The scientific significance of such research is extremely important. Whereas pharaonic civilization has long been studied in the perspective of the great civilizations of the Near East, we have only just begun to examine ancient Egypt from the point of view of its African context. Egypt is clearly located at the meeting-point between three different worlds: Mediterranean, African and Asiatic, and the Nile is an African river par excellence, originating in the great lakes of Uganda via the White Nile, and in the high mountains of Ethiopia via the Blue Nile. The middle section of its very long valley was bordered to the east by the vast Saharan desert, the climatic history of which has had a major impact on the definition of the pre- and proto-historic phases of the Nile valley.

If Egyptologists and Africanists are both to undertake their programmes of research, they must take account of one another's points of view. While debates and discoveries have proliferated in recent years, and some partial syntheses have been compiled, with various refinements, there is now a great need for an overall study of Egyptian prehistory (particularly in the French language, the last great work of this type being more than 40 years old now, see Massoulard 1949).

Midant-Reynes' field experience, wide research and close links with other prehistorians have enabled her to produce a book that will be both new to specialists and useful to a wide public. Starting with a discussion of the essential factors relating to the geographical context and the palaeoclimatic environment, she takes us from the Palaeolithic, through the various stages of 'neolithicization', to the Neolithic of the 5th millennium BC, in the form of the cultures of the Faiyum, Merimda Beni Salama, el-Omari (in southern Cairo), el-Tarif in the Theban region, and finally Nubia (as far as Khartoum) and the eastern Sahara (in the light of recent German and American expeditions).

The Badarian culture identified by English scholars in 1922–3, takes us to the brink of the Predynastic period, with its cemeteries spread over an area of more than 30 kilometres along the east bank of the Nile in Middle Egypt (Mostagedda and Hemamia) – this rich material bears witness to a complex and technically advanced society. A millennium later, the Predynastic cultures emerge, those in the north having been most recently investigated by German researchers (i.e. the Maadian and its variants), and those in the south comprising the Amratian (Naqada I) and the Gerzean (Naqada II), the relative and absolute chronologies of which have been refined by Werner Kaiser and Fekri Hassan.

During this period, the principal culture in Lower Nubia was the so-called A Group, which was identified by George Reisner in 1910 (his use of a simple alphabetic designation being an indication of the comparative obscurity of this phase), while further south, in the region of Khartoum, a late Neolithic culture was still in existence. Considering the uncertainties concerning links between Egypt and the other cultures of Africa, it is to be hoped that we will be able to find out more by examining the materials transported from one region to another, and indeed new factors are already emerging as a result of work currently being undertaken in the Sudan. Another major problem is the study of rock carvings, given that the surveys along the Nile and in the great wadis of Upper Egypt, Nubia and the Sudan have revealed a new offshoot of Saharan rock art. With regard to the cultures of hunter-gatherers and pastoralists, the emergence of a great mass of such rock art shows that there were cultural similarities stretching from the Red Sea to Mauritania, in some cases persisting throughout the pharaonic period itself.

With the two centuries between 3300 and 3100 BC we reach the first pharaohs, which raises the question of the unification of 'two countries', given that Egypt was known in the pharaonic period as the 'two lands'. We must consider the means by which this unification took place – was it a case of military conquest or peaceful integration? The theory of 'invaders from the east' seems nowadays to have been abandoned, while research at the sites of Hierakonpolis and Qustul provides evidence of powerful chiefs who ruled over parts of Egypt and Nubia even before the legendary King Menes, who is traditionally regarded as the first pharaoh. The recent excavations of German archaeologists in the necropolis of the earliest kings at Abydos have provided precious evidence of a so-called Dynasty 0.

Thus, some problems have certainly been solved but many uncertainties still remain. Future discoveries will undoubtedly produce as many questions as answers. This, however, is what we have come to expect from any scientific discipline, as it gradually evolves. Undoubtedly Egyptian prehistory will continue to fill us with fascination.

Jean Leclant, Emeritus Professor at the Collège de France and Permanent Secretary of the Académie des Inscriptions et Belles Lettres

Acknowledgements

I am most grateful to Claude Lechevalier, Professor of Geology at the University of Paris X-Nanterre, Francis Geus, Senior Lecturer at the Charles de Gaulle–Lille III University, and Pierre Vermeersch, Professor of Prehistory at the Catholic University of Leuven, all of whom have read certain parts of the manuscript and provided constructive criticism.

Translator's Note

Since a period of eight years has elapsed since the publication of the original French version of this book, the opportunity has been taken to update both the text and the bibliography in order to incorporate various archaeological discoveries that have taken place during the 1990s. This book is therefore not only a translation of the original but also effectively a revised edition, and the process of revision would of course not have been possible without the generous cooperation of the author. This translation also includes a glossary, providing definitions for the considerable number of technical terms that appear throughout the book some of these are Egyptological while others relate to geological phases or types of stone tools; for further information on the latter, readers can obtain more detailed information from such sources as *Préhistoire de la pierre taillée* by Jacques Tixier, Marie-Louise Inizan and Hélène Roche (Valbonne, 1980) and *Lithics* by William Andrefsky, Jr. (Cambridge, 1998).

Introduction*

In 1922, when Jean-François Champollion announced the decipherment of hieroglyphs with his famous 'letter to Monsieur Dacier', the new academic discipline of Egyptology came into being. Clearly the aims of the subject, in which monumental archaeology played an important role, were to remain closely linked to the reading of texts. In 1968, for instance, Serge Sauneron declared: 'More than any other ancient people, the Egyptians have produced a huge multiplicity of texts, therefore, whatever the importance of the strictly archaeological evidence uncovered up till now, the study and interpretation of Egyptian texts still forms the basis of most of the research that Egyptologists undertake.' (Sauneron 1968: 41). The study of events before the pharaohs still lies outside Egyptology proper. In fact, it was not until 47 years after Champollion's letter that it even began to be suspected that there might have been a Stone Age in the land of the Thutmosid and Ramessid rulers.

The diaries of E. Hamy and F. Lenormant, dated 30 October 1869, note the presence of numerous worked flints on the plateau of the Valley of the Kings (Biban el-Moluk) at Luxor, putting an end to the suggestions that there had been no Stone Age in Egypt. The following year, on the 20th of December, they drew up a list of the Stone Age surface remains which they had discovered between Elkab and Saqqara. Mariette reacted with some scepticism to these findings, pointing out that the Egyptians of the pharaonic period were known to work flint into tools. It is true that the working and use of stone tools continued until the Roman period, and in the late nineteenth century there were still definite doubts as to whether there had ever been any pre-pharaonic period.

Seventy-two years after the decipherment of hieroglyphs, when Flinders Petrie uncovered thousands of tombs in the Naqada cemetery, he was so

* This text was published in *Archéo-Nil* 0 (October, 1990) under the title: 'Prehistory and Egyptology: a century of prehistoric research in the Nile valley'.

startled by the unusual nature of the contents of these graves that he thought he had found evidence of a group of foreigners who had invaded Egypt at the end of the Old Kingdom, thus providing a possible explanation for the chaos of the First Intermediate Period. These bodies in the foetal position accompanied by red polished black-topped vessels, sometimes decorated with white motifs on a brown background (or vice versa), as well as a great variety of zoomorphic siltstone palettes, bone and ivory spoons, hairpins and combs, carved into unusual forms, all contributed to the overall effect of strangeness, and created confusion among the scholars who had spent nearly a century studying purely pharaonic remains.

It was Jacques De Morgan who was the first to recognize the traces of a prehistoric people. De Morgan's 'intuition' – as Petrie waspishly described it in *Prehistoric Egypt*[1] – was unerring, but the task of uncovering the prehistory of Egypt had barely begun. With his customary meticulousness and efficiency, Petrie set about the process of recreating a whole world that existed before the pharaohs. His excavation and analysis of the cemeteries of Naqada, Hu, Abadiya and Abydos allowed him to reach the same conclusion as De Morgan, but on the basis of scientific criteria rather than pure assumptions. In 1901 he produced his famous system of 'sequence dates', starting from the premise that the wavy-handled jars evolved from globular shapes with functional wavy-handles to more cylindrical shapes with purely decorative waves. Without the use of computers he employed a form of seriation to create a relative chronological framework consisting of 50 divisions. Thus, SD30 corresponded to the earliest Predynastic pottery, while SD79 was equated with the time of the 1st-Dynasty ruler Menes, towards the end of the fourth millennium BC (the only 'absolute date' to which the whole relative sequence was attached).

It is easy to imagine the potential flaws in such a system, and there has been no lack of criticism of it; for any object might have appeared before the particular ceramic type by which it was dated, or might have continued in use well after it. Alternatively, some objects derived from graves that contained either no ceramics or types of vessels that could not be classified according to Petrie's system. It might also be argued that this system was based only on Upper Egyptian funerary material and therefore could not be applied to the Predynastic sites that were later discovered in Lower Egypt. Nevertheless, even this flawed system was better than having no system at all, and, most importantly, for nearly a hundred years it was the only method available to prehistorians in Egypt – even to those who were its harshest critics.

---

1   '. . . by happy intuition, though without any definite proof, De Morgan treated the Naqadeh discoveries as being pre-dynastic' (Petrie 1920: 1).

Ironically, no sooner had Petrie left Naqada than De Morgan went there and found the 1st-Dynasty mastaba-tomb of Queen Neithhotep, in which vessels decorated with Petrie's 'degenerate' wave forms were found alongside Early Dynastic material, thus providing evidence which finally clinched the argument for Petrie's theories. It was at around this time, between 1876 and 1889, that Georg Schweinfurth, a German botanist and palaeontologist, travelled through the Nile valley and the surrounding deserts in search of material dating to the enigmatic Stone Age, which had begun to be recognized but was still poorly understood.

In the first few years of the twentieth century several impressive sites were uncovered, including Hierakonpolis (ancient Nekhen, the capital of prehistoric Upper Egypt, where the famous Narmer Palette was found, see Quibell and Green 1902), the Mahasna cemetery (Ayrton and Loat 1911) and the el-Gerza cemetery (5 kilometres northeast of the Meidum pyramid, near the Faiyum), which was the type-site of the Naqada II or 'Gerzean' culture, also providing evidence of its expansion northwards, towards the Delta (Petrie *et al.* 1912). Petrie's chronological system gradually absorbed these thousands of new graves. On the basis of the relative frequency of different pottery types, two main periods could be discerned: Naqada I (SD30–40) and Naqada II (SD41–60), the temporal gaps between each of the sequence dates being indeterminate. A third phase, stretching from SD61 to SD78, was later added; this period (Naqada III) was thought to correlate with the invasion of the Nile valley by a 'new race' from the East: the so-called Dynastic Race, ancestors of the pharaohs, whose early reigns corresponded to SD78–79. While the prepharaonic era of Egypt was being uncovered, the investigations of George Reisner (1910) and G. M. Firth (1912, 1927) in the Sudan, from 1907 onwards, were also revealing funerary assemblages that were similar to those of Predynastic Egypt.

By the beginning of the First World War evidence had emerged of a prehistoric period encompassing the whole of the Sudan-Egyptian Nile valley. In the post-war years there were many discoveries in this area of research: in the south, the Naqada culture was found to be preceded by the Badarian, and in the north, the earliest Egyptian Neolithic cultures were identified. Between 1922 and 1925, Guy Brunton excavated the Badari region, between Matmar and Hemamia, finding graves and assemblages that were similar to those of the Naqada period but which were also noticeably different. In particular, the red and black polished pottery, or black-topped red pottery, had characteristically undulating outer surfaces produced by dragging a bone or wooden comb across the clay before firing. Brunton instinctively dated this material to the period *before* SD30.

In 1924, a young Egyptian called Amin el-Omari was investigating the area beside Helwan (23 kilometres from Cairo), on the advice of Father Bovier-Lapierre, when he found the Neolithic site which is now known as el-Omari. Despite the early death of its discoverer, we know a fair amount about this site because Fernand Debono undertook three seasons of excavation there between 1943 and 1952, the results of which have only recently been published (Debono and Mortensen 1990).

From 1924 to 1926, Gertrude Caton-Thompson and the geologist Elinor Gardner discovered, on the northern banks of Lake Qarun, the Faiyum Neolithic cultures. In 1926, Hermann Junker, a German Egyptologist, uncovered the huge settlement of Merimda Beni Salama, covering several hectares, in the eastern Delta, about 50 kilometres from Cairo. In 1932, the excavations of O. Menghin and M. Amer in the Cairo suburb of Maadi revealed the remains of an important Predynastic settlement and two associated cemeteries, which appeared to be so unprecedented, especially in terms of links with the Near East and copper trading, that the term 'Maadian' was coined to describe them.

Faiyum, el-Omari, Merimda and Maadi are all sites or regions which are distinguished from the Upper Egyptian cultures both by the nature of the excavated material and by the fact that they incorporated settlements. The specific features include circular or oval houses, partly subterranean and with their walls coated in a mixture of mud and chopped straw (Merimda), important storage areas, sometimes lined with basketry (Faiyum), and sparsity of grave goods accompanying the deceased (Merimda and Maadi), all of which indicate the existence of a distinct northern-style sequence of Predynastic cultures, although there are great gaps both in Middle Egypt and the Delta. From a chronological point of view, the Faiyum, el-Omari and Merimda cultures, all of which were devoid of copper, seem to be the earliest, even earlier than the Badarian, in which metal is attested. Maadi, on the other hand, was part of the Chalcolithic era, contemporaneous with the Badarian and Naqada periods in Upper Egypt.

While the overall structure of the Predynastic was being worked out, researches into the earlier Stone Age were still continuing. In 1923, Edmond Vignard's analysis of material from the plain of Kom Ombo led to the definition of various lithic assemblages comprising an industry divided into three phases. The Sebilian industry evolved from Mousterian to microlithic, passing through a number of stages of development equivalent to the Mousterian, Aurignacian, Magdalenian, Solutrean, Azilian and Tardenoisian in prehistoric Europe. Vignard had in effect discovered Egypt's Upper and Middle Palaeolithic.

At about the same time, in 1925, Bovier-Lapierre's study of the gravel quarries of Abbasiya, near Cairo, enabled him to isolate and analyse an important stratified sequence of 'rolled' lithics deposited at the same time as the formation of ancient Nile terraces. The discovery of bifacial

Acheulean tools, which are among the earliest surviving human tools, provided the Nile valley with a Lower Palaeolithic phase and also indicated the essential role played by geology in the study of these very early periods. It was James Henry Breasted, then Director of the Oriental Institute at the University of Chicago, who organized the first prehistoric 'survey' of the Nile valley, along with the study of the ancient terraces. The geologist K. S. Sandford and the archaeologist W. J. Arkell were assigned to this task, eventually publishing, between 1929 and 1939, a four-volume synthesis of the Egyptian Palaeolithic.

By the outbreak of the Second World War, 42 years of fieldwork allowed the basic foundations of Egyptian prehistory to be laid, demonstrating the process of human development along the Nile, from the earliest working of stone to the emergence of the first pharaohs. However, in the 1930s the overall outline of early Egyptian history was mapped out on the basis of mythology and texts, and it is this image that has been perpetuated in the collective memory of Egyptologists, despite the archaeological evidence relating to an area of interpretation with which traditional Egyptologists – more used to dealing with texts – tend to be unfamiliar.

In 1930, Kurth Sethe's celebrated work, *Urgeschichte und älteste Religion der Ägypter*, used literary sources (particularly the Pyramid Texts and the nome lists) to support the theory that, around the last quarter of the fourth millennium, there was a powerful unified kingdom in the north of Egypt, with its capital at Heliopolis, which embarked on a war with a southern kingdom governed from Hierakonpolis. A first unified state emerged under the control of the Heliopolitan kingdom and dominated by the falcon-god Horus, while the south was ruled by Seth. According to this reconstruction, the myth of the conflict of Horus and Seth would therefore have emerged as a reflection of actual historical events. Then the south rebelled, once more splitting the country into two kingdoms, each with its own capital: Pe (Buto) in the north and Nekhen (Hierakonpolis) in the south, until the re-unification was achieved by an Upper Egyptian ruler called Menes.

In a work published in Leipzig in 1941, *Der Götterglaube im Alten Aegypten*, Hermann Kees refuted Sethe's hypotheses and proposed a different possibility, whereby there was no colonization of the south by the north, but the emergence of a powerful confederation of the southern nomes, united around the ruler of Hierakonpolis and leading eventually to the unification of the country as a whole.

Although Sethe himself had conscientiously drawn attention to the uncertain and sometimes audacious nature of his own theories, most Egyptologists accepted the truth of his reconstruction almost unreservedly. We should therefore not be surprised to find that in 1949 Émile Massoulard combined Sethe's version of events with aspects of the archaeological data in his synthesis of Egyptian prehistory: 'We can feel reasonably sure of the emergence of two early Predynastic kingdoms, one in Upper Egypt (the Amratian culture), where Seth was the main deity, and the other in the Delta (the Gerzean culture), worshipping Horus . . . The most powerful of the unified kingdoms was, it seems, created in the middle phase of the Predynastic period, after the king of Lower Egypt had conquered Upper Egypt, perhaps making his capital at Heliopolis. It was then that the Gerzean culture, which had until then been confined to the north, expanded southwards and took over the whole of Egypt' (Massoulard 1949: 512–13).

According to Massoulard, this Gerzean civilization was followed by a dazzling protodynastic state which not only extended throughout Egypt but also included part of Nubia. The state was created by Menes, a southern king from This who conquered the north. The nature of the final Predynastic phase was thought to derive from the invasion of Egypt by a group of Asiatics, the 'dynastic race' who were even given anthropological backing by Derry (1956).

In the years that followed, research into Egyptian prehistory continued in the form of fieldwork, which extended as far as Kharga, an oasis in the Western Desert, where Caton-Thompson (1952) found evidence of a prehistoric sequence stretching from the Acheulean to the Neolithic. In the Sudan, Arkell (1949) defined the Khartoum Mesolithic and Neolithic. The work of Élise Baumgartel (1955, 1960) formed the basis for the final syntheses of the subject before the important fresh advances of the 1960s. This new impetus was to derive primarily from the international rescue project for the monuments of Nubia which took place under the aegis of UNESCO. The urgency of the situation opened up the archaeology of the Nile valley to multidisciplinary approaches, drawing on the talents of many of the leading exponents of various fields at that time: engineers, technicians, architects, anthropologists, geologists and also archaeologists experienced in all of the expected types of remains. Among them were prehistorians, not only equipped with new practical techniques but also taking a new approach to the problems, sometimes creating new debate, and sometimes correcting or clarifying the image of the past conveyed by pre-war researchers.

By 1947, progress in physics and chemistry had allowed Libby to create an 'absolute' dating system, based on a radioactive isotope of carbon (^{14}C), which was first tested on Neolithic material from the Faiyum. Although this technique was by no means perfect and needed to be corrected with reference to the dendrochronological calibration curve, it allowed Nilotic prehistory to be fixed within a coherent framework, which notably facilitated the dating of different geological layers within which precious artefacts were located.

Since geology had been the basis of the work of Sandford and Arkell, it was also essential that this area of study should be re-examined by the new methods and approaches. It was part of the fundamental data for the prehistoric period, and therefore the obvious line of research to explore first. Aware of the lack of a proper basic study of Egyptian geology, Rushdi Said (1962, 1990) undertook this colossal task himself. The terraces that Sandford and Arkell had defined began to appear, in the light of Said's work, to be much more complex than they had at first seemed: rather than consisting of continuous stages they were much more fragmented, with no obvious correspondences between one section and another.

Finally, on the conceptual level, fieldwork became 'palaeoethnological', to use the term coined by André Leroi-Gourhan, a new area of research intended to examine human culture in its full complexity: ecological, economic, technological, social, religious etc. In this regard, the excavation techniques were borrowed from the so-called exact sciences, an exhaustive approach to the archaeological record now replaced the nineteenth-century tendency to select 'interesting' types of artefact. Nothing should be put to one side, and if total excavation was either impossible or unnecessary, a *sample* of the material should be made (the *representativeness* of which could be tested statistically). For prehistorians, these years represent the *age of typologies* whereby they calculated percentages of tools at one site and compared them with others.

Under the direction of Fred Wendorf, several international research teams set out, within the organization of the Dallas Combined Prehistoric Expedition, turning upside down the data relating to the Nubian and Egyptian Palaeolithic, displacing Vignard's Sebilian industry and bringing to light an explosive series of cultural developments that were peculiar to the Nile valley. Pursuing their researches in the eastern Sahara, where Caton-Thompson had tracked down a long cultural sequence, they discovered the earliest Neolithic remains in the region. In the long process of change that transformed the populations on the banks of the Nile into Neolithic settlements, the Sahara, more humid at the beginning of the Holocene, was identified as a potential focus point. With regard to the Predynastic period, the fieldwork of Fekri Hassan (1985) produced many more radiocarbon dates and gave this period the absolute chronological system that it needed.

Petrie's sequence dates, however, having survived a period of about 50 years relatively unchallenged, had already been subjected to 'assaults', in the form of Kaiser's so-called Stufen (Kaiser 1957). Critically reassessing Petrie's data, he analysed the horizontal patterning of the ceramic types in the well-documented cemetery at Armant (Mond and Myers 1937) and succeeded in defining an internal chronology for the Naqada period which was divided into three phases and eleven subdivisions, thus correcting and clarifying Petrie's system.

A fresh chronological framework had become available to a new kind of specialist – more prehistorian than Egyptologist. In the late 1960s, therefore, when Walter Fairservis and Michael Hoffman established a new programme of work at Hierakonpolis, they brought a multidisciplinary team capable of taking on the study of the Great Wadi at the site in its palaeoecological context, from the Palaeolithic through to the beginning of the pharaonic period.

In 1965, W. Hayes published an excellent work dealing with Egyptian prehistory, *Most ancient Egypt*, but it was written before the results of the UNESCO campaign had become available, therefore it was not until 1980 that Michael Hoffman's fine synthesis, *Egypt before the pharaohs*, provided a true summary of the advances achieved in the course of twenty years of intensive research and collaboration. The subject has continued to develop, and new teams have undertaken fieldwork during the 1980s and 1990s. New imperatives have arisen as a result of the increasingly intensive cultivation of the Nile valley along its entire length (including Sudan), thus threatening the total destruction of sites located at the edge of the alluvial plain. Modern prehistoric research in Egypt has necessarily become very much identified with the techniques of rescue excavation. Certain research priorities have been identified, especially the poorly known areas of Middle Egypt and the Delta.

Since 1980, as a result of the work achieved by Pierre Vermeersch and his team (the Belgian Middle Egypt Prehistoric Project), Lower and Middle Palaeolithic sites have been revealed and studied in their environmental context, while it has also become possible to clarify the different climatic phases prevailing at the time of the development of the earliest human cultures in the Nile valley. Vermeersch has found the two earliest Egyptians so far identified: the man at Nazlet Khater, excavated in the 1980s and dated to c.30,000 BP (Vermeersch *et al.* 1984), and the child at Taramsa Hill, near the temple of Hathor at Dendera, discovered in 1994 and dated to c.55,000 BP (Vermeersch *et al.* 1998).

In the uncertain territory of the Delta, efforts have concentrated on several sites: Merimda Beni Salama, where excavation resumed under the direction of Josef Eiwanger (1984); the great Naqada-period cemetery of Minshat Abu Omar, which was excavated by Dieter Wildung's team from the Ägyptische Sammlung at Munich (Kroeper and Wildung 1985); the crucial site of Buto (Tell el-Farain), where Thomas von der Way (1989) needed to use drainage pumps to gain access to the Predynastic strata beneath the level of the water table; and a site in the Faqus region where a mission from the University of Amsterdam, directed by Edwin van den Brink, located several successive phases of a settlement dating from the late Predynastic to the first few dynasties. These discoveries, as well as the recent work at Maadi by Italian and German archaeologists (Caneva *et al.* 1987; Rizkana and Seeher 1987, 1988, 1989), have helped to sketch out the framework of the cultures peculiar to the northern part of Egypt, producing an image of Delta prehistory that contradicts the previously accepted view that it was an uninhabited marsh land infested with mosquitoes.

In the Faiyum, the joint research undertaken by American, Italian, German and Polish teams has enabled the prehistory of the region to be integrated with the study of the palaeo-lakes, thus allowing the elaboration of a complex palaeoclimatic sequence (see Kozlowski 1983). In the Sudan, French, Italian and Polish expeditions have re-examined the areas excavated by Arkell, and extended the range of their investigations southwards (Geus 1984; Caneva 1983; Krzyzaniak 1984). In Upper Egypt, the French Institute have begun fresh excavations at the site of Adaïma, in the heartland of the Naqada culture, which was located and partially excavated in 1973 (Midant-Reynes *et al.* 1990). It is only necessary to glance at the section of the annual journal *Orientalia* in which Jean Leclant and Gisèle Clerc summarize current survey and excavation in the Sudan to see that prehistoric research accounts for a significant proportion of archaeological activity in the Nile valley. Finally, a series of international conferences, held at Poznan every four years since 1980, have brought together specialists in the prehistory of the Nile valley and North Africa to consider particular themes.

The above, therefore, is a basic summary of the course of Egyptian prehistoric studies over the last century. If we return to Serge Sauneron's definition of Egyptology in 1968 as a subject that was still essentially reliant on texts, then we may wonder whether the pre-pharaonic past is still nowadays regarded as a field of study outside the limits of the subject. Certainly, the increasing numbers of specialized publications may well be escaping the attentions of non-specialists, thus reducing the likelihood of change within Egyptology as a whole, or, more optimistically, they may actually be extending the familar scope of the Egyptologist, for the study of prehistoric Egypt is certainly a discipline in its own right. Studies that may initially have been regarded as pure prehistory have been 'Niloticized' as they move into the Neolithic, and Egyptologized as they approach the first dynasties. It is easy to see that this is a continuous process whereby the various phenomena are linked together, transferred and modified but rarely broken up.

The brilliant work of the German Egyptologist, Kaiser (1964), tells us something about the subject. Comparing all the earliest texts with the archaeological sources (each properly analysed and assessed), he reaches the conclusion that there was probably a process of political unification which took place before the time of Menes, under the rule of many small kinglets. This early political unification would correspond both with the cultural homogeneity of the Gerzean and with the appearance of an elite group of leaders, each described as a 'Horus', who are well-attested archaeologically and whose names were written in *serekh*s – these would have been the so-called Followers of Horus mentioned in the Palermo Stone.

The idea of a 'premature' unification is clearly not new, but, based on the recovery of archaeological and textual evidence, the analysis sweeps aside the reconstructions proposed by Sethe and Kees and necessitates some consideration of the idea of the 'two lands' which appeared in historical times.

More than any other ancient peoples, the Egyptians were firmly attached to the very soil of their valley. When they absorbed cultural phenomena, they reinvented them, infusing them with an originality that was almost a form of national genius. Their distinctive method of writing – invented in the Nile valley itself – was only one of these phenomena, and the long history of the valley is much more than just the history of the pharaonic period (although this is the principal subject of Egyptology and the most brilliant cultural phase). Whichever way we view it, the Nilotic adventure can be defined only in terms of the entire process of change.

Traditional Egyptologists now admit that most of the elements of pharaonic civilization derive ultimately from the distant prehistoric past, which we must therefore seek to understand more clearly. For their part, the prehistorians (with the exception, perhaps, of those studying the Palaeolithic) agree that it is not possible to study the Egyptian Neolithic cultures in the same way as other regions of this date precisely because they are pre-pharaonic, and also because the complex process of change amid scatterings of Neolithic data in the Nile valley (from the Tropic of Cancer to the Mediterranean) represents one of the more important stages in the development of humanity. It is by no means easy to understand this kind of process of cultural transition, and specific methods are required. Although scholars who pass back and forth between prehistory and Egyptology are treated well, the languages of the two disciplines are different. What common ground is there between the economic data of the Great Harris Papyrus, the deed of sale of a cow on a demotic ostracon, and the transition from the Qarunian to the Faiyum A culture? There is no more similarity between these three phenomena than between the Chaséen (a Neolithic phase in the south of France) and the La Chapelier law during the French revolution. We should beware of false problems, which can be caused by the rigidity of the words we use.

If there is one period that concerns both prehistorians and Egyptologists, it is the phase which lies at the chronological junction between the two disciplines: the 'protohistoric' period, which, in Egypt, is confused with pre-pharaonic times. As Lionel Balout (1955: 450) remarked, with regard to North Africa, 'Neolithic is a cultural condition, whereas 'protohistory' expresses a state of knowledge'. This is a subjective situation from which it is difficult to escape – by allowing the Egyptian Neolithic into what Balout describes as the 'antechamber of history', we end up with an undetermined period which is neither Neolithic nor pharaonic. If we consider Kaiser's ideas concerning the possibility that there was a political unification of the country prior to the agreed extent of the 1st Dynasty, then we can see the enormous variability of the borderline between prehistory and history, and we can appreciate why it is so difficult to recognize the signs when we find ourselves at this particular crossroads.

The study of the protohistory of Egypt is in fact a discipline in its own right, given that it draws on field techniques which are closer to prehistoric archaeology than to the study of monuments, and considering that it uncovers original material which must be studied without reference to later periods but which inevitably sheds a certain amount of light on them. No one has yet made a semiotic study of the designs on Predynastic vessels, which evidently provide expression for a complex mode of thought and a form of written language. Late Predynastic sculpture evidently lays the foundations for the great pharaonic styles, but it also hints at prehistoric preoccupations that have not always survived into the art of historical Egypt – in this world of continuity, there appear to be certain very basic ruptures between the Predynastic and the dynastic. How many of the images that emerged in the Predynastic had already exhausted their range of expression before they reached the threshold of history? Alternatively, how many of those images that carried on into the historical period became instilled with new symbolic meanings that they had not possessed in their more primitive versions? The universe of the 'protohistorian' of Egypt overlaps with those of the prehistorian and the Egyptologist, borrowing both their techniques and their mental approaches.

The uncovering of a tremendous process of historical change, the definition of research directions and priorities, and the emergence of a new type of researcher (neither prehistorian nor Egyptologist) – these are some of the results of less than a century of prehistoric investigations in the Nile valley.

Part I

The Land of Egypt

1

Between the River and the Desert

The desert dominates Egypt, constituting perhaps the greatest influence over the land as a whole. Jacques Besançon, *L'homme et le Nil*

The northeastern section of the African continent, between 24° and 31° latitude, is part of a series of deserts stretching for almost 1000 kilometres from the Atlantic end of the Sahara to the salt lakes of northern India. In these arid regions the climatic phases of the Quaternary period played an unusually important role in determining life, death and prospects for the human groups who lived there. If the Nilotic cultures were to emerge successfully, it was essential that the desert should be able to support life during those periods when the Nile valley was less hospitable.

The growth and prosperity of pharaonic civilization were both directly dependent on the emergence, climatic development and colonization of three large geographical zones: firstly, the Nile and its flood-plain, comprising a long corridor stretching down into Africa; secondly, the Eastern Desert and the Sinai peninsula, at least one of which had to be traversed in order to reach the great civilizations of western Asia; and finally the Western Desert, a link with the Sahara of the first hunters. The presence of these three zones placed Egypt at a cultural crossroads from the outset.

The Nile Valley: from the Rift Valley to the Terraces

The Nile valley as we know it today (or rather as it has been familiar to us since the time of the pharaohs) is a very long river; at 6670 km, it is one of the longest in the world, described by Herodotus as 'the opposite of other rivers, in that it flows most abundantly in summer and diminishes in the winter'. Although partly Saharan, the system of Nile floods is effectively dependent on the rains of equatorial and central Africa. When the Egyptians made contact with the land of Nubia, they often went up beyond the First Nile Cataract, and the search for the sources of the Nile had occupied the time and mental energy of humanity since ancient times (Mazuel 1935). It was, however, not until 13 August, 1858, that an English explorer called John Speke, who was travelling in central eastern Africa, discovered a great lake which he called Victoria. In 1860, on his second visit to the area, he followed a river that flowed out of the lake, eventually reaching the Egyptian post of Dufilé. His subsequent telegram, almost as famous as the letter from Champollion to Dacier, announced: 'The Nile is settled'.

Emerging from the high plains of the Great Lakes, enlarged by the summer rains, which expand the waters of its tributaries in Sudan (Bahr el-Gebel and Bahr el-Ghazal) and Ethiopia (Sobat, Blue Nile and Atbara), the Nile passes through 2500 kilometres of total desert, before fanning out into a large delta and disappearing into the Mediterranean, thus splitting Egypt into two morphologically distinct regions: to the east, desert plateaus intersected by valleys and ravines, and to the west, a vast peneplain dimpled by depressions. Herodotus distinguished these two areas in terms of their populations, calling them, respectively, the 'Arabian' and 'Libyan' deserts.

The Nile valley was therefore not only part of the east African equatorial forest, but also the Sudanese savanna and the Sudano-Egyptian deserts. As well as this climatic diversity, there was also a complicated topographical and geological sequence. Generally speaking, the substratum of Egypt and neighbouring regions comprised a schisti-crystalline peneplain that formed over a long period during the Palaeozoic age. On this pre-Cambrian crystalline peneplain there formed, in the south, Nubian sandstone, a detritic deposit of continental origin, and, from Esna northwards, limestones deposited by deep seas following the Cretaceous transgression. In the course of the Tertiary age, when the Eocene sea receded, there appeared a primeval Nile (Blanckenhorn's *Ur-Nil*), which has long been considered to be the ancestor of the modern Nile, but flowing further to the west, in the Libyan desert (Said 1975).

The modern course of the Nile valley corresponds to the tectonic movements that took place at the beginning of the Pliocene, some five million years ago, most probably constituting one of the branches of the great African rifts that stretch out towards the Red Sea. Thus the river first appears as a series of interlinked lakes, which, according to some, are interdependent, but according to others are separate from the Ethiopian section. The absolute age of this very unusual hydrographic system is a source of some controversy. Certain writers (de Heinzelin de Braucourt and Paepe 1965; Butzer and Hansen 1968) consider that, during the first phase of its history, the main floods derived from the discharge of wadis supplied by local palaeoclimates. An important modification took place in the late Pleistocene (about 50,000 years ago), when the waters of the Sudanese basin were captured, judging from the deposits of silts and marls left by the floods of the Blue Nile and the Atbara. According to others (Maley 1969; Williams and Adamson 1982), there was already communication with Ethiopia from the beginning of the Quaternary period onwards, or even during the Tertiary, judging from the similarities between pollens and microfauna in Ethiopia and those deposited below the waters of the Nile Delta.

During the first two million years of the Pleistocene, the geomorphological processes controlling the evolution of the valley were themselves dependent on climatic fluctuations of a periodic nature. These fluctuations were expressed by such phenomena as erosion and deposition of alluvium. This process of successive transportation, deposition and erosion of alluvia in these sediments, while they were still not consolidated, had the effect of creating terraces of gravel and nodules. The connections between the phases of these terraces and the occurrences of human industries were revealed by the work of Sandford and Arkell in 1929–39. In fact, it was only fragments of terraces that were discovered, since each readjustment connected with the new climatic conditions brought about the partial erosion of the contours and earlier deposits. The terraces of tributary wadis correspond with these Nile terraces, which formed, according to Sandford and Arkell, as readjustments of the river in response to the eustatic fluctuations of sea level.

Research over the last 30 years has served to demonstrate the complexity of this process of terrace formation, whereby deposits accumulated in various ways, mixing together, intersecting, dividing and combining, and it appears that the earliest terraces, located north of Asyut, are not directly linked with those of Upper Egypt. The conclusions reached by Sandford and Arkell may still be valid in principle, but the processes that influenced the formation of these terrace-levels are now known to be much more complicated, with the cycles of sedimentation and erosion being augmented by climatic fluctuations that have led to significant aggradation and degradation at a regional level. In addition, the base level of the erosion was frequently modified near the coastline, as a result of the eustatic variations in the Mediterranean. This phenomenon of intense denudation of the Pleistocene series has led geologists to make a study by section, accompanied by attempts to make fairly difficult links. The detailed geological and geomorphological analyses of local sequences (essentially by means of granulometry, mineralogy and palynology), have both revealed processes of pedimentation and facilitated the identification of lithological entities known as 'formations', each of which has been named after the town or region where it was first discovered. Thus Sandford and Arkell's 'terraces' have been replaced by the Dakka, Korosko, Dendera and Qena formations (to name only a few), each corresponding to phases in the accumulation of gravels in the wadis or Ethiopian silts; their chronostratigraphy is linked to the study of the human industries that they contain, and has expanded our knowledge of the prehistoric period, particularly the earliest phases.

At a distance of about 23 kilometres north of Cairo, when the Nile has finally begun to slow down after a journey of 2500 kilometres through the desert, it divides into two branches that then meander gradually through the Delta: the western branch reaches the Mediterranean at Rosetta, while the eastern one ends at Damietta.

The fertile soil of the Delta, comprising clay and silt mixed with sands brought from the volcanic plains of Ethiopia, has produced a region of meadows and cultivated land concentrated in an area of 22,000 km^2, which accounts for 63 per cent of the habitable surface of the country as a whole. This hunting ground of the pharaohs, described by Jean Yoyotte and P. Chuvin (1983) as 'an African Sologne created by the Nile, under Mediterranean skies', is a fertile triangle marked in many different ways by the traces of river branches and fossil canals that have been silted up since ancient times. In the fourth century BC, Herodotus identified five branches, with the Canopic branch furthest to the west and the Pelusiac furthest to the east. In the first century AD, Strabo noted seven branches, as did Ptolemy a century later. The numbers and the names may vary from one author to the other, but the fact remains that the Egyptians have continually struggled to prevent the canals from silting up, thus creating a dense network of rivers throughout the Delta.

Two geomorphological regions can be distinguished: firstly, to the south of a fault line stretching southwestwards from Lake Manzala to the centre of the Wadi Natrun, there are the 'turtle-backs' (yellow islets of sand, each between one and twelve metres above the surrounding cultivated land), which may be the remains of ancient silted-up Nile branches. The sediment in this zone is thick and not very homogeneous, containing alluvial silt that has passed through gravel banks. The second geomorphological area is to the north, comprising a fine homogeneous sediment down a gentle slope towards the great coastal lakes along the edge of the Mediterranean. From Alexandria to Port Said, the Mariot, Edku, Borollos and Manzala lakes (the two latter opening out onto the Mediterranean) comprise a hinterland of ponds, lagoons and marshland. It is in the lower Delta that the papyrus plants once flourished, and it is there that the legendary Chemnis floats somewhere, like islands of reeds.

About 80 kilometres southwest of Cairo, the Faiyum semi-oasis is similar to the depressions in the Western Desert, but its natural connection with the Nile and the fact that its soil is made up of alluvial silts both mean that it is usually included within the general area of the Nile valley. At about the level of the town of Dairut, the Bahr Yusef emerges from the Nile, following the course of an ancient Nile branch and zigzagging up to a large plain to the east of the Faiyum, veering towards the latter, which it enters via the Hawara canal. From this point onwards, the Bahr Yusef is lost in a large number of branches and canals that irrigate the entire surface of the depression without ever reaching Lake Qarun (Herodotus' Moeris), occupying the lowest part of the region, to the north-west, 44 metres above sea level.

Since the earliest studies of the Faiyum (Beadnell 1905), opinions have differed as to the origins of the depression itself: tectonic deformation, fluvial erosion and deflation have all been put forward as possibilities at different times. There is a tendency nowadays to consider the Faiyum to be like the oases of the Western Desert, assuming that the variability in the hardness of the rocks facing the erosion is reponsible for the forma-tion of this enormous depression covering 1700 km^2, carved out of the Eocene and Oligocene strata, closed off to the north by an abrupt escarp-ment, and overall sloping gently southwards.

Before it became a depression, the Faiyum had been the delta of an earlier version of the Nile, the evidence for which takes the form of fluvio-marine deltaic deposits in the northern part of the region. It was also in this part of the region, in the Oligocene levels dating to 25–30 million years BP, that fossils of small primates were found (Oligopithecus, Aelopithecus, Aegyptopithecus, Propliopithecus); these were distant an-cestors of the modern 'great apes', precious links in the evolutionary chain of the hominids. After this period, volcanic phenomena resulting from the driving in of the African tectonic plate brought about the formation of the basalt which covers the escarpment to the north of the Faiyum. In the Quaternary period, terraces of gravel and nodules mixed with ar-chaeological material attest to a long hydrological history, along with the rest of the Nile.

When Herodotus saw Lake Moeris, which he believed to have been 'dug out by human agency', it filled up almost the entire depression and was dependent on the Nile, which fed it via the Bahr Yusef. Indeed, four lakes followed one another in succession, brought to light by the studies of Caton-Thompson and Gardner (1934), Sandford and Arkell (1929), Ball (1939), and, most recently, Wendorf and Schild (1976). It is the two latter scholars who have produced a reconstruction of events on the basis of the results of their expeditions in the 1970s:

● A palaeo-Moeris, defined by the earliest deposits, dating to c.7000 BC, was situated at a difficult level to clarify, but which seems to have been more than 16 metres above sea level.

- After a rapid collapse, a new lake, the pre-Moeris, was created in *c*.6000 BC, at a height of 15–17 metres.
- A short period of shrinkage ensued, then the proto-Moeris filled up the basin again, a millennium later, but this time reaching a level of 24 metres above sea level, which has never been surpassed.
- By the end of the 5th millennium, the lake seems to have undergone an enormous reduction which it is difficult to follow or define precisely. When, in *c*.4000–3500 BC, the first Predynastic communities were established along the shores of Lake Moeris which was about 12 metres above sea level, the waters gradually – slowly but surely – rose up, reaching about 23 metres at the end of the Old Kingdom (*c*.2200 BC).

From then onwards, the building works were undertaken by the 12th-Dynasty rulers (*c*.1785–1680 BC), then, in the first century AD, Ptolemy's erection of the Illahun barrage, which was intended to recover alluvium for the agricultural land, severed the link between the lake and the Nile, and once deprived of this supply the level of the waters sank rapidly down to the modern height.

The Eastern Desert: high mountains and 'miraculous rains'

The Eastern Desert and the Sinai peninsula make up a single geomorphological entity comprising alternate zones: high massifs of igneous and metamorphic rocks formed from the pre-carboniferous base and sedimentary plateaus. A large number of wadis pass through the desert, their deep valleys, draining off towards the Gulf of Suez and Aqaba in Sinai, between the Nile and the Red Sea in the Eastern Desert. These massifs, their peaks reaching a height of 2000 metres, gradually widen as they run from a latitude of 29° north down to the level of the Sudan. In Sinai, the massifs form the nucleus of the peninsula, culminating in St Catherine's mountain at 2641 metres. They can also be found, at a more modest altitude, in the Uweinat Oasis, down in the southwestern corner of the country, as well as at several other places in the Western Desert, and it is from these ancient rocks that the Nubian sandstone has emerged most recently. These rocks relate to the most distant past of the land: gneiss, schists and granites, the formation of which was linked to the orogenesis (process of mountain building) that led to the folding up and regional metamorphism of these sediments. A period of volcanic activity was responsible for the formation of diorites and porphyries, while the greywackes and carbonated rocks (the characteristic formations of the

Wadi Hamammat) were deposited in thick beds in the depressions.

The marine transgression that affected most of Egypt during the Upper Cretaceous period, about 90–95 million years ago, was represented by sandstone/quartzitic formations of varied colours, which were well developed in Nubia and are therefore known as 'Nubian sandstone'. This sandstone takes up the whole of the western half of the region, from the 25° 30' line down to the 23° 05' line, lava and tuffs are to be found within the base sediment.

Because of the mountainous nature of the Eastern Desert, an upraised landscape, dissected and dominated by black schists, it was characterized by more humid atmospheric conditions, which facilitated seasonal activity in the wadis and erratically replenished wells. In about 2000 BC, a graffito in the Wadi Hammamat describes the way in which a sudden shower indicated the presence of subterranean water and revealed a hitherto unknown well.

The Western Desert: the flat land of the oases

On the other side of the Nile valley, the Western Desert differs from the Eastern in its flatness, its golden appearance and its aridity. It is a vast limestone plateau gradually rising to 500 metres above sea level towards its southern end, which is the point where it meets another plateau, consisting of Nubian sandstone, overlooking both the high massifs of Gebel Uweinat further to the southwest (only the northern flanks of which are within Egypt) and the plateau of Gilf Kebir, which reaches a peak of 1000 metres above sea level. Covering nearly 681,000 km², this vast eroded surface, which carries on westwards, beyond the artifical boundaries of Egypt, constitutes two-thirds of the entire country.

The presence of large depressions, transformed into oases by artesian springs, not only gave the Western Desert a unique geomorphological appearance but also facilitated human migrations, opening up the valley to the great Saharan spaces. From the southeast to the northwest, the oases of Kharga, Dakhla, Farafra, Bahariya, Siwa and Qattara served as relay-stations along a route which has still not become desertified. Practically all of these depressions are marked, like the Faiyum, by an escarpment to the north and a floor which descended gently southwards until it reached the same level as the surrounding desert. These escarpments were created out of a hard limestone, which was more resistant to erosion than the adjacent marls and schists. According to Said, it was the combined effect of erosion and the thickening of the limestone stratum that created the depressions, rather than any tectonic activity. He suggests that it was in the zones where the limestone layers had not thickened much (and therefore offered less resistance to the wind) that these subsidences took place.

Apart from the artesian springs, to which the oases owed their existence, there is an almost total absence of water. There is no rain and little drainage; the only wells are at the edges of the Mediterranean coast and the massifs of the Gebel Uweinat. Aridity is the principal characteristic of this region; it is responsible for the formation of the dunes, stretching in a south-southeasterly direction for nearly 450 kilometres from Bahariya to Kharga, and giving a 'sea of sand' allure to this otherwise stony desert.

Part II

The Palaeolithic Period

2

The earliest evidence for humans in the Nile valley

It is difficult to pinpoint precisely when human beings first appeared in the Nile valley. Some prehistorians, such as Biberson, Coque and Debono, have suggested that the earliest cultural phase of all – the Oldowan – is attested by stone tools deeply embedded in the geological stratigraphy of the Theban massif and apparently exposed by an excavation undertaken in 1975. However, other scholars (including Paulissen, Vermeersch and Wendorf), argue that the identifications of these tools are by no means certain, given that we currently only have the published drawings rather than the tools themselves.

The presence of the Oldowan may be a matter of debate, but the Acheulean cultural phase, comprising bifacial tools and flakes dating to *c.*300,000 BP, at the beginning of the Pleistocene period, is unequivocally in evidence at a number of sites in the valley, from Cairo down to Khartoum. Acheulean assemblages have been found in Butzer and Hansen's Dakka and Korosko formations (i.e. Said's Abassid gravels), geologically *in situ* but archaeologically unprovenanced. The term 'Acheulean', which Mortillet coined in 1872 to describe the bifacial industries of the Somme valley, was redefined by François Bordes for western Europe and by Mary Leakey for central and eastern Africa. It actually describes a technological stage at which bifacial lithics began to be produced, alongside the (more or less frequent and more or less specialized) production of flaked tools.

Among the techniques for the production of flaked tools, the Levallois knapping techniques represent a turning point. The core was prepared in such a way that several flakes of a required type could be obtained from it. The presence or absence of these flakes, and their varying quantities, enabled different aspects of bifacial industries to be distinguished. These techniques, which had appeared in earlier periods, were fully developed by the Middle Palaeolithic. The classic Levallois knapping technique consisted of the preparation of a platform from which were struck centripetal flakes covering one whole face of the core. From a prepared surface of this type it was possible to strike off – ideally with one blow – a so-called Levallois flake.

Few studies have so far been made into this long period in Egypt. The site of Nag Ahmed el-Kalif, near Abydos, was excavated by Vermeersch, but it is in Sudan that the most productive research has been undertaken. The site of Arkin 8, studied by the Polish archaeologist Chmielewski, and those at Wadi Halfa, analysed by J. and G. Guichard, are the best studied examples of the earliest human occupation in the region.

On the left bank of the Nile, less than 50 kilometres from Wadi Halfa, Arkin 8 was perched 51 metres above the flood plain. A series of eight concentrations occupy an area of 40 × 80 metres stratigraphically sand-wiched between the Nubian sandstone (immediately below them) and a 20- to 30-centimetre thick sandy wadi layer. A total of 3407 artefacts were recovered and analysed; 76 per cent of these were fashioned from quartz, and the rest from ferruginous sandstone, both of these being lo-cal rocks. Generally speaking, the Arkin 8 assemblage comprises a peb-ble industry: 'chopper' tools, discs and half-discs, spherical polyhedra (globular cores), and very few retouched tools from which the Levallois technique was totally absent. The eight distinct concentrations, which make up only part of the site, appear to have moved over time, as if they corresponded to a series of temporary encampments. This hypothesis may well be supported by the presence of sandstone blocks enclosing a semi-circular area in which there is a high density of artefacts – this may be one of the first human structures attested in the Nile valley, and the inhabitants of Arkin 8 certainly belong to one of the earliest periods. Neither stratigraphy nor radiocarbon dating are possible in a site of this type lacking in fauna, therefore only the typology of the tools – particu-larly the presence of spherical polyhedra and the absence of any use of the Levallois technique – indicate that Arkin 8 dates to the Acheulean period.

Not far from Arkin, in the Wadi Halfa region, there are 11 surface sites which shed new light on the period of bifacial tools along the Nile. The statistical and typological analysis of more than 3000 tools enables us to distinguish three phases: an early Acheulean, characterized by Abbevillean bifaces, trihedra and handaxes; a middle Acheulean in which lanceolate forms and micoquian bifaces with light Levallois-style knapping appear; and a later Acheulean which includes a mixture of the aforemen-tioned types. There are no surviving structural components at these sites to allow us to reconstruct the appearance of the encampments, but the proximity of the raw material – a ferruginous sandstone covering the inselbergs (eroded hilltops) – may suggest at least the location of stone-working areas.

In comparison with other known African assemblages, the Nubian Acheulean – as defined by J. and G. Guichard – is an integral part of a complex stretching from Olduvai (in Tanzania) via Khartoum, up to Abu Simbel. Indeed, the same types of bifacial tool have been found everywhere in Africa at this date, although there is one particular aspect of the Nubian Acheulean that distinguishes it from the rest of the continent: the characteristic cleavers of the African Acheulean, made from large flakes partly worked on both faces, are rarely found in the region from Khartoum to the terraces of Abassia.

In Egypt, as we have already noted, the sporadic finds of Acheulean tools in the gravels running alongside the high plains of the Nile valley are lacking in any real archaeological context. At Nag Ahmed el-Khalifa, the only excavated site in Egypt dating to this period, the somewhat 'rolled' lithic material was found among the thick scree which covers the Nilotic silt deposits correlating with the Dendera Formation. These tools consist of crude bifaces with no traces of the Levallois technique, as well as a few cleavers.

Very little is known of the Eastern Desert and the Red Sea coast at this date. The expedition led by Debono in 1949, at the time of the construction work on the Quft-Quseir road, succeeded in locating surface finds dating to the early and middle Palaeolithic on the heights overlooking the Lakeita depression. Archaeological surveys undertaken in 1982–4 along the Egyptian coast of the Red Sea have simply provided confirmation of this very early occupation. The survival of both concentrations and isolated finds of bifacial tools indicates that the flint deposits in the Eocene calcareous formations from the Gulf of Suez down to Quseir and the volcanic rocks further to the south were being exploited from the early Acheulean onwards. But these vital pieces of evidence are so far described in only a few lines of a preliminary report, and until further research is undertaken we can only gloss over the many questions concerning early human activities between the Nile and the Red Sea. In the Sinai peninsula, Acheulean bifaces were found near the Gebel Libni in the northern part of the peninsula, as well as in the Wadi Quderat near Qadesh Barnea (Neuville 1951, 1952). But the search for further information is impeded by the lack of any real archaeological sites, whether of surface material or stratigraphic deposits.

In the Western Desert, Acheulean material associated with artesian springs was first discovered and studied in the Kharga Oasis by Gertrude Caton-Thompson. More recently, Fred Wendorf has moved the investigations southwards, into the region 350 kilometres to the west of Abu Simbel, where he has discovered numerous Acheulean sites in the Bir Sahara-Bir Tarfawi depression. In these extremely arid regions the artesian springs emerging from the aquiferous layer of the Nubian sandstone

18 metres below the surface transformed the depressions in the oasis, allowing fields and villages to flourish in the lowest parts. A few are still fertile in modern times, but in prehistory there were once many more. Most of the latter, however, now survive only in the form of basins filled with red clay and silts out of which appeared cones several metres high, made up of the debris that had accumulated in the springs exploited by early humans. Archaeological material, clearly out of its original context, is concentrated on the surface, where it is mixed with the sediments of ancient channels.

At the eastern edge of the Dakhla basin, near Balat, two fossil springs have been found to contain 7006 and 2847 artefacts respectively, mostly worked from flint nodules obtained from the neighbouring Eocene series. Primary flakes associated with non-specific cores form the essence of the production, which is mainly oriented towards denticulates, notches and scrapers. Bifacial tools, however, are in the majority in these assemblages, making up 82 per cent of one toolkit and 64 per cent of the other. At least five types of biface are represented: amygdaloidal, cordiform, backed, double-backed and subtriangular, but the general shuffling of their positions over time means that their original spatial distribution cannot be studied.

On the carbonated surface of the plateau alongside the depressions at Bir Sahara-Bir Tarfawi, further Acheulean sites have been found. These are not concentrations of worked material, but a scatter of tools consisting mainly of large amygdaloidal handaxes but also cordiform and lanceolate shapes, including only a small number of pieces of debitage, as well as a few cleavers.

To the south of Bir Tarfawi, on the sands above the lacustrine deposits, the same types of amygdaloid biface (although somewhat smaller) occur in displaced concentrations. There are no cleavers and no associated fauna, as is the case in a nearby fossil spring, where 113 late Acheulean bifaces of quartzitic sandstone, mainly subtriangular or cordiform, were covered by a calcareous layer that had formed gradually towards the end of the spring's life at a time of decreased deposition. The fragments of a tooth belonging to a large ruminant were found alongside some pieces of ostrich-egg, the molar of an equid (*Equus asinus*) and the remains of the jaw of a warthog (*Phacochoerus aethiopicus*). These finds suggest savanna fauna based around water sources. Much more data is needed for us to be able to reconstruct the climate of this region, let alone that of a whole continent. In these arid areas, where any changes in rainfall can have a significant effect on the landscape, we are only able to study palaeoclimate on the basis of secondary or circumstantial data.

Certainly, the relative levels of the lakes can serve as an indication of the intensity of rainfall, the silts of a river tend to reflect its hydraulic system, while the pollens and the fossil fauna provide evidence of a specific climate as well as of human occupation and whatever can be deduced concerning their way of life. However, all this evidence must be interpreted carefully. The rainwater may change the levels of lakes, but subterranean reservoirs can also feed extra water into the lakes regardless of the local climate. Although the fauna can be a good palaeo-climatic marker, it only indicates conditions in a relative way (i.e. fairly cold, or fairly humid) rather than directly reflecting the average climatic conditions in a particular period, especially if it is present in such low levels as at Bir Sahara. As for the use of the flora, the initial scenario has been eclipsed by new evidence of the contamination of pollen, which has been obtained over the last 70 years: distant pollens can be brought into a region by the wind or palaeo-pollens deriving from earlier geological strata can lead to exaggerated reconstructions of the landscape. A single piece of pollen evidence is no longer considered to be sufficient evidence in itself; such data can only be taken seriously when they are integrated into a complete statistically validated picture. Thus, the hasty conclusions that once transformed the Saharan Holocene into a Mediterranean biotope with Ethiopian fauna, have been significantly modified by recent critical studies, suggesting that there was indeed a more humid climate in the Egyptian Sahara during this period but that temperate species were unknown there.

At Wadi Kubbaniya, to the north of Aswan, some sondages made in 1978 produced four grains of barley and one of wheat, apparently in association with a piece of wood charcoal radiocarbon-dated to *c*.17,000 BP. The presence of these domestic species of grain in an Upper Palaeolithic complex appeared to overturn the prevailing ideas concerning the introduction of agriculture into the Nile valley. However, the application of more reliable dating tests revealed that these grains were intrusive, thus indicating that the implications of the discovery were somewhat less revolutionary. In what kind of environment should we therefore assume that Acheulean humans lived on the edges of the Nile and in the Western Desert? Unfortunately, very little evidence is available for reconstruction.

The palaeosols of the valley suggest that conditions were more humid. The polygenic gravels of the Cairo region are characterized, according to Said, by an 'Abassid pluvial' which would have taken place in the mid-Pleistocene, between about 120,000 and 90,000 BP. The studies undertaken by Wendorf's team in the Western Desert attest to more complex phenomena comprising brief humid intervals separated by at least two arid phases. An early Acheulean phase would have been contemporary with the artesian springs at Kharga, which were active at that date, as were the lacustrine sediments of Bir Sahara-Bir Tarfawi, the stratigraphic horizon of which suggests the formation of soils in semi-arid conditions with an optimum rainfall of between 250 and 600 millimetres per annum.

Vermeersch and Paulissen have identified a hyperarid phase corresponding with the Dendera Formation, representing the kind of environmental crisis that would have immediately preceded a more humid episode, during which the people of Nag Ahmed el-Khalifa would have appeared, taking advantage of a semi-arid climatic phase (see chart 1).

In the central Sahara, the Acheulean assemblages, although typologically and technologically distinct from those of Egypt and the Western Desert, were associated with lacustrine sediments that were rich in fauna: rhinoceros, elephants, equids, antelopes and hartebeest, indicating a savanna landscape. In the course of several hundred thousand years, the people of the Pleistocene period began to group together around sources of water, on the banks of rivers, by springs and by the lakes that appeared intermittently at the bottoms of depressions, transforming the landscape into a humid savanna region. Although the climate was only ever semi-arid, it was nevertheless capable of supporting a population of higher mammals, providing a source of protein for the first human hunters.

Carried along at the mercy of the seasons and climatic events, these small groups of hunter-gatherers were able to cover several hundred kilometres each year on the trail of the great herds, devoting themselves to the production of bifacial tools, and occasionally also utilizing the flakes that appeared as by-products. One can imagine that these nomadic migrations often led to contacts between different groups, exchanging bifacial tools among themselves en route between the Nile and the Atlantic. This, however, is an image which is contradicted by the precise analysis of the toolkits. Typological and technological changes, due to such factors as the availability of types of raw materials, the nature of the environment and the presence of certain cultural traditions (and sometimes a combination of all three) in fact tend to individualize the stone tools of each region; thus the Nile tools are unique in comparison with those of the Western Desert, while the latter are clearly distinguishable from those of the Maghreb. Within these regions it is also possible to distinguish even more local traditions.

Finely adapted to their immediate environment, the skeletons of these makers of bifaces have not been preserved. It is *Homo erectus* who is usually associated with the creation of the Acheulean industries, but to what human species should we assign the tool-makers in the Acheulean sites of the Nile valley and the neighbouring deserts? So far, none of these Acheulean deposits have been preserved *in situ*, and the only one that was found even geologically in its original position is that at Nag Ahmed el-Khalifa, dating to about 300,000 BP. The sites in the Western

Desert, linked with the Pleistocene sediments, have provided more precise dates, but like those in Nubia, they are purely surface remains.

The arrival of humans in the 'land of the pharaohs' is an unusually low-key event, and this silence is due not only to the erosion of the relevant sites but also probably to the fact that research into this period is still in its infancy. There is reasonable hope that new fossil human remains will soon be discovered, allowing us to gain a much better understanding of the physical appearance of the first humans in the Nile valley.

3

The beginnings of cultural diversity

Judging from the fossil spring that yielded 113 bifacial tools at Bir Tarfawi, the end of the Acheulean period corresponds to a gradual decline in activity and then the drying up of water sources. In the Nile valley, the river no longer deposits coarse gravels, but instead a fine sediment, which is evidence of a weaker current. This post-Acheulean arid phase is apparent in the Bir Tarfawi-Bir Sahara depressions, where concentrations of Mousterian artefacts are scattered over the bottom of a wide deflated area, which attests to an even lower water level than that of the present day. Humans deserted the ancient oases, taking refuge in more favourable locations along river valleys and coasts.

The return to a relatively humid phase corresponds with the reoccupation of regions around water-sources by human groups who had moved on technologically, gradually replacing bifacial tools with flaked tools, often using Levallois techniques. This development towards a lighter, more specialized and better adapted method of making tools characterized the Middle Palaeolithic both in Africa and Europe. It was in this period that the Mousterian, with its multiple facies, constituted the most prevalent industrial complex.

However, a situation developed in North Africa whereby flaked pedunculate tools and retouched bifacial points were mixed together to create a local version of the Mousterian industry. Known as Aterian, after the type site of el-Ater in Algeria, it was spread over the three regions of the Maghreb, across the Sahara down to the Niger, over to western Libya, and, in its final phase, in the oases of the Western Desert and in the Nile valley. In 1946, an Egyptian Middle Palaeolithic phase was recognized by Caton-Thompson and Gardner on solely typological criteria, but the researches of Wendorf, Karl Butzer and Pierre Vermeersch have identified it on more solid geological grounds. All along the Nile the general framework of the phase is provided by a series of deposits of Nile silts separated by strata of material deriving from the wadis, and mixed together with archaeological material *in situ*.

Once again, however, it was in Nubia that the real unearthing of the Middle Palaeolithic industries took place. In the Wadi Halfa region, Jean and Genevieve Guichard defined the 'Nubian Middle Palaeolithic' on typological grounds; as with the Acheulean, their evidence primarily consisted of material situated on the tops of inselbergs. They distinguished three main industries in which the Levallois technique was used, but instead of the so-called 'classic Levallois', a new method of preparing the core appeared – the 'Nubian Levallois'.

Described by Jacques Tixier *et al.* (1980: 50, figure 9), it comprises the striking of two deliberately 'plunging' flakes, producing the very finest Levallois point. Thus Nubian foliated tools, scrapers and cores occur in varying proportions, associated in different ways with Acheulean bifacial tools. Two groups have been distinguished on the basis of the preponderance of bifacials (Group I) or fine foliated tools (Group II). Despite certain resemblances between Group I and the Sangoan industries on the eastern shores of Lake Victoria in Uganda, and between Group II and the north African Aterian, the lithics of the Nubian Middle Palaeolithic, according to the Guichards' definition, represented a specific, unique toolkit.

Arkin 5 is the only Nubian Middle Palaeolithic site to have been studied in any detail. It was located on the west bank of the Nile, covering an area of 70 × 20 metres on a pediment of large slabs of ferruginous sandstone. A 100-square-metre trench was excavated down to the surface of the Nubian sandstone (at a depth of 50 centimetres), revealing three concentrations of archaeological material, each with a diameter of about 3.5 metres. A total of 9769 artefacts, made from the local ferruginous sandstone, were excavated; the vast majority of these were either debitage or unfinished tools, suggesting that this was a quarrying locality with no associated settlement. Among the finished tools, the foliated bifacial points resembled those of the Aterian to some extent.

Another Aterian type site was Khor Abu Anga, on the west bank of the Nile, downstream from the junction of the Blue and White Niles. This site was studied first by A. J. Arkell and later by the fourth expedition of the University of Colorado (Carlson and Sigstad 1973). The latter exposed a stratigraphic sequence of gravel deposits alternating with phases of calcification and erosion which contained archaeological material. Some Acheulean-style bifaces are mentioned in the description of the lower strata, while artefacts comparable with the Sangoan and Nubian Middle Palaeolithic (Group I) assemblages are simply noted in an intermediate layer of gravel. The uppermost layer contained foliated and pedunculate tools reminiscent of the Lupemban (an industry known from sites in Zaire and Angola), the Nubian Middle Palaeolithic (Group II) and the Aterian.

Following the Guichards' work, Anthony Marks explored the region between the Second and Third cataracts, discovering 11 concentrations of material, all clustering to the north of Wadi Halfa. The analysis of these concentrations allowed Marks to define both a Mousterian industry including denticulates and a Nubian Mousterian industry divided into two types: 'A', which did not include bifacials but showed a certain emphasis on Upper-Palaeolithic-style tools (scrapers, burins, borers etc.), and 'B', which *did* include bifacials. Contrary to the situation at Arkin 5, the ratio of tools to debitage indicates that these were not quarries or manufacturing sites but encampments, although no structural remains of any kind have survived – no stone-walling and no post-holes. In addition, the acidity of the soil means that no organic material was preserved.

In the same region, near the Second Cataract, are five sites grouped together under the name Khor Musa. Not only are they still in their original stratigraphic position (i.e. not subject to geological disturbance or rearrangement) but they are also of great archaeological interest. Three of them are both composed of and covered by Nile silts, between 11 and 18 metres below the modern ground surface, while the two others were found in the adjacent sand dunes. Covering very large areas, from 30 to 254 m², these 'Khormusan' sites are characterized by faunal remains, a few polished bone tools, some fragments of haematite and, in a predominantly Levallois lithic assemblage, a distinct preference for burins. The prevalence of the latter tool, which is very common in the Upper Palaeolithic, together with charcoal yielding two radiocarbon dates (20,750 BC ± 280 and 15,850 BC ± 500, see Marks 1968b: 318, 321), quite naturally led to the assumption that the Khormusan was an Upper Palaeolithic industry transitional between the Nubian Mousterian and the better-known cultures that followed. However, more recently obtained dates from three other samples have cast doubt on this view, giving a range of *c*.41,000–33,000 BP, thus pushing the Khormusan back into the midst of the Middle Palaeolithic industries, to which all the elements (except the burins) correspond.

The Khormusan people exploited a variety of different raw materials – ferruginous sandstone, quartzite, quartz, rhyolites, chalcedony, agate and fossilized wood – using specific rocks more frequently for certain types of tool. Thus burins, although occurring in all of the materials listed above, were primarily made from chalcedony. Thousands of remains of bones were excavated, but their poor state of preservation means that we can only make a very cautious reconstruction of the fauna: large herbivores (*Bos primigenius*), donkeys, hippopotami, gazelle, rodents and Nile fowl. Fish remains are also present (*Synodontis, Bagrus, Clarias, Tilapia* and *Lates*), but they appear to have played a relatively minor role in the sites' economies.

The Khormusan people were undoubtedly hunters and occasional fishers, but neither grinding stones nor vegetable remains have survived to inform us of their activities as gatherers. Some 15 kilometres to the south of the Second Cataract, the site of Jebel Sahaba has yielded an abundance of haematite, fragments of which were found (bearing traces of polishing) at each of the Khormusan sites. The presence of burins suggests that bone, wood and reed were being worked. A borer and a small spatula constitute the earliest bone tools so far recovered in Nubia, and it is highly probable that many tiny tools were provided with wooden hafts. Bevelling, cleaving, making notches, piercing – these are the technological developments which appear and diversify among these groups of hunter-gatherers in a limited area.

Although site 440 at Khor Musa (Shiner 1968b: 630–7) is located in the same geographical region as the Khormusan sites, 12 kilometres to the west of the Wadi Halfa airport, it consists of an original assemblage, typologically similar to the denticulate variant of the Mousterian. Two levels of occupation appear in the rough grey sand, separated by a layer devoid of archaeological material comprising 50 centimetres of the same type of sediment. A layer of sandy colluvial sediment covered them, and was itself sealed by a deposit of Nile silts, indicating a major rise in the flood level of the river. The technological and typological analyses of the two horizons, as well as artefacts found on the surface, reveal a great homogeneity in the composition of the toolkit and the knapping techniques employed. The tools were made from quartz, Precambrian ferruginous sandstone and brown pebbles of Nubian conglomerate, and denticulates predominated in assemblages which also included sidescrapers, endscrapers, Levallois points and small numbers of burins. One foliated tool, found on the surface, appeared to J. D. Clark to be reminiscent of the Aterian. Although the two levels of occupation were similar in terms of their lithics, their range of fauna differed widely: mammals (*Bos, Gazella, Equus, Hippopotamus*) were prevalent in the lower phase, while fish remains were extremely common in the upper level, and yet this faunal change does not appear to be accompanied by any change in the toolkits.

Some 12 kilometres to the north of Aswan, the Wadi Kubbaniya, where grains of barley and wheat were once mistakenly attributed to the Upper Palaeolithic (see chapter 2), yielded fruitful evidence of prehistoric geology to an American expedition in 1978–82. Both Middle and Upper Palaeolithic sites, including a human skeleton that will be discussed further below, were found in a stratigraphic position which links them closely with the Pleistocene development of the Nile.

The Wadi Kubbaniya, carved out of the Nubian sandstone of the Eocene plateau, communicates with the Nile from the west, after passing through the Kalabsha plain. Fragments of sand terraces and gravels provide evidence of early phases of sedimentation. It was at the mouth of the wadi that Nile sediments were deposited: their complexity, their depth, their clear association with human activity, as well as the preservation of organic materials, all help to make them a crucial element in the prehistory of the Nile valley.

Most of the sites are part of a group located between dune sand and silty deposits deriving from a time when the Nile was 8 to 10 metres higher than its modern level. The desert environment was then hyperarid and the winds swept the sand down the wadi, where it was caught up by plants, thus leading to the formation of the dunes upon which the annual floods periodically deposited layers of alluvial silt. This interstratification took place in two phases separated by an arid phase. The lower levels contained Mousterian lithics.

Three concentrations of material have been attributed both typologically and technologically to the Middle Palaeolithic. Site E82–5 contained 1480 items, mainly carved from quartz, quartzite and ferruginous sandstone, linked to the Denticulate Mousterian (see Marks 1968a: 280–2 for a definition of the latter). Thermoluminescence dating was undertaken at the base of the sandy layer which covers it, suggesting an age of 89,000 BP. Judging from its position, site E82–4 represents the latest Middle Palaeolithic deposit in the region. A small concentration of 24 items, including scrapers and burins, recalls the Khormusan 'family' of industries. Finally, it is worth noting a small group of 46 quartz artefacts situated under the basic outline of site E82–6.

Between Asyut and Nag Hammadi the fieldwork of the Belgian Middle Egypt Prehistoric Project, directed by Pierre Vermeersch, uncovered several Middle Palaeolithic sites. Surrounded by the more or less coarse accumulated sediments, located several metres above the modern river level, such sites as Beit Allam, near Abydos, Nazlet Khater 1, 2 and 3, near Tahta, Makhadma 6, near Qena and Nazlet Shahaba, near Dendera represent the exploitation of nodules brought by the Nile floods or the wadis' discharges. The assemblages are mainly made up of cores and flakes, all characterized by Levallois knapping, some in the Nubian style and others in the classic centripetal style. The toolkits were primarily made up of notches and denticulates, with no bifaces present.

At Nazlet Shahaba, shafts were cut a metre down through aeolian sand in order to reach nodules of flint in the underlying terrace. The abundance of fragments of tool-making debris inside the shafts suggest that the raw material was being worked *in situ*. To what sites were the finished tools taken? Where were they sharpened, gathered together and used? We in fact know nothing about the people exploiting these stones who must surely have been living lower down in the valley at sites which today are covered by more recent sediments. However, it was in the vicinity of one of these chert-cobble quarry shafts at Taramsa Hill (near Dendera), that excavators in 1994 found the remains of what appears to be both the earliest human skeleton in Egypt and the earliest grave in the Nile Valley (Vermeersch *et al.* 1998). The poorly preserved bones were those of a subadult 'anatomically modern human' similar in appearance to the Mechtoid populations of the north African Epipalaeolithic. The position of the body, as well as the depth of the pit in which it was found (a metre below the surface), suggest that the child had not died in this location but had been deliberately brought here to be buried. Just as in the Acheulean period, the Eastern Desert has preserved no real data from this date. Clusters of cores, flakes and Levallois tools (scrapers, points, backed blades and notch flakes) derive from the exploitation of quarrying sites, and even more exhaustive analysis of these sites is unlikely to provide fresh insights.

In the Sinai peninsula, the situation is hardly more encouraging. A Mousterian working area was excavated by Henry and Goldberg in northern Sinai and in the Wadi T'mila, but the paucity of Middle Palaeolithic sites perhaps derives more from a lack of available evidence than from a real gap in the archaeological record.

In the Western Desert, on the other hand, the study of dozens of concentrations of Middle Palaeolithic material linked with the development of lakes has proved to be a very productive source of information concerning the inhabitants of these regions and provides the best demonstration of the climatic complexity of this period.

At Bir Sahara, five Mousterian horizons have been identified and linked with lacustrine sediments. Badly affected by wind erosion, these concentrations preserve a material essentially made up of grey or brown siliceous sandstone, the formations of which cover an area extending for less than 20 kilometres to the northeast. Brought from quarries, the blocks of raw material were roughly shaped and worked at the procurement sites themselves. The blocks, although incomplete, provide clear evidence of their Mousterian nature through the large amounts of Levallois-style debitage: everywhere, the denticulate tools dominate the assemblage, the development from one site to another being especially evident in the gradual diminution of the tools' size. The discovery of a fragment of a camel's tibia in these Mousterian levels, in association with worked stone, suggests that this animal was already present in early Egypt, despite the fact that it is unknown during the pharaonic period.

At the site of BT–14, in the northern section of the indurated lake deposits at Bir Tarfawi, Aterian points appear among the Mousterian assemblages and the thousands of fragments of bone. Seven individual sites were thus distinguished at Bir Tarfawi, on the basis of geological considerations as well as the changing density of the material. The raw material throughout the entire region was the typical ferruginous sandstone, easily accessible beds of which were located less than 6 kilometres away.

On the great surface of calcareous marls at 'area A' in site BT–14, denticulates, scrapers and Mousterian points (and no other type of tool) were associated with the remains of gazelle, antelope, bovids and rhinoceros, the fore-parts, shoulders and pelvises of which had clearly been taken away – doubtless to be consumed elsewhere. Area A therefore appears to have been an area in which mammals were dismembered (i.e. a huge butchery site); it evidently constituted the remains of a stopping place – perhaps even several successive stopping places – perhaps corresponding to the dry season, thus potentially indicating the storage place, if we knew in what place and at what distance from this site the meat was consumed.

Traces of the 'Aterian people', established near the great internal lakes of the Sahara, are also to be found near the artesian springs at Kharga, where they appear to have adapted their lifestyle to the exploitation of wide open spaces, following animal herds from one water source to the next, from lakes to marshes, from spring to spring. They certainly leave evidence of their passing in the form of such distinctive cultural markers as pedunculates with their bases worked to form points, but they also used sidescrapers and endscrapers of various types, notches, denticulates, bifaces and even – in the Maghreb – some burins. The direct evidence for the fitting of hafts or handles to tools suggests that the Aterians may have been highly mobile groups, provided with a toolkit that was both lighter and more efficient.

In the Nile valley, definite traces of the Aterian people have been found only at Wadi Kubbaniya, in the form of a small concentration of surface material, although they are also perhaps attested both at Arkin 5 and at site 440 in the Khor Musa region (see also Carlson and Sigstad 1973). Given the evidence for the Nubian Middle Palaeolithic (as defined by Guichard), the Nubian Mousterian, the Western Desert Mousterian and the Khormusan, it is clear that there was a general tendency towards cultural diversity.

The common ground between these various Middle Palaeolithic industries is the gradual abandonment of the bifacial tool at the same time as the increased use of flaked tools, the obtention of which corresponds to a particular preparatory procedure. In some sites a 'Nubian' technique was developed for the preparation of the core, and at other sites, on the contrary, the classic Levallois method was adopted, keeping the bifacial style of tool, reducing the sizes of tools, showing a preference for burins or denticulates, or working a pedunculate so as to facilitate the attachment of a haft: each group was established in an ecological niche to which it was adapted with maximum efficiency.

Given the absence of stratigraphy and the lack of sufficiently numerous or precise dates, it is not surprising that it has proved so difficult to establish a chronological framework for the Middle Palaeolithic. The variations from one site to another and from group to group can be explained as much in terms of functional diversity as in chronological differences. Both the sites studied by the Guichards in Nubia and those analysed by Pierre Vermeersch in Middle Egypt are, first and foremost, reflections of quarrying activity. The presence, absence or relative frequencies of denticulates, sidescrapers and tools such as burins, perforators and endscrapers that already foreshadow the Upper Palaeolithic can be interpreted both as techno-economic differences among contemporaneous groups and as purely chronological differences. Consider, for example, the butchery sites of Bir Tarfawi. As for the Khormusan sites, they reveal above all the activities of groups concerned with the exploitation of their immediate environment, having chosen to use burins for reasons which are no doubt far more complex than the mere efficiency of the tool.

For the same reasons, it is difficult to know whether the replacement of the Lower Palaeolithic industries by those of the Middle Palaeolithic is a result of indigenous development or external influences. There is no stratified or transitional site that can explain the passing from one period to another; despite the existence of bifaces, which, in the Middle Palaeolithic, never appear to be in the majority, there is no indication of a smooth transition from bifaces to flaked tools. However, varied as they are, the industries of Egypt and Nubia may also be defined in terms of neighbouring regions where the prehistory is known.

Judging from the Bir Sahara-Bir Tarfawi evidence, the Mousterian and the Aterian correspond to two successive episodes of lacustrine activity, and the Aterian's position in the sediments indicates that it is associated with the final stages of the drying up of the lake. The five Mousterian horizons are characterized only by a gradual diminution in the size of the tools, but this tendency does not continue in the Aterian (i.e. the artefacts of the latter are not smaller than those of the last Mousterian groups).

According to Vermeersch, Paulissen and Van Peer (1990a, 1991), the Nubian Middle Palaeolithic can be divided into three phases on the basis of the tools' morphology: the earliest corresponds to the 'Middle Palaeolithic' as defined by Guichard. This is then followed by Anthony Marks' isolated Mousterian groups, while the last phase is the Khormusan.

We currently have no certain means of assigning site 440 at Khor Musa to any particular stage of the Middle Palaeolithic. Joel Shiner (1968b: 636) suggests that it was occupied between c.30,000 and 20,000 BC, on the basis of geological estimates, although he admits that the sedimentary formations which contain the industries have not themselves been precisely dated. The items that have been able to provide radiocarbon dates at Bir Sahara-Bir Tarfawi suggest that both the Mousterian and the Aterian should be assigned to some period earlier than 43,000 BP. We know that, for periods before 10,000 BP, radiocarbon dates are unreliable, since they are uncorrected by dendrochronology. We must therefore resort to other dating techniques (i.e. thermoluminescence) or use new accelerator techniques of radiocarbon dating. Around this period in time, *c.*40,000 BP, the Aterian is said to have appeared in the Maghreb, although these dates too are lacking in precision.

At this point, it is worth remembering site E82–5 at Wadi Kubbaniya, dated by thermoluminescence to 89,000 BP, and then the Khormusan material *re*-dated by radiocarbon to *c.*40,000–35,000 BP. We might then place the Middle Palaeolithic industries of Egypt, Nubia and the Western Desert, with customary imprecision, some time between 90,000 and 35,000 BP.

What can we say about climatic conditions? The sediments laid down by the Nile, which are finer silts than those of the Acheulean period, suggest that conditions in the Middle Palaeolithic were relatively humid, although these are less evident than in the Lower Palaeolithic. The Khormusan fauna indicates that the landscape along the banks of the Nile was more wooded than it is now, allowing it to support large ruminants and hippopotami attached to such permanent water sources as ponds and rivers, but the '*rufifrons*' gazelle, with its reddish brown forehead, inhabited the thorn-infested sub-desert areas. The intense processes of sedimentation that characterize the Khormusan sites, as well as the presence of the dunes, emphasize a state of relative aridity which would explain the fact that these sites have only been found near the riverbanks.

More than anywhere else, the Bir Sahara-Bir Tarfawi sequence suggests that there were two arid phases separated by two humid post-Acheulean phases, the first corresponding to the Mousterian and the second to the Aterian. The recurrence of identical fauna in both humid phases (with the exception of the warthog) indicates an open biotope comprising savanna or steppes. Between the water-loving white rhinoceros which inhabits grassy or brush-covered savanna, and the gazelle and camels which prefer a semi-desert environment, is the black rhinoceros, which survives on thorn-bushes in dry lands and can sometimes be found up to 50 kilometres from any source of water. Subject to seasonal changes, the inner basins became highly favourable after the rains, although no doubt only for a short time. The desert would at this time of the year have been covered with sources of water around which steppe forms of plants grew up. In the dry season, on the other hand, life would have retreated to the vicinity of artesian springs, great rivers or permanent lakes (such as that of Bir Sahara-Bir Tarfawi).

In the central Sahara, as in the Maghreb, the association between one or more humid phases and the Mousterian industries seems to be well attested. In Lake Chad, the lacustrine sediments indicate a series of lakes dating between 40,000 and 20,000 BP, possibly linked with one or other phase of Bir Tarfawi. At Adrar Bous in the central Sahara, a Levallois site was discovered *in situ* within the calcareous lacustrine clays; in the same area, Aterian artefacts were found in association with a sediment that provides evidence of a drier period of marked aeolian activity. The same situation applies at the Erg Chech, in the western Sahara, where Aterian material was again mixed with lacustrine sediments. In the Maghreb, along the northern coast, numerous sites with associated fauna have been preserved; in general, the animals are similar to those in the Ethiopian savanna (large buffalo, wildebeest, hartebeest, gazelle, *Equus mauritanicus*), as well as a few palaeoarctic species (the merck rhinoceros (*Dicerorhinus Kirchbergensis*), aurochs and wild boar).

At the Wadi Akarit, near the Mediterranean, a rich Mousterian industry is associated with pollens which indicate a steppe-like grassland environment with the presence of tamarisk and very occasional trees. As we have emphasized earlier, however, both the flora and fauna can only suggest micro-environments, and there is not yet any firm chronological famework to provide links between these climatic and cultural occurrences at the various different sites. Generally speaking, the palaeoclimatic trend was heading in the direction of growing hyperaridity well before 40,000 BP. On the basis of the thermoluminescence dates for the Middle Palaeolithic sequence at Wadi Kubbaniya, it was around 60,000 BP that the beginning of this inexorable development should be placed. Despite its brief humid intervals, the Middle Palaeolithic was never characterized by the kind of humidity that we find in the earlier Acheulean phase.

A period of intense aeolian activity followed the Aterian sequence at Bir Tarfawi. In the mouth of the Wadi Kubbaniya, there are 20-metre-thick quaternary sediments, a phenomenon in which the aggradation of the Nile combined with fierce winds to create a stratigraphy in which sand dunes alternated with layers of silt, along the Nile between Esna and Armant. On the east bank, however, the evidence of wadi activity can be explained by rainfall on the Red Sea hills at the same time as air circulation typical of hyperarid periods. Moreover, this hyperaridity is well attested in the Western Desert, in the form of the movements of dunes, the southward retreat of the steppes and savannas, and the absence of any trace of humans throughout the sub-Saharan fringes of Africa. Everywhere in the Sahara itself the lakes disappeared, even as far as Chad, which became totally dry. In Mali and Niger, continous chains of dunes were formed, and the White Nile basin was also engulfed in sand.

In the Maghreb, traces of human occupation became scarce between the end of the Aterian (before c.25,000 BP) and the beginning of the Iberomaurusian (c.15,000 BP). However, the restriction of the sites to the coastal and mountainous regions suggests that there was an environment capable of supporting human occupation beyond the northwestern fringes of the Sahara (Camps 1974: 60).

This erratic but inexorable diminution of the rains which had prevailed throughout the entire Middle Palaeolithic caused the lakes, springs and other water-sources to dry up gradually, forcing the herds and human populations to withdraw from the desert towards more permanent water supplies. The post-Aterian period in the Sahara was characterized by a hyperaridity that emptied it both of water and people. The Nile valley thus served as the principal place of refuge until the Holocene pluvial, acting not only as a physical rallying point but probably also as a cultural melting-pot. It is from this point of view that the site of Nazlet Khater 4 (NK4), excavated in 1980–82 by the Belgian Middle Egypt Prehistoric Project, takes on special significance.

NK4 is a chert-quarrying site in Middle Egypt, 20 kilometres to the northwest of Tahta; it is linked with groups of Upper Palaeolithic industries by the presence of non-Levallois blade debitage and such tools as denticulates, burins and axes. New radiocarbon dates, derived from charcoal taken from the hearths associated with the quarry shafts, assign it to the period between 34,400 and 31,500 BP, which was effectively a time when conditions in the desert would have rendered human survival impossible. The inhabitants of NK4 dug a 9 × 2 metre trench through the thick wadi deposit, and then created several underground galleries and vertical shafts, using a variety of different techniques to extract chert cobbles from the ancient terrace subjacent to the Nile (Vermeersch, Paulissen and Van Peer 1990b).

This emergence of Upper Palaeolithic blade industries is also to be found in Cyrenaica at the sites of Dabba and Haua Fteah, which have been dated to c.38,000–15,000 BP. In the Lagaman sites of the Sinai peninsula and in the Negev (at the site of Boker A), remains dated to c.35,000–33,000 BP present a similar blade industry. At NK4, however, there were also some hitherto unknown types of tools, and the proportion of denticulates was not quite so small. As Vermeersch points out, it is difficult to make comparisons between such functionally dissimilar sites, given that NK4 is a set of quarries while the other places are probably occupation sites. It is nevertheless clear that it was in such favoured coastal, mountainous and riverine regions (provided with continuous supplies of water amid hostile conditions elsewhere) that an important technological development emerged: the lengthening of flake-tools to form blades, which were then themselves knapped into further tools.

At Boulder Hill, 400 metres to the north of the NK4 quarrying site, lay the body of the second-earliest human so far discovered in Egypt. He was lying on his back with his head to the west, and a bifacial axe was placed near his face, this being the first attested piece of funerary equipment in a land that was to become the most prolific source of such grave goods. A second grave, found about 30 metres to the east of the first, consisted only of a skeleton stretched out on its back, completely crushed and with its skull missing. Some foetus bones and fragments of ostrich eggs accompanied this wretched and incomplete corpse, which unfortunately cannot be scientifically dated, since the organic carbon content was insufficient to permit radiocarbon analysis, thus dissuading the excavators from attempting the same procedure on the first, almost complete body. However, certain elements of indirect evidence suggest that the two burials must have been contemporary with the chert quarry. The first grave, carved out of the consolidated clay, 60 centimetres below the modern ground surface, was covered with large blocks of stone, and the gaps between these blocks had been left to fill up with aeolian sand comparable with the drifts blocking up the galleries, shafts and trench of the quarry. In addition, the axe, which was similar in all respects to the tools found in the quarry site, is not of a type attested in the Upper Palaeolithic industries, which occur in the valley from 20,000 BP onwards, and it also differs from the later Neolithic axes. Finally, although the skeleton is an 'anatomically modern human', it has certain 'archaic' features, including an unusually thick mandible (see Thoma 1984).

Thus we have, standing firmly on his own two feet, the second-earliest riverbank-dweller in the Nile valley (the Taramsa Hill body being earlier). With a cranial capacity of at least 1400 cm^3, somewhat negroid features (such as the praenasal fossa and alveolar prognathism), he was an experienced quarrier who knew where to obtain flint and, not content with the mere excavation of several fairly deep shafts (like those created by his ancestors at Arkin 5 or Jebel Sahaba), he worked out several means of gaining access to the terraces hidden under the sediment, where he was able to find the nodules of flint that he needed for his tools.

4

Diversity or Nilotic adaptation

The transition to the Upper Palaeolithic was essentially a process of technological evolution but it was also characterized by the appearance of *Homo sapiens sapiens*. The production of blades, which had already begun in the Mousterian, now intensified, and slowly but surely reached a higher level of technical quality, gradually minimizing the wastage of raw material. Tools such as endscrapers, perforators and burins had been known in earlier times, but these types now diversified, resulting in an increasing degree of functional multiplicity. When this decisive step took place in Europe, the climatic conditions were distinctly icy, comprising phases III and IV of the Würm glaciation.

We know that the northeast African desert was at this date devoid of occupation, with groups of humans only clustering around the edges of water-sources. However, between 40,000 and 25,000 BP, there are very few sites attested, and the process of technological transition is difficult to follow. Sites with mixed tool-types (i.e. Levallois artefacts alongside blades) are both rare and poorly dated. It is therefore possible that the emergence of the so-called Halfan knapping technique may shed new light on the process of cultural transition at this time.

The Halfan technique, discovered by Anthony Marks in the microlithic industry at Wadi Halfa (see below), is a technological process that involves both Levallois-style working and blade preparation. It seems to have involved a core with two platforms, one of which was used to produce six short, fine, parallel bladelets, while the other was prepared for the knapping of a series of convergent flakes, which gave this side of the core a Levallois air. One large first flake was struck off, its distal end bearing a few short marks showing the ends of the bladelet scars, then a second large flake (the Halfan flake itself) was removed. The Halfan flake has distal blade-shaped ridges and a 'bird-wing' stub, characteristic of the removal of a flake from another flake. Known only in Egypt, the

Halfan technique is, however, not present at NK4, the earliest Upper Palaeolithic site so far located in the Nile valley.

Several kilometres to the west of Qena, the two sites of Shuwikhat were excavated in 1985 by Pierre Vermeersch's team. They were found in a contact zone between coarse dark silt formed by the Nile's aggradation (evidence of a hyperarid climate) and the deposit in one of the most important wadis in the Eastern Desert. Since Shuwikhat 2 consisted only of a surface concentration deriving from bladelet-production, only Shuwikhat 1 was actually studied. Mixed with the silt and sealed by a palaeosol, the Shuwikhat 1 artefacts indicated the production of blades without any use of the Levallois techniqe. Denticulates, endscrapers and burins were made from these blades, which were themselves knapped from flint nodules obtained from the neighbouring wadis. The assemblage was dominated by cores with platforms on both sides (i.e. opposed-platform cores). Among the bones were identified the remains of aurochs, gazelle and catfish, while fragments of burnt clay associated with the occupation have given a date of 24,700 ± 2500 BP.

Other sites similar to that of Shuwikhat 1 have been noted in the region of Esna-Edfu by Fred Wendorf's team, but there have been no further investigations to clarify the situation. A date obtained from burnt clay, 21,590 ± 1520 BP, certainly presents no obstacle to the assumption that we are dealing with a coherent group of sites between Qena and Edfu, occupied by fisher-hunters who had forgotten or abandoned the Levallois technique but were not yet initiated into the wonders of a microlithic toolkit.

What is left of the 'Halfan transition', then, if there is not the least surviving trace of the Levallois technique at Nazlet Khater 4, Shuwikhat 1, or any of the sites related to the latter, nor any sign of a Halfan core either? Pierre Vermeersch suggests that these mixed groups of material might be found among Wendorf and Schild's Idfuan sites with Levallois debitage. Six concentrations have been found in the great el-Kilh plain (Wendorf and Schild 1976: 27–30) on sandy hills at a height of 5–7 metres above the flood plain. The only one of these to be studied in any detail was E71P1, where test-trenches were excavated. From a technological point of view, half of the cores were Levallois (including some with Halfan-style Levallois), while the rest had one or two platforms for the creation of flake tools, blades and bladelets. A large variety of tools were being produced, ranging from burins, endscrapers, blades and retouched flakes to 'scaled pieces' (*pièces esquillées*), and for the first time we encounter bladelets bearing so-called 'Ouchtata retouch'. The latter were defined by Jacques Tixier (1963: 48) in the Epipalaeolithic industries of the Maghreb; this direct retouch, 'short or very short, never cutting beyond the edge with which it is concerned, semi-abrupt or slightly abrupt', is essentially an abrasive movement achieving a kind of nibbling of the edge of the blade.

The problem is that this assemblage, which incorporates the remains of hartebeest, aurochs, hippopotami, gazelle, rodents and catfish, produced five radiocarbon dates from *Unio* shells, ranging from 15,000 to 15,850 ± 300 BC, whereas Vermeersch, Paulissen and Van Peer would like to date them at about 40,0000–30,000 BP on the basis of techno-typological considerations. There must presumably be some doubt about the shell dates, given that we have only a poor knowledge of the original carbon content. Another element must be taken into consideration, which in no way simplifies the interpretation of this fundamental site: the concentration of different types of lithics in different parts of the site. At areas A and B, in the northern part of the site, the excavators found that the Levallois index was higher, there were no burins and Ouchtata bladelets were rare, whereas in the south, in areas C and D, the toolkit comprises numerous Ouchtata bladelets, burins and scaled pieces, and the latter can only be described as 'appearing to have been worked into the form of intermediate hammered tools' (Leroi-Gourhan 1988). Do these patterns reflect areas where different activities were taking place, or do they represent, as Vermeersch suggests, areas exploited at different times by successive groups?

Thus, the derivation of the Upper Palaeolithic from a slow transition between the Levallois techniques and the blade-making techniques, via the Halfan core, remains, for the moment, rather too much of an unproven hypothesis. Although the theory in itself is convincing, this reconstruction has not yet been backed up archaeologically. No Halfan technique has yet been definitely found before 20,000 BC, while the first blade industries stretch back to 35,000 BC.

Because of its geographical isolation, Egypt has not tended to be much influenced by the outside world. Certainly it seems likely that the transition from Levallois flaking to the creation of blades from a unipolar core took place at the site of Boker Tachitt in the Negev. The Levallois point became the Emira point and then disappeared in the later levels, between 45,500 and 40,000. However, although the Negev industries are certainly much earlier, they cannot seriously be regarded as the antecedents of the tools from Nazlet Khater 4 or the Shuwikhat-Edfu assemblages, since the Egyptian tools differ both technologically and typologically from the Boker Tachitt assemblages.

Although the people of the Nile valley might have been influenced *indirectly* by cultural phenomena outside Egypt, they were probably evolving independently to a greater extent than our research currently indicates (given that the exact role played by the Halfan technique is far from clear). They were thus in a sense already entering into the modern age.

Equipped with their blade-based toolkits – which were not only lighter and more efficient but, above all, more diverse – they were launching themselves, from about 20,000 BP onwards (i.e. 12,000 years before their European counterparts) into a new technological venture: with a cut-down tool, in that the blade became the basis for other tools. This stage of material culture is known as microlithism – the process of knapping the maximum cutting edge from the minimum amount of raw material.

Let us return to Lower Nubia, and specifically to Wadi Halfa. In association with the sand dune deposits of the Ballana formation, six concentrations of lithics that included microlithic tools were studied by Wendorf's team: this was the Halfan industry, which has yielded the famous cores (described above) that are part Levallois and part blade-producing, thus providing the term to describe the '**Halfan** technique'. Because of the geological contexts of each of these sites, Anthony Marks believed that he could discern a development, notwithstanding the somewhat schematic nature of this evolution, given the small number of sites from which it derived.

The interest of these assemblages lies in the fact that Levallois, Halfan and microlithic typologies were all found together, the latter consisting entirely of backed blades. Five phases can therefore be distinguished, moving gradually towards a decrease in the production of Halfan flake tools and an increase in the production of blades from flint nodules. The manufacture of further tools out of these backed blades (such as truncated tools, denticulates and notched perforators) never accounts for any more than 10 per cent of the entire toolkit, leaving a large proportion consisting of sidescrapers, burins, denticulates, notches and truncated flakes, as well as 'scaled pieces'.

The choice of flint nodules as the raw material seems to go hand in hand with the microlithic option in an environment where ferruginous sandstone, fossilized wood and pebbles of quartz and agate were all available.

- The first – purely hypothetical – phase rests on the supposed development from the Levallois technique to a Halfan style of tool production, although none of the sites actually corresponds to this initial phase in concrete terms.
- The second phase, represented by sites 1020 and 1018, is characterized by the Halfan core and flakes. Although a small number of micro-flakes and backed bladelets are present, the toolkit continues to be made up essentially from flake tools.
- Site 624 is the only example of the third phase, in which the toolkit of the second phase was augmented by 'scaled pieces' (which were to account for a consistent proportion of the tools in the fourth and

fifth phases) and a type of bladelet-producing core, which, on the basis of its distinctive shape, is known as a 'wedge-core'.

- In phase 4, represented by sites 443 and 2014, the backed bladelets became the predominant feature of the toolkit, while the Halfan flakes, in contrast, became the fossil elements of the assemblages.
- The final phase, exemplified only by site 1028, was characterized by the virtual disappearance of the Halfan technique, replaced by microlithic tools.

The site 443 occupation also incorporated indications of the presence of domestic structures of some kind: a hearth, 23 centimetres below the modern ground surface, and six pits cut into the virgin sand containing concentrations of burnt rocks, bone, wood charcoal, bladelet tools, as well as five ostrich-egg discs at various stages of manufacture. It is also notable that there were fragments of burnt sandstone yielding a powdery red substance (iron oxide) which is a pigment comparable with haematite. Twelve fragments of mica-schist deriving from the Batn el-Hagar could also have served as colouring agents, in one instance mixed with animal fat.

Three radiocarbon dates have provided a global estimate of 19,500–17,500 BP for the entire group of Halfan sites.

In 1920, Edmund Vignard (1923) discovered a number of lithic assemblages in the Kom Ombo plain, which he named after the nearby town of Sebil. The **Sebilian** industry thus made its appearance in Egyptian prehistory, raising a series of questions, some of which are still far from being resolved today. All of these Sebilian sites were surface remains, but they corresponded to several stages of lake-terraces created by the Silsila barrage. Vignard distinguished three techno-typological stages of development within the Sebilian, ranging from a Mousterian-like industry to a Tardenoisian (i.e. microlithic) type.

The Sebilian I phase (or Lower Sebilian) was characterized by a toolkit using diorite, quartz and Nubian sandstone. The cores were small and disc-shaped but not worked according to the Levallois knapping method; the tools included flakes deriving from the discoidal core, often taking the form of points truncated (i.e. deliberately snapped off) at the base. The tools developed towards trapezoidal and triangular shapes, one or two of the edges being truncated (the terms 'trapeze' and 'triangle' being used here only in a straightforward descriptive sense rather than with the more technical connotations of the terms for specific microlithic tool types used by prehistorians). Blades rarely appeared, while microliths were not yet found at all. A few hammer-stones and an anvil also featured in the inventory.

In the Sebilian II phase (or Middle Sebilian), flint became the primary raw material, and the style of core began to diversify, with the early types being supplemented by some that were flake-producing and others with blades produced from platforms on either side. The Levallois flake disappeared and simultaneously it became more common to find flake points with basal retouch, which removed the bulb of percussion and was accompanied by lateral and/or distal truncation, thus creating subgeometrical forms such as scalene triangles and lunates. The production of microburins first happened in this phase, while sandstone pestles and mortars still bore traces of ochre, and anvils and hammer-stones grew in number. Hearths, consolidated by clods of earth, have been found in abundance and, according to Vignard (1923: 27), 'give the impression of a long period of occupation, with their substantial build-up of ash'. Heaps of mussels and broken bones accumulated, forming what amounted to 'kitchen middens' several cubic metres in volume.

The Sebilian III (Late Sebilian) phase was characterized by the use of flint and chalcedony alone. Discoid cores became rarer, being replaced by opposed-platform cores, while the toolkit evolved towards a genuine geometric microlithic technique linked with the microburin production method. In these assemblages there were many retouched blades and bladelets. The retouch was sometimes developed in a notch style, removing a pedunculate which can give certain tools the appearance of unilateral arrow heads. Endscrapers made from flakes are found alongside this microlithic uniformity. Six hearths derive from these late Sebilian levels, and kitchen middens, although less common than in the Middle Sebilian, preserve a certain number of bone tools polished 'by the hands of man but also by sand' (Vignard 1923), a pierced bovid toe-bone, fragments of sandstone grinders, a double-perforated shell (*Corbicula consobrina*), and a pierced flake of schist. The rich Late Sebilian inventory also includes a small receptacle worn naturally into the sandstone bedrock and still bearing traces of ground-up red ochre.

According to Vignard, the Early Sebilian phase derived from the Egyptian Mousterian, and evidently plummeted back into the Middle Palaeolithic (compared with Europe), while the Middle Sebilian corresponded to the Aurignacian, Magdalenian, Solutrean and Azilian, and the Late Sebilian was the equivalent of the Tardenoisian. Thus Vignard's Sebilian covers the entire length of the European Upper Palaeolithic, comprising an ideal bridge between the Levallois-tradition industries and the microlithic industries. In this reconstruction there is barely any sign of the traditional blade industries of the Upper Palaeolithic, which Egypt seems to lack.

However, in the 1960s, the researches of the geologists Butzer and Hansen, de Heinzelin and Paepe clarified the complex sequence of the Nile's cycle of sedimentation and erosion, and a certain number of radiocarbon dates sketched out a chronological backdrop that resulted in a total revision of the view of the Sebilian described above.

In the Wadi Halfa region, Anthony Marks discovered nine sites attributable to Vignard's Early and Middle phases of the Sebilian, radiocarbon-dated to $c.12,000$ BP. On stratigraphic grounds, the earliest occupation would therefore have stretched back to $c.20,000$ BP, but could not have been any earlier than this because all of the sites were associated with the Sahaba formation, which consisted of a deposit of sands and clays rich in shells, and the dating of which was between 20,000 and 12,000 BP. This redating therefore presented problems in terms of linking the Early Sebilian with the Mousterian.

Further to the north, on the west bank of the Nile, about 10 kilometres from Abu Simbel, Wendorf examined three Sebilian assemblages in the Ballana region. Sites 8899 and 8898 included large sandstone flake-tools struck from discoidal cores with a minor Levallois component. The toolkit, comprising truncations, backed flakes and some microburins, therefore related to Vignard's Early and Middle Sebilian. Site 8899, consisting of two stratified Sebilian horizons, has the advantage of placing the Sebilian after the Halfan and before the Qadan, but nevertheless still suffers from a severe lack of absolute dating evidence.

Even further north, in the Dishna plain near Qena, two Sebilian sites can be linked with the final phase of the Sahaba formation, preserving a macrolithic toolkit with a high Levallois index, in which truncations were the dominant tool type (Hassan 1972). As in Nubia, this pair of sites are assigned to phases I and II of the Sebilian – especially phase I.

Site E71P3, situated between Edfu and Esna (Hassan 1974a), is possibly associated with the Sahaba formation and it includes material resembling that of Vignard's Sebilian I, although it also incorporates a reasonably large microlithic component. One point appears to have emerged in the light of these various areas of new research: the likelihood that Vignard's Sebilian III should actually be replaced by more microlithic industries. Donald O. Henry suggests that the 'Late Sebilian' should be assimilated, purely and simply, into the Silsilian.

It has been suggested that the origins of the Sebilian might lie in the Khargan industry (i.e. the Khargan Levallois defined by Caton-Thompson), but, as with the Nile valley Mousterian, the chronological hiatus between the two is too great. Connections have been made with the Tshitolian, an industry which, apart from the presence of bifacial tools, appears to have been similar to the Sebilian; it was described by J. Desmond Clark (1970) in Angola, but has also been found in northern Congo and Gabon at around 15,000 BP. Nevertheless, the geographical distance between these two cultural heartlands is quite significant, and no attempt to reconstruct a route linking the two has yet been successful.

It remains the case that the Sebilian, an exclusively Nilotic industry between Wadi Halfa and Qena, is regarded as intrusive, with its geo-metrical macroliths, its Levallois-like knapping technique and the tenta-tive emergence of the microburin technique. The industries that flourished in the valley between 20,000 and 12,000 BP were basically microlithic.

Might this originality be explained by the idiosyncrasies of different groups, described by Hassan (1974a: 219) as mobile hunters of large mammals, if we take into account the small scale of the sites? Alterna-tively, is it necessary to push the Sebilian back to an earlier date, like the second phase of the Halfan and site E71P1 at Edfu, as Vermeersch, Paulissen and Van Peer (1990a, 1991) suggest? Given the vagueness of the available dates (mostly relying on carbonated sediments or shells), Vermeersch *et al.* attach greater importance to techno-typological crite-ria, suggesting that there must have been a much more complex Middle Palaeolithic, of which the Sebilian, the Halfan and the Idfuan with Levallois component would constitute different facets. This would help to explain the lack of any Levallois technique in the blade industries of the Upper Palaeolithic in the Nile valley. Its discrete presence in the com-paratively well-dated microlithic industries of Wadi Kubbaniya could then be regarded as a resurgence of the technique.

In Wadi Kubbaniya, the accumulation of sand dunes in *c.*20,000 BP resulted in the creation of a lake, fed initially by the Nile floods and then later by the water table, after it had become entirely cut off from the river by the rising sands. In such a favourable environment, the human popu-lation settled in the safety of the high dunes at the time of the annual flood, only occupying the flood plain itself during the dry season. A first season of excavation was undertaken by the Combined Prehistoric Expe-dition, led by Fred Wendorf, in 1978, revealing a series of bladelet sites, the general nature of which was defined as 'Kubbaniyan' (see Wendorf *et al.* 1980, 1989). A good series of radiocarbon dates were obtained for this industry, placing it between 19,000 and 17,000 BP. Because of the discovery of grinding stones associated with these remains, and therefore the possibility (now discounted) that grain was being cultivated, the Americans returned to the region for further seasons from 1981 to 1984. They discovered sites that were slightly earlier than the Kubbaniyan in-dustry, as defined in 1978, including a human skeleton dating to *c.*30,000–20,000 BP.

These early Kubbaniyan sites (E81–3 and E81–4) were characterized by the predominance of the use of quartz, and about half of the debitage consisted of single-platform cores. The main features of the toolkit were backed bladelets, sometimes with Ouchtata retouch, perforators (made from blades with two worn-down edges), notches, denticulates and 'scaled pieces'. Numerous radiocarbon dates have placed this indus-try at *c.*21,000–19,000 BP, and there are striking typological similarities between it and the **Fakhurian** industry, which had been defined by D. Lubell (1971) on the basis of a number of sites in the vicinity of Esna (E71K1–5). Although the radiocarbon dates obtained from *Unio* shells from Lubell's Fakhurian sites are slightly later (18,020 ± 330 BP and 17,590 ± 300 BP), and the technology is also slightly different (with greater importance of bipolar production at the Esna sites), some scholars (e.g. Vermeersch 1992: 128) nevertheless include the early Kubbaniyan sites within the Fakhurian industry.

The eight 'classic Kubbaniyan' deposits which were located and studied in 1978 are all marked by debitage comprising bladelets made from either single-platform or opposed-platform cores and a toolkit largely dominated by bladelets with Ouchtata retouch. Scaled pieces are rare or even totally absent, apart from sites E78–2 and E78–4 where they occur in extremely high percentages. Endscrapers made from flakes, as well as notches and denticulates, appear in fairly significant numbers, along with a few burins.

Chert nodules from the Nile valley and the wadis accounted for 80 per cent of the raw material used, while the remaining 20 per cent comprised fossil wood, flint, chalcedony, agate, granite, sandstone and basalt. Although not very commonly found in the debitage, flint seems to have been brought in the form of prepared cores intended for the manufacture of a specific range of tools: Levallois flakes, Halfan flakes and burins. It seems that these techniques reappeared for particular limited types of tool, a high percentage being found at E78–2, where their frequency was equalled by that of scaled pieces, as mentioned above. These types of tool were found in smaller quantities at E78–3, E78–9 and E78–4. Such a technological 'throwback' in a microlithic context was also found at Esna (site E71K13), where Levallois flakes were used to produce burins!

Six of the eight sites yielded sandstone grinding stones. Altogether, 34 mortars and 32 pestles were found scattered in the occupation areas linked with the dune formations. The presence of grinding materials is not in itself a major occurrence, given that fragments of grinding stones were found at Sebilian sites in the Kom Ombo region (in association with ochre), and also at el-Kilh. However, their sheer abundance at Wadi Kubbaniya, together with their archaeological contexts, increase their significance here. Despite a homogeneous lithic inventory, both the stratigraphic positions of the sites and the associated faunal remains are sufficient to allow them to be split up into two groups: the sites on the dunes and those of the flood plain.

The dune sites, high enough to be safe from the annual flood, appear to represent something of a peak in terms of fishing. The lake, flooded during the time of maximum Nile indundation (August–September) was populated by aquatic species comprising huge numbers of fish, left stranded by the retreating waters and therefore easy to catch. The abundance of fish bones speaks volumes in this regard. W. Van Neer (1986) has shown that fishing was also practised at the beginning of the flood, when the *Clarias* fish had just began to gather at the edge of the waters. It is particularly interesting to note that heads rather than post-cranial skeletons tend to be found, suggesting that the fish were immediately gutted and, perhaps after drying and smoking, were taken away to be consumed elsewhere, in areas which, despite the efforts of fieldworkers, have not yet been identified. This practice, attested at sites E71K1 and E71K3 at Esna and also at Makhadma 4, may be interpreted as a first step towards a form of food storage which, along with the intensive use of grinding stones to process tubers, place the people of the Kubbaniyan industry at the beginning of a tradition of 'hunter-gatherer-storers' which was to have significant consequences.

The snaring of birds was a winter activity, judging from the species excavated, all of which visited Upper Egypt in the winter months. Few birds, on the other hand, appear to have been hunted on the plain, where sites have yielded few bird bones and, compared with the dune area, little in the way of fish. The remains of hartebeest (*Alcelaphus buselaphus*), aurochs (*Bos primigenius*) and gazelle (*Gazella rufifrons*) all suggest that there was a certain amount of hunting of mammals, perhaps geared more towards the season when animals left the low desert as it became too dry, and moved down to the river to quench their thirst.

Thus, 20 metres of sediments at Wadi Kubbaniya allow us to follow – more precisely than at any other comparable site – the lives of these communities of 'hunter-fisher-gatherer-storers', admirably adapted to the regularly changing conditions of their ecological context. These people were semi-sedentary occupants of a number of sites, still scattered at some distance from one another. The diversification of their exploitation of food resources (hunting large mammals and birds, catching fish, and gathering plant food) was accompanied at Wadi Kubbaniya by the phenomenon of storage.

In a study of hunter-gatherers, A. Testart (1982) has shown how much distance there usually was between the producer and the stored product. The decision to defer the consumption of a product until a later time implies a social and ideological transformation. Testart (1982: 45) discusses the implications of the use of storage:

'There is an abandonment or transformation of the rules of distribution, a change in attitudes towards others; people rely less on links based on kinship, affinity or friendship in the course of preparing for the future. There is a change in attitude to time, with greater importance being attributed to the past (i.e. goods that have already been accumulated) rather than the present, in terms of satisfying subsistence needs. There is a change in attitude to work, favouring work already done, invested in reserves, rather than work still to be done. There is a change in attitude to nature, which becomes a less important factor, compared with human labour.'

This socio-economic transformation was achieved without any fundamental change to the lithic inventory (apart from the appearance of grinding stones). At all of the Kubbaniyan sites, bladelets dominate, all knapped from the same basic raw material. Only in the case of sites E78–2 and E78–4 is the assemblage instead dominated by scaled pieces, which are not even present at the other sites. Another unusual aspect of site E78–4 is the presence of discs made from ostrich-eggshell, thus introducing an aspect of human activity which was unrelated to subsistence. Plant remains comprising tamarisk, acacia and *Salsola baryosma*, were found at both of these sites (with particular abundance at E78–4).

Between October 1962 and April 1963, the Canadian team led by P. E. L. Smith returned to re-examine Vignard's sites in the Kom Ombo plain. In the lower part of the Wadi Shait, near Gebel el-Silsila, they found GS-III: a stratified site consisting of two horizons sealed by later deposits of the Nile. At the base of the stratigraphy, Smith identified a microlithic industry incorporating the microburin technique: the **Silsilian**. This industry has great similarities with an industry discovered in Nubia by Wendorf (1968: II, 831–55), at a distance of about 50 kilometres to the north of Wadi Halfa: the **Ballanan**. Triangles and trapezes appear alongside burins, but the most frequent tool in Ballanan assemblages is a pointed type made from a blade or bladelet, which was totally or partially backed, in other words, a point made with the Levallois technique. The fairly small cores are bipolar and derive from pebbles of chalcedony, agate, jasper or carnelian. Several surviving surface scatters also correspond typologically to this industry.

In the absence of an exhaustive publication of the type-site, we must draw on two publications: firstly an article published by J. Phillips and Karl Butzer (1973), describing site GS2B-II on the surface of the Kom Ombo plain, and secondly the description of site E71–K20, near Esna, provided by Wendorf and Schild (1976: 269–72, figs 181–3). The toolkit is rich in truncated bladelets, backed bladelets and the microburin responsible for so-called La Mouillah points: 'bladelets, the edges of which were removed with abrupt retouch, resulting in a sharp distal or proximal trihedron' (Tixier 1963: 106), which are frequently found in the Iberomaurusian sites of the Maghreb. The associated fauna: catfish, shoveller-ducks, geese, wild asses, hippopotami, aurochs, hartebeest and gazelle (see Churcher and Smith 1972) suggests an economy based on hunting and fishing; GS2B-II, situated in an early Nile channel, must only have been occupied for part of the year, during the dry season.

The site of Arab el-Sahaba, 25 kilometres downstream from Nag Hammadi, studied by Vermeersch, is the northernmost Silsilian concentration (Vermeersch *et al.* 1985). Consisting of surface remains on top of a silt terrace, the assemblage is characterized by a strong tendency towards microlithic tools (the artefacts are often smaller than 1.5 cm), dominated by backed bladelets (often pointed) and truncations. A few 'true' microliths can be distinguished, in the form of scalene triangles, as well as blades and bladelets which had been retouched at the base, rounded off, or worked into a conical point. The microburin technique is frequently used, while the Levallois style of knapping is still unknown. There have been no finds of hearths or faunal remains to facilitate dating, therefore the chronology rests solely on techno-typology in this case.

In Nubia, five radiocarbon dates from charcoal have provided a range stretching from 18,000 to 16,000 BP. In the Kom Ombo region, a date of 15,300 BP has been obtained from a piece of charcoal and one of 14,400 BP from an *Unio* shell. Vermeersch, Paulissen and Van Peer (1991: 13) concede that, 'since the dates do not match very well, it seems that this industry should be placed between 16,000 and 15,000 BP'.

In the region of Esna, at the edge of a fossil lake which was perhaps associated with the Sahaba-Darau formation, six concentrations of lithic material studied by Wendorf (E71–K6B and K18A–E) were the first indication of the **Afian** industry, named after the nearby village of Thomas Afia (see Wendorf and Schild 1976: 280–7). This industry has also been found at Kom Ombo (GS–2B-I), where grinding stones have also been found, as well as at Wadi Kubbaniya (E83–4). In addition, the site of Makhadma 4 is evidently linked with the Afian.

The cores are essentially of the opposed-platform type, producing elongated flakes and bladelets (50 per cent), and some of them show signs of preparation reminiscent of Levallois cores. There are also 'true' Levallois cores in this industry (20 per cent) but they are of a distinctive type, described as 'bent Levallois', producing somewhat curved debitage. The toolkit is mainly dominated by micro-flakes and backed bladelets. The Afian is a geometric microlithic industry (scalene triangles and lunates) in which the microburin technique plays an important part, suggesting a familiar role in the development of composite tools. At Kom Ombo, a radiocarbon date from a piece of charcoal and two from shells have produced an overall date of about 13,000 BP, which appears to confirm the range of 13,500–12,500 BP obtained at Makhadma 4, on the basis of about ten dates derived from charcoal.

In the Wadi Halfa region, 16 **Qadan** assemblages (named after the type-site at Qada) were studied by Shiner (1968a). They comprised a

microlithic flake industry, in which the artefacts were almost all fashioned from Nile pebbles. The most typical artefact in the Qadan industry
is the lunate, a type of geometric microlith which is defined by Tixier
(1963: 129) as having the silhouette of a segment of a circle or a semicircle, the curved edge being obtained by careful retouching, while the
straight edge (i.e. the chord) is a rough, rectilinear cutting edge. The frequent glossy sheen of these lunates, together the presence of numerous
grinding stones *in situ* at Tushka (site 8095), indicates the role in the
Qadan economy played by the collection of wild *Gramineae* (a wheat-
like grass) from 14,000 BP onwards. Shiner distinguishes three phases of
occupation, each exemplified by three or four assemblages, extending
from 14,000 to 12,500 BP, and during this period the lithics were joined
by a few potsherds, which prefigured the next cultural phase: the Abkan.
Although the most recent estimates of date appear to be confirmed by
site E78-10 at Wadi Kubbaniya, dating to 12,500 BP, Shiner's hypothesis
of a long process of development has not yet been backed up by solid
evidence.

We need to return to the Esna region to consider the **Isnan** industry,
which, like the Sebilian, stands out clearly because of its macroliths, and
is dated to *c*.12,500 BP only on the basis of associations between surface
sites and the Sahaba-Darau formation. There are three large areas in the
regions of Esna, Naqada and Dishna where fairly rough Isnan material is
preserved, deriving from large chert cobbles from the Eocene limestone
formations of the Theban massif.

The cores, the dimensions of which are often more than 7 cm, are
globular in shape, indicating the production of large flake tools. Examples with one or two platforms are rare, as are blades. Large endscrapers
made from flakes are the most common tool type, along with notches
and denticulates, while bladelets are rare and sometimes totally absent. It
is particularly significant that some fragments of grinding stones are
present given that fish remains are notable by their rarity (having been
found only at one Isnan site) but 15 per cent of the retouched tools have
cutting edges bearing the characteristic glossy sheen associated with the
cutting of stalks of *Gramineae*. It is worth mentioning a small slab of
flint bearing, engraved into its cortex, a set of lines interpreted by its
discoverers as the head of an elephant.

Toolkits similar to those of the Isnan culture were found by Smith in
the region of Gebel el-Silsila; they were remarkable for the abundance of
the endscrapers (56.5 per cent) along with a set of non-microlithic blades
and flakes. These sets of material are known as **Menchian**, after the modern village of Menchia, which is located in the Kom Ombo plain, and
beside which Vignard had identified and published such assemblages. In
the absence of a basic study – given that the industry was discussed by

Smith (1967a: 201) in only about twenty lines – it is difficult to assess the 'cultural density' of the Menchian. The same applies to the **Sebekian**, a poorly defined occupation level above the Silsilian assemblage at GS-III (see Smith 1966, 1967a: 200).

On the other hand, in the Qena region, the so-called **Makhadma** sites have been the subject of research undertaken by Belgian archaeologists (Vermeersch, Paulissen and Van Peer 1989: 87–114). The Nile terraces and wadi deposits combine to form a complex system of landscapes within which the Makhadma sites 1–5 are located. Makhadma 1, first examined by Wendorf (Wendorf and Schild 1976: site 6104), represents the earliest of these sites, both in terms of its stratigraphic position and the typology of its lithics.

In 1983 and 1984, the Belgian team excavated Makhadma 2 and 4, both situated halfway up the slope of a wadi deposit. Two post-holes and two hearths were recognized at Makhadma 2, where the archaeological material was spread over the entire exposed surface, without any obvious clustering. The lithic material, fashioned from the terrace pebbles, which were rich in chert, comprised some 2000 items. The method of production was both flake and blade, obtained from single-platform cores (66 per cent). Only a few (46 per cent) were actual tools, and among these the most common were denticulates made from blades (9 per cent) and also from flakes (7 per cent), as well as endscraper-denticulates (8 per cent).

At Makhadma 4, numerous pits had been cut into the ground, sometimes pierced by post-holes. The archaeological layers consisted of fine sediments, coloured brown by ash, charcoal and deposits of black silt. As at Makhadma 2, the terrace pebbles were the main raw material being used. Single-platform cores dominate amid debitage relating to the production of blades and flakes. The 168 tools recovered (including items with continuous retouch) have been split up into 36 groups, the most outstanding of which are the burins, which account for 37 per cent of the total. The group of backed bladelets includes some atypical examples that are more flakes than bladelets. Notches and truncations are also prominent. Geometric microliths are rare, occurring in the form of trapezes, lunates and triangles. The microburin technique was not used.

The study of faunal remains at Makhadma shows the prominent role played by fishing in the economy of these sites. Three polished bone objects with double point and oval section should probably be interpreted as fish-hooks. Among the species of fish that have been identified, the catfish (*Clarias*) predominates. Mammals, on the other hand, are less numerous: hares, hippopotami, aurochs, hartebeest, and small carnivores such as otters. The discovery of a marine gastropod's shell (*Engina mendicaria*) indicates contacts with the Red Sea. Seven radiocarbon dates on charcoal have allowed the occupation period to be dated between 12,450 and 12,050 BP.

The Belgian archaeologists suggest that Makhadma 2 and 4, exploiting the riverine resources from their position of safety above the catastrophic floods of the so-called 'Wild Nile', are comparable with the snail-based economies (*'escargotières'*) of the Maghreb, with the role of the snails being taken by fish. The study of the ichthyofauna led by W. Van Neer reveals 99 per cent of *Clarias* at Makhadma 2, and 30 per cent at Makhadma 4, where *Tilapia* (68 per cent) predominated. *Tilapia* prefer deep, well-oxygenated water, while *Clarias* are usually found in residual water channels. Thus, the high proportion of *Tilapia* at Makhadma 4 is an indication of fishing during the high-water season when the river valley was flooded. However, the location of the sites on the wadi slopes must have enabled the fishing season to be prolonged, with the more continuous exploitation of stagnant ponds and marshes left behind by the flood (this being the period when *Clarias* were caught in greater numbers). It appears, however, that the fish must have been dried and smoked, judging from the survival of piles of charcoal. Perhaps even the two pits at Makhadma 2 were part of the set-up of a drying area. The Makhadma sites relate to the Afian-Silsilian industry, which is dominated by truncations, but the Belgian researchers are cautious about using purely typological evidence to integrate such specialized, seasonal occupations into the larger cultural spheres outlined above.

We have now reached *c*.12,000 BP, having following a plethora of small hunter-fisher-gatherer communities who are relatively limited in their movements and certainly obtained the protein in their diet by hunting large mammals. However, these groups were gradually 'squeezing' their micro-environment more and more with their extensive exploitation of aquatic resources, their clear tendency towards storage, and their equally intensive collection of wild *Gramineae*.

Such terms as Halfan, Sebilian and Qadan designate only the specific nature of toolkits within limited regions. Their cultural or functional specificity is therefore part of the microlithic-style culture in which the Levallois element survives to a greater or lesser extent. From another perspective these phenomena could perhaps be reorganized into a more restricted number of designations. In his study of the areas covered by these sites, Hassan (1980) notes that from 18,000 to 16,000 BP the average size of the occupations varies between 400 and 800 m². It progresses from 800 to 3500 m² over the next 2000 years (16,000–14,000 BP), and reaches 12,000 m² by 12,000 BP, with the latter period of growth evidently roughly corresponding to the increasing appearance of grinding stones. If we agree that the area of 20–400 m² corresponds on average to a community of 5 to 40 people, the vaster sites, with homogeneous material, indicate the regular reoccupation of the site, doubtless on a seasonal basis. It appears that during the period under consideration the population regularly increased, with a clear acceleration corresponding to the exploitation of tubers and the storage of food.

It has already been pointed out, with regard to the Wadi Kubbaniya remains, that there are social and ideological implications resulting from the practice of deliberately delaying the consumption of a product. There is no doubt that the sense of security to be gained by keeping food in reserve for months of penury must have served as a motivation towards more intensive storage. The immediate corrolary of this intensification was an increase in the available food resources, as well as a leap forward in the direction of a fully sedentary lifestyle. It appears, however (and we will return to this in connection with the Neolithic below), that, from both ethnological and archaeological points of view, the process of increasing sedentism played a fundamental role in population growth, the very fact of immobility having a beneficial effect on the birth-rate. It is indeed well-attested that the continual movement of women, either travelling in the wake of hunters or indeed in their own activities as gatherers, make it necessary for them to space out the births of their children over a longer period.

All the data at our disposal suggest that the process of Nilotic adaptation favoured partial sedentism and encouraged food storage. It was therefore part of the beginning of a long evolutionary process through which the people of the Nile valley embarked on the Neolithic period. But what is the meaning of the smaller scale of the toolkit, and what were the origins of this gradual diminution in the size of the lithics? The production of microliths is an indication of significant technological progress in that it inverts the links between raw material and available cutting edge. The tool, struck off in the form of small flakes, becomes a composite artefact and implies the use of wooden or bone supports. A group of fitted lunates in the groove of a handle forms a sickle. In the 1980s, advances in trace analysis allowed a French CNRS team to determine that the repeated presence of ochre on the non-active edges of a series of Capsian bladelets (eighth to fifth millennia BC) was linked with the fact that they were rubbing against wood and skin. This has thus been interpreted as proof that these tools had handles made from wood and leather ligature, the ochre being left behind by the strap as it decomposed or, conversely, having been deliberately used to speed up the drying process of the ligature and prevent putrefaction (see Beyries and Inizan 1982).

The transition from a toolkit that is simply reduced in size to one that is truly microlithic is reflected in the passage from a micro-support (flake or bladelet) produced directly from the core to the creation of a fragment of material from a flake, blade or bladelet. In the first instance, the traces of the knapping technique still leave a mark on the tool, whether it is retouched or not, whereas in the second instance these traces disappear and the process of fashioning by truncations produces a geometric shape such as the trapeze, triangle or lunate. It is this which enables us to understand the role of the microburin – it is not a tool in itself but simply the chacteristic by-product of the technique by which geometric microliths are produced. This technique, which has been studied and well defined by Tixier (1963: 39–42) in connection with the Maghreb Epipalaeolithic, consists of the pressure flaking of a notch as a result of which an oblique fracture is produced. The part which is detached and falls off at this point has rather misleadingly become known as a microburin because it resembles a small burin, but it is actually only a piece of debitage, and its sole significance for the flint-knapper lies in the piece of stone which remains in his hand, the sharp trihedron which can be altered by various retouches to serve as the basis for many of the characteristic tools of this epoch. The microburins, blending in with the tools themselves, may not be indispensable to the microlithic assemblage but they unfailingly indicate the practice of this method of knapping and allow its importance to be assessed.

Where did these bladelet and microlithic industries originate? Far from being restricted to the Nile valley, these industries constitute the essential components of neighbouring cultures in the Near East and the Maghreb. They run from the Euphrates to the Atlas mountains, along the entire Mediterranean coast, and their regional variants cover the entire African continent. In South Africa, the Howieson's Poort industry includes the production of bladelets, lunates and trapezes even before 50,000 BP (Clark 1978).

In the Maghreb and Cyrenaica, the Iberomaurusian followed the Aterian, after a considerable hiatus. Given the lack of any intermediary stage, it seems that the Levallois pedunculate points were simply replaced by the backed bladelets of the Iberomaurusian, which account for anything between 40 per cent and 80 per cent of the toolkit. Among these bladelets, La Mouillah points and Ouchtata retouches are found in varying proportions. Microburins are present (sometimes in very small numbers) at all of the sites, while the geometric microliths are also rather poorly represented, consisting only of lunates. The percentages of 'scaled pieces' vary from one site to another, burins are hardly abundant, and endscrapers (generally short and made from flakes) are found everywhere, although in small numbers. This whole toolkit is made from pebbles of flint, sandstone, quartzite and volcanic rocks, while the cores, which are small in size, frequently have one platform. Polished bone was used for knives, smoothing tools, pins, bradawls, fish-hooks and punches. Chronologically, the Iberomaurusian extended from the sixteenth to the tenth millennium BP (Camps 1974: 68): six millennia during which an evolution can be discerned (Camps 1974: 70–80) but no loss of the microlithic component.

In Cyrenaica, in the cave of Haua Fteah, the eastern Oranian industry defined by Charles McBurney (1967), which was contemporaneous with the Iberomaurusian, is similar in many respects, with the proportion of bladelets sometimes as high as 98 per cent. The Dabban, on the other hand, was earlier than the eastern Oranian and paralleled the Aterian; in about 40,000 BP, it already included backed blades and bladelets. In its later phases, c.32,000–17,000 BP, rectangular microliths with double truncations appeared, eventually reaching a proportion of 18 per cent of the toolkit, while burins eventually accounted for 18–40 per cent.

To the east was the site of Boker-Tachitt in the Negev, which has already been mentioned above. The lithics at Boker-Tachitt suggest that, around 40,000 BP, there was a transition from Levallois production techniques to a unipolar method of blade production in a style that was already clearly Upper Palaeolithic (Marks 1983b).

Two technocomplexes characterize the final phase of the Levantine Palaeolithic: the Ahmarian and the Levantine Aurignacian. The Ahmarian, which developed out of the local Mousterian, is defined on the basis of the site of Erg el-Ahmar in the Judaean desert, and its blade-dominated industry contains a high number of tools made from bladelets. The tool inventory of the Levantine Aurignacian, situated in the north, consists largely of flake-tools rather than blades; endscrapers and burins still account for more than 50 per cent of the tools, and some el-Wad points are present, particularly in level VII at Ksar Akil, in Lebanon, which dates to 3200 BP (Tixier and Inizan 1981: 360). These two complexes, each of which pulls together a number of different sites and variants, went through an uninterrupted process of development between 39,000 and 17,000 BP. The Ahmarian tradition is the only one of the two which is represented in the Sinai. The sites, a cluster of small scatters covering 10–100 m² at the foot of Gebel Lagama, are known as 'Lagamean'. Since the climate at that date was colder and more humid than it is today, there were two springs (now fossilized), providing a meeting point for the communities in this region. The lithic inventory was dominated by retouched blades and bladelets, including several el-Wad points, endscrapers and burins. The sites as a whole have been dated to the period between 34,000 and 30,000 BP on the basis of radiocarbon dates obtained from hearths. Similar occupation-sites were studied by Phillips (1987) at Qadesh Barnea, some 100 kilometres to the east of Gebel Maghara.

There then ensued a dry period (traces of which have survived in the form of phenomena indicating erosion), between 28,000 and 14,000 BP. This seems to correspond to an arid phase across North Africa generally.

Both in the east and the west, the deserts became devoid of human population. Traces of humans reappeared in *c*.14,000 BP in the form of a microlithic industry known in the Levant as 'Geometric Kebaran' (consisting of two phases, A and B). The non-geometric Kebaran complex – out of which the Kebaran industry had evolved – is a set of Epipalaeolithic industries attested in Syria-Palestine from 19,000 BP onwards, which, although involving multiple facies, was characterized by a considerable proportion of non-geometric microliths (85 per cent) within a context of blade production. The toolkit also includes a few polished stone awls, as well as pestles and mortars. When it was followed by the Geometric Kebaran A, *c*.14,000–12,000 BP, the percentages of 'true' microliths (especially trapezes and rectangles) increased to as much as 60 to 80 per cent of the toolkit. Wherever we find the Geometric Kebaran in a stratigraphic context, it is situated above the Kebaran proper. At Yabrud III and at el-Khiam, it is situated below the levels containing material of the Natufian culture, the first sedentary group attested at around 12,000 BP in these regions. This Geometric Kebaran A was found at Gebel Maghara in the Sinai, in association with grinding stones at North Lagama VIII (see Bar Josef and Phillips 1977).

A group of sites clustered together in Wadi Mushabi, still in the Gebel Maghara region, have preserved traces of a blade industry which involves extensive use of the microburin technique. Arched backed bladelets, La Mouillah points and asymmetrical trapezes are also present between 14,000 and 12,500 BP, in association with ostrich-eggs and the so-called *dentalium* shells which resemble hooks. This complex, the 'Mushabian', is similar to the last phase of the Geometric Kebaran in that it includes microburins, but, on the other hand, there are no lunates, despite the fact that these are the most diagnostic tools of Geometric Kebaran B.

Amid this vast network of bladelet industries, several cultural centres can be distinguished both on the basis of their earlier date and in view of the fact that the transition from one industry to another can be discerned. This is the case at Howieson's Poort in South Africa, which is probably the earliest bladelet industry of this type, at Boker-Tachitt in the Negev, at Ahmarian sites in the Levant, at Dabban sites in Cyrenaica (where blades and bladelets have been found alongside a strong Levallois-Mousterian tradition), at Sebilian sites in Egypt (where the Levallois method was still used alongside the newly introduced abrupt retouch and microburin techniques), and at Halfan sites dating to *c*.19,000 BP (which include a high proportion of backed bladelets and use of Ouchtata retouch along with a Levallois tradition). Compared with all these complexes and industries, the Iberomaurusian is one of the latest variants.

Tixier (1972) suggests that northern Sudan might have been one of the main 'centres of differentiation' that produced the bladelet industry of the Maghreb which is so similar to the final Palaeolithic of Upper Egypt. It is still not clear where the Sebilian ought to be placed in chronological terms, but we cannot deny the originality of Halfan techniques with regard to the development of the micro-support. One point remains problematic: the archaeological void in Middle and Lower Egypt. Given that the Nile Delta is located directly between the Levant and North Africa, it must have played an essential role in the development of microlithic cultures, and some scholars argue that the Mushabian complex in the Sinai might have originated in the Delta.

With a probable 'centre of differentiation' in the south and evidence for diffusion in the north, the Nile valley, between 20,000 and 12,000 BP, was not only part of a major techno-cultural process but one of the driving forces. A major climatic change now took place: the rains had returned in about 14,000 BP, and these were followed by the great early Holocene wet phase from 12,000 to 7500 BP (see chart 2). Groups of people were thus able gradually to reoccupy the zones of the Sahel and Sahara that had until then been deserted.

Paradoxically, it was around this period, corresponding to the end of the catastrophic floods of the 'Wild Nile', that virtually all trace of human occupation disappeared in the Nile valley. Abnormal floods, reaching heights of 8 or 9 metres above the modern flood-plain, and characterized by deposits of clayey silts, were detected by Butzer (1980), who argued that they reflect climatic anomalies in sub-Saharan Africa, between 14,000 and 12,000 BP. The sites of Makhadma 2, 3 and 4 were contemporary with these high floods.

This episode was followed, at round 11,500 BP, by a brief hyperarid phase during which the height of the Nile flood sank again, consideranly reducing the extent of the alluvial plain. The end of the period of high floods produced a state of disequilibrium which engulfed the process of Nilotic adaptation. No site from the period of 12,000–8000 BP has been found, apart from Qadan sites in Wadi Halfa. It was once thought that human occupation throughout the length of this narrower Nile valley had simply been covered up by the wider area of modern sediments. Another hypothesis, however, was put forward by Connor and Marks (1986), who suggested that the adaptation to a high-water environment, based on the significant potential of resources, was ultimately unsuccessful, forcing these groups to move away in search of fresh sources of subsistence, and thus destroying the fragile equilibrium of the communities. This situation was no doubt accompanied by violent competition between different groups, and we might ask whether a cemetery of 59 human skeletons found at site 117, Jebel Sahaba, constitutes evidence of this aggression.

Site 117, located 3 kilometres to the north of Wadi Halfa and just to

the south of Jebel Sahaba, is one of the earliest surviving cemeteries in
the history of the Nile valley. A total of 59 skeletons were excavated
(Wendorf 1968: II, 954–95). The bodies were all laid out in semi-flexed
positions, on their left sides, with their heads to the east, facing towards
the south, in simple pits covered with sandstone slabs. The remains were
sealed by a calcified crust, and then this crust was covered by sloping
heaps of debris from the nearby inselbergs. As these piles of debris were
eroded by the wind, the sandstone slabs covering the graves were exposed here and there. In Nubia, this layer never covers anything as late as
Neolithic or historical material, therefore it would appear that the cemetery must be pre-Neolithic in date. However, the dating of the cemetery
rests largely on the typology of the lithics associated with the skeletons.
The toolkit, including burins, truncations made from flakes, backed flakes
and bladelets, endscrapers and various geometric microliths (including
lunates), resembles that of the Qadan industry, particularly the phase
dated at around 12,000 BP.

The excavators found 110 artefacts, including 97 simple un-retouched
flakes, embedded in the bones and inside the skulls of 24 of the skeletons, perhaps representing the cause of their deaths. These possible indications of brutal killings were exacerbated by the presence of multiple
inhumations, with two graves containing four bodies each. The eight
bodies had been buried simultaneously as an undifferentiated group of
men, women and children. Fractures of the forearms, as well as traces of
cut-marks on some of the long bones in their legs, evidently caused by
the deep penetration of knives into the flesh, further reinforce the impression of extreme violence.

Contemplating the possible explanations for this situation, Wendorf
reached the conclusion that it was an exceptional site. The women and
children made up nearly 50 per cent of this macabre population, therefore the continuation of such a mortality rate – when combined with the
'normal' percentages of births and deaths calculated for groups of hunter-
gatherers – would have quickly led to the total extinction of the entire
group. Either site 117 represents an exceptionally dramatic event perhaps connected with the disequilibrium following Wild Nile floods, or it
was an unusual site plagued by violent deaths and constituting evidence
of a custom of selective burial. If the first possibility were correct (i.e.
ecological causes), then we would have to assume that the cemetery was
used for a relatively short period corresponding to a sudden staggering
drop in the group's population. According to the second interpretation
(i.e. violent deaths and selective burial), the site might have been occupied for a much longer period, and during this time it would have been
repeatedly visited by one or more groups of hunter-gatherers.

At around the same time (1962–3), 39 skeletons were exhumed from a site on the west bank of the river, almost exactly opposite Jebel Sahaba. Although these were also laid in flexed positions, the orientation of the body varies, and, as far as multiple burials are concerned, the number here dropped to only three double inhumations. The complete absence of 'projectiles' incorporated into the bones, and the presence of only one case of traumatic pathology suggest a much calmer situation. Nevertheless, the anthropological study of the two populations reveals great physical similarities.

A fossilized skeleton at Wadi Kubbaniya (Close 1986: site E82–6), partly exposed on the surface and embedded in a block of calcified sandstone, has some affinities with the two groups just described. It is a male human aged 20–5 years, buried with its face against the ground and probably in an extended position (the back of the body having been partially destroyed) in a simple shaft excavated prior to the accumulation of a silty deposit dating to c.20,000 BP. On the left-hand side of its abdominal cavity were two bladelets of Final Palaeolithic type, which may possibly have been responsible for his death. This is reminiscent of the violence that seems to have brought about the many deaths at Jebel Sahaba – violence that is also attested by the reduced fracture of the ulna of the man at Wadi Kubbaniya, as well as the stone flake that partially damaged his left humerus.

At Tushka, 250 kilometres upstream from Aswan, site 8905, on the west bank, consists of a vast collection of Qadan remains among the sand-dunes, at the edge of a marshy area. On and around an oval mound, about 5 metres in diameter and about 30 centimetres high, 21 graves have survived, corresponding to at least two periods. The first graves, apparently contemporary with the Sahaba formation, are earlier than the plant types developed at a time of maximum high waters. The second group cannot be dated with any precision but appear to be considerably later than the first.

The individuals in the earlier Toshka graves – buried on their left sides, facing to the east, and mostly in a flexed position – are poorly preserved but present morpohological similarities with the nearby Jebel Sahaba skeletons. The occupants of graves 12, 13 and 18 had bovid horns placed by their heads. It is certainly tempting to see here all the first signs of the privileged relationship which existed in later times, during the Egyptian pharaonic period, between men and cattle/bulls (still favoured by Upper Nile pastoralists in modern times). We should, however, remain cautious in this repect, especially as Wendorf (1968: II, 875) points out that 'In all instances the horn-cores were above the skeletons and not clearly associated with them.'

Two skeletons were found near Esna, apparently in association with Fakhurian material (Lubell 1971). From an anthropological point of view, all the human skeletons in the Nile valley that have been found in association with microlithic industries (totalling a little more than a hundred so far) are of the Mechta-el-Arbi (or Mechta-Afalou) type, which was defined partly on the basis of about 30 skeletons discovered in one of the great snail-consuming communities ('*escargotières*') of the Upper Capsian at Mechta-el-Arbi in Algeria. This type, the north African Cromagnoid, is the only form of human associated with the Iberomaurusian; the evulsion of the incisors is a cultural trait peculiar to this group, a 'mutilation' which was totally unknown among the Nilotic people.

What then are these 'Mechtoids' doing in the Nile valley? Several characteristics differentiate the Nile examples from those of north Africa, such as higher cheekbones in the face and a more exaggerated prognathism; in addition they never practised dental extraction. Where, then, did they come from? Certainly not from north Africa, since they are thousands of years earlier than the people of the Iberomaurusian complex. They may possibly derive from the proto-Cromagnons of Qafzeh, as Vandermeersch (1981) suggests (see also Tillier 1992). Alternatively they may have simply evolved towards this physical type independently within the Nile valley, although unfortunately this is difficult to prove since we know nothing of the human types who preceded them. It is therefore with a certain degree of circumspection that modern humans, emerging from unknown stock, first appeared and established themselves along the Nile valley.

Part III

The Neolithic Period

5

The process of 'Neolithicization'

The great Holocene wet phase (c.12,000–8000 BP)

From Mauretania to the African rift valley, via the Maghreb, the central and southern Sahara, the Nile valley and Ethiopia, the whole series of wet phases underway from 14,000 BP onwards is a phenomenon which also affected the modern arid and semi-arid areas of Africa. Overall, the levels of the Saharan lakes gradually increased until c.9500–9000 BP, when they reached their maximum (Muzzolini 1983).

Between the Atlas Mountains and the Nile valley, the climate across the Saharan massifs in about the seventh millennium BP was sufficiently humid to support hardwood forests in their heights and Mediterranean-style plants in the lowest regions. The intensive drainage system (visible under the sands by means of satellite photography), which is a fossil of the Plio-Pleistocene period, came back into operation and lakes were supplied with fresh water enabling the renewal of fauna, flora and human communities. However, these people brought with them the first indications of the Neolithic period, in the form of pottery types with wavy-line decoration well-known from A. J. Arkell's excavations at Khartoum in 1949. The intensive research projects of the last 20 years, in the central and southern Sahara, have shed new light on the emergence of the Neolithic.

The central Sahara

The site of Tagalagal, discovered by J. P. Roset in 1978, was perched up in the Aïr mountains, at a height of more than 1820 metres above sea level. Covering an area of about 20 × 40 m, cleared of the enormous granite boulders which cover the surrounding surface, the site consists of an accumulation of worked stone, the remains of grinding stones and sherds of brown pottery decorated with wavy lines. In the southern part of the site, a rocky overhang preserves a fossiliferous deposit which extended over several square metres and was less than a metre thick. This was probably a dumping ground, comprising scattered fragments of archaeological material which were piled up and mixed with pieces of charcoal. Two astonishing radiocarbon dates have been obtained: 9370 ± 130 BP and 9330 ± 130 BP. The outline study indicates that there was already a well-developed pottery tradition, with both open and closed forms, with spheroid bases, sometimes with very short, slightly splayed necks. Several techniques are prominent in the decoration of these pots. Wavy lines, applied with a flexible fish-bone comb, covered the entire surface of most of the vessels; some are decorated with impressed spirals, flambé decoration (i.e. the uneven or streaky application of colour), impressed opposed chevrons, wedge shapes and incised parallel lines. The poor standard of the lithics is in stark contrast to the variety of ceramic types; the quality of locally available stone – volcanic rocks and quartz – is doubtless suitable for most purposes, but the search for stone with a more homogeneous grain for the purpose of creating fine examples of arrowheads provides a good indication of the ability to work stone. As a general rule, they chose to use straightforward thick flakes, without retouch, for endscrapers, transverse sidescrapers and a few angle burins. It is also possible to find examples of so-called 'accidental burins', usually interpreted as knapping errors whereby the flake is split into two halves along the axis of percussion (often because of the coarse grain of the material). No microliths have been found, but a notable quantity of axes and adzes with polished cutting edges; this does not constitute evidence of agriculture, but it is an indication of grinding, showing the important role of wild grains in the subsistence pattern.

Far from being an isolated instance, Tagalagal seems, so far as we can tell, to be one element of a coherent group, judging from the discovery of similar sites at the edge of the Aïr region that have been radiocarbon-dated to the same period.

The site of Amekni, located at the confluence of two wadis in the Hoggar region (Camps 1968), was dated by its many hearths heated by stones: the calibrated date of 6700 BC can be retained for the beginning of this occupation, which lasted for nearly three millennia (recent levels: 3500 BC). There is no trace of domestication in the early strata, but the wild fauna suggests a landscape of marshes and savanna, which is also indicated by pollen analysis suggesting temperate species. There are grinding installations in the form of depressions hollowed out of the granitic outcrop that makes up the bedrock of the site. Taken together with the discovery, at a depth of 1.4 metres, of two grains of *Pennisetum* (millet), these installations not only indicate the essential role played by plants but also suggest that there may possibly also have been some practice of agriculture.

There are sherds from this early phase at Amekni that evidently derive from simple, large-sized open bowls. The diameters of some of these vessels are greater than 50 centimetres. The fabric of the ceramics is hard and essentially tempered with grains of quartz, and it is always decorated with impressed motifs executed before firing, while the fabric was soft, using a comb or natural implements, such as *Silurus*-fish spikes or stripped twigs. As at Tagalagal, the diversity of the ceramics contrasts with the unimpressive range of stone tools, and once again this can be at least partly ascribed to the relatively lack of good quality of the local stone with regard to tool production: volcanic rock, quartz, poor quality obsidian and rock crystal. The quartz that was primarily used for their toolkit, found in the lower strata, took the form of backed bladelets as well as a few endscrapers and arrowheads. The influence of the microlithic style of toolkit, without microburin technique, was steadily weakening, leading gradually to the preponderance of an increasingly diverse range of pebble-based tools. Burins, rabots, endscrapers and then perforators began to appear, while arrowheads also became slightly more common. The range of bone tools is, on the other hand, of very high quality, taking the form of fine polishing tools, borers, chisels, awls, hairpins, pendants and abundant beads. Small discs made from ostrich-egg shells and stone bangles complete this rich inventory of artefacts.

Three individuals, identified as 'negroid', comprising a woman and two children, were buried at Amekni towards the end of the seventh millennium BC (one of the children's burials having yielded a calibrated radiocarbon date of 6100 BC).

Concerning daily life in these first Neolithic settlements, the inhabitants of which were presumably agriculturalists but had not yet begun to rear animals, Gabriel Camps (1974: 234), the excavator of Amekni, writes: 'Hunting, fishing, gathering and plant cultivation were their external activities; within their encampments, between the huts, built in the midst of large stones, the women pounded the millet and ground up the grains of wild cereals, cooking porridge in the large vessels made from silt collected from the river banks. The preparation of the skins of antelope or cattle, and the making of basketry using bone awls would have still left plenty of time for loafing around and idleness. At the end of spring, when the fruits of the nettle-trees were ripening, they would pick great quantities of them in the nearby woods, and perhaps with fermentation in the large vessels they would make a form of beer.'

Similar traces of occupation, either contemporary with Amekni or earlier, have been found elsewhere on the Hoggar massif (e.g. Maitre 1971). In the granite massifs of Tadrart-Acacus, in southwestern Libya, several sites preserve an Epipalaeolithic industry associated with high quality pottery decorated with typical dotted wavy line motifs. Radiocarbon dates of 8640 ± 70 BP for Ti-n-Torha (Barich 1978) and 8070 ± 100 BP for Fozzigiarien (Mori 1965) indicate that these sites were roughly contemporary with Amekni, in the second half of the seventh millennium BC.

The Western Desert

In Kharga Oasis, after the post-Aterian hiatus, the beginning of the final Palaeolithic period appears to have been contemporary with the formation of the Holocene playas, c.9000 BP, and it seems to have lasted until about 7200 BP. Gardner and Caton-Thompson (1952), who surveyed the region in the late 1940s, discovered surface sites indicating the presence of two distinct cultural groups. The first of these, characterized by a microlithic toolkit consisting of blades and backed bladelets, including the type with two backed edges, was attributed to the 'Bedouin Microlithic'. There were few 'true' geometric tools and no sign of microburin technique among these artefacts, which included arrowheads made from transverse flakes, Ounan points and fine rhomboidal armatures, with bifacial knapping. Fragments of grinders and ostrich-eggshells (including disc-shapes) give this group an Epipalaeolithic flavour that is further accentuated by the total absence of pottery. However, pottery vessels are certainly found in association with the concentrations of 'Neolithic' material, comprising axes, chisels, planes, bifacial knives and hollow-base arrowheads, characteristic of the second group: the 'Neolithic farmers'. The extremely weathered potsherds (never decorated), are made from a brownish red fabric, but there is little more that can be said about them.

Further to the north, in the Siwa Oasis, the fieldwork undertaken by Fekri Hassan (1976, 1978) has revealed the presence of many sites associated with early Holocene deposits. About 30 kilometres to the east of the modern town of Siwa, a set of concentrations form the complex of Hatiyet Um el-Hiyus. Mainly dominated by straight backed bladelets (sites 75/5, 75/6 and 75/31), burins, microburins and perforators are well attested, alongside several bifacial points. The radiocarbon dating of one of the many ostrich-eggshells places this group at around the beginning of the Holocene: 8154 ± 65 BP. At site 75/31, burins outnumbered perforators, microburins and backed bladelets.

The Garra Oasis, 130 kilometres from Siwa, was a depression fed by brackish springs where they became vast *sebkhas*. A group of seven sites, each comprising sub-concentrations of material, contained a toolkit made up initially of burins, then denticulates, perforators, blades and backed bladelets, endscrapers, scaled pieces and notches. There were no microburins but there were numerous small points made from pedunculate blades (Hassan 1976: figs 7a, d). An ostrich-egg yielded a date of c.8258 BP.

At Shiyata, another depression 37 kilometres from Siwa, there is a site located on an area of high land overlooking a small salt lake occupying part of the bottom of the depression. A semicircle of limestone slabs surrounds a concentration of lithic items, with a diameter of 11.7 metres. These lithics were not spread randomly over the whole area but roughly grouped together into subconcentrations of various types: the cores were separated from the waste flakes, and the latter were found in a different location from blades, tools and ostrich-eggshells. One of the shells has yielded a radiocarbon date of 8817 ± 77 BP for this temporary occupation. Although typologically linked with the microlithic material of the Egyptian Sahara, the final Palaeolithic industries of Siwa are particularly distinguished by the frequency of burins.

Nearer to the Nile valley, at Nabta Playa, Fred Wendorf's team found three pluvial phases separated by arid intermediate phases, stretching althogether from 9000 to 5800 BP (Wendorf and Schild 1980: 236–41). About 20 kilometres further to the north, two small basins filled with playa deposits, el-Kortein and el-Beid, reveal the same basic sequence of pluvials and intermediate phases (Wendorf et al. 1984).

Two archaeological phenomena are associated in these regions with the dune formations and the playa sediments; one dates to the final Palaeolithic while the other is essentially Neolithic. Six concentrations (E75-6–7, E75-9, E77-3, E77-6–7), which have been studied in detail, correspond to the first humid phase (Playa I). Taking into account variations from one site to another, the proportions of tools made from bladelets generally predominate, consisting largely of backed bladelets. The microburin technique had not yet appeared, but the so-called 'Krukowski microburin' is present; the latter is defined by Jacques Tixier (1963: 142, no. 103) as follows: 'end of a blade or backed bladelet removed by the "microburin blow" technique applied on the side of the backed edge'. Lunates, trapezes and triangles cover the whole range of geometric microliths. Small points made from pedunculate bladelets are linked with the Ounan points of the Maghreb (Tixier 1963: 149, no. 844) and the el-Harif points in Sinai (although those from Nabta are rather squatter than the two latter types). While quartz and igneous rocks provided a range of raw material in situ, this toolkit, clearly dating to the Upper Palaeolithic, was essentially made from a fine Eocene chert deriving from the gebel, the procurement of which indicates transportation of materials. Pestles and mortars, although still far from abundant compared with later periods, nevertheless indicate a degree of perseverance in the gathering and use of cereals. Ostrich eggshells are common, on the other hand, either in the form of fragments decorated with incised motifs or as discs at various stages of manufacture. A coherent group of radiocarbon dates obtained from charcoal and ostrich-eggs show that the occupation stretched from 8960 to 8300 BP.

No sites corresponding to these periods are either associated with wadi sediments or situated in the depressions of Bir Sahara and Bir Tarfawi, which are otherwise so rich in material from earlier periods. There seems, in fact, to have been a major change in settlement strategy, with the areas of occupation moving to the edges or to the regularly inundated surfaces of the playas.

On the basis of geomorphology, as well as the surviving traces of flora and fauna, the landscape of Nabta can be reconstructed; it appears to have been semi-wooded, bushy, and focusing around sources of water, the geology being dominated by Eocene limestones of the Gebel, occasionally interrupted by exposed surfaces of Nubian sandstone. The fauna, essentially made up of gazelles (*Gazella dorcas* and *G. rufifrons*) and hares, suggest a semi-arid country of sub-desert steppe with scattered bushes and thorny plants. It therefore seems that the only areas of humidity took the form of these ephemeral lakes which cover the bottoms of playas.

The insignificant scale of these concentrations of material, together with the overall structure of the encampment at Shiyata in Siwa Oasis, suggests that they were only temporary settlements, each with their individual characteristics; the presence of hearths and grinding stones, however, makes it likely that these areas were favoured places that were regularly reoccupied.

The time of these encampments was followed by a period of aridity and erosion, characterized by the formation of dunes. Next, however, the return of humidity is indicated by the fact that vegetation can be seen to have invaded the dunes. New groups of people then arrived, very often reoccupying final Palaeolithic sites; their lithic traditions were different from their predecessors, but their strategies for use of the land, together with the first traces of pottery and cultivated cereals, show that this was an important turning point.

Five sites at Nabta Playa corespond to this second litho-stratigraphic phase (Playa II). Moving their investigations further to the west, into the area of Bir Kiseiba, Wendorf's team were able to clarify and refine the study of Nabta by the study of 13 further localities.

The vast depression of Bir Kiseiba, the main stopping point along the Darb el-Arbain (the 'forty-day route' linking the Nile valley with the Sudan, via Kharga Oasis), was surrounded to north, east and west by an enormous Nubian sandstone escarpment topped by a bank of ferruginous conglomerate, yielding the many chert pebbles that form the main high-quality raw material for the groups settled on the edges of basins at the bottom of the depression.

The earliest known Neolithic groups (el-Adam type, according to Wendorf *et al.* 1984: 409ff) correspond to the playa sites located at the foot of the Kiseiba escarpment (E77–7 at Gebel el-Beid, and E79–8 and E80–4 at el-Adam). Ten radiocarbon dates from these three sites suggest that they were occupied between about 9500 and 9000 BP.

The toolkit, 60 per cent of which is made from Eocene chert, was still mainly microlithic, dominated by the backed bladelet, usually pointed; the microburin was well represented, as well as endscrapers, perforators and notches. Few burins, however, figure in this group, in which truncations, denticulates and geometrics are rare. Many pestles and mortars were found, alongside ostrich-eggshell beads at all stages of manufacture; it is likely that the latter are associated with grooved stones, which were probably involved in the manufacture of eggshell discs. The incised decoration on the eggshells is sometimes filled with ochre. It was at two of these sites (E79–8 and E80–4) that the first known pottery appeared in this region. Three decorated sherds at site E79–8, and four very eroded and apparently undecorated sherds at E80–4 were linked with layers datable to 9000 BP, thus situating these early ceramics in the second half of the eighth millennium BC, as at Tagalagal. The sandy, well-fired fabric with mica inclusions, has a brownish red to brownish grey colour; the impressed motifs on the outer surface consist of parallel bands of curved lines, each a sort of long comma, being oblique in relation to the rim. Among the fragments of bone that have been identified, the gazelle predominates at both sites. Some remains of *Bos* may represent the domesticated species of *Bos primigenius*.

There are also five later sites ranged between 8800 and 8500 BP, on the basis of four radiocarbon dates obtained from charcoal and ostrich eggs at three of the localities (the el-Kortein Neolithic type, according to Wendorf *et al.* 1984). The typology remained microlithic; the most characteristic tool is the small point with a sharpened base, made from a bladelet, already encountered in the final Palaeolithic, reminiscent of the el-Harif and Ounan points. The microburin technique continued to be used; notches and denticulates are found, but few geometrics, burins and perforators. The gazelle is still the dominant animal represented, alongside the same remains of *Bos* that were perhaps domesticated. No sherds have been found in these concentrations, which are of limited extent, the locations of which within the playas suggest that they were occupied during the dry season.

Seven sites, from Kharga to Kiseiba, cover the next phase from 8500 to 8200 BP, on the basis of four radiocarbon dates from three sites (all el-Gorab Neolithic types according to Wendorf). The scalene triangle is the dominant tool in an inventory which was still microlithic. The backed bladelets, often sharpened, the trapezes and the microburins are found in significant numbers, while endscrapers, perforators and burins are rare. Many potsherds derive from site E79–4, some of them decorated with incised and dotted lines. Few animal remains have survived at these sites, apart from a few *Bos* bones at site E79–4. Site E72–5, in the Dyke region, some 500 kilometres west of Nabta, virtually in the centre of the playa, indicates either a long period of occupation during a fairly extensive time of aridity or seasonal reoccupation of the place.

The period around 8000 BP seems to correspond to the final episode of this early Neolithic phase in the southern part of the Egyptian Western Desert, defined by the work of Wendorf. A total of five occupation sites at Nabta Playa and Bir Kiseiba have provided radiocarbon dates spaced out between 8100 and 7900 BP (Wendorf's el-Nabta Neolithic). Although the basic lithic technology, based on the knapping of blades and bladelets deriving from single-platform or opposed-platform cores, scarcely differs from material at earlier sites, the specific typology had undergone radical change: artefacts worked with continuous retouch, as well as burins and perforators, which had until then been the 'poor relations' of the assemblage, became much more significant, alongside backed bladelets and a few geometrics (principally scalene triangles). The pottery, which was frequently found at these sites, was decorated with dotted lines or combed impressions; the sherds evidently derive from simple, large bowls.

The animal remains suggest that there was an increase in the proportion of hares compared with gazelle and *Bos*. The size of the sites was growing, and the systematic patterns of the settlements suggest that this group, if not sedentary, at least occupied a certain region relatively permanently. Site E75–6 at Nabta is significant in this respect. Located in the middle of the playa, in an area unaffected by the seasonal flooding, an area of 1000 m² has been uncovered, revealing the remains of one of the first villages brought to light in this region (Wendorf 1980: 131, figure 3.60). The construction and spatial organization of the settlement at this site expresses a state of relatively sedentary occupation, as well as undeniable signs of a social structure. The bases of huts, comprising basins with a diameter of 3 metres, each contained one or two hearths, and several were surrounded by post-holes, aligned in parallel alignments, spaced out at more or less equal intervals; silos, consisting of circular pits with diameters of around 1.5 metres, were found in association with the huts, while two wells with carved out steps inside them provided access to the subterranean water table.

The lithic assemblage pertaining to this settlement, essentially made from quartz but also from clear grey chert, comprises perforators (especially double backed types), backed bladelets, notches and denticulates, sometimes made from large flakes and blades. The geometrics often take the form of triangles; less important types are burins and scaled pieces, but the most rarely found types are small truncated bladelets, a tiny number of endscrapers and microburins, and finally a few stemmed points.

Pottery is present to a small extent, comprising less than twenty sherds, all decorated with deep V-shaped incisions covering the entire surfaces of the vessels. The rim sherds indicate that these were fairly simple types of bowls. Ostrich eggshells in the form of fragments and beads are found alongside bone points. The fauna is represented by hares and gazelles, as well as a few examples of *Bos*. Finally, important grinding materials have been found in connection with plant remains, including two grains of six-row barley, in other words, definite evidence of cultivation.

The Nile valley

What was happening meanwhile in the Nile valley? On the west bank, the investigations of Polish researchers from 1963 and 1965 uncovered four important sites covering a period of nearly four millennia in the region of Arkin, at the Second Cataract, or, more precisely, between Shamarki and the villages of Nag el-Arab. These remains are linked with the Arkin formation, which is made up of silty sediments mixed with micaceous sands, an accumulation which is evidence for an increase in the Nile floods, reaching a high point at around 9500–9000 BP, and then dropping down gradually by successive stages over the course of the next few millennia.

The Arkinian   The site of Dibeira West 1 (DIW 1), on the west bank in northern Sudan, is situated in the higher layers, between silts and sands, making up the earliest stage of the sequence of 'Arkinian' industries. These remains have been radiocarbon dated to 10,580 ± 150 BP (Wendorf *et al.* 1979). Three areas of high ground parallel to the Nile must have made up an island or at least a bank of land which was safe from the high waters; these three small hills were covered with artefactual material, as well as burnt stone and bone, in the form of 13 concentrations comprising a total of 97,157 lithics. The raw material consisted only of pebbles scattered across the site. Chert, agate, jasper, igneous rocks, fossil wood and ferruginous sandstone were all used as the basis for a microlithic toolkit in which, however, the endscrapers (26 to 50 per cent) played as important a role as the backed bladelets (29 to 53 per cent), one of which bears traces of 'sickle sheen' on its un-retouched edge.

Ouchtata retouch is an important element in this industry, as well as scaled pieces, from which nearly half of the endscrapers are made. The geometrics are represented only by a small proportion of lunates (5.79–6.74 per cent), and there is no trace of the microburin technique. Some large quartz pebbles bear slight dimples (in the centres of which there are traces of flaking), indicating their use as 'anvils', which ties in with the increased quantities of scaled pieces. Scattered across the surface are several fragments of burnt and broken grinding stones, only one of which still bears traces of grinding, the rest having been too severely eroded. Three burnishing tools make up the total number of polished bone tools from the site.

Despite the undeniable homogeneity of the Arkinian industry as a whole, there are differences in percentages of the various types from one concentration to another, although these are sometimes explicable as the result of environmental influences: the accumulations of bladelets at the edges of certain concentrations seems to correspond with the 'washing' effect of the Nile floods. However, the presence of thick lunates (found only in 'concentration B' at DIW 1) suggests an alternative possibility, relating to chronological or functional differences between the concentrations. The excavators suggest that DIW 1 should be regarded as a small seasonal encampment, located on an islet. The hartebeest is the most common component among the faunal remains, which also include the aurochs, the gazelle, the hippopotamus, a few *Bos*, and fish.

From a typological point of view, the Arkinian is part of the wide range of North African Epipalaeolithic industries, and the statistical analysis of the group of backed bladelets reveals similarities with the Iberomaurusian. But these affinities with the latter are only one aspect of the Arkinian industry. The high percentage of endscrapers, together with the rarity of burins and microburins, and the predominance of lunates among the geometrics, all suggest connections with the north African Keremian industry, the type site of which is Kef el-Kerem in Algeria. The Keremian was itself initially assumed to be part of the Iberomaurusian complex, but Jacques Tixier suggested that it was a separate industry precisely because of its higher proportions of endscrapers and backed bladelets. The radiocarbon dates from the Keremian site of Bou Aïchem (10,215 and 9800 BP), although slightly earlier than those obtained for DIW 1, are within the same basic chronological range. However, in view of the fact that the Keremian heartland and Dibeira are separated from one another by a distance of 3300 kilometres and a time lapse of several centuries, it seems unlikely that this typological similarity is any indication of direct contact between the two groups, even taking into account the more humid conditions that prevailed at that time. Moreover, there are even typological differences between the two, such as the lack of scaled pieces in the Keremian. It would thus perhaps be more prudent to regard the link between the two as something along the lines of a common source, reserving judgment on the significance of similarities in percentages of lithics until our researches have reached a more advanced stage.

The Shamarkian The five sites of the Shamarkian industry are situated on 'regressional beaches' at Dibeira West, at a height of 120–131 metres in the case of DIW 51, 127–128 metres in the case of DIW 53, and 126–127 metres in the case of DIW 3, DIW 3A and DIW 6. These five sites (ignoring DIW 50, a sixth site in the same vicinity, which is Neolithic in date) include the same types of tools in similar proportions.

Using raw material consisting of 80–90 per cent Nile pebbles, the people of the Shamarkian industry produced large numbers of backed bladelets (some with Ouchtata retouch) and geometrics (trapezes). In contrast to the Arkinian, there were few endscrapers and only a small number of Krukowski microburins. There are also a few Bou Sââda points, arrowheads with transverse cutting edges, and some scaled pieces. There are scant remains indicating the grinding of plant material, but there are numerous fragments of ostrich-eggshell beads, particularly at DIW 3A, and a few Ounan points at DIW 3.

From a chronological point of view, there is a stratigraphic link between, on the one hand, sites DIW 53 and DIW 51, covered by 120 centimetres of sediment, and, on the other hand, DIW 50, which is situated above this sediment. Site DIW 51 yielded a radiocarbon date of 7700 ± 120 BP, while DIW 50 was dated to 5600 ± 120 BP, suggesting a gap of about two millennia between the sites, which would explain the undoubted typological differences between them. New dates, however, suggest that DIW 51 was considerably earlier: 8860 ± 60 BP (Wendorf *et al.* 1979). With an average area of 1200 m², comprising zones of obvious knapping debris, the occupied surfaces at Dibeira West quadrupled and quintupled between the beginning and end of the period, clearly indicating a change in the way of life of the Shamarkian group. However, we know little concerning the economic aspects of these sites where the bubal antelope is still well represented among the faunal remains.

The Shamarkian, which is part of the large family of bladelet industries, is surely related to the Capsian industry, which developed between the eighth and fifth millennia BC in North Africa. Similarly, it is also possible to link the Shamarkian with the East African 'Kenya Capsian' (or Eburran) industry, based on the working of obsidian bladelets (Clark 1970; Ambrose 1984). In the case of both of these groups, the connection can hardly be anything other than the existence of a common origin, since the evidence is insufficient to show that one rose out of the other.

Nearer to the valley, there are typological similarities with the 'Bedouin Microlithic', in the Karga Oasis, mentioned above, although their manufacture of fine bifacial arrowheads differentiates this Kharga industry from the Nubian groups.

The Elkabian   Turning instead to the heart of the pharaonic city of Elkab, down by the river itself, the Belgian excavators working in 1967, within the town wall, discovered concentrations of worked flint. During the two subsequent years, the team led by Pierre Vermeersch uncovered a new Epipalaeolithic industry: the Elkabian. In the Nile alluvia deposited at the mouth of the Wadi Hellal, they found and studied four concentrations (some disturbed in ancient times by the digging of Predynastic graves).

Most of the artefacts in this homogeneous set of material were made from rolled pebbles out of the Wadi Hellal, while a smaller number were made from chert, also from this wadi. The toolkit is almost entirely made from blades and bladelets, giving the industry as a whole a somewhat microlithic air, despite the relatively low number of geometrics. Backed bladelets – sharpened with rectilinear backs or notched – still dominated the assemblages. Double backed perforators, although far from numerous, were still present, along with geometrics in the form of elongated stepped triangles and lunates. There were many microburins, including Krukowski types, the latter consistently occurring, but only in small numbers. Notches and denticulates were also common, but there was little or nothing in the way of burins, endscrapers and truncations. Fragments of polished and rough sandstone must be linked with the grinding of minerals, judging from the traces of ochre on them. Bone spatula burnishers and ostrich-eggshell discs completed the inventory in by now almost customary fashion.

On the basis of radiocarbon dates, the different strata of occupation at Elkab were set at around 8000 BP (i.e. the end of the sixth millennium BC). The study of the faunal remains shows that fish formed an important element of subsistence (*Synodontis*, *Lates* and *Claridae*, all species that are still attested in the modern Nile), along with aurochs, dorca gazelle, moderately sized bovids (maned mouflons?), soft-shell turtles, hippopotami and, in smaller numbers, hartebeests, jackals and porcupines. The catchment zone included, first, the grassy and wooded savanna, and secondly the flood plain. The gazelles came down from the sub-arid hills to the flood plain in order to quench their thirst in the annual flood, during warm periods. The likelihood that the sites are seasonal encampments occupied only during the summer months (i.e. mid-July to mid-November) is also suggested by the evidence for the fishing of catfish (*Claridae*), which tended to be caught in the shallow waters of the inundated flood plain. The lack of evidence for migratory birds associated with the winter months also argues in favour of a summer encampment, and, given the evidence already cited, Vermeersch argues that the absence of these birds is unlikely to be simply the result of defective sampling of the archaeological record. The hartebeest is also absent, despite its ubiquity at Arkinian and Shamarkian sites, the catchment areas of which also incorporated the flood plain. Achilles Gautier (1978: 111) suggests that these sites were only being occupied during the summer, because they would have been too marshy for human habitation outside this season. There was certainly no danger of encountering such problems in the summer, and the hunters would have been able to concentrate on the pursuit of aurochs, hippopotami and gazelle, which were the main sources of protein, judging from the careful calculation of frequency of species.

Periodically nomads – hunter-fishers – reached this early branch of the Nile at Elkab, which was gradually silting up and usually flooded during the summer months, while the Wadi Hellal must have served as a supplementary source of food in winter. Their somewhat ephemeral encampments, with hearths only consolidated by sandstone blocks, no indication of any plant harvesting (given that the grinding stones were more concerned with the processing of minerals), and the presence of pointed bladelets (essentially designed for hunting), all point towards a Palaeolithic way of life which was in contrast with the earliest villages, the first ceramics in the Sahara, and – as we shall see below – their contemporaries in the Near East.

The Qarunian The Faiyum Oasis, 600 kilometres downstream from Elkab, is the next stage in our sequence of evidence. It formed the target of four seasons of survey undertaken by Caton-Thompson and Gardner (1934), from 1924 to 1928. Since they assumed that the lake was gradually shrinking over the course of several phases, they suggested that a clearly Neolithic cultural group (Faiyum A) had settled at the edge of the lake-shore at a height of +10 metres, but that this actually *preceded* an Epipalaeolithic group (Faiyum B), which was located at the lower height of +2 metres. They therefore formulated the idea of a kind of cultural degeneration from the Neolithic of Faiyum A back to the Epipalaeolithic of Faiyum B.

Thirty years later, however, A. J. Arkell and Peter Ucko (1965), and then Wendorf and Schild (1976) demonstrated, on the basis of radiocarbon dating and new geomorphological analyses, that the cultural sequence suggested by Caton-Thompson and Gardner actually needed to be inverted. The history of the different Faiyum lakes during the Holocene was in fact a much more complex sequence of floods, comprising alternating highs and sudden lows.

During the 1970s, Wendorf's exploration of a number of sites to the north of Lake Qarun, on the plateau of Qasr el-Sagha, revealed an Epipalaeolithic encampment linked with the pre-Moeris lake; this culture has become known as the Qarunian. The concentrations of artefacts at site E29-H1 (which have been assigned a radiocarbon date of 8100 ± 130 BP) correspond to Caton-Thompson's Faiyum B culture (Wendorf and Schild 1976: 182). The chert pebbles deriving from the Oligocene conglomerates of Gebel Qatrani, which overlooks the Qasr el-Sagha plateau, formed the raw material for an industry that consisted of 50 per cent bladelets and backed bladelets (most of which, i.e. 18–30 per cent of the total assemblage, had an arched back with retouched base). Notches and denticulates accounted for 9–17 per cent of the tool kit, while the geometrics made up only 5 per cent (mainly triangles and trapezes). The distally truncated bladelets (3–9 per cent) and the microburins (4 per cent), including a number of Krukowski types, all comprised only a small proportion of the toolkit. Perforators were rarely used, and there were few endscrapers and no burins. Some harpoons were made from the jaws of catfish.

The analysis of the fauna suggests, moreover, an economy founded essentially on fishing, while the hunting of large mammals and the gathering of plant foods were evidently of less importance (Brewer 1987). In 1966–8, however, the Institute of Palaeoethnology at Rome identified a group of similar assemblages to the northeast of the sites examined by Wendorf; the proportions of tool types in these new Qarunian-like assemblages differed sufficiently to suggest the practice of other activities (Mussi *et al.* 1984). A year later, a team of Egyptian, American and Polish archaeologists (under the aegis of the so-called Combined Prehistoric Expedition) discovered site E29-G1 (between Qasr el-Sagha and Kom Aushim), which was a human burial associated with the Qarunian settlement layer (Henneberg *et al.* 1989). The skeleton, laid out on its left side in a flexed position, with its head to the east and face towards the south, was found in the lacustrine sands of the pre-Moeris lake at about 17 metres above sea level. The body was that of a forty-year-old woman with a height of about 1.6 metres, who was of a more modern racial type than the classic 'Mechtoid' of the Fakhurian culture (see pp. 65–6), being generally more gracile, having large teeth and thick jaws bearing some resemblance to the modern 'negroid' type.

Not far from the Faiyum is a set of sites at Helwan (about 25 kilometres south of Cairo) which were probably linked with the developments taking place at that time in the Near East. It was at Helwan that archaeologists from 1871 to 1950 found thousands of blades, bladelets and geometric microliths (particularly lunates), but the most characteristic tool was a 'sharpened bladelet, sometimes with retouched edges, bearing proximal, bilateral notches' (Brezillon 1971: 252), known as a 'Helwan point', which was very similar to the 'el-Khiam point' (Brezillon 1971: 320). M. C. Cauvin (1974) suggested, in the conclusion to his diachronic typological analysis of Syrian notched arrowheads, that the term 'Helwan point' should be entirely abandoned. Dorothy Garrod (1932, 1937) saw great similarities between this industry and that of the Natufian culture in Palestine. Fernand Debono (1948), who was one of the most recent archaeologists working at Helwan, recognized hearths, animal bones, ostrich eggshells, as well as *dentalium* shells that suggest links with the sea. We cannot yet reach a more precise idea of the Helwan industry, which has not yet been fully published and therefore cannot be properly distinguished from the general mass of bladelet and geometric industries.

The Near East

In the Near East, an impressive process of cultural change took place between 12,000 and 7000 BP, magisterially studied by a team from Lyon led by J. Cauvin (1994), whose researches form the basis for the description which follows.

The phenomenon of 'sedentism' began in about 12,000 BP with the emergence of the Natufian culture in Palestine. However, Cauvin (see Aurenche *et al.* 1981) regards the different Epipalaeolithic cultures that preceded the Natufian (the Kebaran Geometric A, the Mushabian in the Sinai, and the Kebaran in the Negev) as the 'establishment of the geographical parameters of the Natufian culture' (Cauvin 1994). In other words, it was during this period leading up to the Natufian that its essential elements were evolving: the habitation area which, from 14,000 BP onwards, began as a kind of natural cave shelter and developed into an open-air semi-subterranean building, as well as evidence for grinding. But it was between 12,000 and 10,000 BP that whole villages of 2000–3000 m^2 flourished at sites as important as Mallaha and Hayonim, established at the edges of lakes or water-courses. These settlements consisted of circular or oval semi-subterranean houses, with diameters varying from 2.5 to 7 metres, built from paving slabs, pits, mortar and built hearths. Remains of rough stone walls were juxtaposed – without mortar – with mud-brick walls (built upon foundations of stones at Beidha, and covered in a coating of plaster at Mallaha), and are a sufficient demonstration of the standard that had been reached with regard to the construction of domestic buildings. These villages were, for the first time, transformed into settlements that, although not necessarily permanent, were at least major sites, and compared with these, the sites without any trace of architecture would simply represent seasonal encampments.

The toolkit associated with these settlements was still microlithic, in the tradition of the preceding culture, made from backed bladelets, but there were increasing numbers of lunates, which have long been considered to be the characteristic tools of this culture. Alongside these omnipresent microliths were backed blades, el-Khiam points, truncations, endscrapers, burins, perforators, notches, denticulates and retouched blades and flakes, which express, via their multiple internal variations, the 'classic' range of the hunter-gatherers of the end of the Palaeolithic, but amid these there were also a few new groups of tools that foreshadow those of later times: sickle teeth with 'sickle sheen' on their edges, arrowheads, picks and bifacial tools.

Limestone, basalt and sandstone were used for the manufacture of simple vessels (bowls, cups and goblets), as well as pestles, mortars, grinding stones and polishers. Although these first stone vases first appear (along with pestles) in the Kebaran levels at En Gev (c.15,700 BP), they only began to be made in large numbers by the people of the Natufian culture. Bone-working was mainly represented by harpoons, points, fish hooks, polishing tools and sickle handles.

Eventually there was a veritable explosion of art that could not have been foreseen, given that there was nothing in the preceding cultural stages to suggest it. It was not simply a case of shell necklaces, pierced teeth, bone elements, bilobed pendants or small cylinders, for all of which straightforward polishing was required, but human figurines and, above all, three-dimensional representations of animals, sometimes decorating the ends of tools. According to Vala (1975: 111): 'By the quality and variety of its manifestations, it [i.e. art] helped to accentuate the impression of the apparent material prosperity of the Natufian culture'. It was hunter-gatherers who were responsible for this 'material prosperity', settled as they were in their natural ecological zones incorporating wheat and barley, but without having developed agriculture, domesticated animals or pottery.

In the case of the Natufian graves, situated within their villages, there is some debate concerning the graves' relationships with the houses. The burials consisted of single individuals or multiple inhumations (primary or secondary) in simple pits. Neither the foetal position nor the orientation of the body were subject to any consistent rules, and the only funerary offerings were necklaces or bracelets.

The next phase (c.10,300–9600 BP) was characterized by a continuation of the basic Natufian culture but with very important architectural and technological innovations. The decrease in numbers of settlement sites was offest by the appearance of large agglomerations of populations with monumental constructions, as in the case of Jericho, where walls were built out of worked stone or moulded mud bricks. The number of microlithic tools decreased to the point of disappearance, while arrow-heads proliferated and the first polished axes appeared.

At Mureybet, in the Jordan valley, the earlier style of Natufian art, which essentially revolved around animal forms, gave way, in about 10,000–9800 BP, to schematic female figurines made from limestone or pottery, almost a millennium before the emergence of pottery vessels as domestic artefacts. This almost stereotyped representation of the female image is linked with the discovery of cattle bucrania, from about 10,300 BP onwards, in small banks of clay within the houses. These buried bucrania indicate the inhabitants' preoccupations with symbolic order, and they suggest to Cauvin (1994) that from the end of the ninth millennium BC onwards, the two dominant motifs of the Near Eastern Neolithic period – the woman and the bull – had already been established.

It was in this peripheral area of the Natufian culture, in Syria, that the first agricultural practices developed, from 9850 BP onwards (Aurenche and Cauvin 1989). In the middle Euphrates region, phase III at Mureybet has yielded evidence of an abrupt increase in artefacts showing sickle sheen, material associated with grinding, and grain deriving from wild species of cereal, but at Tell Awad, on the other hand, with its round semi-subterranean houses, excavators have found morphologically domestic types of starchy wheat (*Triticum dicoccum*), peas (*Pisum sativum*), and lentils (*Lens culinaris*). Similarly, there were also domestic forms of barley found at Netiv Hagdud, in the lower Jordan valley, and both starchy wheat and barley in the PPNA (Pre-Pottery Neolithic A) level at Jericho.

The period from 9600 to 8600 BP, which corresponds to the PPNB phase at Jericho, was characterized by the transition to rectangular architecture, the appearance of a sophisticated range of weaponry consisting of points with flat retouches, the spread of agriculture and the deposition of gypsum-covered human skulls at Jericho. This culture began to diffuse first to the northeast, into southeastern Anatolia, and then in the opposite direction, into the southern Levant.

The domestication of the goat and the sheep had possibly occurred by this date, but it has not been definitely proved. Although there is a distinct increase in remains of ovicaprids at all of these sites, the morphological criteria linking them with domestication have not yet been found. Between 8600 and 8000 BP, the Levantine process of Neolithicization sprang into action, spreading out from the core zone into central Anatolia, the Mediterranean fringe of the Levant, with the foundation of Byblos, and the desert regions stretching from Sinai to southern Mesopotamia, which had been abandoned at the end of the Epipalaeolithic. The rearing of ovicaprids is already attested by then, and the domestication of cattle had begun by 8000 BP. Finally, at the same as the appearance of the famous 'white vessels', in plaster or in lime, the first ceramics are found at several sites in the northern Levant (Le Mière 1979). But it was especially in the next period, from 8000 to 7600 BP, that people throughout the whole of the Near East began to produce a diverse range of pottery shapes and types of decoration.

Around 8000 BP, the PPNB, both in Sinai and over a large area of the Near East, came to a sudden end, doubtless as a result of the increasing aridity, in a process of climatic change similar to that in North Africa. The reoccupation of the desert regions at this date, by groups practising a different economy from that of the sedentary agriculturalist-pastoralists whose expansion we have already followed, puts a new slant on the origins of nomadic pastoralism in the Levant. Many aspects of the archaeological record suggest an intinerant subsistence pattern involving adaptations to a less favourable environment, such as the return to circular houses with stone bases, the adoption of a specific toolkit ('sites with burins'), and the clear domestication of ovicaprids at certain sites, compared with the presence of hunted species only at others.

It is this impressive phase in the prehistory of the Near East that has long been assumed to be the actual stimulus for the Nile valley Neolithic. Sedentism, agriculture, domestication and pottery are all found earlier in the Near East, clearly suggesting a gradual westward diffusion. However, in the scenario that we have just discussed in the light of recent research, the processes of cultural change seem to be much more complex than was once thought.

The very concept of the Neolithic has become a much more complex issue in recent years, throwing into doubt many previous ideas. Since Gordon Childe's formulation of the 'Neolithic revolution' in 1930, the general tendency was to stress the significance of the transition from a state of 'predation' (the hunter-gatherers) to one of 'production' (pastoralist-agriculturalists), a fundamental change that necessitated a whole range of social and cultural modifications. This definition might well be judged too schematic, given that groups of humans, both in Africa and the Near East, cluster together, settle in one place, and undergo technological change even before they have begun to cultivate plants or rear animals.

Such phenomena as sedentism, population increase, demographic concentration, changes in the toolkit, the domestication of plants and animals, which represent a complete ensemble in the 'full' Neolithic, all played different roles in the various regions, each progressing at different speeds. It is only necessary to consider first the absolute pre-eminence of sedentism, associated with sickle sheen, in the Palestinian Natufian, and secondly the raising of caprids alone in the first villages constructed in the Zagros region from the eighth millennium BC onwards (Dollfus 1989).

In the case of the Natufian culture of Palestine, the emergence of two distinctive aspects of the Neolithic was achieved on a microlithic basis, in a society where the 'broad spectrum' strategy of food procurement remained essentially Epipalaeolithic. With regard to the Zagros region, the transition to a new way of life took place in a high altitude ecological niche where they undertook no agriculture, no pottery production, no polishing of stone tools, and no domestication of animals apart from the rearing of goats. J. and M. C. Cauvin (1985: 1073) thus point out: 'What matters is not so much the concept of the Neolithic (which, in its full sense, designates only the end of a process) but that of Neolithicization, which stresses the actual dynamics of the process and takes into account the diversity of the particular routes taken towards the Neolithic.'

Faced with these precocious developments to the east, the Nile valley continued with its own traditions, retaining a way of life based on hunting, fishing and gathering (Arkinian, Elkabian and Qarunian) and the seasonal occupation of sites based around the regular, natural changes of this particular ecological zone, responding primarily to the annual Nile floods. This systematic exploitation of the residual channels full of *Claridae*, together with the exploitation of the neighbouring savanna populated with aurochs, the waiting for the return of the gazelles to the river (at the beginning of the warm season), the harvesting of the wild cereals that flourished at the edge of the terraces, the maximum exploitation of local lithic resources – all these strategies of food procurement removed the need for the great seasonal population movements during the Palaeolithic, encouraging instead the development of a certain sense of territory. This 'territoriality' not only led to the process of 'Nilotic adaptation' in such an arid period but was also an attitude that the Epipalaeolithic people in some sense inherited. In addition there was the increasing role played by wild cereals in food procurement, the tendency towards a more intensive use of land, and the practice of storage suggesting slow processes of maturation.

It is particularly in regions to the west of the Nile that the data of the last twenty years have shed light on the problem of the Neolithicization of the valley. At the edges of the Saharan mountainous zones, at the bottoms of depressions fed by playa lakes, semi-nomadic groups began to appear from the eighth millennium onwards. These groups, whose origins are unknown, emerged from areas that had continued to be occupied during the arid post-Aterian period, living by hunting, fishing, gathering, and producing all the earliest ceramics in the region. According to J. P. Roset, the Tagalagal ceramics, far from suggesting the feeble beginnings of pottery production, instead indicate the full possession of the means of production. This situation may be compared with that in Australia, where A. Testart (1977) has demonstrated that the precocious invention of pottery was closely linked with the control of plant resources, from the end of the Palaeolithic onwards. According to Roset, there are two possibilities at Tagalagal: either the beginnings of pottery production are to be sought further afield, or the pottery producers at this site are close to the beginnings of their craft. Further to the east, at el-Kortein, the same type of pottery can be found in a different environment, suggesting an unknown strong microlithic tradition in the central Sahara, where the stone working technology is in inverse proportion to the quality of the pottery. However, the fine workmanship of the bifacial arrowheads suggests that this situation may simply have been a cultural choice rather than an inevitability.

What are the implications of the presence of two grains of plain six-row barley in the early Neolithic phase of Nabta Playa (c.9000 BP)? The Braidwood model concerning agriculture suggests that its beginnings, like the beginnings of animal domestication, have only tended to take place in favourable ecosystems (i.e. in situations where potentially cultivable wild species were widely represented), while the Binford model argues that it took place in marginal zones, as a result of population explosion and the migration of semi-sedentary hunter-gatherers towards a less favourable periphery. The Nabta depression, however, does not correspond to either of these models. The natural habitat of wild barley in Africa is nowadays limited to the Cyrenaic region, and wheat is unknown (el-Hadidi 1980); this however implies nothing with regard to the likelihood that one or other of these species was present in the area under consideration. A transfer of population is, moreover, always possible to envisage, but it remains, in our current state of knowledge, very difficult to discern. It seems, however, somewhat rash to start talking about the emergence of agriculture purely on the basis of two grains with domesticated morphology. As Muzzolini (1989: 156) points out: 'If a variety of barley was flourishing prolifically in the steppe land of the Western Desert, and the local Epipalaeolithic groups began to collect it, perhaps intensively (or even to subject it to "incipient" cultivation), then this practice would no doubt have had the same significance as the collection of other wild cereals.'

The problem is posed in a different way with regard to bovids, which Achilles Gautier (1984: 64–72) believes to have been domesticated in the depressions of the Western Desert. Gautier argues that the climate was too severe to support the herds of aurochs (with less than 400 millimetres of annual rain, whereas 400–625 millimetres are needed for the wild herds to flourish in the Kordofan-Darfur region), and osteometric data provide distinctions between the 'small' wild cattle and the 'large' domestic beasts. He envisages the possibility that the Bos species might have been brought under human control at this time. He also argues that the Nile valley may possibly have been their place of origin: first, the herds of wild cattle are well-attested; secondly, a symbolic link was long established between humans and cattle, judging from the horns found in connection with the deceased in cemetery 8905 at Tushka; and thirdly, the Arkinian toolkits show similarities with those of North Africa and the Sahara. Gautier therefore suggests that it is not impossible that an incipient domestication of bovids was introduced from the Nile valley into the eastern Sahara, as a result of contacts between the Saharan hunters and the riverine populations (i.e. Arkinian sites) based by the Nile, which had long been a favoured location. A completely domesticated species of cow might therefore have been re-introduced into the valley in the following period, when, pursued by aridity, the Saharan hunter-pastoralists reached the banks of the river, this time with the intention of permanent settlement.

Gautier's hypothesis is an attractive one, but it needs to be backed up by more solid archaeological evidence, given that no domestic cow has yet been found either in the Arkinian sites or at any similarly dated site in the valley, and the apparent links between the animal skins and human skeletons in the Tushka cemetery are not definitely proven. Muzzolini (1989: 154), unconvinced by Gautier's arguments, suggests an alternative model based on the idea of 'a herd of aurochs living in the aforementioned steppe-land environment but definitely linked with sources of water at Nabta Playa: this type of exploitation is therefore comparable with the much described Magdalenian hunters who subsisted on a herd of reindeer actually penned within their natural territory'.

Up to the tenth millennium BC, human evolution along the Nile was influenced by local peculiarities but was not fundamentally different from that of the neighbouring regions; the complexity and diversity which is to be found in the Nile-valley Middle Palaeolithic opens up vast areas of research; we have already seen what a dynamic role it played in the introduction and development of microlithic cultures.

From the tenth to the sixth millennium BC, the Nile valley continued its own Palaeolithic traditions, avoiding the formidable processes of change that affected the areas to the east and west, and the explanation for this situation is probably to be found in the abundance of natural sources of nutrition: fishing, hunting and gathering, constituting a way of life to which the Nilotic peoples had been perfectly adapted for thousands of years. The arid phase of the mid-Holocene would eventually upset this harmonious state of affairs, once more pushing into this refuge zone the Saharan communities as well as those from the Eastern Desert.

The mid-Holocene arid phase (c.8000/7500–7000/6500 BP)

In about 8000/7500 BP, the arrival of a new arid phase had the effect of
emptying the deserts, forcing human populations to settle closer to the
surviving sources of water. The Nile was about to serve once more as a
refuge zone.

This severe climatic phase, which is well-documented throughout the
Sahara (Muzzolini 1983: 108–10), is known in even better detail in the
Western Desert, thanks to the work of Wendorf and Hassan (see Hassan
1986b). Short intervals of high aridity punctuate the general development towards a climate that was considerably drier than in the previous
period. Thus, at Nabta Playa, the second arid phase is represented only
by a short interval (c.7900–7700 BP) followed by the humid 'pulse' of
Playa III, during which the middle and late Neolithic phases (as defined
by Wendorf et al. 1984) flourished in this region.

The Western Desert

At Siwa Oasis, Hassan identified a period of erosion between 8000 and
7000 BP, during which the level of the lakes dropped and the dune formations advanced along their shores. In Bahariya Oasis, several generations
of playas indicate alternating humid and arid phases, as at Nabta Playa
(Barich and Hassan 1987).

Generally speaking, the sites in the Western Desert that are linked with
this period of erosion are characterized by a radical change in their inventory of tools: the microlithism was gradually abandoned in favour of
a technology based on flakes, aimed at the creation of notches and
denticulates, in other words large retouched tools that became, along
with bifacial tools, the dominant categories. This is the case with the six
sites at Bir Kiseiba (E79–2, E79–4, E79–5A, E79–6 and E79–7, Bir Murr
I), from the lower level of E75–8 at Nabta, and from E77–5 and E77–5A
at Kortein, which represent the middle Neolithic defined by Wendorf.
Five radiocarbon dates on charcoal place the phase between 7700 and
6200 BP. In place of local quartz and the surrounding cherts and metamorphic rocks used during the preceding periods, flint extracted from
Eocene limestones was imported in large quantities in order to manufacture retouched flakes, perforators, notches and denticulates, a few bifacial
arrowheads, as well as backed bladelets, the number of which steadily
decreased. Finally, the first polished axes make their appearance. The
sheer volume of material devoted to grinding is an indication of its importance, while pottery, the complete outer surface of which is decorated
with an impressed matting motif, is omnipresent.

The fauna scarcely differs from that of the preceding period, essentially consisting of *dorcas* gazelles and hares. The dimensions of the sites are revealing – either they are isolated units at the centre of playas or much larger settlements in which the overlapping of wells indicates reoccupation of the same sites. The locations of these latter types, at the fringes of the playas, suggest that they may have been winter encampments.

At Bahariya (Hassan 1979), a collection of surface material dated to *c.*7000 BP shows a technology based on blades and flakes in which the dominant tools are endscrapers, notches, burins and denticulates; some bifacial pieces were mixed in with them, but no microliths.

In the northern part of the Kharga Oasis, at Umm el-Dabadib, a certain number of sites associated with playa deposits indicate a succession of humid phases between 8600 and 7100 BP; these were examined by Hassan and Holmes (1985). Here too the toolkit, made from flakes, takes the form of notches, endscrapers, retouched flakes and a few pointed bifacials, again with no microliths present.

The Nile valley

We know nothing of events in the Egyptian section of the valley; doubtless because, as Hassan (1988a) suggests, the Nile was exceptionally low at this time, therefore the sites established then at the edge of the river were destroyed later by the annual floods of the next humid phase, when the waters were generally rising considerably higher.

The Khartoum Mesolithic

We now need to look much further to the south, parallel with Khartoum, for the place where the first Neolithic cultures in the valley developed from the seventh millennium BC onwards. In the 1940s, A. J. Arkell's excavations at the confluence of the Blue and White Niles had revealed a vast area of settlement that he called 'Early Khartoum'. Located on the top of a sandy-clay area of high ground at the edge of the Blue Nile, it took the form of an ashy layer, between one and two metres in thickness, stuffed with quartz flakes, sherds of the characteristic brown pottery decorated with incised wavy lines, fragments of shells, and sandstone grinding stones. In its first phase, the settlement was situated below the level of the annual inundation, therefore it could only have been inhabited during the dry season. There were no hearths or post-holes, only traces of wattle, and, in the excavated area, 17 graves dug into the ground within the settlement.

The very frequently surviving faunal remains show the importance of river-based animals, including crocodiles, turtles and hippopotami. The presence of porcupines, warthogs and buffaloes indicates a humid savanna landscape. Compared with the small numbers of carnivorous predators and birds, fish remains vastly outweigh all other types of fauna. Among the diverse species of fish, it is possible to distinguish several types of catfish, including the *Synodontis,* the finely denticulate dorsal spine of which was used to impress decorative motifs into the soft unfired fabric of pottery vessels.

Nearly 300 fragments of bone harpoon heads serve to emphasize the fundamental role played by fishing in these semi-sedentary communities. The Khartoum harpoons are equipped with one row of barbs (or in a few instances two rows) which are left sticking in the body of the prey, a notable technological development that would have increased the chances of success in hunting small fishes. Two methods of fixing the barbs would, according to Arkell, have corresponded to two different types of hunting weapon. One type with a bluntly pointed butt (marked with notches and often ridged with parallel grooves in order to attach it into a haft) was actually the head of a type of assegai spear. The other type, however, had a perforated base that was intended to receive a tightly bound strap for the handle (a procedure which allowed the weapon to be removed at the moment of impact and, when unleashed, allowed control of the grip over a longer distance) – this type was therefore probably a genuine harpoon. If the many grooved stones can be assumed to have been used as net-weights, the very early inhabitants of the Khartoum region were evidently efficient fishers. Moreover, Arkell suggests that the harpoon points could have been used as arrowheads for fishing with bow and arrow.

The people of the Khartoum Mesolithic were also hunters. The thousands of quartz flakes that have been analysed indicate an industry which was basically microlithic and dominated by lunates. The use of small pebbles of quartz and chert petrographically linked with the local geological zone initially suggested that the search for raw material was unremarkable, but rhyolite was also being used, and the nearest source of this was in the Sixth Cataract region, 80 kilometres from Khartoum. The pestles and mortars found at the site seem to have been used for the grinding of pigments (traces of which have also been found) rather than the processing of wild cereals. Finally the numerous stone rings, each measuring about 10 centimetres in diameter, could have been attached to digging sticks, thus serving as quasi-maceheads, foreshadowing later examples further to the north, in the form of the disc-shaped maceheads of the Naqada I phase.

Only a few offerings accompanied the contracted bodies of the deceased, one of whom was wearing body jewellery made from ostrich-eggshells. With regard to the anthropological evidence, only very miner-alized fragments of skeletons have survived in 17 of the graves. In one instance (M20), it has proved possible to reconstruct the skull, which is apparently somewhat long and straight (a trait that is undoubtedly exag-gerated by the absence of any anatomical connection with the torso), with a massive mandible; the large lower mandible (interpreted by Derry as a negroid characteristic) is exaggerated by the removal of the incisors from the upper jaw. This trait of incisor extraction is found both in mod-ern African populations and in the skeletons from Jebel Moya, a cem-etery of uncertain date situated to the west of Sennar (in the latter case mainly among women). Derry's attribution of these Early Khartoum skel-etons to the negroid race rests on assumptions that are nowadays re-garded as controversial (and to which we will return later).

The pottery consists of large open forms (essentially bowls) made from brown, well-fired fabric with quartz inclusions, the rim being of a slightly finer composition than the rest of the vessel. They are smoothed on the inside but their outside surfaces are never polished, being decorated in-stead with the famous wavy-line motifs, evidently intended to suggest the appearance of basketry. A second type of pottery, probably based on the first, comprises vessels decorated with dotted wavy lines made with a curved comb; these types have nearly all been found at Neolithic sites dating to the next period (the Khartoum Neolithic).

Given the lack of radiocarbon dates, Arkell based his dating of these astonishing fisher-hunter-potters on the material culture, which, judging from the fauna, existed in conditions that were more humid than those prevailing in this region in modern times. Entirely ignorant of the domes-tication of plants and animals, and thus generally closer to the Palaeolithic than the Neolithic, they are best described as 'Mesolithic', a term that was first applied to the European transition from Palaeolithic to Neolithic, when the glaciers were retreating and humans were adapting to new eco-logical circumstances. In the game of definitions, the presence of pottery – especially in an African context – hardly ties in with the conventional idea of the Mesolithic, as some specialists have pointed out (e.g. Balout 1955: 156). On the other hand, the Early Khartoum material lends itself readily to the concept of Neolithicization, as defined above by the Cauvins (see J. and M. C. Cauvin 1985: 1073). For convenience, however, we retain here the term 'Khartoum Mesolithic' simply because it is now en-shrined in the literature (while acknowledging, nevertheless, its true Neolithicizing nature).

Researches undertaken since the 1970s have yielded information con-cerning other sites contemporary with Early Khartoum, allowing the chronological aspects of this cultural phenomenon to be clarified on the basis of about a dozen radiocarbon dates. Sorurab 1 and 2, Shabona,

Shaqadud, Saggai, indirectly Tagra, and most recently Abu Darbain and Aneibis, at the confluence of the Nile and the Atbara, cover nearly two millennia, from 9370 ± 110 BP and 9330 ± 110 BP (at Sorurab 2) to 6408 ± 80 BP (at Sorurab 1); most of the dates are situated in the mid- to late seventh millennium BC.

The site of Saggai, carefully investigated by a team from the Institute of Palaeoethnology at Rome (Caneva 1983), consists of an area of 36,000 m² of archaeological deposits, averaging 70–135 centimetres in depth, situated on a natural rise at the confluence of the river and the wadis, on the right bank of the Nile, 40 kilometres to the north of Khartoum. As at Early Khartoum, there are no surviving traces of the structural ground plan, but differences in the types of artefacts found in various zones suggest that the settlement was spatially differentiated.

The fauna corresponds to species which are still present in modern Sudan, although their habitat is now about 400 kilometres to the south, in a more wooded savanna landscape with annual rainfall of 400–800 millimetres. About thirty types of mammal were found: mongooses, grivets (northeast African guenon monkeys), jackals, wild cats, warthogs, lions, hippopotami, giraffes, and buffaloes, but the most common mammal remains derive from two hoofed animals: kobs (African water-antelopes) and small antelopes (mainly oribis), which are never found far from sources of water. Along with turtles and crocodiles, the ichthyofauna has survived in large numbers, comprising ten species, including *Polypterus*, *Clarias*, *Synodontis* and *Lates*. This diversity, like that at Early Khartoum, can certainly be explained by the adoption of techniques that were better adapted to all-year fishing. However, the sedimentary history of the site and its location in an area that would have been covered by the annual flood suggests that this was primarily a dry-season occupation (characterized by intensive fishing both with harpoon and net); during the wet season, the population would have dispersed into the hinterland, stretching the extent of the catchment area as far as the dry savanna, where the kobs and antelopes were to be found, as well as incorporating the wooded areas containing the grivet monkeys with white side-whiskers. The accumulation of shells (*Pila wernei*] and the high level of strontium measured in the bones of the skeletons suggests that molluscs were an important source of nutrition. Some examples deriving from the Red Sea, used as beads or pendants, indicate links with the Eastern Desert that have still not been properly studied.

These fisher-gatherers inhabiting the site of Saggai (the importance of plant gathering being indicated by extensive remains of grinding stones) were also hunters. Their quartz-based microlithic toolkit, including a minor element of rhyolite (as at Early Khartoum), is dominated by lunates, some of which were retouched. Denticulates and notches are also well represented, as well as perforators made from crescent-shaped flakes.

Among the bone artefacts were fragments of smoothers, knives, curved-fronted combs for decorating pottery, tubular and disc-shaped beads, awls, needles, and finally harpoons with rows of barbs and tips prepared for the attachment of handles. Although not one entire pot has been found, the thousands of sherds are often large enough to show, as at Early Khartoum, that the shapes of the vessels were bowls polished only on the inside. The decoration – consisting of a varity of motifs made up of wavy lines traced out with a comb – includes continuous sets of lines, groups of waves, arcs of circles and sporadic sets of lines. Dotted wavy lines were often combined with continuous ones to add variation to the decoration, and sets of double lines were sometimes created with the use of a comb with two sets of teeth.

Six graves dug into the archaeological deposits have been found in the excavated area. The bodies, all in foetal positions, are located at the base of the occupation debris, with no consistent orientation. Only a few shells are associated with these burials, which are otherwise devoid of grave goods. From an anthropological point of view, the four women and one man (the skull of the latter having not survived) show a certain homogeneity in their appearance, notwithstanding a few minor variations. The robustness of their mandibles, compared with the forehead and temples, may reflect functional adaptation indicating greater mastication along with greater general use of the teeth.

No hearths have survived at the site, therefore radiocarbon dates have been obtained from the shells of freshwater molluscs (the *Pila wernei* gastropods eaten by the Saggai population): 7410 ± 110 BP, 7320 ± 110 BP, 7250 ± 110 BP and 7230 ± 100 BP. Fragments of charcoal deriving from the occupation layer at Sorurab 2, opposite Saggai, on the left bank of the Nile (Hakem and Khabir 1989; Khabir 1985) have provided the earliest dates for the Khartoum Mesolithic: 9370 ± 110 BP and 9330 ± 110 BP.

Further to the south, 200 kilometres from Khartoum, near the village of Tagra, Adamson (1982: 205) discovered, three metres below the modern level of the White Nile, two barbed harpoon fragments, small mammal and fish bones (including catfish). He assigned all these to the Khartoum Mesolithic on the basis of two radiocarbon dates obtained from *Pila wernei* associated with the assemblage: 8700 ± 350 BP and 8130 ± 225 BP.

The site of Shabona, on the east bank of the White Nile, 110 kilometres south of Khartoum, was excavated by Clark (1989), revealing an occupation zone of about 52,000 m². Buried under 10–30 centimetres of loose dark brown sand, it has fortunately preserved seven depressions (within an excavated area of about 83 m²) hollowed out of the brown sandy silt that covers the base layer of carbonized gravel. Three of these depressions – each about 13 cm in diameter and 5 centimetres deep – were full of burnt bird bones and lumps of burnt earth (the latter possibly indicating the cooking method). A larger pit, 60 centimetres wide and 28 centimetres deep, contained a mixture of unburnt fish bones, mammals' bones and one end of a harpoon. In an adjacent area of the site, an 82-centimetre-deep conical depression was found to be full of *Pila* shells. In another instance, the *Pila* shells were pile up in an irregular depression, along with a complete skull of a catfish (Clarias) and various other bones of fish and mammals. Finally, the largest depression (about a metre in diameter) contained a harpoon broken into two pieces, as well as fish and bovid bones.

Five graves were found in the settlement at Shabona; the two most complete consist of bodies laid out in extended positions, one of them looking to the east and the other to the west. As at Early Khartoum and Saggai, there were no grave goods accompanying the deceased. The radiocarbon analysis of a fragment of bone provided a date of 7470 ± 240 BP. Another date, obtained from a *Pila* shell, placed the graves at around 7050 ± 120 BP. The seven bodies – three men, three women and a sub-adult – all have straight skulls with striking occipital regions, robust faces, varying degrees of prognathism and rectangular orbits. The robustness of the mandibles indicates, as at Saggai, a functional adaptation corresponding to 'masticatory stress'. One individual suffers shows signs of dental caries, one had an alveolar abscess, and another had osteoarthritis in hands and feet, as well as a fractured rib that had healed and fused back together. As in the case of some of the Early Khartoum skulls, the upper incisors of one of the women had been deliberately removed.

The lithic industry at Shabona includes a 36.6 per cent microlithic component, made from local quartz and essentially comprising lunates and trapezes; rhyolite, the more distant raw material, was used for large crescent-shaped tools, backed tools, perforators and a specific type of sidescraper. Sandstone, the nearest source of which was only about 40 kilometres away, was used for pestles and mortars. The most unusual item in the toolkit was a polished triangular piece of haematite with a hole pierced at one corner. Single-barbed harpoons appear in a variety of different sizes, usually pointed at one end for the attachment of a handle, and sometimes also with incisions designed to help fix the handle in place. The repertoire of polished bone included only needles and smoothers.

On the basis of the analysis of 2094 potsherds, two types of fabric were identified: one with mineral inclusions and another with inclusions of plant material. The vessels were not polished, but all had been burnished before decoration and firing. The mineral-based fabric may sometimes have been coated with a red pigment, which might possibly account for the bringing of haematite into the settlement. Although no complete vessels have survived, the original forms can be reconstructed, consisting of simple hemispherical bowls and globular pots. The dotted line style of decoration is particularly common on pottery made from the mineral-based fabric typical of the Khartoum Mesolithic, while 75 per cent of the vessels made from clay with inclusions of plant material are decorated around their middles with cord impressions, reminiscent of the 'basket imitations' that are noted by Arkell at Khartoum but are unknown at Saggai. According to Clark, the lack of this motif at Saggai suggests that the site of Early Khartoum represents the northernmost limit of this cord-impressed decorative tradition.

The fauna at Shabona also largely comprises either riverine species – fish, turtles, crocodiles, hippopotami, monitor lizards, various other types of lizard, and snakes – or those types of animals, like the kob (*Kobus kob*) and the oribi (small south African antelope: *Ourebia ourebi*), that are found not far from water. The presence of remains of the roan (*Hippotragus equinus*) and the buffalo indicates a landscape consisting of a plain scattered with trees and bushes, while traces of warthogs and elephants suggest waterlogged terrain.

In a possible indication of dietary preferences, the absolute count of bones shows a partiality for lizards and, to a slightly lesser extent, antelopes. The abundance of *Pila wernei* again suggests that this mollusc was being consumed on a regular basis, and the presence of shells in pits suggest that quantities were being stored. As far as the exploitation of plant foods is concerned, the remains of the plants themselves, together with impressions of carbonized grains in pottery fabric, indicate the presence of *Digitaria*, a species of the *Panicoidae* family, a wild plant which is still found in the pluvial zones of modern Sudan and one species of which has been cultivated in West Africa.

Situated in a part of the valley that would have been flooded during the annual inundation, the site of Shabona, like Early Khartoum and Saggai, must have been regularly occupied during the time of low waters by the last groups of hunter-fisher-gatherers, earliest users of pottery in the Nile valley. Generally speaking, all of these sites appear to consist of semi-permanent settlements adapted to the exploitation of the river and its surrounding ecological zone, where wild cereals seem to have played a crucial role in the subsistence pattern (judging from the evidence of dentition, grains included in pottery fabric, and grinding equipment).

The Khartoum Mesolithic evolved at a time when the Sahara was enjoying favourable climatic conditions in lacustrine environments; the representation of the harpoon is indicative of an economy based on fishing (along with hunting and gathering). The earliest harpoons derive from

Ishango, in the Congo (Heinzelin 1957), in strata dated to 11,000–8500 BP. At a later date they have also been found at Gamble's Cave in Kenya (Leakey 1931: 90–175), and, somewhat later again, they appear at Khartoum Mesolithic sites. The presence of bone harpoons in Central Sahara, as far away as Mauritania, has led to intriguing observations as much with regard to typology as chronology (see Huard and Massip 1964). The same situation applies to the diffusion of wavy-line pottery: Arkell noted that *unpolished* pottery decorated with wavy lines and wavy dotted lines was typical of the Khartoum Mesolithic, while *polished* pottery decorated in the same way typified the Khartoum Neolithic. However, it is in general the polished type with wavy dotted lines that is mostly found in the Central Sahara, while the wavy-line type *stricto sensu* is only found in the Nilotic sector of Sudan. It therefore appears difficult, considering the lack of large numbers of precise dates, to establish the routes of diffusion taken by these earliest African pottery producers.

Is it, however, necessary to attempt to establish these patterns of diffusion out of Nilotic Sudan? In the initial aftermath of Arkell's discoveries, it seemed likely that Sudan was the formative centre of a current of Neolithicization that would have moved westwards, and the term 'Sudanese tradition Neolithic' creates the image of Nilotic people leaving their rich valley and migrating across the immense Sahara desert, taking with them their precious ceramic invention. Nowadays, however, the central Sahara has ousted the Nile valley as the home of the first pottery-producers, who, according to Zarattini (1983: 256), make their appearance in communities that tend to be sedentary in exploiting a broad spectrum economy in similar coastal environments from the Nile to Mauritania. This 'aquatic' way of life is interpreted by John Sutton (1974) as a specific cultural type, source of the modern distribution of Nilo-African languages. It is true that the rate of population increase in favourable ecological niches must have risen, and contacts between groups must have been inevitable. But these seem to have been more limited than we would necessarily expect, if we observe closely the typological variety of harpoons and pottery.

The question of the origins of this first pottery-using culture is still open to debate. No final Pleistocene site, such as those downstream from Wadi Halfa, has been found in this part of the valley. The Second Cataract region actually appears to have become a frontier between these pottery users and the hunter-gatherer Epipalaeolithic people who were gradually extending southwards, a buffer zone that can be understood in topographical and geological terms, in that the immense granite region of the Batn el-Hajar ('belly of stone') opens up and the Nile cuts through it without leaving much in the way of fertile sediment. After 125 kilometres of arid terrain, however, the geology reverts to Nubian sandstone and the floodplain widens out, now supporting luxuriant vegetation. No site of the final Pleistocene has yet been discovered in the 625-kilometre stretch between Dal and Khartoum, despite the fact that the later sites of the first pottery-producers in Nubia are to be found in this very section of the valley.

Should we assume, like Isabel Caneva (1988: 362), that the reason for this lack of final Pleistocene sites is to be found in the ecological conditions prior to the sixth millennium BC? The vigorous flow of the Nile at that time, together with the irregularity of the floods, might well have destroyed or buried the traces of sites left behind at this date by groups who would only very occasionally have settled on the banks of the river, which no doubt then held little attraction for them. Caneva suggests that in this region the archaeological remains become visible only when the river has begun to cut into the Nile valley, in other words, at precisely the point in time when the first pottery-using cultures flourished.

The contacts with the first Saharan pottery-producers – even perhaps the first pastoralists – could well have been made in this context. But there was also a vast well-watered region to the east of Khartoum, which has also shown itself to be worthy of note: the Atbara, and in particular the Butana, an enormous area of grassland to the east of the Middle Nile and to the west of the Red Sea hills. In 1981, an expedition led by Anthony Marks (Marks, Peters and Van Neer 1987) discovered a large number of final Palaeolithic sites that are, however, typologically distinct from those that have been found to the north of the Second Cataract, and also radically different from the Khartoum Mesolithic culture.

The Eastern Desert

Until recently, no prehistoric sites had been excavated in the Eastern Desert, but such researches have begun to proliferate in recent years, thus providing fresh insights, especially with regard to certain aspects of the diffusion of the Neolithic. Vermeersch (1994), for instance, has uncovered the remains of goats and sheep in the Sodmein cave, near the Red Sea, dated to c.7000 BP. Until the 1990s, the researches undertaken by Fernand Debono in 1949 (Debono 1950, 1951) were the only sources of information concerning the prehistory of the region. These researches indicated the survival of microburins and points made from bladelets in the Lakeita area, suggesting that there were Epipalaeolithic industries present in this part of the Eastern Desert.

6

The Neolithic period (fifth millennium BC)

In about 5000 BC a humid phase began; it was weaker than in the preceding period, but it nevertheless had the effect of raising the level of the Saharan lakes and water table. This new climatic episode took the form of an increase in the quantity of rain, although temperatures continued to be high. The episode appears as a series of humid oscillations in an environment that remained essentially sub-arid. As Muzzolini points out (1983: 113), the streams in the Aïr, Tibesti-Djado and Ennedi regions, towards Chad, petered out, and the definitive decline in the lake levels began. The new occupants of the Sahara were at this point fully Neolithicized: these pastoralists and makers of paintings and rock-carvings were about to enliven the massifs of North Africa from the Atlantic to the Red Sea.

The Faiyum Neolithic

The investigations undertaken between 1924 and 1928 by Caton-Thompson and Gardner (1934), to the north of the Faiyum lake, uncovered two areas of settlement taking the form of elongated kôms (archaeological mounds) labelled W and K by the excavators, where a great deal of surface material was found associated with the settlement remains in the ground: all of this belonged to the Faiyum A culture, so-called in relation to the Faiyum B (which was initially regarded incorrectly as a 'degenerate' phase later than Faiyum A). Flint flakes, tools, quartz, dolerite and fossilized wood hammers, mixed with shells, bone fragments and potsherds. Between these two kôms, a zone of silos making up two distinct topographical groups (somewhat separated from one another) make these remains a potentially rich source of evidence.

The excavations of each of the kôms revealed a considerable number of basin-like depressions hollowed out of the lacustrine deposits: 248 in

Kôm W and 60 in Kôm K, Some still contain charcoal, having clearly been used as hearths. In several cases jars were found *in situ*, and in others artefacts similar to those found on the surface and in the course of excavation were found at the bottom.

The study of the published lithics of the Faiyum Neolithic reveals a total break from the preceding microlithic cultures. A total of 17 arrowheads, mainly of the hollow-base type (although 356 pedunculate examples have been found on the surface), and 31 sickle blades with glossy denticulation, along with chipped stone axes, make up the essential core of a bifacial industry. Leaf-shaped points were added to the repertoire, as well as a halbard type of weapon which foreshadows the 'fishtail lances' of the Predynastic. The axes alone accounted for 40 per cent of the toolkit; small in size and usually rectangular or triangular in shape, they are made from dolerite, limestone, volcanic stone and flint. Three such axes found on the surface were totally polished rather than chipped, but the vast majority (60 examples) are fashioned with a combination of both techniques in that the tool as a whole was chipped while the cutting edge was polished. Some gouges were also made with a combination of chipping and polishing techniques. A small bladelet core and five bladelets (two of which were double backed) hark back to the Epipalaeolithic assemblages.

The origins of these techniques can certainly be traced back to the Near East. It is true that the polishing of stone (using some kind of specialized tool) was attested from the Natufian onwards, and the practice of polishing the cutting edges of chipped stone axes was characteristic of the Yamukian, a cultural phase in Palestine, from the beginning of the fifth millennium BC onwards. We must also bear in mind, however, the fact that, if the recent discoveries at Tagalagal are confirmed, this North African site already includes axes and adzes with polished cutting edges from the mid–seventh millennium BC onwards. On the other hand, the picture of a bifacial lithic tradition that emerges from the studies undertaken by Caton-Thompson is muddied by the fact that she selected particular tools from an assemblage that is now known to be much larger and more diverse. The researches undertaken in the 1980s by Polish archaeologists from the University of Cracow have facilitated the definition of two Neolithic units in the Qasr el-Sagha region: first the Faiyumian (which corresponds to Caton-Thompson's Faiyum A) and secondly the Moerian, which is later in date (see Kozlowski and Ginter 1989).

The Faiyumian Neolithic is represented by an industry comprising 90 per cent flake tools: flakes struck from cores with unprepared platforms and opposed platforms, or discoids and subdiscoids made from terrace pebbles. Notches, denticulates, sidescrapers and retouched flakes make up the main classes of tools, with bifacial tools turning up only occasionally. In order to verify this new definition of the Faiyum Neolithic, the

Polish researchers undertook surface surveys both in the vicinity of Kôm W and in areas explored by Caton-Thompson: in both cases large quantities of flake tools were found.

We must therefore radically revise our definition of the lithic industry in the Faiyum during the Neolithic, which, instead of being regarded as bifacial, must be viewed as a flake-based industry including a minor bifacial element. This discovery significantly modifies our research questions concerning the origins of these first Neolithic cultures in Egypt.

The many sherds scattered over the surface, originating from excavation trenches and from several depressions, can be joined together to form complete shapes of vessels made from a coarse fabric comprising silt mixed with chopped straw. The outer surfaces (as well as the interiors of the cups) are often red polished – more rarely black polished – or simply burnished, but never bearing any decoration. Five groups have been distinguished on the basis of shape: the first is made up of spherical or globular cups and bowls, with flat or rounded bases. The second category comprises 'cooking pots and bowls', defined as such because they tend to be found in the hearth areas of the kôms; they were similar to the first types but larger and often with very thick walls. The third type consist of pedestalled cups, one example of which survived intact; with regard to the fourth type (a small cup with three knobbed feet made up of small irregular protuberances) there is also only one surviving near-complete example. The final category consists of large rectangular dishes, the edges of which had been moulded in such a way as to end up with four 'ears' or 'peaks' at the corners, which have been interpreted as early handles.

Six large pestles, accompanied by their mortars, were made from sandstone, whereas palettes were carved from limestone or diorite, suggesting the grinding of grain in the case of the former and pigment in the case of the latter. Many objects of polished bone (needles without eyes, pins, borers, small fine harpoons without notches or ridges at the base, nearer the Natufian than the Khartoum Mesolithic) were found alongside seashells, which seem to have been used as spoons, judging from the fact that they tend to be found in pottery vessels. The repertoire also includes numerous ostrich eggshells (including two pierced fragments), several pierced stone discs and amazonite beads. The first use of this fine greenish-blue gemstone in Egypt has led to suggestions of contacts with the Tibesti region, but Lucas (1962: 393–4) notes natural occurences of amazonite in the immediate vicinity of the Nile valley.

Two zones of granaries, situated roughly midway between the two kôms, consisted of a group of 168 silos and 18 depressions for sunken pottery vessels. The upper set of granaries were 67 depressions cut into the gravel of the Pleistocene layer; 57 of them were covered with mats and straw. The diameter of these depressions varied from 30 to 150 centimetres, while the depths varied from 30 to 90 centimetres. Grains of wheat (*Triticum dicoccum*), sometimes carbonized, as well as grains of six-row (*Hordeum hexastichum*), four-row (*Hordeum vulgare*) and two-row barley (*Hordeum distichum*) represent the first traces of cultivated plants in Egypt. Flax (*Linum usitatissimum*) has also been found. When Willard Libby was experimenting with his revolutionary radiocarbon-dating technique in 1955, he used carbonized grains from these granaries, obtaining a date of 5145 ± 155 BC. In several cases, mud-covered baskets were excavated from the bottoms of the pits, along with other objects, such as flint artefacts, sherds and shells. A boat-shaped basket, filled with shells, was found *in situ*, as well as three straw trays and a barrel-shaped basket. Two sickles consist of a 50-centimetre-long tamarisk handle, curving slightly inwards, with a central groove and three bifacial flint denticulates, the one in the middle being rectangular, and the two others being triangular points (see figure 1). Several fragments of curved or forked tamarisk sticks have been interpreted as possible flails. The pottery vessels found *in situ* were of the same type as those in the kôms.

Length: 7.62 cm.

Figure 1 Sickle dating to the Faiyum Neolithic (after Caton-Thompson and Gardner 1934: 1).

The lower-level granaries, some 9 metres below the upper set, comprised 109 silos and 9 depressions for sunken pottery vessels. Despite their poor state of preservation, these lower granaries had sufficient similarities with the upper set to suggest that they were contemporary with them.

Concerning the fauna, the range analysed by the British archaeologists has not yet been subjected to any re-examination; it included large mammals such as elephants, hippopotami, crocodiles, fish and freshwater mussels from the lake, but it is the presence of the bones of domesticated goats, sheep, cattle and pigs that shows the progression of the Faiyum culture into one that was fully Neolithic. The Polish excavators in 1981 found remains of all of these domesticated animals (goats, sheep and cattle), except for pigs, but they appear to have played only a secondary role in the diet. It appears that the goat and the sheep were the first animals, after the dog, to be domesticated, and the place where they originally developed into domesticated species seems to have been the Near East, the ecological niche where their wild ancestors lived (notwithstanding arguments concerning an African species of sheep). Indeed, we have seen that the domestic goat is attested at Ganj Dareh in Iran, in levels dated from 7300 to 6800 BC; it is also found in Anatolia, in association with the sheep, in the upper layers of çayönü, in about 7000 BC, where the archaeozoologist Achilles Gautier (1990: 31) noted a shrinking of the size of caprines, compared with those in the lower layers. In Syria-Palestine, it is possible that ovicaprids were being reared in Jericho and Beidha, from the Pre-Pottery Neolithic B period (PPNB) onwards, judging from the size of the surviving remains of the animals. It therefore appears that the goats and sheep of the Faiyum Neolithic can only have come from the Near East. We have still not found any evidence of wild sheep or goats in Africa, except for the 'mouflon à manchettes' (*Amnotragus lervia*) which has nothing in common with the domesticated species of goats and sheep.

We know that Caton-Thompson and Gardner, who worked on the assumption that the lake was gradually diminishing, deduced quite logically that the Epipalaeolithic-style industries were later, because they were situated at a lower point in the Faiyum. They thus assumed that Faiyum A was followed by Faiyum B, the latter apparently representing some kind of cultural degeneration from the former. In the 1950s, Jacques Vandier (1952: 94) pointed out, 'Human development has not always been in the direction of what might be called progress; although the people of Group B existed significantly later than those of Group A, they were a long way from equalling them in cultural terms'.

It has become apparent that fluctuations in the level of the lake were actually more complex, taking the form of a succession of lows and highs, and consisting of five stages between the Palaeo-Moeris lake and the Moeris. The joint American and Polish researches in the 1980s were helped by numerous radiocarbon dates, which enabled them both to verify this more complex chronology and to clarify the accepted image of the earliest Neolithic cultures. By analysing Holocene lacustrine deposits, it is possible to distinguish two stratigraphic and geomorphological units linked with climatic fluctuations. The first of these (LMD, or lacustrine marl-diatomites) developed between 8835 ± 990 and 7440 ± 90 BP; it corresponds to a phase of recession in an arid period, in other words, the Pre- and Proto-Moeris transgression identified by Wendorf and Schild. Several Epipalaeolithic sites were found together, their dates corresponding with those of Qarunian encampments. A hiatus separated this formation from another later formation consisting of grey indurated silt and containing traces of earlier Neolithic settlements. The stratigraphic position of the sites shows that the early Neolithic phase (the 'Faiyumian') appeared during a dry period and evolved simultaneously with increasing humidity, as we can tell by the discharge of rainfall from the wadis of the Western Desert into the Faiyum lake. The dates of 6480 ± 179 and 5540 ± 70 BP (i.e. 5200 and 4500 cal. BC) indicate, on the one hand, a millennium of separation between the end of the Epipalaeolithic (c.7440 ± 90 BP) and the beginning of the Neolithic, and, on the other hand, a long process of development covering nearly 900 years from the early Neolithic until the time when the first Predynastic sites were established.

Identifiable as concentrations of material at the foot of small natural hillocks, the Faiyumian sites have been studied with surface collection and excavation, and we have already discussed the lithic industry of Faiyum A above. The fragments of pottery show a reasonable degree of variability in the very composition of the fabrics; generally speaking, these materials derive from local Tertiary formations and Nilotic clays deposited to the east of the zone being studied. The temper is often organic, sometimes formed from grains of sand or miniscule pieces of shells. In most instances, the shapes are barely recognizable, but when they are discernable they essentially tie in with the categories determined by Caton-Thompson. No ground plans or silos have been found in nearly a millennium of Faiyumian occupation remains.

To the northeast of the zone that has been explored, several sites enclosed in the upper part of a formation of sandy white silts, the results of a new period of recession, provide a chronological sequence from 5410 ± 110 BP to 4820 ± 100 BP, a development of 600 years in a dry climate. From a typological point of view the material found at these sites is characterized by a homogeneity that is quite different from preceding periods in that they can be grouped together under a common term: Moerian – the lithic industry, based on blades made from small pebbles of flint comprising cores which are either simple or double-platform. The tools are especially manufactured from blades and bladelets: two-thirds of the repertoire comprises backed blades, blades and bladelets with micro-retouches, retouched blades, and perforators. The endscrapers, burins and truncations are found only in isolated instances, while retouched flakes appear steadily but far from abundantly. A fragment of a sickle or blade and a hollow-base arrowhead are the only two bifacial elements in the repertoire, but the technique does survive in the form of small flakes in the knapping debris.

The sherds indicate a type of pottery made entirely from local Tertiary clays. The reconstructed vessel shapes include hemispherical bowls and cylindrical pots with necks, but no sign of the footed vessels or large basins characteristic of the Faiyum A culture. On the basis of radiocarbon dates, a hiatus of nearly a century, at the very end of the fifth millennium BC separates these two Neolithic groups: the Faiyumian and the Moerian. In the light of this new information, the Neolithic occupation of the Faiyum has been defined, corrected and fixed in its chronological and palaeoecological contexts, but there are still questions to be asked concerning its origins.

The presence of domesticated ovicaprids, as well as techniques of bifacial knapping with use of polishing, all point towards the Neolithicized Near East. However, Caton-Thompson herself, while taking into account the Oriental possibility, could not exclude the possibility of a more autochthonous origin in the Nile Delta. We have already discussed the thick clouds of mystery that surround the events in the valley during the sixth millennium BC, and we cannot entirely rule out the possibility that an earlier 'ancestral' phase of the Nile valley Neolithic is simply buried under the alluvia of the flood plain. The excavations that have begun to be undertaken in the Delta during the 1980s and 1990s may perhaps shed light on this. Wenke and Casini (1989) point out that the ecological conditions were favourable for the flourishing of cereals and domesticated animals adapted from the Near Eastern species.

Since there were very early cultures with ceramics and perhaps also with domesticated cattle in the regions to the west of the Nile valley, it seems possible that the Nile valley Neolithic might have emerged from the eastern Sahara; the Faiyum could therefore have been one of the first occupied areas at the time of the displacement of populations towards the river, under the pressure of the arid conditions that prevailed in the sixth millennium BC. It is for this reason that Kozlowski and Ginter (1989) interpret the Moerian (the *second* phase of the Faiyum Neolithic) as a late echo of these Saharan traditions, given its blade/bladelet technology reminiscent of the lithics found at Siwa Oasis. The Faiyumian (the *first* phase of the Faiyum Neolithic), on the other hand, might have had its origins in the Near East.

In a more general study, Diane Holmes (1989b: 377) considered the clearly Saharan character of the Faiyum Neolithic industries. The flake industry, with a proliferation of retouched items, notches, denticulates, hollow-base points, grinding stones and ostrich-eggs, is remininiscent of the sets of lithics in the Kharga Oasis, in the more westerly areas investigated by the BOS (the 'Besiedlungsgeschichte der Ost-Sahara': a multidisciplinary programme of research in the 1980s). The Faiyum Neolithic should thus be viewed as a culture at the intersection of three routes: one from the eastern Sahara, one from the Near East and one from the Nile valley itself.

From the point of view of human interaction with the landscape, it should be noted that the hearths in kôms W and K, as well as the silos, were all situated on natural elevations and used throughout the year, although it is clear that they would have been particularly beneficial locations during the humid season, when the lake level was higher. However, apart from these silos and hearths, no actual dwellings have been excavated (such as the semi-sunken houses of the Natufian culture in the Near East). It is evident that the high level of sedentism – full-scale villages – that characterizes the Natufian version of the Neolithic is alien to the Faiyum, where the strategy of land use seems instead to be still linked to a broad spectrum form of seasonal exploitation. Indeed, although agriculture and domestication are attested, the fishing-hunting-gathering combination (reflected both in the toolkit and in the surviving remains of animal species) continued to be the dominant element in their way of life. In this sense, the Faiyum Neolithic recalls that of the eastern Sahara: the sites found by the joint American-Polish teams, located as they are in areas of the Faiyum that would have been covered by the annual flood, would have been able to serve as short-term base camps, which would therefore explain the absence or non-survival of the ground plans of dwellings.

The archaeozoologist, Douglas Brewer (1989b), proposes – in his recent study of the fauna from Neolithic sites in the Faiyum – a model of exploitation based on the very precise seasonal use of lacustrian resources. Fish figure strongly in his analyses since they are the best represented species. Catfish (*Clarias*), found in well-oxygenated marshy waters, account for 66 per cent of the ichthyofauna at certain sites, but it is clear from the presence of Nile perch (*Lates niloticus*), which, in contrast, tend to favour deep waters, that the methods of fishing were varied. The *Clarias*, which is a large fish swimming in relatively shallow waters, can be harpooned, trapped in nets, or even caught by hand, whereas the procurement of the *Lates* necessitates the use of more complicated nets in deep waters, and this implies a more collective style of fishing, doubtless undertaken from a boat. A precise analysis based on the growth cycle of the *Clarias* has shed a certain amount of light on the techniques of Faiyum fishers, since its pectoral spine has growth rings which are thin and dark in the winter months, when the fish tends to lie still in the cold waters, but large and clear in the warm season, when it is active, feeding and growing considerably. The statistical analysis of these growth rings has demonstrated that, at both Faiyum B and Faiyum A sites, the fish were caught at the end of spring and beginning of summer on the one hand, and the end of summer, on the other hand. If the lake was well connected with the Nile and therefore subject, like it, to fluctuation of levels, the whole beginning of the summer corresponded to the low waters and to the formation, in vast depressions, of vast marshy zones where the *Clarias* proliferated. The end of summer, in contrast, was the season when the fish laid their eggs and therefore gathered together, making them easier to catch. In terms of such fishing practices, the Faiyum Neolithic sites differed very little from those of the Epipalaeolithic Faiyum B.

Linked to the great western zone first by their geographical position to the west of the Nile valley, secondly by their lithic technology, and thirdly by their exploitation of the landscape, the first known Neolithic people of Egypt proper borrowed from the Near East the species that they domesticated; possessors of an original range of ceramics, they seem to have participated in several different cultural universes.

The Faiyum depression was an oasis in the Sahara Desert; it was linked with the valley but nevertheless was different from it, and it also lay at the western end of the route from the Near East via the Delta. It engendered a Neolithic culture which was initiated by individuals perhaps coming from the west, pushed by the terrible climatic conditions of the sixth millennium BC, and finding ecological conditions in the Faiyum favourable to the farming of domesticated species that might already have been present in the neighbouring Delta region. In this sense, the hypothesis of an earlier form of the Neolithic buried in the Nile silts must without doubt be examined in more detail.

Merimda Beni Salama

Discovered by Hermann Junker under the auspices of the Vienna West Delta Expedition, this large site in the western Delta was the object of seven seasons of excavation from 1929 to 1939 (four of these seasons being collaborations with the Swedish archaeologists of the Egyptian Museum in Stockholm). The publication of Merimda is limited to preliminary reports (Junker 1929–40) because of the outbreak of the Second World War, which resulted in the loss of a great deal of the documentation; the rest of the information is spread across a number of different museums (Cairo, Stockholm, Heidelberg and Vienna), as regards the Palaeolithic material.

In the 1960s, the Egyptian Antiquities Service undertook a rapid rescue excavation in an endangered part of the site (Badawi 1978), and in 1977–83 excavations were resumed by the German Institute of Archaeology at Cairo, under the direction of Josef Eiwanger (1984, 1988), the main item on the agenda being the difficult problem of the site's stratigraphy.

Junker uncovered almost 6400 m² of a total area of occupation extending for nearly 200,000 m², the thickness of the excavated deposits being close to 3 metres in certain parts of the site. He only took account of the statigraphic variation at a comparatively late stage (see Junker 1940), eventually distinguishing three layers of occupation. Eiwanger's excavations essentially undertook a reassessment of the stratigraphy by means of a series of sondages in the area between the two zones excavated by Junker.

At a distance of 45 kilometres to the northwest of Cairo, between the el-Beheri canal and the desert edge, the Merimda settlement is situated in the valley, on a terrace spur made up of pebbles from a wadi disgorging to the north. The site developed within a sedimentological unit formed by white Aeolian sand. The terrace contained both rolled Palaeolithic artefacts, which have been studied by K. Schmidt (1980), and the raw materials from which the lithics of the lowest occupation layer (level I) were made. Five archaeological levels (corresponding to three cultural phases) have been distiguished altogether:

- Level I (Eiwanger 1984), named the *Urschicht* by the German excavators, is clearly differentiated from the four levels above it; this material indicates the presence of a hitherto unknown culture that, according to Eiwanger, was in contact with the Levant.
- Level II (Eiwanger 1988) seems to contain material indicating African influences.
- Finally, levels III, IV and V (Eiwanger 1992) constitute a more classic regional culture, similar to that of Faiyum A.

The *Urschicht* – the deepest archaeological unit, situated on the terrace itself – contains unusual original material. The excavators identified three post-holes comprising fairly shallow round or oval pits, two to three metres in diameter, and a few hearths. Parts of level I are covered by a layer of sterile Aeolian sand, but in other areas it lies directly beneath level II.

The many potsherds are characterized by untempered fabric; they have a reddish appearance, as well as thick walls and a lack of variety in shapes. The polished ceramics, generally well fired, can be categorized as red-brown to purple-violet in colour, while the vessels that have been burnished by hand vary from a clear orange colour to red. Typical of this stratum is a form of herring-bone decoration that is incised before firing into the fabric of some polished pottery (and exceptionally also applied to miniature burnished pottery vessels); the band of decoration, always left unpolished, presents the whole range of decorative varieties on thin- or thick-walled vessels, finely or coarsely polished. The shapes are limited to cups, basins and hemispherical bowls. A separate group comprises miniature vessels generally made from a burnished fabric. The variety in this area of ceramics increased in the upper layers, where bottles appeared and such features as lips, necks and feet were added to the vessels. However, receptacles with handles figure in the repertoire of the lower level but are not found otherwise. The bases of the vessels are essentially rounded, very occasionally flat, and never pointed. Fired clay ladles appear in level I, one example having been found by Eiwanger and several others being noted by Larsen (1962) among the burnished ceramics.

The lithics in level I at Merimda differ from those in the upper levels even more than the pottery does. The terrace pebbles, generally small, served as cores for the production of short, wide blades and rather blade-like flakes, often produced from the actual cortex of the pebble. The retouches on the blades are above all direct and lateral, sometimes inverse. The use of large flakes struck from the pebbles as the basis for retouched endscrapers, whether coarse or fine, unifacial or bifacial, is quite characteristic of this level, as are the numerous perforators made from flakes or pebbles. The bifacial retouch was essentially used to create cutting edges on pebbles, thus functionally linking this set of tools with axes. The only true axe in level I is triangular and lightly polished along the edges. One remarkable aspect of this industry is the presence of a type of small arrowhead made from a flake, entirely retouched on its upper face, with pedunculate and fins, and with two notches, which recall the Helwan points and the series of armatures with notches in the Near East.

Pestles and mortars have been found in all of the levels; those in level I amount to 60 fragments of local siliceous sandstone, oval to subrectangular in shape. Sherds from the burnished pots were used as grinders and doubtless also as smoothers. Among the stones, red haematite is common, presumably having been ground up into body paint. Fairly local sources of fossilized wood, quartz, sandstone, limestone and basalt were also exploited, while schist must have been brought from further to the south.

There is one peculiarity which makes this level I material at Merimda entirely original compared with the rest of the Nile valley: the presence of clay figurines. An anthropomorphic figure and fragments of bovids represent the first examples of Egyptian sculpture in the round.

The radiocarbon dates deriving from this *Urschicht*, although considered too recent by Eiwanger, actually correspond with those published by Olsson in 1955 (see Hassan 1985): 4795 ± 105 AQ.BC and 5005 ± 125 BC (180 centimeters below the surface, according to Olsson), which suggests that this first phase of the Merimdan culture should be dated to the very beginning of the fifth millennium BC. We hope that new dates will soon be available to confirm, clarify or modify these data. From this point of view, we should not ignore the doubts expressed by Eiwanger (1988: 54 n. 312), who considers the radiocarbon sequence to be too short, and is tempted to 'push back' the *Urschicht* to the sixth millennium BC. Indeed we have noted above that the first Neolithic cultures in the Faiyum, Caton-Thompson's Faiyum A and Ginter and Kozlowski's Faiyumian, stretches back to *c.*5200 BC. However, it is the upper stratum at Merimda that includes material comparable with that of the Faiyumian culture – there thus appears to be poor correlation between the radiocarbon dates and stratigraphy.

The fauna, studied by Angela von den Driesch and Joachim Boessneck (1985), reveals the existence of domestic species from the first stratum onwards: sheep essentially, then also cattle, pigs, and, in very small proportions, the goat. The dog is also present. Although it is uncertain where the domesticated cattle came from, the presence of ovicaprids suggests that the Near East may have been the place of origin for each of these species. Although a wild species of pig could have existed in Africa, it was domesticated for the first time at çayönü, to the south-east of Anatolia, from 7200 BC onwards; it could certainly be found in about 6500 BC at Jarmo in the hills of Iraqi Kurdistan overlooking the Zagros (see Gautier 1990: 137–40).

Among the wild species represented is the hippopotamus – only one of which could supply as much meat as four to five head of cattle or 40 to 50 sheep – while its enormous skeleton also provided material for numerous objects, such as harpoons, fish-hooks and boring tools. According to Eiwanger, the earliest Neolithic stratum at Merimda has connections with southwest Asia. In a study of the ceramics from Merimda at Stockholm Museum, Larsen (1962) points out that the incised herringbone motif is found on pottery from levels I–IV at Hassuna; the lithics were characterized by the beginning of the bifacial technique with flat retouch and the first appearance of the polishing technique. We should add to this the Oriental trilogy of domesticated animals (sheep, pigs and goats) as well as all early clay figures attested in Palestine since the Natufian. All these factors tend to place the *Urschicht* in the well-known sixth-millennium hiatus between the Helwan Epipalaeolithic and the Faiyum A culture.

Level II at Merimda comprises the remains of a more intensive phase of settlement, judging from the extensive traces of post-holes, pits and hearths; this layer is brownish in colour, due to the presence of larger quantities of ashes and organic remains. There is in general more surviving material, including large amounts of fauna and plant remains.

The level II pottery differs radically from that of the *Urschicht*, in that the latter is tempered with chopped straw, suggesting the making of larger receptacles. Polished ceramics appear in quantities almost equal to the burnished vessels. The colour of the polished pots vary from red to grey, eventually resulting in the deep black pots of levels III to V, which Junker regards as archetypal Merimda pots. On the other hand, in stark contrast to level I, none of the pots in level II are decorated. The shapes are all still simple: numerous cups with fairly vertical sides, conical and hemispherical bowls, the bases of which are more often rounded than flat, while the rims are straight or turned slightly outwards. It is in level II, however, that a characteristic Merimda-style vessel appeared: the oval vessel, usually forming part of the burnished category, which occurred in level I only as a miniature vessel but appears in all sizes in level II, from voluminous to very small.

It is clear, however, that, compared with the change in pottery, the lithics in level II are even more distinct from those of level I, becoming less numerous and essentially bifacial. The flint knappers stopped using the wadi pebbles and instead exploited the flint nodules in nearby limestone formations. Two factors appear to have led to this change: first, the burial of the wadi terrace under a thick organic deposit, thus creating difficulties in gaining access to the raw materials, and secondly, the introduction of technological innovations (bifacial flat retouch, pressure flaking and polishing) which required the use of homogeneous flint cores that were larger in size and of better quality.

It is interesting to note that the 'winged' arrowheads appear in level II, often with broken wings. Certain examples show traces of a pre-polishing stage designed to prepare the surface for long flat retouches created by pressure flaking, doubtless with the use of bone points, a technique which was later to be used for the production of the distinctive Naqada II knives (see Midant-Reynes 1987). Pressure flaking was generally used for larger items and for elongated triangular or lozenge-shaped blades.

As in the Faiyum, chipped stone axes were made with polished cutting edges, although in level II at Merimda the polishing was often executed over a larger area of the tool. One particular shape of axe at Merimda has a transverse cutting edge similar to that of the gouge (or adze) in the Faiyum and Khartoum Neolithic cultures; one face is flattened by large retouches or in its natural state, while the other was rounded, with a series of transverse retouches creating a fine straight cutting edge.

Sometimes bifacial sickle blades are characterized by pre-polishing and there are often traces of sickle sheen in the denticulations. Bifacial perforators are fairly common, some of them still being made from blades, like those of the *Urschicht*, while others were made from pebbles and retouched flakes struck from pebbles. Blades are much less common than in level I, but tend to be longer, while retaining roughly the same width, some having been subjected to lateral retouch.

In contrast to the lithics, objects made from baked clay, bone, shell and ivory began to occur in large numbers in level II. Fragments of clay modelled bovids, beads and spheroids have been found, while fish-hooks made from mussel shells and beads made from ostrich eggshells were only found in the first two levels. Boring tools appear in large numbers as well as many fragments of needles. More specific to level II are bone harpoons, with rows of three barbs and a flat base without incisions, as well as pendants made from canid teeth, and an ivory bracelet. Two small transverse-edge axes were fashioned from the rib of a hippopotamus.

The working of hard stones is attested by several fragments of Egyptian alabaster that are probably the remains of vessels, polished schist axes, and, above all, two piriform maceheads, one made from alabaster and another made from a type of volcanic rock found in Palestine and Anatolia. The many pestles and mortars are made from local sandstone, and fragments of haematite are still present.

A pottery vessel embedded in the ground, near the hearth, contained several objects covered over with a mat. This vessel is a conical, flat-bottomed bowl belonging to the burnished pottery group, and the objects found inside it were five small polished schist axes, a fragment of a bracelet or anklet made from hippopotamus ivory, two enigmatic conical objects made from the same ivory, and a small animal of uncertain identity sculpted in bone (perhaps a hippopotamus).

The fauna in level II is also quite different from that of level I, and much more similar to that of levels III to V. Domesticated cattle become more common and continue to increase in number throughout each of the different occupation levels. The percentage of fish and pigs follows the same basic upward curve, whereas molluscs decrease from level I to V. Only Nile mussels (*Aspatharia Rubens*) were still widely used, both pierced for decorative use and worked into the form of fish hooks. Hunting for wild animals is well evidenced, particularly the pursuit of ruminants and hippopotami.

Although showing continuity with the *Urschicht* – or even evolution out of it – in terms of the polished pottery, modelled figurines, mussel-shell fish hooks, ostrich-eggshell beads, and certain aspects of the lithic toolkit, level II is also clearly marked by the very nature of the material that forms the basis of a new cultural landscape. Zones of sterile sand may reflect the arid phase of the sixth millennium BC, detected in Palestine between 5500 and 4500 BC, during which the human population of southern Libya almost entirely disappeared; this would push the date of the *Urschicht* back to 5500 BC.

In contrast to the Asiatic-influenced level I, the cultural influences perceptible in the novel aspects of level II, were, according to Eiwanger, more African than Asiatic. Thus the bone harpoons and the hard stone adzes originating in the First-Cataract region both 'draw' on the Saharo-Sudanese periphery. No radiocarbon dates have yet been obtained for level II.

The third phase of occupation at Merimda, comprising strata III–V, must be treated as a single entity in the absence of detailed publication. This third phase is the one that has usually tended to dominate the classic descriptions of the site, such as those given by Jacques Vandier (1952: 95–153) and William Hayes (1964: 229–42). Although processes of development can clearly be discerned within strata III–V, none are as radical as the differences between level I and all the later levels.

The pottery found in level III indicates a growing tendency towards the closed forms that had appeared in level II. Polished pottery flasks characterize levels IV–V, and it is noticeable that changes of orientation in the actual process of polishing a vessel – horizontal on the neck, and vertical on the main body of the pot – could produce a kind of decorative effect. Finally, the large receptacles of coarse pottery make up half of the repertoire of pottery in levels III–V.

During phases IV and V, the polished pottery developed towards red and dark black types, indicating an increasing mastery of the process of firing, and towards oval, closed, globular or cylindrical forms, or even large dishes; the 'extremities' of the pots are elaborated in various ways, with lips, necks and annular or anthropomorphic feet. All of these variations also applied to the smaller vessels, which were present throughout the site. Finally, the coarse and burnished categories were decorated with protrusions or incisions.

The lithics of levels III–V show a development of the bifacial tendency of level II. In addition to the groups previously mentioned, there were multiple perforators made from pebbles, numerous sidescrapers and endscrapers made from flakes; the wide bifacial pieces with flat retouches take on particularly significant proportions in levels IV and V, where they are sometimes made by the 'burin blow' technique. The excellence of the Merimdan flint-knappers can be deduced from the very finely worked lancehead in the Cairo Museum (JE 57920, see Baumgartel 1955: pl. IV/1), combining pre-polishing, pressure flaking and a beautiful sense of equilibrium in terms of its form. The probable existence of a flint-knapping workshop at Merimda, noted by Junker, serves to reinforce the image of a fairly specialized workforce that is independently suggested by the analysis of the tools.

Several hundred objects of bone, horn, ivory, baked clay and shells indicate the high level of activity of the last inhabitants of Merimda. Small limestone weights with longitudinal grooves were probably used in net fishing, while clay spindle-whorls – which must surely be linked with the presence of flax grains – attest to spinning and doubtless also weaving. Junker refers to a fragment of a sieve or strainer, made from an indeterminate material, that is the first example of this type of artefact on an Egyptian site. Beads of bone, ivory, clay and various gemstones (turquoise, cornelian and agate), although not common, are nevertheless present both in the settlement and, to a greater extent, in the graves.

Finally, the later phases at Merimda have yielded the first representations of the human figure, including a roughly cylindrical baked clay statuette provided with hair, eyes and chest, which is the first definite three-dimensional human image that has so far been found in Egypt. An oval clay head, measuring 10.3 centimetres high, with two gaping holes for eyes, a flat nose and a small open mouth, constitutes the first schematic depiction of a face (Cairo, Egyptian Museum, JE 97472). Holes distributed across the forehead presumably indicate the means by which some kind of hair was secured (perhaps in the form of feathers), while another set under the chin may indicate the presence of a beard, and a further hole, at the base, raises the possibility that this enigmatic head was originally attached to the upper end of a wooden pole, as if it were a kind of puppet.

It is in the uppermost layers of the site that the remains take on a genuinely village-like appearance. The oval houses, measuring roughly 3 x 1.5 metres and partially dug down into the earth, were built of irregular masses of clay and chopped straw, preserved up to a height of slightly less than a metre. Both the upper part of the walls and the roof must have been made of plant materials: branches, reeds and stubble. Entrance to the houses was facilitated by a threshold made either from a simple hippopotamus tibia or a fragment of wood placed on the inside, against the wall. A jar, pushed down into the floor, presumably held a supply of fresh water. The presence of hearths and animal remains suggests that meals were consumed inside these houses, sheltered from the wind and sun.

Primitive though they may seem, these dwellings were not scattered at random but aligned with one another and lined up in rows, along which streets can be assumed to have passed. Groups of post-holes mark out the ground-plans of huts made from lighter material and horseshoe-shaped shelters opening towards the southeast, which were probably more ephemeral structures serving as workrooms or summer kitchens, protected from the north wind. Finally, a reed enclosure fence, laid out across the ground and very well preserved, made of lines of stalks bound together by two horizontal ties, strikingly recalls enclosures for livestock in modern Egypt.

The evidence of burning includes a degree of complexity not previously encountered in Egypt. These 'hearths' are not simply hollows dug into the ground or even hollows consolidated with rings of stones, but actual small ovens built of mud bricks or balls of clay laid out in circles.

In one hearth, Junker describes a pair of clay cones, each about 20 centimetres high, which could have been used to support a cooking pot, a procedure which is depicted hundreds of years later in one of the *mastaba*-tombs of the Old Kingdom.

As well as these light shelters, more permanent dwellings, hearths and enclosures, granaries are also to be found, just as in the Faiyum. The granaries, made up of large baskets set into pits lined with clay, and huge jars, nearly a metre high and embedded in the ground, are not arranged in groups for communal use, as in the Faiyum, but spread around in such a way as to suggest that each individual house had its own. The difficulties of excavation and the confusing of different stratigraphic layers means that it is actually difficult to assess whether this is indeed the case, but it is nevertheless undeniable that no *clusters* of granaries have yet been found at Merimda.

In the immediate vicinity of many of the silos were groups of four depressions, each four metres wide and not very deep, their bottoms covered with reed matting, which have been interpreted as areas for the threshing of cereal; Vandier (1952: 122) notes, 'In historical times, the threshing area was a round surface, covered with a layer of hardened earth and surrounded by a low wall. The earliest hieroglyphs show us an area that is already circular but surrounded by a ring, sometimes striped with green lines, which, according to Junker, must represent the matting that has been placed in the pit, with its edges protruding upwards at ground level.'

Just as the distribution of the silos poses a stratigraphic problem, so the patterning of the graves at Merimda also is also still a somewhat controversial aspect of the site. About 180 graves were excavated by the Austrian expedition. The bodies were wrapped in mats or animal skins, and in 85 per cent of cases they were laid on their right sides, in oval, fairly shallow pits, often covered over with plant fibres. Usually laid in a contracted position, preferably with their heads towards the south and the face looking towards the north-northeast. The extreme rarity of adult males compared with the large numbers of young children has led to the suggestion that the latter (and sometimes also women) were buried within the dwellings or in their immediate proximity, while men, perhaps often killed in the course of hunting or war, might have been buried in those parts of the outside world where they died. The absence of grave goods further bolstered this interpretation, stressing the possibility that the necessary means of survival in the afterlife were located within the dwelling place which the deceased thus never left. The contrast with Upper Egypt was therefore couched in 'sociological' terms: cemeteries in the south were located alongside a more ephemeral set of dwellings, thus implying a more nomadic population, while the burials in villages in the north were regarded as proof of a more sedentary group. This viewpoint was, however, eventually refuted by Barry Kemp (1968), who recognized that the stratigraphic confusion at the site could have been a misleading factor in terms of the interpretation of the burials. Karl Butzer (1959), considering the total area of the site (200,000 m²), reached an estimate of more than 160,000 for the population of Merimda, on the assumption that the entire site was simultaneously occupied, but it is clear that this assumption is incorrect. There were considerable abandoned areas of the site at different times during its occupation, and these deserted zones must thus have served as burial sites, with only young children being buried within the settlement, which is a well-known custom elsewhere in ancient Egypt. Indeed, the conclusions of the German excavations of the 1980s appear to concur with this general trend.

The discovery of graves spread around in different occupation strata correlates with the discovery of funerary assemblages in which the offerings (not occurring in any quantity but nevertheless sometimes present) allow the inhumation to be dated to one specific period or other. F. A. Badawi (1980: 75) notes, with regard to a group of burials found in a sector not excavated by Junker, that the settlement corresponding to these tombs must be sought elsewhere in the site, and such a comment completely contradicts the idea of burials *in situ* within the houses at the time that they were actually being inhabited. Eiwanger (1982: 70) reports 40 graves belonging to level I, consistently oriented, the skeletons with heads to the south and face towards the northeast, with all ages represented, apart from very young children . . .

In its complexity, Merimda provides evidence for a long development over at least 400 years, during which the site underwent both horizontal and vertical processes of change.

Although there is a considerable difference between the level I occupation at Merimda and the subsequent phases, the creation of the various elements of Neolithic culture appear to have been in place from the beginning; thus the economy relies partly on the exploitation of domesticated species of animals and plants, species that were first domesticated in the Near East (wheat, barley, sheep, goats and pigs), but at the same time, the more traditional resources provided by the environment were certainly not being neglected, since hunting and fishing are great providers of protein. Pottery immediately fitted into this Neolithic way of life, thus inaugurating the use of the earth for less immediately material purposes. In other words, the symbolic 'vocabulary' was already elaborated and, as far as we can tell, the bovid played a role in this symbolism, but not one that we are yet able to understand fully.

The equipment found in the upper levels at Merimda does not modify this first image in any way, tending not only to accentuate the agricultural aspects of life with the increasingly common instances of sickle sheen, but also stressing the continued importance of hunting with the presence of arrowheads and spears, which were more and more carefully worked, and providing more evidence of hunting techniques, with fish hooks, harpoons and net weights.

In this context, it is worth discussing further the ways in which people have interacted with the Nile flood. The regular return of the inundation may be regarded as a kind of game of hide and seek which has been played since the earliest times. Indeed, more than any others, the Nilotic peoples were at the whim of seasonal changes caused by the peculiar ecology of the valley, and they were unusually well adapted to the 'management' of the flood. It is more than likely that permanent villages were constructed only outside the areas of land that were subject to flooding. Other factors must certainly have influenced the gradual introduction of a fully sedentary way of life at Merimda, a lifestyle that was of the 'Oriental' type, and not the type that we have observed in the Faiyum, despite their proximity and their many similarities. The first indications of a primitive form of urbanization, the distribution of houses according to a system of alignments, the creation of silos (whether individual or communal), threshing areas and livestock enclosures, all of these elements of life at Merimda suggest a degree of organization, a collective way of life, a community in which activities were undertaken simultaneously, and a set of common spiritual interests of which the first sculptures, mentioned above, are dim reflections.

It is almost as difficult to define the origins of Merimda as to define those of the Faiyum cultures. From this point of view, it will be crucial to obtain a more precise date for the *Urschicht* – if, as Eiwanger suggests, it appeared in the sixth millennium BC, the level I pottery would be the earliest in this part of the valley, and perhaps the common ancestor of the ceramics in Merimda III–V and Faiyum A. It goes without saying that if this were the case, it would be a clear indication of the adaptation of cultivated and domesticated species in the Delta, from the sixth millennium onwards. The people of the Faiyum would have adopted these species from the Merimda culture at the time when they came into the region from their original homeland in the Western Desert. At the same time, the Faiyumians might also have adopted the polished pottery, which is very similar at both sites, although more sophisticated and more skilfully made at Merimda.

El-Omari

The recently published sites of the el-Omari culture (Debono and Mortensen 1990) provide new data concerning the earliest Lower Egyptian

Neolithic cultures. Located at the mouth of the Wadi Hof, 3 kilometres north of Helwan, and about 4 kilometres from the modern course of the Nile, el-Omari is actually made up of three main localities: el-Omari A, el-Omari B and Gebel Hof. El-Omari A and B are separate parts of the same site, situated at the edge of a terrace of Pleistocene gravel, at the mouth of the limestone massif of Ras el-Hof, while the Gebel Hof region is located 5 kilometres north of Helwan and at a height of 90 metres above the floor of the Wadi Hof.

Initially uncovered in the course of surveys undertaken in 1918 in the region of Helwan by Father Paul Bovier-Lapierre, the main site was actually identified in 1924 by Amin el-Omari, a young mineralogist, who died a short time later; Bovier-Lapierre therefore named the site after him, and began to excavate it in 1925.

Situated in a vulnerable area, el-Omari at one stage looked likely to be wiped out entirely through the greed of plunderers, the diggers of sebakh and the interests of the military. Three further seasons of excavation took place under the direction of Fernand Debono (in 1943–4, 1948 and 1951), but it was another 40 years before this work was finally properly published under the auspices of the German Archaeological Institute at Cairo.

The main site consists of two excavated areas (A and B) and five other areas (D, E, F, G and H) were only surveyed, covering a total area of 750 × 500 metres. The excavations revealed pit-structures cut into wadi deposits and sometimes also into the underlying limestone *gebel* itself. With shapes including circular, oval and sometimes irregular, these pits had diameters of 50–250 centimetres and depths of 50–110 centimetres; the walls and floor of the larger structures comprised mats and clay (a form of wattle and daub), while the smaller structures (perhaps storage rooms) were lined either with coarse clay or with basketry. Occasionally there are post-holes within these pit-structures; some, on the other hand, have a small semi-circular depression next to them, constituting an intermediate level, perhaps helping the inhabitants to step down into the main pit-dwelling.

Remains of posts, each 2–4 centimetres thick, were preserved up to a height of 5–40 centimetres; they are also occasionally found in the fill of the pits. In view of their isolated character and the fact that they were sometimes held in place by stones, it seems that the posts were possibly supports to which the cords of light reed superstructures may have been attached. However, there are also post-holes (depressions with diameters of 20–40 centimetres) which suggest heavier, more substantial superstructures. In some parts of the site, the dwellings appear to be linked together by shallow trenches, perhaps indicating the presence of reed fences similar to enclosures (*zeriba*s) in modern Egyptian settlements. The few hearths that have been found at the el-Omari sites are usually located outside the pit-dwellings, the stratified contents of which represent precious evidence for chronological developments. This stratified material did not form as a result of patterns of behaviour in the pit-houses themselves, but as a result of activities some distance away, with the many depressions forming zones of refuse.

The refuse takes the form of a brown deposit consisting of organic materials mixed with other types of debris and artefacts. There are also two other significant deposits: first a layer of yellow sand (the thickness of which varies, judging from the depressions) containing no archaeological material and therefore suggesting a dry phase, as at Merimda, and secondly a layer of saline material of varying thickness, at the base of the the brown deposit, presumably indicating a more humid period. However, some pits contain only the yellow deposit, some only the brown layers of refuse, and others have both; in those pits that have both yellow and brown deposits, the yellow one is almost always lower down in the stratigraphy (apart from a few cases where either the order is reversed or the yellow is sandwiched between two layers of brown. It seems clear that there is a vertical stratigraphy whereby the yellow sandy layer is earlier, given that when two pits with different fills were sectioned, the blackish sediment was later than the yellow in both cases, but across the site as a whole it is also possible to see a horizontal chronological development. Debono and Mortensen (1990) suggest that there were nine occupation phases during which the site would have evolved from area B.III, which essentially consisted of small pits that were probably used only for storage, towards areas A and B.I, where there were larger depressions lined with basketry; then finally the whole site (A and B) was used as a settlement, judging from the post-holes, the presence of pots inside pit sediments, and the existence of large depressions and hearths. As if designed for specific units of the population (perhaps family units), each large depression tends to be surrounded by smaller ones, and between these there are traces of light structures attested by post-holes and trenches for low reed barriers.

The pottery, always tempered with plant material and also incorporating some mineral inclusions, was made from two types of marl clay obtained from the wadi, sometimes used separately and sometimes mixed together (Nile silt being rarely used). The resulting fabric is hard, tough, non-porous, brown-coloured when the firing temperature is below 800°C, and red when it is fired any higher; often poor control of the fire means that many pots are mottled with brownish marks. About two-thirds of the vessels are polished, while the rest are smoothed, and sometimes an ochre slip is applied. The shapes are always simple open or half-open types, with flat or slightly concave bases, usually comprising oval plates, bowls, goblets and hemispherical jars.

This pottery is an original group that cannot easily be compared with the ceramics from Merimda and the Faiyum. There are greater similarities with the Neolithic A and B pottery of Palestine, as much in terms of technology as shapes; two clays also formed the basis of the Palestinian pottery production, and, just as at el-Omari, these two clays were either used separately or as a mixture.

The lithic toolkit at el-Omari was made first from pebbles deriving from the local terraces, secondly from larger nodules brought from further afield (perhaps from Abu Rawash, about 20 kilometres away), and thirdly from grey flint which was clearly imported in the form of large blades.

The small cores were used to make bifacial tools such as small conical chipped stone axes (8 × 4 centimetres) with polished cutting edges, as in the neighbouring sites of the Faiyum and Merimda cultures, but there were also a small number of purely polished examples noted by Bovier-Lapierre. Hollow-base arrowheads, thick triangles and sickles complete the range of bifacial pieces. Sickle blades made with blade technology seem to have been used throughout the history of the settlement, only being joined by bifacial sickle blades in the final phase. Sidescrapers made from flakes are common in all phases, as are drill bits, backed blades and composite tools made from short flakes, combining perforators, endscrapers, burins and denticulates. In addition, microliths of a final Palaeolithic style appear in most of the pits.

Finally, a very characteristic type of object begins to appear: a long pedunculate blade, the rectilinear cutting edge of which is often left rough and unworked, while the back, arched at the distal end and then softly convex, is backed by a series of inverse or direct retouches. The larger examples are made from fine imported grey flint, while the smaller ones are evidently imitations made from local raw material in the form of terrace pebbles. All of these date to the final phase of the settlement, like the picks made from silicified limestone, sandstone and flint. In a general sense, the development of the el-Omari lithics mirrors that at Merimda, in that an early toolkit made from flakes and blades gradually becomes dominated by bifacial tools.

Stone vases appear in the form of fragments of calcite and a basalt three-footed base, which probably came from Palestine. A few stone gouges, probably serving as whetstones, were made from nodules of silicified limestone, and a number of limestone pierced discs were probably used either as spindle-whorls or as fishing-net weights. Percussors and pestles made from petrified wood, sandstone, quartz, flint and limestone, must have been used with the small limestone palettes and sandstone mortars that have also been found. Polished bone is represented only by a few pins, borers and a single fish-hook, and there are no surviving artefacts of ivory or copper. However, in a dish sealed under the yellow sandy deposit and turned upside down, in one of the pits, the excavators found fragments of a heavy metal, perhaps galena, wrapped in an animal-skin bag.

The excavation of el-Omari A and B resulted in the discovery of 43 graves, containing 28 adults, 12 children and 2 individuals of undetermined age. These are usually simple oval pits measuring 90–120 × 70–110 centimetres and not very deep (about 40 centimetres), which are often visible on the surface; they were either deliberately dug or re-used pits. Two of them may have had superstructures, judging from the postholes surrounding them. The deceased were laid out in the foetal position, on their left sides, with their heads to the south and faces to the west in most cases. A kind of pillow of stones or plant materials seems to have been used to support their heads. It appears that a mat was placed under the body, and sometimes also over it (even, in one case, totally enveloping the corpse). Grave goods are rare, but there is one persistent feature whereby a small pot was placed in front of the face, arms or legs. Of the two types of pottery that were regularly used, one was polished and seems to be restricted to the larger graves of men or women. Grave A35 contained an intriguing object in the form of a stick 35 centimetres in length and bulging at both ends, suggesting the shape of a phallus. Its presence in the hand of a man suggests that it may have had a specific meaning, possibly symbolizing power or magic (Debono and Mortensen 1990: pl. 28.1). Items of jewellery are represented by numerous pierced Red Sea shells, as well as bone and stone beads. Two pendants are made simply from pierced pebbles. The body of one of the children was accompanied by ibex horns, while another body was covered in the remains of flowers.

It is not possible to discern any evolution in the funerary practices across the horizontal stratigraphy of the site. The graves have obviously been dug, as at Merimda, in parts of the settlement that had been abandoned. Men, women and children each appear to have been buried in particular areas; thus, men seem to be more concentrated to the west of area A, while the women and children were buried mainly in the east. With the exception of a woman buried with a foetus, no babies have been found, perhaps because of the relative fragility of their bones.

Initially serving as a storage zone, and later as a zone of land and settlement, el-Omari – like the neighbouring sites of the Faiyum and Merimda cultures – was characterized by a production economy. From the beginning of the occupation, carbonized grains indicate the existence of several types of wheat (*Triticum dicoccum, Triticum compactum, Triticum monococcum*), barley (*Hordeum vulgare*), rye (*Lolium temulentum*), legumes (e.g. peas and broad beans), and flax, as well as various herbs that flourished in the fields of cereals. The fact that this is such a diverse mixture of food sources suggests that they had not reach a very advanced stage of agriculture, and the few sickle blades found might well have been simply used to chop down stalks for the manufacture of mats and baskets.

The surviving remains of domesticated animals comprised goats, sheep, cattle and pigs, the latter playing an important role in the economy, but the inhabitants of el-Omari are especially fishers, preferring deep high-water catches, judging from the abundant remains of Nile perches, alongside catfish (*Synodontis*), much sought after for its pectoral spike, in more peaceful waters. The people of el-Omari also hunted crocodiles and hippopotami, an important source of protein, but showed little interest in the pursuit of desert animals and marsh fowl, preferring to exploit an ecological niche between the wadi and the alluvial plain.

This is just the opposite of the usual situation with riverbank settlements. El-Omari was located in a particularly high place and at some distance from the flood plain, at the mouth of a drainage system that brought together the accumulated waters of Gebel Abu Shama and Gebel Gabo to the east, depositing the sediments to the north of Helwan and thus causing the Nile itself to be forced into a narrower course over to the west. This regular replenishment by rainwater combines on the one hand with the particular capacity of the limestone massif to retain water in the depressions and natural basins, and on the other hand with the numerous springs of mineral water, the existence of which is due to a system of geological faults. Thus the immediate environment was conducive to the exploitation of natural resources, such as plant life and animals, which flourished around semi-permanent sources of water. The people of el-Omari clearly developed a close knowledge of their environment, only using the clay from 'their' wadi to manufacture their pottery; they nevertheless also exploited the attractions of the valley, which was beneficial in terms of sowing and harvesting, and it was there that they hunted precious extra sources of nutrition in the form of turtles, crocodiles, fish and hippopotami.

The site of Gebel Hof, situated on a terrace some 100 metres above the floor of the wadi, is, from this point of view, more significant. It was discovered in 1947 and has now almost entirely disappeared, but in 1954 the Egyptian Department of Antiquities made a sondage through the remains, uncovering a reed enclosure within which they found a large jar and an oval pit full of carbonized cereals. The archaeological material is similar to that at el-Omari, thus suggesting that this was a settlement of comparable type and date, perhaps an observation post, perhaps a cool refuge in the heat of summer, or, on the contrary, a shelter from the annual floods (to which the saline layers in pit-dwellings at the el-Omari A and B sites no doubt bear witness).

The more distant contacts, with Sinai and the Red Sea – the regions from which seashells and galena were obtained, and doubtless also the source of fine grey flint – might all have been facilitated by the use of domesticated donkeys, el-Omari being the first Egyptian site where the bones of these animals have been found.

The settlements of the people of el-Omari are comparable in their basic structures with those of Lower Egypt, but they nevertheless constitute an original group in that they were less complex than Merimda, having neither their polished black pottery nor their artistic production and architectural development. The el-Omari remains indicate a simple cultural level and a way of life particularly embedded in their micro-environment. Radiocarbon dates from the site reveal 200 years of occupation (c.4600–4400 BC), corresponding to the most recent strata at Merimda, assuming, of course, that the range of dated materials are representative of the *entire* occupation and that the remains of the final phase of the site had not been eroded away. The existence of an unsuspected microlithic-style industry at el-Omari still makes it possible that these Neolithic people were the direct descendants of the Epipalaeolithic hunters of Helwan.

El-Tarif

Back up the Nile in Upper Egypt – soon to be at the heart of cultural developments in the valley – it is now necessary to look at the very beginning of the Neolithic period in the Theban region. The research undertaken at the end of the 1960s by a joint expedition of the Jagellone University of Cracow and the German Institute of Archaeology at Cairo, under the direction of the Polish Centre for Mediterranean Archaeology, discovered an occupation layer most probably dating to the fifth millennium BC (Ginter *et al.* 1979).

On the desert edge, at the limit of the cultures, the site includes a group of Middle Kingdom *mastaba*-tombs, which were the initial focus of the German excavators. A 50-centimetre thick layer of Predynastic settlement remains was discovered when the 5-metre gap between two mastabas was excavated. This layer was situated on top of the pediments created by the destruction of the Theban limestones and Esna schists, deposited later than the silts of the Sahaba-Darau aggradation. Middle and Upper Palaeolithic artefacts, no longer in their original contexts, were mixed with the gravel of the base pediment, and typical late Palaeolithic tools (i.e. backed bladelets and Levallois elements) are spread over the surface of this formation. A layer of clay sediment, between 2 and 20 centimetres thick and probably of Aeolian origin, has been deposited on top of this gravelly material, and it is this context that has produced the heavily weathered artefacts making up the basis of a new industry: the Tarifian. Above the Tarifian material is another clay layer containing no archaeological material, and finally a Naqada-period occupation layer, darkly coloured by the ash and organic remains, is superimposed over this earlier material.

The Tarifian comprises 5400 flint items, including 110 cores and 561 tools; it is an industry in which flake tools both account for 90 per cent of the knapping and serve as materials from which most of the tools were made. The local grey flint that derives originally from the Theban limestones represents 80 per cent of the raw material used at the site. The knapping technique is simple, often without any preparation of the core, and the flakes are essentially cortical. There is no trace of the Levallois technique, and the main category of tool is the retouched flake (30 per cent of the total), with blades making up only a small proportion. Sidescrapers are the second most characteristic Tarifian lithic artefact, accounting for 20 per cent of the toolkit. The rest of the industry is made up of notches and denticulates, made from large, robust flakes; endscrapers made from the ends of flakes and blades; perforators made from short square flakes; a few burins and truncations made from blades; and finally the microlithic elements of the industry comprised only three atypical trapezes, a point with burin removal, and a Krukowski microburin. Twelve retouched bifacial tools can probably be interpreted as axes, while three worked pebbles are probably to be assigned to the same functional category.

This Tarifian assemblage was part of the general trend towards flake industries at the beginning of the sixth millennium BC, whereby flake tools gradually replaced microliths in all of the Western Desert sites. The microlithic component, although negligible, is not completely absent, and the Neolithic announces its presence with the bifacial items. Ginter *et al.* (1982) suggest that it may have been a northern variant of the post-Shamarkian industry in northern Sudan (see pp. 144–5). In both Tarifian and post-Shamarkian assemblages, the pottery occurs in small fragments – therefore reconstruction of the shapes of the original vessels tends to be difficult. A hemispherical bowl, a spherical vessel with a thick rim, another bowl with a conical neck, a conical bowl and a fragment of a plate – these give some idea of the limited range of shapes. The fabric is essentially tempered with plant material, but sometimes also with minerals added. There are two basic types of technology involved: first, hand-made pottery that mineral analysis shows to be made from Pleistocene silts from the Sahaba-Darau formation, and secondly, vessels made on turntables, using clay extracted from the flood plain. The hand-made pots were fired at temperatures between 350 and 650°C, and the others between 600 and 900°C.

Since no radiocarbon dates have been obtained from the el-Tarif material, it has been dated on stratigraphic grounds. The Tarifian deposit is situated between the gravels probably relating to the Dishna recession (eighth millennium BC) and the Naqada-period stratum just above it (radiocarbon dated to 3150 ± 60 BC). On the other hand, the Aeolian sediments that contain the Tarifian industry were formed during the dry period from the sixth millennium to the early fifth millennium BC; the archaeologists have therefore suggested dating it to the very beginning of the fifth millennium.

Although geographically limited to only one site, which is not very informative concerning the inhabitants' way of life, the Tarifian nevertheless appears to be an important stage in the process of Neolithicization.

The Khartoum Neolithic

The village of Shaheinab, 50 kilometres to the north of Khartoum, on the west bank of the river, is the type site of the Khartoum Neolithic. Discovered and excavated by A. J. Arkell (1953a) in the 1950s, it consists of a gentle hill, about 200 metres long and 60 metres wide, along an early Nile terrace situated about 850 metres away from the modern river bank. Darkly coloured by organic materials known locally as *umm ruweida* ('mother of ashes'), the surface of this small tell-site is covered by an accumulation of potsherds, lithic items and fossilized bones. Tombs dug in later times, from the late Neolithic to the Islamic period, have disturbed many parts of the site.

Shaheinab

Located on a thick bed of clay alluvia covering a terrace of quartz pebbles, Shaheinab is characterized by radical renewal in terms of its toolkit and the presence of domesticated animals. One unique aspect of sites of this date in this region is the fact that there are a series of hearths in basins lined with sandstone blocks, filled with ashes and the remains of bones, the largest measuring 1.5 metres in diameter.

The local quartz continued to be used for the manufacture of microliths, among which crescents were still well represented. However, the geometric triangles and the scalene points that were found in the Mesolithic had disappeared. At the same time, they began to produce new types of tools made from rhyolite, described by Arkell as 'gouges'. He argued that they were the key artefacts of this culture, which he initially designated the 'gouge culture', later opting for Khartoum Neolithic instead. The gouge is a kind of small axe with a concave cutting edge, one face being totally or partially polished, and the other chipped into shape. The opposite end to the cutting edge was usually carefully trimmed for insertion into a wooden handle. It must have been used rather like an adze, and it is notable that Jacques Tixier (1962: 340) uses the term adze to describe similar tools in the Tenerian Neolithic industry (6500–4500 BP) at Adrar Bous. The gouge – a very specific kind of tool – is distinguished both by the presence of axe blades and by a rougher style of manufacture; gouges are generally chipped into shape and less standardized than usual. When provided with handles, they can be used as axes or adzes.

Conical and disc-shaped maceheads in gneiss or granite (made out of ochre grinding stones) had diameters of 56–76 millimetres and a thickness of about 50 millimetres, the central concave area being pierced. One example, 46 millimetres thick, has been reconstructed, and thirteen fragments of a similar type have been found. The site has also yielded a number of sandstone discs and rings of uncertain purpose. Pebbles of quartz, rhyolite and fossilized wood were used to make a range of percussors, grinders and smoothers.

The pottery was now characterized by polishing on all surfaces. Dotted line motifs formed a link with the preceding period, but pottery decoration generally became more diverse, combining triangles, zigzags and fish scales. The whole surface of some pots was covered with incised horizontal or irregular lines achieved by means of a comb with widely spaced teeth. The decoration only occasionally extends to the rim of the vessel, where it may take the form of small fuzzy black inverted triangles, which were first incised initially on the red polish and then executed directly into the surface of the pot. The black colour of the triangles seems to have been created by the burning of animal fats, and ultimately the tendency to blacken the whole of the rim of the pot with a band of varying width became established. This 'black-topped' effect was later to become a successful aspect of Predynastic ceramics, although by then the effect seems to have been achieved by a different means: inverting the pot and burying the rim in ashy material, thus creating an oxidizing atmosphere around it during firing, the effect being to blacken the entire inside of the pot as well as the rim. At Shaheinab, only 60 sherds indicate that this latter technique was used, while the rest (amounting to several hundred) are characterized by the earlier method of blackening the rim alone, through the burning of fats.

Arkell (1960) put forward a convincing hypothesis concerning the origins of the practice of blackening pots' rims. A Sudanese friend drew his attention to the fact that gourds were still being used as vessels (calabashes) by cutting them into two hemispherical halves, and the rim of each half was burnt in order to prevent their rims from crumbling. It was possible therefore that ancient calabashes had provided the model for the first black-topped pots.

Beads and pendants made from shells, ostrich eggshell, cornelian, amazonite or simple pebbles have been found in their thousands at Khartoum Neolithic sites, along with perforated canine teeth and fragments of bracelets and rings made from shells and ivory. The main group of quartz perforators among the lithics must doubtless be linked with the manufacture of these items of jewellery.

The working of bone, attested by numerous remains of needles and borers, reached a new level with the production of axes made partly from the bones of large mammals. There were also two types of harpoons, one with perforated base and the other with a flat base for insertion into a haft.

The rich array of fauna was first examined by Dorothy M. A. Bate (see Arkell 1953a), who claimed to have identified the dwarf goat among the repertoire, but this suggestion was rejected by J. Peters (1986) when he re-examined the material. The analysis of the faunal remains shows that the animals exploited during the Neolithic differed little from those of the Mesolithic, apart from the appearance of hares and, on the other hand, the near-disappearance of the cane rat (a small amphibious rodent similar in appearance to a large guinea pig) and the Buffon's kob (*Kobus kob*), an antelope of the savannas and irrigated plains. Gautier (1989: 366) suggests that this faunal change may be explained by dessication within the Nile valley, combined with the effects of excessive hunting: the Buffon's kob, which tends to be very attached to its own territory, would have been particularly vulnerable in both respects. As for the hare, it is possible that a decline of the kinds of animals that were usually hunted might have led the Neolithic peoples to add this rodent to their menu. Among the shells, the *Pila wernei* remained the most popular species.

However, it was particularly in terms of domesticated species of animal that the people of Shaheinab advanced further into the Neolithic. Cattle (*Bos primigenius*), sheep and/or goats (*Ovis ammon* and *Capra aegagrus*) often make up a fairly high proportion of the bones, indeed to such an extent that pastoralism seems to have been an important element of the economic basis of the Khartoum Neolithic peoples.

Benefiting from the then newly invented radiocarbon-dating technique, Arkell was able to place the Neolithic occupation at Shaheinab in the second half of the fourth millennium BC (the actual dates being 5446 ± 380 and 5060 ± 440 BP). Another pair of dates obtained in 1979 by Randi Haaland (5360 ± 80 BP and 5260 ± 80 BP) give a calibrated average date of 4165 ± 105 BC (see Hassan 1985).

El-Qoz

A short distance to the south of Khartoum, Arkell made test excavations at another locality: el-Qoz. This small site, unfortunately very disturbed, yielded material identical to that at Shaheinab, but this time it lay immediately above a layer of Mesolithic remains, thus providing crucial stratigraphic proof that the Khartoum Neolithic assemblage was the later of the two. However, although the chronological order of the two cultures is well attested, the question of whether the Neolithic carried on continuously from the Mesolithic is less clear. As we have noted above, recent studies of the Mesolithic place it in the seventh millennium BC, suggesting that there may be a gap of as much as 2500 years between it and the Neolithic.

In order to attempt to answer this question concerning Mesolithic–Neolithic continuity, and more generally to shed light on the Sudanese Neolithic, as defined at Shaheinab, quite a number of investigations have taken place during the 1980s and 1990s. A number of sites, from south to north, Umm Direiwa (Haaland 1981), Kadero (Krzyzaniak 1984, 1986), Zakiab (Haaland 1981), Geili (Caneva 1988) and el-Ghaba (Lecointe 1987; Reinold 1987) have considerably enriched our knowledge of this period. In addition, the researches undertaken at Shaqadud, in the Butana, have yielded some possible answers to the question of the Mesolithic–Neolithic transition in the Khartoum region.

Umm Direiwa

About 15 kilometres to the north of Khartoum, on the right bank of the Nile, the site of Umm Direiwa has been the object of several sondages (Haaland 1981). It takes the form of two fairly eroded hillocks (Umm Direiwa I and 2), a few kilometres apart. The excavated areas have yielded material similar to that of Shaheinab, associated with fauna including a high proprtion of domesticated species: *Bos primigenius*, *Capra aegragus* and *Ovis ammon*. Several calibrated radiocarbon dates have been obtained: 4890 ± 110, 4475 ± 210 and 3765 + 120 BC for Direiwa 1, and 3825 ± 320 BC for Direiwa 2 (see Hassan 1986a).

Kadero

Situated 18 kilometres to the north of Khartoum, Kadero comprises an eroded alluvial clayey mound on the east bank, a little less than 2 metres above the wide flat plain of the valley. Excavations undertaken by an expedition from the Polish Centre of Mediterranean Archaeology directed by Lech Krzyzaniak identified two settlement areas to the north and south of the mound, with graves along the edges of the occupied zones, to one side of the central part of the mound.

Quartz and rhyolite were the fundamental raw materials employed in the lithic industry, which was essentially based on flakes. While rhyolite is almost absent from the knapping debris, it accounts for 56.45 per cent of the tools. Quartz cores with discoidal flakes are widespread across the site. The assemblage is characterized by almost equal proportions of notches and denticulates, perforators, gouges, partially retouched flakes and blades. Backed bladelets, truncations and burins are hardly present at all, and the same applies to lunates, endscrapers, sidescrapers and axes. The lithics as a whole are similar to those at Shaheinab, apart from lunates (more abundant at Shaheinab), and notches and denticulates (better represented at Kadero).

As far as the thousands of excavated sherds are concerned, it is possible to recognize Nile silt pottery with mineral (sand) temper, the interior and exterior surfaces of the pots being red, usually polished, and more rarely marked with a comb to create a slightly undulating effect. The shapes are simple: hemispherical and ovoid bowls, usually with rounded bases, rims continuous with the vessel walls, and rarely modelled with any relief decoration. Eighty per cent of the sherds are covered with decoration comprising continuous or dotted parallel lines, impressed zigzags, cross-shaped compositions, as well as crescents and triangles. In 25 per cent of the cases, the rims are decorated at the top; as at Shaheinab the red polished pots bear incised triangles or a simple band along the rims, thus constituting 'black-topped' types.

Like the lithics, the Kadero ceramics are similar to those at Shaheinab; although there are no dotted wavy lines, there are more variations in the combination of triangular motifs and dotted lines, as well as hatched lines, giving the impression of a partial contemporaneity between the two sites, with Shaheinab being slightly earlier in date.

The fauna, analysed by Gautier (1984), indicates a pastoral economy dominated by cattle and sheep. The abundance of gastropods and freshwater bivalves suggests important nutritional supplements. Wild species derive almost entirely from the riverine environment, thus indicating a fairly limited catchment area. It is uncertain whether agriculture is being practised, but two species of *Gramineae* (sorghum and millet) were identified by Klichowska (see Krzyzaniak and Kobusiewski 1984: 321–6) from grain impressions in the fabric of pottery vessels. These cereals must have been ground in the many mortars found at the site. However, A. Stemler (1990) has raised doubts concerning this identification, emphasizing the problems involved in differentiating wild and cultivated grain.

Finally, the human population at Kadero has survived in the form of about 40 burials contemporary with the settlement, divided into two groups, one at the far north end of the tell, and the other at the edge of the settlements. The intense phenomenon of erosion at the site has caused many of the skeletons to be visible on the surface, leading to great deterioration of the bones. In the northern cemetery, about 15 burials contained individual bodies of adults of both sexes and children. The grave goods were particularly rich in this part of the site, combining disc-shaped maceheads, thin-walled pottery, necklaces, pendants made from cornelian, Red Sea shells and zeolite (the latter being a stone from the Ethiopian plateau, perhaps rolled into pebbles in the river Atbara). At the edge of the settlements, on the other hand, 11 individual burials (men, women and children) contained hardly any grave goods.

Six radiocarbon dates have been obtained from Nile bivalves, clearly brought into the settlement for consumption (Krzyzaniak 1982). With regard to the southern sector, they provided the following dates: 5280 ± 90 BP, 5030 ± 70 BP, which result in a calibrated average of 4015 ± 35 BC (Hassan 1985); in the northern sector, the dates are 5610 ± 55, 5500 ± 70 and 5380 ± 65, which produce a calibrated average of 4330 ± 95 BC (Hassan 1985). This places the Kadero Neolithic at the very end of the fifth millennium BC, with a gap of 300 radiocarbon years between the two areas of settlement.

Although no immediate difference between the two settlements was initially perceived by archaeologists, a deeper study of ceramics and lithics in each of the two areas tends to corroborate this chronological gap. The northern settlement contains more sherds with red slip, more closed forms of vessel, less black-topped types, less triangles and zigzags, less gouges and flake-based lithic technology which was perhaps more highly developed. In this light, Krzyzaniak (1986) suggests that the northern sector is similar to Shaheinab, while the south owes more to the later phase of the Neolithic represented by the material at el-Kadada (see below).

Zakiab

Further to the north, about 20 kilometres from Khartoum, on the east bank is Zakiab. Discovered by Arkell and excavated by Haaland in 1978, it consists of a mound of gravel covering an area of about 2000 m², only 3–4 kilometres from the Nile and about 1.3 metres above the level of the floodplain (see Haaland 1981). The material at Zakiab, which is similar to that at Kadero in terms of the toolkit, includes numerous remains of domesticated species (*Bos primigenius, Ovis ammon* and *Capra hircus*), as well as fish and molluscs, and it has been interpreted by Haaland (1987) as an encampment of fisher-pastoralists exploited during the dry season.

Geili

Still further to the north, 46 kilometres from Khartoum, the site of Geili, which has been under investigation since 1972 by an Italian team from the Institute of Palaeoethnology at Rome, consists of an archaeological deposit measuring more than a metre in thickness. Situated on the east bank of the Nile, opposite Shaheinab, it constitutes a cruciform area of high ground about 4 metres above the level of the flood plain. The complex stratigraphy indicates that there was a Neolithic occupation at the site, and that when this was abandoned it was used as a burial site from the late Neolithic to the Meroitic period. The graves are distributed at a rate of three to five pits for every 10 m².

The study of the palaeoenvironment of the region has allowed the formation of the mound to be placed in the context of the history of the river. A compact brown clayey fluvial deposit with a thickness of about 1.8 metres, created by the Nile during humid climatic conditions, between 9000 and 6000 BP, created the basis of this mound; layers of molluscs located on top of the lowest stratum have actually provided a radiocarbon date of 8440 ± 120 BP.

A layer of clayey sand, pale grey in colour, varying in thickness from 70 down to 20 centimetres, contains a confused mass of archaeological material deriving from the Neolithic settlement. A date obtained from a *Pila wernei* shell is 5570 ± 100 BP, but the sedimentological analysis of the site showed that this stratum corresponded to the gradual retreat of the river's waters because of the effects of increasing aridity, the Nile moving westward away from its early course. Over the course of 3000 years, during which the river added to the height of the levee, and while the Mesolithic was flourishing some 7 kilometres to the south at Saggai, the site of Geili was occupied only by shellfish! It was not until the end of the fifth millennium BC that pastoralists brought their herds of animals to graze a short distance away from the bank, in the heart of pasture-land.

The faunal remains, although very much modified by later processes of erosion, revealed a rich range of domesticated livestock (cattle, sheep and goats), while wild species still account for an important part of their economy. The collection of *Pila wernei* molluscs must have dominated the dry seasons, along with the catching of large numbers of catfish. The turtles, reptiles, green monkeys, carnivores, gazelle, antelopes, buffaloes, hippopotami and giraffes suggest a system of complex constraints, based on the exploitation of both wild and domesticated species. As Gautier (1988: 62) remarks, the search for pasture-land for herds, which was doubtless an increasingly important priority in a Sudano-Sahelian environment, must have necessitated population movement combined with the exploitation of natural resources.

Considering the thousands of excavated sherds, it is impossible to differentiate those that derive from the beginning of the later occupation. The fabric of the pottery is homogeneous, fine-grained, tempered with quartz, well-fired and always polished, certainly very different from the Mesolithic ceramics, which were characterized by a coarse temper probably consisting mainly of feldspar (Hays and Hassan 1974); the surface colour varies from buff/orange to red and from greyish brown to black, depending on the degree of firing. The thinness of the sherds suggests that they derive from small, light pots, while the Mesolithic receptacles were generally much larger. The shapes of the Geili vessels were simple, including both open and closed forms, but without necks, feet or handles. It appears that certain types of decoration were applied to specific shapes of vessel; thus, for instance, the red polishing technique was used on cups with tapering rims, while the simple impressed motifs and black polishes appear primarily on globular vessels.

The application of impressed decoration with some kind of rocker remains the essential decorative technique, but the range of motifs becomes more diverse, no longer being limited to the wavy line but including alternating curves, zigzags, triangles, commas and chevrons either executed across the whole surface or in decorative plaques. Decoration applied by combs made its appearance at Geili, eventually becoming a characteristic feature of the next ceramic phase. The Geili pottery therefore seems to be midway between the Shaheinab culture and the late Neolithic exemplified by el-Kadada.

The lithic industry uses locally available materials, either *in situ* or nearby, such as quartz, chert or agate pebbles, Nubian sandstone, rhyolite, basalt and fossilized wood. Here, as in the majority of the Khartoum Neolithic sites, quartz accounts for most of the debitage (92 per cent at Geili, 81–6 per cent at Kadero, 92 per cent at Zakiab, and 77 per cent at Umm Direiwa), but most of the actual tools were made from rhyolite. The need to obtain especially large flakes of rhyolite for the manufacture of large sidescrapers, gouges and axes led the tool-makers to transfer their activities nearer to the sources of raw material, so that they were only bringing back to their settlement the finished or semi-worked tools; the quartz, on the other hand, within easy reach, continued to be knapped for the obtention of microliths, comprising small proportions of the toolkit, and flakes which had not been retouched but were nevertheless clearly used as tools.

From the statistical analysis of frequencies of different lithics, it is possible to distinguish two well-attested groups: first retouched pieces made from large rhyolite flakes, and secondly notches, which account for a quarter of the quartz-made tools. Denticulates and perforators, followed by endscrapers, reflect the development of an industry that included only a minimal percentage of lunates and other microliths. Large rhyolite flakes with retouched backs are comparatively rare, as are axes and gouges, and the percentage of the latter is particularly low (1.3 per cent) compared with Kadero (15 per cent) and Shaheinab.

The bone artefacts at Geili have been subjected to poor conditions of preservation, and their numbers are hardly any higher than in the Mesolithic period. There are two surviving harpoons, one with two barbs and another with one barb and a notch to which the line could be attached. A few fragments of needles, awls and beads (along with ostrich eggshell beads) complete this meagre range of tools. Only a small fragment of an *Aspatharia* shell suggests the preliminary stages of the manufacture of a fish hook.

The grinding equipment, made from sandstone, consists of discs, 9–12 centimetres in diameter, and grinding stones of various types, ranging from fairly cube-shaped blocks to more cylindrical shapes, but there were no pierced discs of the sort found at Shaheinab.

El-Ghaba

The site of el-Ghaba (Reinold 1987; Lecointe 1987), some 150 kilometres to the north, in the province of Taragma, and less than a kilometre from el-Kadada, includes 250 Khartoum Neolithic burials excavated into a layer of settlement with a thickness of about 20 centimetres. The individuals are buried separately, on their sides, in flexed or contracted positions (sometimes on their backs) and without any consistent orientation. The poor preservation of the bones (as is often the case in central Sudan) has prevented the study of anthropological data. Almost 230 pottery vessels (40 per cent showing traces of decoration) correspond to the ceramics at Shaheinab and Kadero. A few types, however, such as chalice shapes or juxtaposed quadrangular decorative motifs, are similar to those of the late Neolithic at el-Kadada. The items of jewellery comprise lip ornaments made of white rock, ivory bracelets, agate beads, and pendants made from small flat pebbles. Fragments of malachite are sometimes placed in the tombs, and the possibility that they are linked with a funerary rite is suggested by the greenish coloration of the skeletons, around the teeth, and certainly the facial area. It was also in relation to the funerary world that bucrania were placed at the bottoms of the pits.

The particular way in which these bucrania were cut, leaving the horns and the upper part of the frontal bone, is similar to the method employed at el-Kadada. Deposits of freshwater molluscs (essentially *Aspatharia*) are fairly frequent, and their occurence in clusters suggest that they were being kept in small bags, probably of leather. The lithic material rarely occurs in the graves, apart from such instances as a perforated disc of polished rock, and a gouge, an extremely rare item at el-Ghaba (see figure 2).

Two groups have been distinguished, differing both spatially and in terms of the funerary rituals that they imply. A rectangular empty space of 10 × 3 metres (perhaps the negative indication of a building) separates the graves into two clusters, corresponding in a general sense to those that contained bucrania (in the north) and those provided with flat-bottomed ceramics and chalice-like vessels (in the south).

Four radiocarbon dates have been obtained from *Aspatharia* shells that indicate that the history of the site was contained within the outer dates of the Khartoum Neolithic: 4990 ± 110 BP (grave 6), 5660 ± 120 BP (grave 7), 5660 ± 120 BP (grave 27) and 5020 ± 100 BP (Geus 1986: 24, 34). However, it represents an important variant of this culture, like that defined at Shaheinab, where it seemed to Arkell that the people were not burying their dead.

With the presence of certain types of ceramics and bucrania – and, more generally, because it consists of funerary material – the el-Ghaba culture foreshadows that of nearby el-Kadada, thus integrating it into the process of development of the Neolithic period in central Sudan.

Shaqadud

Back in the Butana region, the site of Shaqadud, discovered by K. H. Otto (1963) and revisited by A. S. A. Mohammed Ali (1987), 50 kilometres to the east of the Nile, consists of a complex of several different sites rather than one single locality. Of particular significance is the 3.5-metre deposit that has accumulated in the interior and entrance-way of a cave next to a canyon. The lower strata of this deposit correspond to the Khartoum Mesolithic, with a microlithic industry made from quartz and dominated by lunates, and a hard, well-fired type of pottery, tempered with quartz, unpolished and comb-decorated with wavy lines, straight lines, and rocker impressions forming zigzags. In the middle strata, this pottery tends to become more friable, and the dotted line gradually becomes more prominent in the decoration. Finally, the material in the upper strata is typically Neolithic, with the usual polished, chracteristically decorated pottery, and the usual lithics, apart from axes and gouges (Mohammed Ali 1987). All

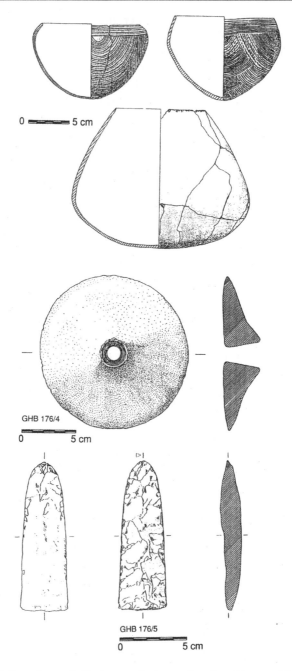

Figure 2 Pottery from el-Ghaba, conical macehead and 'gouge' from tomb GHB176 (after Lecointe 1987: 80, 81).

of these upper strata derive from a new settlement corresponding to the late Neolithic, like the culture defined by François Geus at el-Kadada.

The recent study made by Isabela Caneva and Anthony Marks (1990) on the techniques for decorating pottery at Shaqadud tends to corroborate the assumptions made by Mohammed Ali. The new study emphasizes a long process of Mesolithic development in the course of which the authors discern two phases: the earlier of the two comprises similar material to that found in the valley, at Khartoum, Saggai, Sorurab and Shabona, while the later phase, characterized by a high incidence of double dotted lines, is not so well represented in the valley, having instead a somewhat 'indigenous' air. The upper levels, dating to the Neolithic period, are characterized by a Saharan character, marked for example by sherds with light impressions consisting of small, spaced out points, well polished after the application of decoration.

One radiocarbon date from the Neolithic strata is 4460 ± 195 BC, while another from a higher layer (2095± 155 BC) suggests that the latest phase of the Khartoum Neolithic may have even extended into the second millennium BC (see Hassan 1986a: 89). But here, as elsewhere, it is important to be aware of the potentially misleading nature of isolated radiocarbon dates, which cannot ever be regarded as absolute chronological references. The long stratigraphic sequence at Shaqadud needs to be clarified in many respects, and its various developments need to be placed within a dense network of dates which might then perhaps shed some light on the chronological gap between the Khartoum Mesolithic and Neolithic.

The adoption of a production economy in the Nile valley appeared in a context of adaptation to the exploitation of seasonal resources in a riverine environment. From this perspective, the leap forward seems to be more of a *choice* than a *necessity*. For many years, there has been a strong tendency to take Gordon Childe's view that climatic dessication pressurizes humans to invent new strategies for survival. Certainly climatic variations have very often dramatically influenced human groups, pushing them towards new lands, forcing them to react to new environments. However, at the time that the first potters of Khartoum were established along the Nile, ecological conditions were fairly optimal, the Sahara was scattered with lakes supporting semi-sedentary populations who knew how to make pottery and living in such a state of symbiosis with their herds that it is difficult to describe this scenario with any certainty as domestication (perhaps 'proto-domestication' would be more appropriate).

There seems to be no doubt that contacts were established between the inhabitants of the Nile valley and their close neighbours in the desert; it is easy to imagine communications between the desert and the valley, a coming and going which is sufficiently well expressed by the regional

differences in the various stretches of the Nile valley. However, the river
dweller adapted to the annual sequence of natural resources would have
felt no 'need' at all to develop new strategies of food procurement, which
would in effect be new restrictions.

Doubtless it is this situation that explains the lateness of Neolithicization
in the valley. The adoption of animal rearing and agriculture, during the
sixth millennium BC appears more as an option than as a deliberate response to a drastic environmental change. These sixth-millennium sites,
however, have either been destroyed or are buried under Nile silts (see
Holmes 1993). Certainly it was initially as a result of the wave of aridity
that began in c.8000 BP that the desert occupants began to settle in the
valley, bringing with them their precious livestock, and gaining from the
indigenous inhabitants the ability to derive benefit from magical natural
processes.

According to Hassan, the climatic instability of the period from 7800
to 6500 BP was the main reason for this east–west demographic movement (and also west–east, if we take into account the Eastern Desert),
whereby, following routes that must already have been familiar to them,
the groups based in the Siwa and Bahariya oases moved eastwards into
the Faiyum and Delta, the people of Farafra, Kharga and Dakhla moved
into Middle and Upper Egypt, and the inhabitants of Nabta Playa returned to Nubia, bringing to these Mesolithic peoples the Neolithic touch
that was primarily represented by domesticated species.

For despite the chronological gap that exists between the two cultures
discovered by Arkell, the Khartoum Neolithic does appear to evolve out
of the Mesolithic, given that the Shaqadud material seems to follow on
naturally from that at el-Qoz, and given also the detection of numerous
links between the characteristic artefacts of the two cultures, particularly
in terms of pottery and lithics. Thus the occupants of such Mesolithic
sites as Early Khartoum, Sorurab, Shabona and Saggai (see pp. 91–8)
appear to be the ancestors of the people of Shaheinab, Kadero and Geili.

We must not forget, however, that our perceptions of these fundamental changes have all the sketchiness and fragility of reconstructions that
are based only on meagre remains – those incomplete surviving materials
that are incapable of revealing the full original cultural complexity. As
Hassan (1987: 29) has pointed out, repeating the fine parable from Le
Petit Prince, we have to accept that 'the essential is invisible' (i.e. the
truly fundamental aspects of prehistory are probably not the ones that
have survived in the form of material remains).

The mechanism of climatic transformations (the consequences of which
are impossible to predict) stands in stark contrast with the fluidity of
human behaviour, in such a way that it is impossible to reduce to one
single cause, even a primary influence, the full scale of a phenomenon

such as this. We should therefore be investigating the process of Neolithicization in terms of social relations.

The Nilotic adaptation implies the existence of a network of changing degrees of cooperation, which in certain seasons would have been tight links, but at other times much looser relations. It was during the time of the annual flood, from July to November, that deep-water fishing was undertaken, mobilizing human resources and calling for a collective effort in the manufacture of such things as boats, nets and traps. We have already noted that from 8000 BP onwards, at Elkab, in the Faiyum and in the Khartoum region, fishing techniques became more complex, with those species that were caught individually (e.g. *Clarias*) being in competition with deep-water fishes (e.g. *Lates*); harpoons and fish hooks became more and more common.

The retreat of the annual flood waters provided the ideal opportunity for the capture of catfish and marsh-fowl, as well as the gathering of certain plants (the latter taking place during the winter months, followed by the collection of molluscs). Women in particular must have been involved in this kind of work, while the men concentrated on the hunting of big game (see figure 3). The numerous perforators that began to appear in the toolkit, as well as large sidescrapers, endscrapers and denticulates, then axes and gouges, all suggest the working of such materials as wood, animal-skins and bone: cutting, splitting, chipping, scraping and piercing, making up a whole range of craft activities all geared towards a common end. The notion of *collectivity* had appeared with the first traces of storage. It developed further with the invention of pottery, which was already present in an essentially Epipalaeolithic context, implying, as Testart (1982) has shown, a profound ideological change.

The simple act of deferring the consumption of a product, which was practised for millennia in the Nile valley, may be – as this author suggests – the starting point and the principal source of economic and social inequalities, for the product, once transformed, might not only be the object of exchange, covetousness and monopolization but also *surplus*, thus enabling a whole class of non-producers to be supported, a class that could well have undertaken all of the crafts implied in the Nilotic cycle. On the other hand, complete 'specialists', totally sustained by the community as a whole, had not yet emerged at this date. Nothing among the archaeological remains allows us to envisage such specialization but Testart (1982: 53) points out that 'the specialist's total production may far exceed the needs of the local group with which he can regularly exchange'. Thus the transition to a production economy took place on a mental level, in a society that was already highly structured and where dominant groups must have exercised 'powers', already controlling most of the goods obtained through storage and exchange.

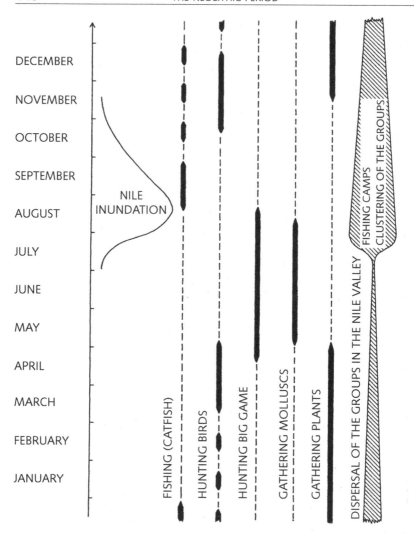

Figure 3 Diagram outlining the processes of Nilotic adaptation (after Gautier 1990: 237).

This was a society 'rich' in traditions, the symbolic aspect of which – already emerging in rock carvings – is well expressed in the favoured relationships between humans and animals.

The introduction of new modes of production only had the effect of encouraging closer collaboration and increasing social inequalities by creating chiefdoms and by legitimizing new roles that were intended to maintain, control and stablize a fresh cultural complexity that would inevitably be expressed in symbolic forms. We have already noted the definite introduction of agriculture at the same time as domesticated livestock in the Faiyum and at Merimda, but its introduction into the central Sudan seems more problematic (Stemler 1990). Indeed, there is no evidence at any other Neolithic site in Egypt or in the Western Desert, for the systematic juxtaposition of agriculture and domesticated animals. Could it be that it was a later introduction? Several possibilities suggest themselves:

- Faunal remains tend to be part of the aspect of the archaeological record that is generally visible through standard excavation, whereas the agricultural macro-remains, assuming they have not been destroyed, require more concentrated methods of investigation.
- The palaeobotanist defines cultivated grain in terms of morphological changes that take place *both after and because of* the selection of species.
- The human exploitation of plants had been going on for thousands of years without the morphology of grains being affected; our proof of this is the practice of collecting plants, by means of which humans familiarized themselves with many types of flora.
- The regular harvesting of wild ears of grain before they had reached complete maturity was in effect a kind of *proto-agriculture*, the evidence for which cannot, however, easily be recovered.
- It is also possible that some of the grains harvested in this 'proto-agricultural' way might have been sown back in the soil, without the harvesting necessarily creating any morphological changes in the grain.

As Gautier (1990: 203) has pointed out, there is no need for any extensive knowledge of biology for plants to be domesticated; he suggests that it may thus have been achieved more easily and more rapidly than the domestication of vertebrates.

We should therefore keep a close eye on these aspects of archaeological data. Human control over the plants and animals surrounding them has a very long history in the Nile valley, a 'long saga' during which regular juxtaposition in a well-defined restricted area would have led to processes of familiarization culminating almost inevitably in the selection of particular species.

A new disturbance to the ecological balance; the arrival of pastoral groups from Sahara (and doubtless also the Eastern Desert), who were forced to move by dessication; the social 'coming of age' of groups structured around shared desires for collective effort and propriety; and the incontrovertible move towards a set of common symbols – all of these factors were essential ingredients of the Nile valley 'Neolithic revolution'.

The earliest pottery in Nubia

Between 5000 and 4000 BC in Nubia, in the vicinity of Wadi Halfa, new technocomplexes were emerging from the microlithic industries of the Second-Cataract region. A radical development of the toolkit was marked by the gradual abandonment of microlithic tools, the increasing dominance of denticulates, sidescrapers and perforators, and the appearance of new polished and bifacial tools, as well as the first pottery in this region.

These changes in material culture indicate such factors as changes in subsistence patterns and new attitudes to the surrounding environment, linked with outside influences which may have had greater impact at a time when the climate was more favourable.

The Khartoum Variant

In the Wadi Halfa region, ten sites are directly linked with the Khartoum Mesolithic, as defined by Arkell. Eight of them were discovered by the Combined Prehistoric Expedition in the 1960s (Shiner 1968c); six were situated on the silty land of the flood plain, two immediately beside the river, and two in the outlying desert zone. Each consisted of shallow concentrations (about 20 centimetres deep) with diameters varying from 20 to 100 metres, and the presence of hearths is mainly indicated by occasional finds of burnt stones. At site 2016, however, the discovery of 2 m² of beaten earth covered by a large concentration of burnt stones suggests the existence of more coherent areas of the site that have now disappeared (especially as this Second-Cataract region is now submerged under Lake Nasser).

The enormous quantity of debris from stone working indicates an industry with a preference for Nile pebbles as well as fragments of quartz and imported Egyptian flint. The microlithic tools were still the main point of reference, and at some of the sites, backed tools and geometrics were made with particular care. However, the most common tool was the concave sidescraper, sometimes taking the form of one of the larger flakes, 30–50 millimetres in length, and virtually all made from Egyptian flint. Types of 'micro-borers' were fashioned in the form of blades with retouched edges and a pointed tip, similar to the drill-bits identified by Tixier (1963: 66, no. 16) in the Maghreb Epipalaeolithic. Notches and denticulates appeared in significant quantities alongside a few bifacial tools consisting of pedunculate arrowheads and oblong 'knife' blades, sometimes with bifacial retouch only along the edge. The term 'proto-gouges' has been given to pebbles with concave fronts (produced by uni-directional retouch), which gives them the appearance of rabots (plane-like tools). There are no indications of polishing on these artefacts. In one instance a flake has been struck from another flake, producing a heel-shaped 'side-blow flake'.

At site Dibeira West 5, blocks of chert and quartz were used as percussors. Grinding activities are indicated only by pestles and mortars. Ostrich eggshells were also being exploited, judging from the small fragments scattered across most of the sites, and the beads found at site 626.

All Khartoum Variant sites contain pottery, of which there are two types: one is similar to that of the Khartoum Neolithic (i.e. grey to reddish coloured, unpolished, bearing fabric impressions as decoration, and occasionally dotted wavy lines), while the other, accounting for only a tiny percentage of the sherds, is undecorated. Apart from a few exceptions, these are very small sherds, making it difficult to guess at the size and shape of the actual vessels; nevertheless, they seem to have been simple bowls which were of fairly large dimensions (with diameters of about 40 centimetres).

Both in terms of these ceramics and in terms of the groups of stone tools used, the Wadi Halfa sites recalled the Khartoum material, but in a minimal way, without the abundance and complexity of the Khartoum culture. On the other hand, we should be careful to note the presence of sites 626 and 628, 15 kilometres west of the valley. Situated at the edge of a small depression at the foot of a massif, providing a source of water between 5000 and 4000 BC, these two sites attest to the abundant use of a type of flint that might have come from the limestone plateaus of Sinn el-Kaddab, 170 kilometres to the north of Wadi Halfa (Nordström 1972: pl. 2) or even, as Randi Haaland suggests (see Nordström 1972: 114), via even more distant contacts, such as the Kharga Oasis or the Faiyum region.

It is difficult to reconstruct the economic aspects of the Khartoum Variant groups, given the rarity of faunal remains. No animal domestication is evidenced, and the remains are primarily those of fish and freshwater molluscs, particularly *Aetheria elliptica*, indicating that these people were still very much directly dependent on riverine resources. The frequent occurence of grinding stones and ostrich eggs at these sites serves to indicate both the exploitation of local wild plants and the hunting of the ostrich. Given that all this is happening at such a great distance from the valley, Shiner (1968c: 785) suggests that the relatively high density of population along the Nile valley may have forced some humans to rediscover hunting zones in less populous regions that were nevertheless both well-watered and in contact with now-precious sources of flint.

Should we then perhaps look to the west for the potential origins of this culture, which, unlike the Abkan and post-Shamarkian (see below), does not seem to have emerged out of any local cultural tradition? Arkell envisaged the distant Tibesti region as the homeland of the pottery-using Khartoum groups, encouraged by the presence of beads of amazonite among the latter, although, as we have noted above, Lucas (1962: 393–4) has subsequently indicated that there were naturally occurring sources of this stone in the immediate vicinity of the Nile valley. It is worth noting, in this context, that recent German fieldwork in the region of the Laqiya Arbain Oasis, 500 kilometres west of Wadi Halfa, has brought to light Khartoum-type sherds in a lacustrine environment dating to the fifth millennium BC (Schuck 1989).

Hassan (1986a) has published radiocarbon dates for the Khartoum Variant, obtained from an ostrich eggshell (5410 ± 140 BC) and charcoal (5070 ± 115 BC and 5005 ± 90 BC).

The post-Shamarkian

Both the stratigraphic evidence and the study of the toolkit suggest that the post-Shamarkian industry, found at two sites on the west bank of the Nile in the Second-Cataract region, DW4 and DW50, constitute a later development of the Shamarkian. The two sites each consist of large concentrations, measuring some 250 × 50 metres in area but very shallow in depth, made up mainly of chert and quartz debitage but also including an element of Egyptian flint (36.8 per cent of the toolkit at DW50).

The industry comprises flake tools, primarily notches, denticulates and perforators, the latter consisting of points made from flakes (sometimes worn down) and drill bits. Backed blades decreased in number along with microliths, although the quantities of geometrics remained similar. The trapezes took the form of arrowheads with transverse cutting edges, while two fine bifacial points with pedunculates were found at each of the sites. The presence of several rabots made from chert pebbles, a few small chipped stone axes, and transverse sidescrapers made from 'side-blow flakes' gives these assemblages a Neolithic air, which is further emphasized by the survival of a few potsherds.

Despite these differences from Shamarkian sites, DW4 and DW50 seem to develop out of the underlying Shamarkian material. Shiner suggests that it is as if the Shamarkian people, based in this area since the seventh millennium BC, had changed their way of life as a result of pressure from new influences. As in the Faiyum Neolithic (see above), the presence of a possible amazonite bead, suggests that there may have been contacts with the Tibesti region (although, as before, see Lucas 1962: 393–4 for Egyptian sources of this gemstone). The inhabitants of

DW4 and DW50 were grinding grain (judging from the surviving fragments of grinding stones) and manufacturing ostrich eggshell beads, but no faunal remains have survived to suggest any other aspects of the subsistence patterns of these relatively large communities. The sites have yielded two radiocarbon dates: 5600 ± 120 BP (4475 ± 270 BC) and 5220 ± 50 BP (Hassan 1986a).

The Abkan

Numerous Abkan sites, representing the final outcome of the long Qadan development, were spread out along both banks of the Nile in the Wadi Halfa region. The name of this cultural ensemble derives from Oliver Myers' discovery of Mesolithic-style sets of material in the district of Abka in 1947–8. The main site in the Abka area (no. IX) comprised several occupation levels, with Khartoum Variant material at the bottom of the stratigraphic sequence; the various strata overlying the Khartoum Variant made up the Abkan sequence. Seven Abkan sites were located and investigated first by the Combined Prehistoric Expedition (Shiner 1968a: 611–29) and later by the Scandinavian Joint Expedition (Nordström 1972: 12–17).

The Abkan industry, dominated by perforators made from flakes retouched on the upper face (i.e. groovers), was still essentially microlithic (71 per cent). It consisted primarily of flakes struck from Nile pebbles, quartz, agate and Egyptian flint. A process of evolution can be traced, with reference to the characteristic traits of the Qadan culture that preceded it. An early form of the Abkan culture, which emerged from the final phase of the Qadan, has been detected at two sites, both of which contain no pottery and have a lithic typology more similar to that of the Qadan industry.

A 'developed' phase of the Abkan followed this early phase. During the developed Abkan – which has been found at five sites – the sizes of tools gradually increased, with the perforator becoming the most important type. Denticulates, notches and sidescrapers increased in proportions, while blades gradually disappeared; at the same time, the repertoire began to include a few hard-stone axes and numerous potsherds.

Finally, the 'terminal' Abkan, the lithics of which were similar to those of the 'developed' phase, was characterized by an increasingly complex pottery typology: the polishing and the rippling effect were adopted when contacts were established with a new culture in Lower Nubia: the A Group (or, alternatively, these traits might have been adopted by the A Group from the Abkan).

Abkan ceramics are made from a sand-tempered fabric varying from friable to hard; the hand-smoothed or well-polished surface tends to be a combination of colours, ranging from red to brown. The vessels are rarely decorated, but when they are the motifs consist of parallel rows of impressed triangles or rectangles, as well as zigzags and herring-bone designs; occasionally they are marked with small incisions parallel with the rim. The shapes, although simple, are more varied than those of the Khartoum Variant culture, comprising bowls, cups, plates, and hemispherical and ovoid forms, sometimes with slightly protruding rims.

There is evidence of the grinding of pigments in the form of sandstone pestles, sometimes stained with ochre, as well as disc-shaped stones possibly used as palettes. The survival of a few borers indicates that some tools were being made from polished bone. Finally, there are also beads made from ostrich eggshells, as well as a small unidentifiable amulet carved from talc. With the exception of stones from disturbed hearths, no ground-plans of buildings have yet been found, although a large number of post-holes were found at site Abka IX.

Favouring fairly high locations, on the east bank of the river, Abkan sites are situated in rocky areas, transected by wadis, in complete contrast to Khartoum Variant sites, which are located in the wide open spaces of the alluvial plains. Indeed, it seems that the Abkan people were essentially exploiting the river valley, judging from the remains of molluscs and fish (*Lates niloticus*, *Clarias*). The latter must have been caught with traps and nets, given the absence of fishing tools from the Abkan assemblages. Land-based creatures, such as the gazelle, the ostrich and the goose (*Alopochen aegyptiacus*), are also represented among the faunal remains. Finally, the metatarsal bones of a domesticated goat (*Capra hircus*) may possibly be linked with an Abkan stratum at site AS–6–G–25, excavated by the Scandinavian Joint Expedition. The Abkan radiocarbon dates that were obtained by the SJE stretch from 6000 to 4500 BP (i.e. the fifth and early fourth millennia BC; see Nordström 1972: 30).

The Sahara Neolithic

The 'extreme east' of the Sahara, to the west of the chain of oases in the Western Desert, had never, until recently, been the object of anything more than brief and incomplete investigations. In the 1980s, a vast programme of multidisciplinary research was undertaken in this zone of potential contacts between North Africa, the central Sahara and the Nile valley. Directed by the universities of Cologne and Berlin, this project, the 'Besiedlungsgeschichte der Ost-Sahara' (BOS), set out to follow the development of human groups over the last 10,000 years, investigating the economic and cultural responses that they made to the processes of environmental change, which were sometimes totally drastic in their impact.

Four seasons of archaeological study were undertaken between 1980 and 1984 (amounting to 15 months of fieldwork altogether), 400 sites were identified and described, and more than 200 radiocarbon dates were obtained. These researches took place along a north–south axis of 1200 kilometres, from the Qattara-Siwa depression down to the Wadi Howar in northern Sudan. Five regions were thus examined in detail, each separated by 300–500 kilometres: the Qattara-Siwa depression, the area of large dunes in the Libyan Erg, the plateau of Gilf Kebir, the region of Laqiya Arbain, and the Wadi Howar.

The density of settlement between 7000 and 4000 BC has been shown to be surprisingly rich, compared with the semi-desertification of modern times. A hiatus in 5500–5000 BC corresponds to the well-known arid phase which occurs elsewhere in the Sahara and the Near East at the same time. In particular, it turns out that the immense 'Sand Sea' situated at the border between Libya and Egypt has not always represented the kind of insurmountable barrier that we tend to assume.

The Sitra region (Czielsa 1989), to the south of the Qattara depression, has been found to contain occupations remarkable for their bifacial toolkit made up of long flat retouches, associated with retouched blades and burins. At site 83/12, 45 per cent of the toolkit was made up of burins, many of which were multiple types, and which might have been used as cores for the production of bladelets. There were also numerous burin spalls resulting from frequent sharpening. There were also a number of elongated triangles. Of the 400 sites recorded by the BOS, only two contained large numbers of burins, one in the Farafra Oasis (site 81/55) and the other near the Libyan border (81/61), radiocarbon-dated to 6900–4100 BC.

Several so-called *Steinplätze* have been examined; these sites, consisting of concentrations of stones, were discovered by Gabriel (1976, 1977). Isolated or in clusters, they correspond to the encampments of Neolithic nomadic pastoralists who followed the valleys that had remained periodically humid, abandoning the great plains, which had now become arid. Hearths associated with these settlements have enabled researchers to identify an early occupation dating back to the ninth millennium BC. Two *Steinplätze* studied by the BOS provided radiocarbon dates: 4840 ± 65 BC and 4340 ± 65 BC.

Further to the south, the site of Lobo (Klees 1989) near Abu Minqar is a small oasis midway between Dakhla and Farafra; it has yielded more than 100,000 artefacts from a sequence of five sondages and a wide-ranging surface survey. These finds include ostrich eggs, several hundred pestles and mortars, as well as a few potsherds. The associated lithics indicate a long occupation of several cultural units with two main phases radiocarbon dated to 7800 and 6100 BP.

Site 81/55.1 is dominated by scaled pieces, double backed perforators and retouched flakes made from the local nodular chert. The arrowheads are represented by bifacial pedunculate points. Site 81/55.2, on the other hand, contains an industry essentially comprising retouched blades, where the bifacial element is made up of pedunculate arrowheads and elongated 'leaf-shaped' points. Decorated fragments of ostrich eggs are associated with these lithics.

It should be noted that the presence of fossil springs at Lobo indicates that there must have been permanent sources of water during a long occupation period that has still barely been 'unravelled' by archaeologists; since there were also salt mines (clearly linked with the water sources), it seems likely that an important route of diffusion passed through this region.

These industries, situated between North Africa and the Nile valley (via the Dakhla, Kharga, Farafra and Bahariya oases) may represent a western extension of the Nile valley Neolithic. Alternatively, it might even be suggested that the Neolithic cultures of the oases and the Faiyum could be regarded as the eastern fringes of the Sahara Neolithic groups.

In the southwestern corner of Egypt, 600 kilometres from the valley, the Gilf Kebir is an enormous Nubian sandstone massif in the vertical escarpments that dominate the plain at a height of 200–300 metres. The area was discovered only in 1925 by Prince Kemal el-Din and John Ball, and ten years later it was visited by the Bagnold-Mond expedition, which included the archaeologist Oliver Myers and the great rock art researcher, Hans Winkler. The Wadi Bakht, in the southern region of the Gilf Kebir, was explored by Myers who recognized Aceulean bifaces mixed with wadi sediments and a Levallois site of which we know very little. Sets of Neolithic artefacts, found in the silts adjacent to a fossilized dune, date to an arid phase in the narrow bed of the wadi, a phenomenon similar to that at Wadi Kubbaniya. It was another forty years before the material collected from this site (now in the Musée de l'Homme, Paris) was studied by William McHugh (1975).

The lithic toolkit, made from silicified sandstone, has a high blade index and very few microliths. Notches and denticulates dominate the assemblages (17.3 and 13.4 per cent), followed by sidescrapers (8.7 per cent), perforators (7.7 per cent) and burins (2.9 per cent). A total of 21 pestles were found, without any mortars. As far as pottery is concerned, 700 very eroded sherds were found, but the shapes of the original vessels could not be reconstructed. The fabric was sandy, with organic inclusions, and the decoration took the form of dotted lines.

In 1975, Wendorf's team re-visited the Wadi Bakht (Wendorf *et al.*

1980: 217–22), where surface sites were found to contain lithic material similar to that found by Myers, as well as 117 sherds of fine, sandy, well-fired, brownish red fabric, the polished external surface of which was decorated with combs, cords, roulettes, incised lines and groups of chevrons. A radiocarbon date obtained from an ostrich eggshell is 6980 ± 80 BP.

In the 1980s, three BOS seasons of fieldwork re-examined the regions of the Wadi Bakht and Wadi el-Akhdar, both of which are characterized by the same geological situation as in the preceding period: fossil dunes behind which large playas developed (see Schön 1989). In the Wadi el-Akhdar, the analysis of these sediments, with a suggested thickness of 15 metres, indicates a lengthy period of sedimentation lasting nearly four millennia (8000–3000 BP).

Of nearly 100 of the sites discovered, 23 were excavated and a number of radiocarbon dates indicate that they were in use between 5500 and 5000 BP. The sites take the form of concentrations with diameters of about 5 metres, incorporating a lithic toolkit made from quartzite, dominated by large denticulates and sherds decorated with wavy lines. The motif that is most frequently encountered on the sherds is a herring-bone design running all around the upper part of the vessel, while the base seems to have been pointed. It is occasionally possible to distinguish a rippled surface, but, because of the very small size of the sherds, it is difficult to tell whether this rippling was present across the whole repertoire of ceramics.

The analysis of 46 samples of charcoal deriving from these two wadis has allowed K. Neumann (1989) to reconstruct the surrounding flora between 7700 and 4300 BP. The fact that the most abundant aspect of the vegetation was the tamarisk suggests that the environment was fairly arid, comparable with the modern conditions in the wadis of the central Sahara mountains. The second most prolific element of vegetation was the Christ's-thorn bush, probably the Sahelian species (*Zizyphus mauritania* or *Z. spina-christi*). Acacia trees are rare, but at around 6600, 5700 and 5000 BP they combine with *Balanites* and *Maerua crassifolia*, both of which are tropical species, thus reflecting periods during which the water supply must have been sufficient to support this kind of vegetation.

The rich fauna identified in the 1930s, including elephants, bovids, addax, gazelle, ostriches, jackals, wild asses and goats, has been confirmed by the more recent researchers (Wendorf 1980) who, however, have pointed out that there are also significant traces of domesticated species of sheep, goats, cattle and dogs. In this context, it is worth looking at the evidence provided by the rock carvings and rock paintings of the Gilf Kebir, often studied along with those at nearby Gebel Uweinat (although of uncertain date). Whether carved on the rocks along the sides of the wadis or painted in caves, these images of wild beasts, especially giraffes, ostriches and oryx, or domesticated species such as bovids, are effectively the first utterances of a world that had hitherto been rather uncommunicative, but was now part of a great explosion of Saharan rock art towards the end of the fifth millennium BC. Large-horned cattle are often depicted in the company of human figures, and the care lavished on the representation of the cows hints at the possibility that their milk was already an important aspect of human sustenance.

Further to the south, in an area 180 kilometres from the Egypto-Sudanese border, the BOS reached the Wadi Shaw in the Laqiya Arbain Oasis, a contact zone between southern Egypt and the northern Darfur (Schuck 1989). A short survey and a small area of excavation were conducted in 1982, resulting in the discovery of 90 sites associated with lakes of the sixth and fifth millennia BC. A wavy-lined sherd was found near an elephant molar in a sandy layer between two lacustrine deposits, thus providing a *terminus ante quem* of 4600 BC. Other sherds derive from contexts that are sometimes less precise, bearing a typical hatched decoration (Laqiya type), the distribution of which seems to extend over a distance of nearly 300 kilometres, as far as Wadi Howar. The radiocarbon analysis of a bone associated with pottery of this type produced the date 4250 ± 350 BC.

Finally, the Wadi Howar, located precisely at the southernmost limit of the B.O.S., constituted a natural corridor, during favourable climatic phases, linking the massifs of eastern Chad with the plateaus bordering the Nile (Richter 1989). No Palaeolithic or Epipalaeolithic sites have so far been found in this region; the first inhabitants of the Wadi Howar, who appear to have already been using pottery, settled there in about 6000 BC, colonizing the edges of the wadi and the surfaces of consolidated dunes. They exploited the permanent aquatic resources during the dry season and the seasonal pastureland during the humid months. The earliest assemblages include a microlithic toolkit, pierced discs of hard stone, abundant grinding materials, and sherds of a Khartoum Mesolithic type.

The next phase at the Wadi Howar is characterized by pottery of Laqiya and Shaheinab types. The radiocarbon dates indicate a long spell of occupation during this period, covering the third and second millennia BC, thus in a sense filling the hiatus marking the end of the Sudanese Neolithic.

Leaving the BOS at this point, and considering developments in the north again, it is worth noting a cultural grouping discovered by McDonald (1985) in the Dakhla Oasis; this material comprises a set of about thirty surface concentrations, to which the term 'Bashendi archaeological unit' has been applied. The Bashendi industry consists of flakes struck from chert or quartzite nodules; the arrowheads (either partially or totally bifacial) make up 27 per cent of the toolkit, followed by retouched pieces, notches and denticulates, perforators and sidescrapers. These lithics are found alongside numerous pestles and mortars, ostrich-eggshell beads, bone points and small polished stone palettes. It is therefore not particularly surprising to find that potsherds are another feature of this Neolithic combination. Although not very numerous and considerably eroded, they show fairly thin-walled pottery vessels with sandy temper, coloured brown to reddish and with burnishing of the surface. The only recognizable vessel shape has a pointed base.

The Bashendi unit is difficult to date but it has points in common not only with the Middle and Late Neolithic phases (7700–6200 BP and 6000–4600 BP respectively) determined by Wendorf for the Western Desert, but also with the 'Bedouin Microlithic' (see chapter 5 above) defined by Caton-Thompson in the nearby Kharga Oasis. Radiocarbon dates from ostrich eggshells taken from five different Bashendi localities indicate a chronological span of 6200 ± 130 to 5170 ± 90 BP.

During the humid Neolithic, which began in the first half of the fifth millennium BC, pastoral cultures spread throughout the Sahara, from the Nile across to the Atlantic, leaving behind them the first rock carvings and paintings in this region. The Sahara as a whole was covered with pastoral sites, not only on the massifs, which were sources of water and centres of life (Acacus, Tibesti, Tassili, Enedi and Uweinat), but also in certain areas of the great plains, the *serir*s that have nowadays become deserts. It is on the plains that concentrations of stones, the *Steinplätze*, indicate a traditional way of life that was the only viable strategy in these difficult regions: nomadism. Local rainfall during the humid Neolithic facilitated this way of life adapted to the specific ecological conditions. A similar strategy had already been adopted in the Near East at about 6000 BC (see discussion of the Natufian culture above).

The question of the dating of the rock art is controversial and will undoubtedly only be resolved when absolute dates are able to be obtained. A. Muzzolini (1986a) argues that they were all executed by Neolithic pastoralists. He emphasizes the fact that the earliest carvings portray, alongside the wild fauna, numerous domesticated cows and scenes of pasturage. This was the time of the famous decorated rams of the Saharan Atlas, which were once thought to have been influenced by the ram of the Egyptian god Amun (despite the fact that several millennia separate the Saharan representations from the Egyptian depictions of the sacred animal, which do not appear until the beginning of the 18th Dynasty, *c*.1580 BC).

The rocks of Upper Egypt and Nubia are covered with thousands of carvings; the earliest ones, which are often executed in a schematic style, portray large wild fauna: giraffes held on leashes, hippopotami, gazelle, ostriches, lions and above all elephants. In an important publication concerning hunters in the Nile and the Sahara, Paul Huard and Jean Leclant (1980) have identified a set of common stylistic traits expressing what Muzzolini (1989: 167) calls: 'a conceptual entity that contrasts with the local particularism of the other cultural features'.

The Badarian culture

Discovered between 1922 and 1929 by Guy Brunton and Gertrude Caton-Thompson, the 'Badarian culture' is the first element of the 'Predynastic period', in the sense that it is radically different from everything that we have so far discussed. It consists of 'wealthy' graves covering a strip extending for more than 30 kilometres at the foot of the limestone cliffs along the eastern bank of the Nile in Middle Egypt. With this culture we unexpectedly plunge straight into a symbolic universe of incredible richness, reflecting an increasingly structured and complex society, and this process was to accelerate enormously throughout the fourth millennium BC, eventually significantly contributing to the emergence of 'Egyptian civilization'.

The Predynastic, a vague term that apparently comprises everything that took place before the first dynasties, in fact serves to define the time when the people of the Nile valley, between the First Cataract and the Mediterranean, were emerging from their long period of Nilotic adaptation. The Predynastic Egyptians developed a cultural diversity that allowed them to forge ahead, in contrast to the Neolithic populations of the Sahara and the Sudan, thus enabling them eventually to begin to deal as equals with the dazzling civilizations of the Near East and Middle East.

Although it was in the region of the type site, el-Badari, that the culture was first identified by the British archaeologists Guy Brunton and Gertrude Caton-Thompson (1928), they subsequently turned their attention northwards to Mostagedda (Brunton 1937) and Matmar (Brunton 1948), uncovering nearly 600 graves and about 40 areas of settlement in a 35-kilometre stretch of the Nile valley. It was in this region, at Hemamia, that Caton-Thompson conducted the first excavation of a vertically stratified site dating back to the Badarian period, thus revealing the sequence of cultures through from the Badarian to the late Predynastic.

Although the Badarian culture appears to be limited to this section of the Nile valley, Badarian artefacts have been found at Armant and Hierakonpolis (Hoffman 1984). Fernand Debono (1951) even found a Badarian cemetery in the Wadi Hammamat. Apart from the work undertaken by Sami Gabra to the south of Deir Tasa, little fieldwork has been undertaken to continue the British research. In 1989, a joint Anglo-American team (Holmes 1989a) reinvestigated the Badarian region in order to make a study of the impact of modern activities on the site and to identify suitable new sites for excavation. The first results of their investigations are of great interest (see end of chapter).

The Badarian culture is best-known from tombs, or rather it is the preservation of material in cemeteries that presents us with the best opportunities to define the culture properly. We will therefore deal with the funerary material first.

The graves – grouped into separate sections of the desert strip that separates the cultivated land from the limestone massifs – take the form of simple oval pits in each of which a single individual is buried, in a contracted position, on the left side, with the head to the south, facing west. Like all general rules, there are of course exceptions to these: some tombs, for instance, are rectangular in shape (primarily in cemetery 1200), while the positions and orientations of the bodies sometimes vary. There are also occasionally multiple inhumations, consisting of two or three individuals, one of which was frequently a new-born infant (perhaps being buried with its mother?).

Each burial was carefully arranged. A mat was placed on the ground to accommodate the contracted body (which was presumably tied up before rigor mortis set in), while the head was sometimes laid on a pillow made from straw or rolled-up animal skin. The whole body was then either covered or completely wrapped up with a mat or gazelle-skin, the latter with the hairy side on the inside (unless it had been tanned). Most of the time it appears that this skin also covered one or more pottery vessels placed as funerary offerings, although the survival of some unrobbed graves has demonstrated that pots were placed at a higher level, as if they had not been added to the burial until the body itself had been at least partly interred. In certain cases, a piece of cloth was placed between the animal skin and the body. Remains of clothes suggest that some kind of short loincloth (made from linen or animal skin lined with linen) was worn.

Although no wooden coffins have been found, reeds have been excavated from the soil surrounding burials, suggesting that some bodies may have been wrapped in a kind of armature which would also have served as a form of roofing. In one case, a small wickerwork receptacle seems to have accommodated the remains of a young child, the accompanying pottery vessels being found on the outside. Only one burial so far includes a small separate 'room' intended specifically for the funerary offerings.

The pottery vessels placed by the side of the deceased constitute the most distinctive characteristic of this culture; hand-made, using clay of varying fineness, tempered with chaff, they nevertheless show great finesse in their execution, attesting to the great pyrotechnical mastery of the Badarian potters. The classification system proposed by Brunton is based on variations in the surface quality and the finish, the generally simple shapes amounting to straight-sided bowls, sometimes carinated, with rounded bases. It is thus possible to distinguish a finely polished type from another which has either a burnished or rough surface. Generally speaking, however, the surface is 'combed' before firing, then polished, thus producing a light, very aesthetically pleasing 'rippling' effect.

The first type (i.e. the highly polished vessels) comprises the red-polished, black-topped pottery, which were foreshadowed in the Khartoum Neolithic. Here it represents, in terms of both quantity and quality, the high point of a tradition that was to continue to be used in later cultures (with the exception of the rippling effect, which is the distinctive sign of the Badarian culture, and does not reappear in later vessels of this type). Sometimes it is decorated with simple floral motifs incised around the base with a burnishing tool, in such a way that they stand out clearly from the matt-finish rounded base. Brown polished black-topped vessels from Badarian sites are simply 'dark' versions of the red polished type, but they form a unique group that would not appear again. Few examples of entirely red polished vessels appear to have been made, and the same applies to the black polished types, which take the form of closed necked vessels, as well as the usual bowls.

The second type comprises the brown burnished pottery and rough ware, with undulating surfaces that the potter apparently created simply by running his fingers over the wet clay. These include large cooking vessels, the function of which is clearly indicated by the burnt black marks usually covering their bases; they are rarely found in tombs, but have most frequently been found *in situ* in settlements. When dried by the sun, they are also used as silos for the storage of quantities of grain.

There is a third basic type of Badarian vessel that effectively comprises anything that does not fit into the other two categories. Some vessels and sherds, for instance, are incised with motifs in the form of crosses, triangles and spirals (perhaps imitating basketry), while others bear painted geometrical motifs or protrusions moulded in relief, as at Merimda Beni Salama. Finally, there is also a unique type of vessel: globular, bottle-shaped, and with four handles forming a kind of girdle at the widest point; its similarities to vessels of the Ghassulian culture in Palestine have been discussed by W. F. Albright (1935) and G. E. Wright (1937).

The frequent occurrence of bone tools (such as curved and straight eye-needles, pins, and awls made from birds' femurs) in the settlement and tombs must undoubtedly have been connected with the working of animal skins and textiles. Ivory formed the basis for an important area of craftwork: bracelets, beads, rings, small rods sculpted in spirals (the purpose of which is uncertain), more or less cylindrical vessels which probably held cosmetics (judging from the malachite found in one example), and very finely carved spoons with handles in the form of animals (often difficult to identify). Also indicative of Badarian culture were the ivory or bone combs with long teeth, spaced at varying intervals and surmounted by a more or less stylized animal motif; one example had a curved shape and very fine, small teeth. Siltstone palettes – usually rectangular in shape (with notches on their shorter sides) or occasionally having an elongated oval form – were always found in direct association with the items of bodily adornment; sometimes they bear traces of ochre or stains of malachite, leaving little doubt as to their use for grinding pigments, especially as stone grinders of various types were often found in association with them. Several ivory tusks were found in three of the tombs, one of them clearly used as a container for ground-up malachite.

Wooden items comprised small pointed sticks and two small curved sticks, bearing a triple line of points along their entire length, 'as if beads had been hammered in', and incised with chevrons on their bases. Brunton (1937: 32), comparing them with the decoration of a later pottery vessel at el-Amra, which depicts two men holding similar objects in front of a (dancing?) woman with upraised arms, suggests that they may possibly have been used as a type of castanet instrument.

Ostrich eggs used as vessels attest to the presence and the importance of this great bird, feathers of which were found in tomb 5754 at el-Badari. Necklaces were certainly particularly popular, made up not only of pierced shells from the Red Sea (*Nerita, Conus, Ancillaria, Oliva* and *Natica*) and stones carved into disc shapes (carnelian, jasper, Egyptian alabaster, breccia and limestone), but also copper and steatite.

Copper, hammered into shape, gradually began to be used for the manufacture of pins and beads, the latter usually either cylindrical (made from a simple rolled sheet) or ring-like (made from a single strand of metal twisted into a spiral). It seems likely, however, that there were originally many more metallic items; thus, for instance, traces of green oxidization are still visible on the remains of small leather bags or baskets, indicating the very early pillaging of these precious accoutrements. In necklaces worn by the deceased, blue and green steatite beads were used as substitutes for the all too rare turquoise. Frequently used in tombs, thousands of these steatite beads adorn the waists of 'wealthy' indivdiduals in the Mostagedda cemeteries.

Finally, as at Merimda Beni Salama, the human figure began to be fashioned in clay and ivory, and here once again it is the female figure that is preferred. Three of these figurines are so far known, deriving from tombs 5107, 5227 and 5769. One of them (British Museum, EA 59679;

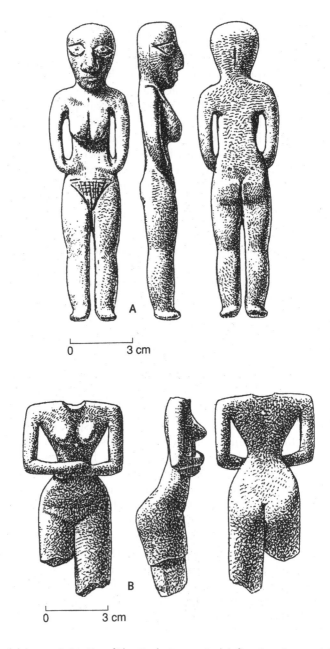

Figure 4   (a) Ivory statuette of the Badarian period (after Brunton and Caton-Thompson 1928: pl. XXIV, 2); (b & c) two baked clay statuettes of the Badarian period (after Brunton and Caton-Thompson 1928: pl. XXIV, 1 & 3).

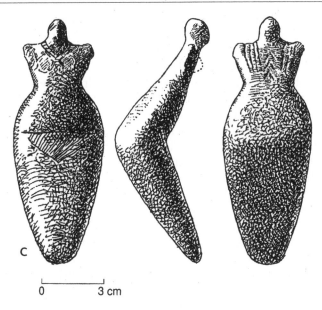

C

0　　　3 cm

figure 4b) is made from red-polished baked clay, and has no head (pre-sumably broken off). The upper part of the body is roughly triangular, with small, highly placed breasts; her hands are clasped (elbows forming right angles) in front of her slim waist, which contrasts sharply with her expansive hips; the pubic triangle is carefully indicated, and her legs are broken off at the thighs. In profile, her figure has a distinctly steato-pygous appearance.

The second figurine (British Museum, EA 58648; figure 4a), carved from ivory, is complete, but its head is far too large for the body; it has enormous incised, almond-shaped eyes, a rounded nose and a delicate little mouth. The upper torso is straight, with pendulous breasts, and the cursory carving of her arms, like jug-handles and without proper hands, gives the distinct impression, when viewed in profile, that she has her hands in her pockets! Her legs are heavy and lacking in detail, and her feet are almost non-existent. There is no sign of any steatopygy, but her femininity is emphasized by the large pubic triangle marked by numer-ous incisions.

The third figurine (London, Petrie Museum, U.C. 9080; figure 4c), moulded from unbaked clay, is extremely schematic in appearance, with a very small head barely emerging from the shoulders, and a triangular upper torso on which the arms are simply stumps. The enormously ste-atopygous lower torso accounts for three-quarters of the figurine; it converges to a point at the base and bears no indication of legs, as if it were enveloped in a long robe clinging tightly down to the feet. Its large pubic triangle is the only aspect in which it resembles its two 'companions'. Finally, its overall shape also draws attention to the buttocks, since it has been 'folded' in such a way that, seen in profile, it appears to lean forward, creating a triangular shape, the tip of which is formed by the buttocks, while the base is an imaginary line drawn between the head and the feet. As well as these three figurines, Tomb 494 at Mostagedda also yielded a small schematic female figurine, made of re-painted pottery and broken into four fragments.

Apart from the 'Venus-figures', the rest of the repertoire of figurines consists of animals: two ivory amulets representing a hippopotamus and possibly the head of a gazelle. Finally, there is also a hippopotamus figurine from Mostagedda (British Museum, EA 63057; Spencer 1993: figure 8), carved out of of a hippotamus tooth, which had been hollowed out to serve as a vessel, with its neck and broad flattened rim emerging from the middle of the animal's back. Three baked clay boat models, schematically modelled, represent the first funerary references to the river.

Compared with the wealth of the graves, the settlement remains are somewhat less attractive, comprising shallow layers (each about ten centimetres deep) of burnt brown deposits of organic materials, often affected by erosion and the superimposition of later settlements. It is possible to discern about forty living areas making up three large zones, each probably comprising several little villages or hamlets which seem to gradually move horizontally after fairly brief periods of occupation.

Certain parts of the sites contain surviving traces of circular pits interpreted as silos. Several irregular cuttings, about 130 centimetres wide and 100 centimetres deep, were covered, in their lower sections, with basketry or hardened mud; many pottery vessels were found *in situ*, pushed about 25 to 40 centimetres down into the ground. Some of these vessels were made from rough clay (sometimes only baked in the sun rather than fired), while others consist of fine fired ceramics, such as the magnificent brown, black-topped cup from Matmar, which was published by Brunton (1948: pl. XVIII), the frequent repair holes suggesting that it was a solid container of the type that might have held dates or grain.

In one part of the settlement were six hippopotamus tusks piled up by the side of a hard limestone block, which might represent a storage area for raw materials being kept in readiness for the creation of vessels and objects.

In addition to bone tools (such as needles, pins and awls) and a few attempts at female figurines (Brunton 1937: pl. XIV), there was an abundance of pottery, shattered into many fragments, which add nothing to the study of the pots found in graves. However, the thousands of lithics that characterize the Badarian stone tool industry relate primarily to the settlements. The lithics that derive from graves are exceptional not only in the quality of their workmanship, but also in terms of what they may have represented in the eyes of the deceased. Brunton and Caton-Thompson (1928: 35–7) divided the 'carefully finished' tools into three bifacial types: winged arrowheads (sometimes also pedunculates), parts of sickles, and elongated leaf-shaped types, four fine specimens of which derive from tomb 5116 at el-Badari (Brunton and Caton-Thompson 1928: pl. XXIX/6), as well as adzes. If the lithics are to be understood in their entirety, then these three tool types should be studied alongside the cores, the flakes and the flint pebbles. Brunton's three types, however, derive mainly from tombs and are notable for their very elaborate working, but Caton-Thompson's study of the lowest stratum at Hemamia enabled her to reach more general conclusions with regard to Badarian lithics. She concluded that it was a pebble-based industry, and that the principal tools were a kind of heavy rabot (a push-plane or steep-ended scraper) manufactured from pebbles or roughly plano-convex nodules, which were picked up from the ground (rather than quarried), judging from their orange patina resulting from prolonged surface exposure. Another re-markable piece is a type of 'knife' made from a blade of brownish grey non-local flint, one edge of which is rectilinear, while the other is slightly convex from its distal end by a series of fine, regular retouches, which either affect only the distal section of the blade or extend along this en-tire edge. The proximal end is characterized by direct and/or indirect retouches which obscure all traces of the original working of the blade. Caton-Thompson points out that a blade of this type, reminiscent of a Chatelperronian 'pseudo-point', was found under a ripple-burnished sherd in a depression filled with purely Badarian material; similar types, how-ever, have been found in the upper layers at Hemamia.

A study of the lithic material in the Petrie Museum (University College London), undertaken by Diane Holmes (1989b) included the re-exam-ination of 45 items from domestic contexts and 266 from graves. The results of her analysis suggest that the Badarian industry is based funda-mentally on flakes and blades, and that – as in the Faiyum – the overall significance of the bifacial toolkit has been over-estimated. The end-scrap-ers, circular sidescrapers, notches, denticulates, burins and perforators are well-represented alongside fine sickles and bifacial arrowheads. If the particularly shiny appearance of certain items suggests the use of heat treatment on the flint, a heating process designed to facilitate the knapping, the orange patina noted by Caton-Thompson appears to characterize Badarian flint.

We only have a relatively vague idea of the nature of Badarian faunal material, since it has not been subjected to any truly modern archaeo-zoological analysis. Animal skulls regularly appear in graves alongside the body of the deceased; these crania derive from cattle, sheep, antelopes, cats and jackals or dogs, and it is highly probable that at this date they were domesticated species (including the antelopes). Indeed, human contact with animals is also indicated by the presence of animal burials, found here and there among the human graves. Like the humans, these animals (comprising an antelope, a dog and a sheep) were were wrapped in a skin and deposited in the ground without grave-goods, thus indicating their social status and foreshadowing the role that the animal kingdom was to play in the symbolic and mythical worlds of the Egyptians.

The types of grain found in the pottery vessels have been identified as the castor oil plant (*Ricinus communis*), barley (*Hordeum vulgare*) and wheat (*Triticum dicoccum*), an agricultural aspect of the culture which is backed up by the frequency of sickles among the tools used. The people of the Badarian culture were agriculturalists, probably pastoralists, doubtless fishers, and certainly also hunters, judging from the many arrowheads found; like the people of the Faiyum Neolithic culture, they do not appear to have made any great impact in terms of the tilling of soil.

Their settlements. situated on the desert edges, in regions that were barely affected by the Nile floods, mainly seem to be the result of pastoralism and the storing of materials. But it seems likely that the exploitation of the resources of the floodplain in the low water seasons led some groups to establish settlements near the river which have long since been either buried under the alluvium or destroyed.

The emerging image is of a relatively mobile existence, combining the annual flood cycle with agricultural, pastoral and hunting activities; this was the way in which new modes of production were introduced in the millennium during which the Nilotic adaptation took place. It is clear, however, that compared with their contemporaries, the Badarian people, with their development of contacts with neighbouring regions, had a culture that was instilled with great dynamism. The presence of objects made from turquoise, copper, steatite and sea-shells shows that they looked towards the east, where the earliest Chalcolithic cultures had developed from the end of the sixth millennium BC onwards (Tell Halaf in northern Mesopotamia, and Mersin, Haçilar and Çatalhöyük in Anatolia).

Copper objects are rarely found at el-Badari; a few beads of hammered native copper have survived the pillaging of the graves, but presumably the search for precious metals must have been one of the main motives for plundering cemeteries. There were three principal regions where copper-bearing minerals were to be found: the Eastern Desert, Sinai and the Sudan. It is tempting to assume that the Eastern Desert was the first to be exploited, but there is not yet any indication that it was exploited for copper before the pharaonic period. It should be noted, however, that procuring native copper and hammering it into shape are not operations that require any great infrastructure. The Egyptian sources of turquoise are located amid the copper-bearing regions of Sinai, therefore the presence of turquoise and steatite beads at el-Badari emphasizes the early exploitation of this peninsular zone squeezed between Egypt and the Near East.

In 1974, an expedition organized by the Institute of Archaeology at Tel Aviv (Beit-Arieh 1980) discovered a set of remains relating to turquoise extraction in the vicinity of Serabit el-Khadim; the artefacts date to the Ghassulian culture of Palestine, and, considering the relative paucity of turquoise at Palestinian sites, it seems likely that these workings were undertaken in order to provide turquoise for Predynastic Egypt. This would suggest that groups from Palestine were based in Sinai with the aim of obtaining and polishing turquoise, then even transporting it to Egypt. The Ghassulian culture, the heartland of which was situated in the Negev region, to the northeast of the Dead Sea, during the fourth millennium BC, is the earliest known Chalcolithic culture in Palestine.

At the same time, the site of Abu Matar (Perrot 1984), which belonged to the Beersheba culture, was an important copper-working centre, comprising workshops, smelting furnaces and moulds. The pure copper at this site was extracted from an exceptionally rich mineral found at Wadi Feinan, on the eastern slopes of the Wadi Arabah massif, some 100 kilometres to the south. Among the objects discovered at Abu Matar were marine shells from the Red Sea, turquoise from Sinai, and shells from a particular species of fresh-water snail that came from the Nile valley.

However, although there is not yet definite proof that the turquoise and copper at Badarian sites derived from Sinai, the possibility that this was the case can hardly be denied, and, on this basis, the discoveries made by Debono in the Eastern Desert (see pp. 162–3) are of some significance. Indeed, if there were contacts between Upper Egypt and Sinai at this date, they might well have been taking place via direct trade-routes, across the Red Sea, thus bypassing Lower Egypt, where the contemporary cultures (Faiyum and Merimda) involve no use of metal.

It seems extremely unlikely that the northern sites could have served as transit points for the movement of copper if no traces of the metal have survived there, although they are found closer to the mines. Few contacts between Upper and Lower Egypt are attested before Naqada II, and S. Tutundzic (1989) has suggested that this lack of contact should be ascribed to an absence of motivation for exchange, given that there was no geographical barrier between what we might describe as 'the two Egypts'. From this point of view, the direct relations between Upper Egypt and the Near East, via Sinai, might even have accentuated the gulf between the two cultural groupings in the Egyptian section of the Nile valley.

The same problem arises if we consider the glazed steatite that was evidently intended to be an imitation of turquoise. A soft stone, creamy to the touch and similar to talc in its texture, steatite is a form of magnesium silicate that hardens when heated, leaving it shiny and aesthetically pleasing. Brunton himself argued that this glazing technique was probably invented at el-Badari, and therefore that the beads must have been locally made. In an article dealing with this topic, Finkenstaedt (1983) points out that thousands of similar beads have been found at Tell Brak, in Syria, and at Tell Arpachiya, in northern Mesopotamia, in fourth-millennium contexts, probably earlier than the Badarian culture. Either the Badarian beads were imports from the Near East that were being elaborated *in situ*, or we should look for a common ancestor for both Badarian and Asiatic glazed steatite in the fifth millennium BC. Considering the enormous quantity of glazed steatite objects deriving from north Mesopotamian and Syrian sites, Finkenstaedt suggests that this is the most likely area where we might look for origins of the glazing technology. We still need to clarify the geographical route by which the two regions were making contact.

However, the manufacture of beads at el-Badari itself cannot be systematically excluded; Alfred Lucas (1962) notes that sources of steatite can be found within Egypt, in the Eastern Desert both at Gebel Fatira, at least 160 kilometres from el-Badari, near Aswan, and at Wadi Gulan, north of Ras Benas, on the Red Sea coast. Thus the importance of Debono's discoveries in 1949, during the construction of the Quft-Quseir road, cannot be over-emphasized. In the Lakeita region, the remains of a Predynastic village were identified. Among the sherds at this site were several made 'with the Badarian technique' (i.e. 'combed' before firing, to produce the typical rippling effect). Debono (1951) indicates that there was also a large quantity of lithic material, including 'polished hard-stone axes and flint hatchets, knives made with blade and even bifacial technology, numerous different types of end-scraper, picks, saws etc.'. A fragment of a forked 'lancehead' from this site indicates the presence of the Amratian culture. Hard-stone pestles and mortars are found alongside a set of polished bone tools (mostly broken), as well as pierced Red Sea shells, ostrich-eggshell beads, stone pendants and many un-worked fragments of copper. Several hearths have survived, yielding faunal remains, including fish vertebrae. Among the graves found by the expedition, Debono mentions two child burials, probably of the Badarian culture.

Not far from here, a village dating to the Early Dynastic period seems to be linked with the exploitation of copper: 'This mineral, without the slightest shadow of doubt, was extracted from the minor copper sources in the vicinity, then it was processed in the village itself, judging from the slag found there' (Debono 1951: 71). It appears that the settlement also served as a workshop for the production of mother-of-pearl bracelets, the main raw material for these being large *pteroceras* sea-shells collected some 120 kilometres away, on the Red Sea coast, where there are indications that the shells were broken in order to extract only the spiral central part, which was then taken to the village to be worked.

In the course of investigations further to the east, in Wadi Hammamat, Debono found a Badarian grave and several Badarian potsherds. The Wadi Hammamat, the favoured ancient route between the Nile and the Red Sea, was at this time much more humid, and well shafts were supplied by a water table that was then much more regularly replenished; indeed the 'miraculous' rains were not so rare on the high plains. The discovery of actual workshops, from the Early Dynastic period onwards – evidently serving as relay points between the centres of production of raw materials and the peak of consumption which the Nile valley represented – suggests that a similar occupation might well have existed at an earlier date, at the time of the Badarian period proper, for instance. Indeed, it is worth pointing out that there has been no systematic survey or large-scale excavation undertaken in this region for 40 years, therefore the questions raised by Debono's work remain unanswered. Considering the intensity of the archaeological work that has taken place in the Western Desert, a region of such crucial significance as the Eastern Desert has been almost entirely neglected with regard to prehistoric and protohistoric sites. There can be little doubt that the Eastern Desert will be an area of study that will surely flourish in future years (see, already, Bomann and Young 1994; Bomann 1995 for discoveries of prehistoric material in the Wadi Abu Had).

Krzyzaniak (1977: 81) stresses the fact that the characteristic rippling effect on Badarian pottery was also practised at Jericho, from 4500 BC onwards, and that it appeared at Byblos, in southern Anatolia and in northern Mesopotamia at about the same time, leading him to suggest that the Eastern Desert, and ultimately southwest Asia, should be regarded as the points of origin for Badarian culture. A. J. Arkell (1975), on the other hand, takes into account the typical black-topped vessel, which is not found in any place outside the Nilotic region but is present at Khartoum since the Neolithic period, and suggests that the Badarian culture must instead have emerged from the south. He also associates the Badarian with the disc-shaped macehead, although, as K. Cialowicz (1987) notes, no macehead has been dated with any certainty to a Badarian context.

Élise Baumgartel, like Arkell, considers that the people associated with Badarian remains must have been a mixture of populations moving up from the south, while at the same time there were purely Asiatic influences coming from the east in the form of agriculture and domestication. This was also the opinion of Caton-Thompson (Brunton and Caton-

Thompson1928), who based her assumption on the very distinctive type of flint that was being used: the kidney-shaped cobbles with orange patina collected from the desert surface. She suggested that this use of surface flint indicated an ignorance of the seams of excellent raw material within the Eocene limestone formations. Thus, she argued, the Badarian people must have come from geologically different southern regions, below 24° latitude, reaching the region of Asyut by way of the Red Sea massifs. Diane Holmes (1989b: 183), however, convincingly rejects this argument, on the grounds that the choice of raw material was actually perfectly attuned to Badarian requirements, while the search for large blocks of fine-grained flint would have been triggered off by the increasing scale and quality of artefacts that predominated in subsequent cultures. With regard to lithics, she points out that there are some similarities with the post-Palaeolithic culture in the Sahara (an industry based on blades and flakes, in which polished axes and hollow-base arrowheads are not lacking), which means that we cannot exclude the possibility that the semicircle formed by the Bahariya, Farafra, Dakhla and Kharga oases might have been the point of origin of populations who were perhaps already pursuing a pastoral mode of subsistence; these people might have been pushed eastwards by increasing aridity and would eventually have settled in the region of Asyut and Tahta. The plant species that began to be cultivated by the Badarian people would be a potential problem with regard to this theory, but their introduction from the Near East *via* the Neolithic sites in northern Egypt is envisaged. Thus, the Faiyum and Merimda cultures would have passed southwards the technique of polishing pottery vessels, which would then have been elaborated in a distinctive fashion at el-Badari.

We therefore have a whole range of different opinions: the Badarian people are said to have come from the south, from the east, from the west, and even from the north – from all of the cardinal points. But there is one of these points of view that can be supported without any difficulty: the view expressed by Holmes (1989b: 185), since it is she who argues that the single most definite feature of the problem is the fact that the Badarian cannot be regarded as a tradition that emerged from one simple, unique source. We are thus dealing with a complex culture, which was already deeply 'Egyptian' in the sense that it appears to have assimilated, and converted into powerfully original forms, traits that are rarely encountered elsewhere.

Last, but by no means least, is the question of the dating of the Badarian culture. Brunton had almost instinctively placed it before the Amratian culture, from which it differed essentially in terms of pottery. Then Caton-Thompson had apparently obtained stratigraphic proof of the fact that the Badarian was earlier by excavating the site that we shall now discuss: Hemamia.

From February to March in 1924 and 1925, she 'trenched' an area of 8600 m², divided into units of 3 × 1.5 metres, into a number of 10-centimetre-deep transects. The depth of each artefact was recorded, apart from undiagnostic sherds. She was thus able to distinguish a process of cultural evolution, at the beginning of which appeared the Badarian material, partly sealed by a compact gravel deposit (which she described as 'breccia') and partly immediately beneath the later artefactual material. Fifty years later, she was able to confirm this relative chronology by means of thermoluminescence dating on sherds at Oxford, chosen on the basis of the traces of their burial soil still adhering to the surface (Caton-Thompson and Whittle 1975). Two dates were obtained for the sub-breccia Badarian layer: 5495 ± 405 BC and 5580 ± 420 BC, while the pottery above the breccia was dated at 4690 ± 365 BC and 4510 ± 475 BC (all of these dates having large standard deviations). During a visit to Hemamia, T. R. Hays and Fekri Hassan collected several pieces of wood charcoal from a Badarian context, allowing them to assign radiocarbon dates between 4400 and 3800 BC for the earliest culture represented at Hemamia (Hassan 1985: 19). Caton-Thompson's stratigraphy at Hemamia has now been confirmed by the work of Diane Holmes and Renée Friedman (1994); two samples from the sub-breccia layer have yielded radiocarbon dates confirming an estimated age of 4400–4000 BC.

We cannot leave the discussion of the Badarian culture without mentioning Deir el-Tasa, the type-site for Brunton's 'Tasian culture', which he considered to have predated the Badarian, on the basis of its lack of copper. He suggested that about fifty of the burials that he had found during his excavations between the village of Deir el-Tasa and Mostagedda, mixed in with Badarian and Naqada graves, contained such a specific range of artefacts that they deserved to be regarded as a separate group. The pottery, although clearly of an early date, nevertheless contained a number of original features. He distinguished three types: (1) reddish brown and grey sherds made from a rough ware, with the surface sometimes burnished and covered in brownish marks due to inconsistent firing, (2) greyish black sherds with a burnished surface and vertical and diagonal ripples, and (3) black, more or less polished, sherds with incised geometrical decoration filled with white paste (including chalice forms that are reminiscent of some of the vessels found at late Neolithic sites in the Middle Nile). One unusual form is a red polished rectangular vessel with a rippled surface. Generally speaking, it is in terms of its pottery shapes that Brunton's Tasian culture is most aptly characterized, the most typical vessel being a deep bowl with a small flattish base and angular sides narrowing towards the rim, thus creating a carinated shape. Thus it was the combination of the anglular bodies of the pots and the flat, straight bases that was regarded as the essential characteristic of the Tasian (see Brunton 1937: 28).

Five palettes were found in the 'Tasian' graves, one carved from siltstone and the others from calcite or limestone. There appears to be no difference between the lithics of the Badarian and the Tasian, apart from the fact that the latter sometimes includes small polished axes of calcite or igneous rocks.

It should be noted, however, that Holmes (1989a: 15) found no trace of the Tasian culture in her survey of the Badarian region in the 1980s. Baumgartel was the first to suggest that there was no such thing as a Tasian culture, on the grounds that there were too few graves of this type and too many cultural similarities with the Badarian; she suggested instead that it should be regarded simply as a local variant of the Badarian. Her point of view has generally been accepted (Krzyzaniak 1977: 68 n. 15; Hoffman 1980: 142) although it has been questioned by Werner Kaiser (1985), who points out that the pottery is indeed somewhat unusual compared with other Badarian ceramics, and suggests, primarily on the basis of the flat bases, that they might be linked with the pottery found at Neolithic sites in the north, as well as that of the Amratian period. It has also been noted that the 'Tasian' culture is not geographically restricted to the Tasia-Mostagedda region, since similar sherds have been found at Armant, and numerous pots of this type have also turned up on the art market.

The 'Tasian question' is therefore more complicated than it was initially thought to be. According to Kaiser, the location where the Tasian first emerged, at the northern end of Upper Egypt, might correspond to a buffer zone through which northern influences could have filtered southwards, exerting a certain amount of influence on the forms of the pottery of the Naqada I period.

Part IV

The Approach to the Pharaonic Period (fourth millennium BC)

7

The Predynastic period (c.4000–3000 BC)

In one sense it is somewhat artificial to make a distinction between the Neolithic and the Predynastic, given that the Neolithic was *already* Predynastic, and the Predynastic was to some extent *still* Neolithic. But the most appropriate term with which to encapsulate the fourth millennium BC, in the section of the Nile valley between the Mediterranean and the First Cataract, is one that makes reference to the astonishing pharaonic explosion that took place in *c.*3000 BC. It was during this relatively short period that all of the cultural elements that had gradually been accumulating in earlier periods finally began to gel together, forming the raw material from which Egyptian civilization was to be fashioned. Although new ingredients – sometimes in large quantities – would undoubtedly be added to the basic cultural recipe, no subsitite would ever be found for the original formula.

Upper Egypt: Naqada I/Amratian and Naqada II/Gerzean

The region of Upper Egypt between Qena and Luxor is the fountainhead of Egyptian prehistory. It was there that Jacques de Morgan, at the end of the nineteenth century, effectively dug up the first prehistoric artefacts, and it was there, above all, that Flinders Petrie uncovered the vast cemeteries that would allow him to develop his sequence dates (see Appendix 1) and therefore to create the first great chronology of Predynastic Egypt.

The Amratian (Naqada 1)

The Amratian culture derives its name from the site of el-Amra, at the beginning of the Naqada meander of the river, but it is represented by numerous sites, from Matmar in the north down to Wadi Kubbaniya and Khor Bahan in the south. The extensive excavations undertaken by Petrie and Quibell resulted in the discovery of many thousands of graves (about 3000 of which date to the Predynastic period) and two large zones of settlement: Naqada South and Naqada North.

In 1975, 1976 and 1978, a series of prospections and sondages were made by T. R. Hays in the el-Khattara region, extending for 18 kilometres, from Danfiq to Ballas. They revealed a large number of settlement sites and produced numerous radiocarbon dates (Hassan 1988: 154).

In its essential characteristics, the Amratian was very similar to the Badarian. The dead were usually buried on their left-hand sides, in a contracted position, with the head to the south, looking towards the west. A statistical study undertaken by J. J. Castillos (1982) indicates, however, that there was an increase in the number of bodies buried in small pits, while simultaneously a small number of individuals began to be buried in larger, better equipped graves. In this regard, the example of Hierakonpolis is instructive (Hoffman 1982): the Amratian graves at this site, although plundered, are remarkable in their rectangular form and unusual size (the largest being 2.50 × 1.80 m). In the case of two of these graves, the equipment includes a magnificent disc-shaped porphyry macehead, a symbol of power. The practice of covering or wrapping the body in an animal skin tends to die out, and the first wooden or clay coffins make their appearance. As in the Badarian, men, women and children are each buried throughout the cemetery, without any zoning by sex or age. The differences between these two cultures can be especially observed in modifications to the range of artefacts. The black-topped red ware gradually became less common, and this trend was eventually to lead to its total disappearance at the end of the Predynastic period. The rippling effect on the surface of the pottery had until this time been restricted to the Badarian culture, but it now also figured – to a much smaller extent – among the Amratian artefacts. The fine black-polished pottery gradually became rarer, while the totally red-polished ware became increasingly common. The shapes of red-polished pottery also became more diverse, eventually reaching a degree of complexity that enabled Kaiser (1957) to distinguish between different chronological phases, including the phasing out of the style involving a rounded base. The red-polished vessels were occasionally decorated with white painted designs comprising geometrical, animal and vegetal motifs. The fauna represented on the vessels was essentially riverine, dominated by images of crocodiles and hippopotami, but it also included scorpions, gazelles, giraffes, ichneumons and numerous schematic bovids, the particular species of which are often difficult to identify. Finally, in a very significant development, the animals began to protrude from the surface of the vessel in a kind of raised relief decoration in which the animals were depicted as if standing on the lower edge of the pot – as in the case of the elephants, crocodiles and lizards on pots in the Ägyptisches Museum, Berlin, the hippotami on a cup from el-Mahasna published by Garstang (1903: pl. XI) and on another in the Egyptian Museum, Cairo (Quibell 1905: pl. 24, no. 11570). Theriomorphic vessels, the origins of which can be seen in the Badarian ivories, became more numerous and more varied as the centuries passed.

Although less common than animals, depictions of people nevertheless also appeared. The human figures were schematic, with small round heads (frequently sporting headdresses of feathers or reeds), triangular torsos, thin hips, and elongated 'stick legs', often without feet. Similarly, the arms were only represented 'when necessary'; thus, the inner surface of the famous 'Moscow cup' (figure 5a), dating to the Naqada I phase, is decorated with a person holding a bow in his left hand, while in his right hand he holds four leashes (perhaps symbolic), linking him to four greyhounds. In the same hunters' world, a vase from el-Mahasna (figure 5b) is decorated with a figure who this time is rendered completely schematically: the torso is reduced to a stick, the legs are shown wide apart, to indicate the act of walking and the exertion of a certain amount of effort, and the depiction of a bump suggests the presence of a penis-sheath. This figure is confronting a harpooned hippopotamus. The cord of the harpoon, piercing the animal between its ears stretches out horizontally, joining up with the hunter in a kind of ball reminiscent of a reel. There can be no doubt that it is in the figure's hand, either in actuality, in which case the arm has disappeared, or symbolically, in which case the arm never existed. On a cup from el-Mahasna (figure 5c), in an equally schematic depiction, it is the head of the harpooner which has disappeared; this scene also includes two complete figures whose arms are raised as if in a dance.

One whole side of the vessel in figure 5d (Petrie Museum, UC) is decorated with two possible dancing figures whose appearance is enhanced by the elongated form of the pot itself. Petrie (1920: 16, pl. XVIII/74) first interpreted this scene as one of combat between two men, but Vandier (1952: 287) and Baumgartel note the contrasts between the two figures which appear to accentuate their sexual dimorphism: one is large and the other small, one has a phallus, the other a small bulge which could perhaps be interpreted as a penis sheath. However, considering the small build of the individual, the 'penis sheath' might also have been intended to represent the vulva depicted as if in a frontal view in order that the female sex should be made visible, as a 'response' to the masculine sex. This frontal view of the vulva would therefore have replaced the exaggerated portrayal of the pelvis, which is often chosen as the female characteristic par excellence. However, the only two surviving parallels to the

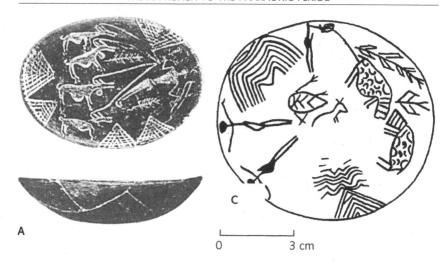

A

C

0   3 cm

B

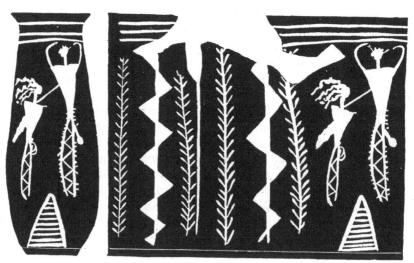

D

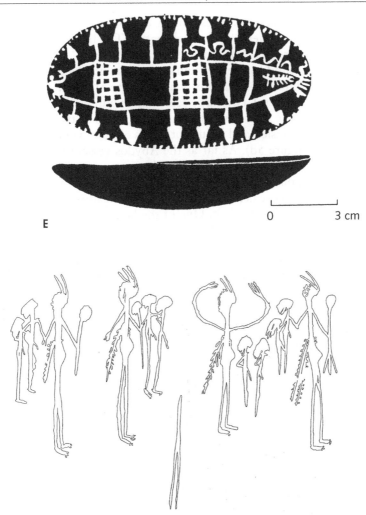

0   3 cm

E

F

Figure 5 (a) Interior painted decoration and side-view of a Predynastic bowl in the Moscow Museum (after Scharff 1928: pl. XXVII,4); (b) painted decoration on the exterior surface of a Predynastic bowl from Abydos, Cemetery B (after Ayrton and Loat 1911: pl. XXVII,13); (c) painted decoration on a bowl from Mahasna (after Petrie 1920: pl. XXVIII/74); (d) Predynastic vessel in the collection of the Petrie Museum, University College London; left: side-view of the vessel, right: view of the entire external painted decoration (after Petrie 1920: pl. XVIII/74); (e) bowl from Mahasna, the interior surface of which is painted to resemble a boat (after Petrie 1920: pl. XV/49); (f) painted figures on a vessel from the late Predynastic tomb U-239/1 at Abydos (after Dreyer et al. 1998: Abb. 13).

decoration on this vessel suggest that we should view this group as a depiction of the conqueror and the defeated. The first of these is in the collection of the Brussels Museum (see Scharff 1928: pl. XXXVIII), while the second was found by the German excavators at Abydos in the 1990s (Dreyer *et al.* 1998: 111–14, Abb. 13; see figure 5f here).

On the Brussels vessel, two large-scale male figures, with feathers fixed on their heads, raise their arms above three groups of two small figures, the latter having tousled and luxuriant heads of hair, as in the Petrie Museum example (figure 5d). As far as the Abydos vessel (figure 5f) is concerned, there are four groups depicted on the upper part of a flat-bottomed, cylindrical, red-polished pot. Each of these groups is dominated by a figure shown at a larger scale, wearing two or three feathers on his head, and with an animal's tail at his belt. One of the larger figures raises his arms above his head, while the rest of them each hold an object with a rounded end, which is possibly a mace but should presumably be interpreted as a symbol of their power. In each instance, a bulge at the level of the penis serves to indicate the sex of the larger figure. Two small individuals – clearly shown to be long-haired men – are linked with each of these large figures. Although it is difficult to discern whether these small figures' hands are tied behind their backs, a solid line physically connects them to the large figures, who are actually 'holding' them on leashes (except in the case of the one larger figure whose arms are raised over his head). It is therefore difficult to sustain the view that the figures on the Petrie Museum vessel are a dancing couple. Instead they must surely be expressions of power-based relationships, and this kind of image was later to become a stereotypical symbol of the exultant victor and the stricken enemy.

To conclude our discussion of the painted universe of the Amratians, we should consider a few representations of curved boats, which are usually depicted in profile, but in the case of one pot from Mahasna, a splayed-out view from above is provided, comfortably occupying the entire bottom of the dish (figure 5e, see Petrie 1920: pl. XV/49). A tiny schematic human figure is shown seated at the front of the boat. Drawing on the intrinsic boat-shape of the dish itself, the small craft is provided with eight pairs of oars (plus an extra one) forming a frieze of triangles along the inner edge of the vessel.

The riverine world, which was the source of life for Nilotic groups over the course of thousands of years, was portrayed at that time in a pictorial language whereby the dominant animals were those that were feared, hunted, killed or raised, observed and respected. It was behind such animals that men crept along in the role of hunters (we might compare, for instance, the schematic representations of the harpooners with the much more detailed depictions of hippopotami), beginning to express their presence in scenes that sanctify their sexuality. The cautious appearance of the boat – the principal means of communication in this river-dominated land – represents the beginning of an enduring scenario.

The human figures that appear on decorated pots – with varying degrees of importance – had already burst onto the scene in the form of clay and ivory figurines, but in the Amratian period they acquired a certain élan. It is in fact very difficult to differentiate between the sculpted figures of the various periods of the Predynastic. It is at present something of a lottery to attempt to distinguish Amratian figurines from the rest. Out of a total of 226 figurines published by Peter Ucko (1968) in his synthesis of the available evidence, only 84 derive from excavations, and 76 were found in tombs, most of which were plundered. The vast majority of the evidence, therefore, derives from the antiquities market. Nevertheless, very important deductions may be made on the basis of Ucko's study, which must continue to figure in the preliminaries of any future analysis on this subject.

Only a few of the thousands of excavated Predynastic tombs contained figurines, and usually they occurred singly, with groups of three or more being comparatively rare. The maximum number found in a single Amratian burial was a set of 16 figurines. The analysis of the other grave goods shows that the burials containing figurines were not particularly 'rich' in other respects, and in fact such sculpted figures might sometimes be the only funerary offering in the tomb. As in the case of certain fine flint knives found among grave goods (Midant-Reynes 1987), the figurines may rather have been intended to express some particular aspect of the deceased, a social particularity, but also perhaps an anatomical one, judging from the recent discovery of a vessel that had been deformed before firing in a tomb at Adaïma belonging to an old man who suffered from a monstrous hump due to tuberculosis of the spine (Midant-Reynes et al. 1991). This point raises a number of elementary questions concerning funerary offerings: for whom were they intended, according to what criteria were they chosen, and how did they actually function?

With regard to our statuettes, 68 per cent are made from clay, the rest from ivory, a plant-based paste, or, more rarely, bone; the carving of stone is still very exceptional in the Amratian. Usually men and women are represented standing, more rarely seated, with the emphasis on the primary sexual characteristics: the breasts, the development of the buttocks, the pubic triangle, the penis or the penis sheath. The legs were evidently regarded as insignificant: sometimes they are vaguely indicated by a median line, but most often the lower part of the human body corresponds to a simple tenon doubtless intended to be pushed into the earth beside the deceased, although figurines were sometimes placed in some form of basket. The arms were also occasionally regarded with the same indifference, perhaps being made simply as stumps, but they can sometimes appear along the length of the body or they can be raised up in a curved style over the head, somewhat in the manner of the dancers depicted on the pottery vessels. Their noses, resembling the beak of a bird of prey, protrude, sometimes being the only element of the face portrayed. However, the mouth and eyes are often indicated, as well as the hair (or wig) in the form of braids or curls. The modelling of the ears is usually present in the case of chiselled ivory figurines, but rarely occurs on clay examples. As in the case of the pottery vessels, certain baked clay figurines (figure 6a) are decorated with stripes of geometric motifs and geometrical quadrupeds, which, according to Keimer (1948), are unlikely to be tattoos.

It seems to be impossible to categorize the entire corpus of figurines so far studied into a limited set of types; rather, as both Ucko (1968) and Needler (1966) have argued, there seems to have been a variety of accepted formulae which could be combined with a certain degree of freedom. It might be said that 'art feels its way along', in that no set of standards or artistic rules had yet begun to regulate the way in which the human image was portrayed. In general the figurines, like the designs on the vessels, appear to us to be centred on sexuality. If we are to link them with some kind of social setting, we must understand what role they played in the graves. Why do some individuals have the 'right' to be buried with figurines, while others do not?

Another category of figurative representation of humans also stands out, however, and we do not yet know whether the study of these sculptures is proceeding along the correct lines. They take the form of schematic human forms, often simply bearded faces on small incised rods of ivory, or on the pointed ends of hippopotamus tusks (figure 6b). Here too there are a number of variations within a general overall concept. A triangular beard seems to be the most common element, sometimes surmounted by eyes (once containing inlay), giving the individual a strange bird-like appearance, and sometimes balanced – in a geometrical sense – by 'Phrygian' headgear pierced by a suspension hole. The purity of the lines of composition results in the famous schist-carved 'Bearded Man of Lyon', which was found in an unstratified context at Gebelein.

The intention here is not to attempt the enormous study of the figurines which remains to be made, on the basis of Ucko's initial spadework, but instead to emphasize certain analytical points which may at least succeed in indicating some potential lines of future research. With regard to the evidence discussed above, we must single out those pieces that were obtained from dated graves rather than simply purchased on the art market, although unfortunately virtually all of the best examples derive from the latter source. E. Finkenstaedt (1979) has tackled the fundamental problem of the chronology of these pieces, and her conclusion

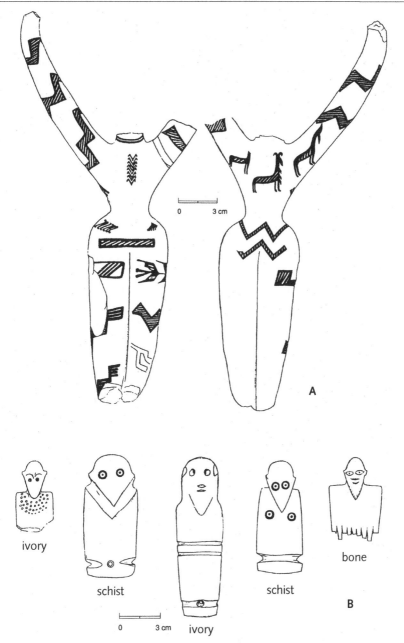

Figure 6 (a) Baked clay Predynastic figurine with geometrical motifs (after Petrie 1896: pl. LIX/6); (b) Predynastic figurines of bearded individuals, from Naqada (after Petrie and Quibell 1896: pl. LIX/1–5).

is clear: this type of evidence derives from the final phase of the Predynastic period, not the Amratian. Although her study still needs to be both widened and properly confirmed by fresh excavations, there is no doubt that the masculinity of the individuals is exclusively indicated by the beard, a secondary sexual characteristic rather than a primary one (such as the phallus or the penis-sheath). Thus, men (as opposed to women) are not represented by their sexual aspect in itself but by the social status that it confers upon them. This is reminiscent of the role of the 'false beard' in the pharaonic period, which could only be worn on the chins of the kings and certain gods.

We can see, moreover, that the rapid rise of a particular social group – a class of chiefs – is indicated by the larger dimensions of their tombs, as well as the equipment placed within them. If only a reliable diachronic analysis of these figurines can at some stage be achieved, it might corroborate Finkenstaedt's conclusions, thus providing us with the 'living' images of the first bearded rulers, the direct ancestors of the kings of Egypt.

We cannot leave the topic of human representations without mentioning two specific pottery vessels: a black-polished vessel fashioned in the shape of woman, from a grave at Diospolis Parva, and a red black-topped vessel, extracted from an unrobbed tomb at Naqada, that bears an enigmatic relief, the interpretation of which is at the very least subject to caution (figure 7). It is a human figure, the pointed nose and eyes being easily recognizable, with a line extending downwards to indicate the torso. Under this head, on either side of the supposed body, are two other lines in the form of horns which stretch up towards the top of the vessel. In the

Figure 7 Predynastic potsherd from Naqada, decorated with relief depiction on the external surface (after Capart 1904: 121, fig. 88).

lower part of the vessel, it is possible to distinguish two balls of clay from which two further lines extend, initially horizontally but then rising up towards the vessel rim. Jean Capart (1904) interpreted this as a man clinging on, embracing the entire vessel with his arms and legs. Both Vandier (1952: 288) and Baumgartel suggested that it was a double representation of a human head and a pair of horns: a fertility goddess who might have been the prototype for Hathor.

However, our current perception of this relief does not seem to be sufficient to allow us to interpret it properly. There are so many aspects of the piece that are unknown to us that we cannot reliably link it with any known symbolic vocabulary. The combined relief depiction of parts of the human body with those of animals (horns?) is certainly not accidental, but it is constructed according to a system of cultural references that is now lost to us. We can occasionally find elements of the Predynastic cognitive scheme that have survived into the pharaonic world, but to attempt to extrapolate back from the Dynastic period into prehistory is somewhat dangerous, since concepts become crammed with new cultural nuances over the course of time, acquiring different appearances, and new myths are grafted onto old rites until almost all sense of their original identity has been erased.

It was in this period that the working of hard and soft stones (schist, granite, porphyry, diorite, breccia, limestone and Egyptian alabaster) triggered off an inexorable process whereby Egypt was to become the 'stone-working civilization' *par excellence*. The first stone vessels were made at this date, initially mainly carved from soft stones, their shapes being more or less cylindrical, with a conical base and with two pierced vertical lugholes. One particular type, shaped like an inverted 'top hat', was once attributed by Petrie to Libyan invaders, on the basis that similar vessels were found at Mersa Matruh, 800 kilometres to the west of Alexandria. However, we now know that this vessel shape occurs from Naqada I onwards, and may well be a development from an ivory-carved prototype dating to the Badarian period. An excellent example from Adaïma has been published by Winifred Needler (1984: no. 116).

This period is also characterized by disc-shaped maceheads, mostly flat but some with carefully rounded surfaces. They were most frequently carved from hard stones, but there are also surviving examples in soft limestone, pottery and even unfired clay, although it tends to be assumed that these latter types were simply models made for the grave, sometimes even provided with handles. Two maces were found at Abadiya (Petrie 1901: 33, pl. 5) with handles made from ivory and horn respectively; their very small perforations (diameter *c*.6 mm) suggest that breakages must have been common, and helps to explain the presence of particularly solid binding at the junction of head and handle, and the prologation of this binding along the whole length of the handle is indicated on a painted model mace from a tomb at el-Amra (Randall-Maciver and Mace 1902: pl. XII,1). This binding is also shown on the depictions of disc-shaped maces which eventually became the hieroglyphic phonogram *mnw* (Gardiner 1969: signlist, T1). It is clear that these artefacts were serving as portable symbols of power from the fact that they were placed in large tombs, such as those at Hierakonpolis, forming essential aspects of the chieftaincy. One tomb in the Mahasna cemetery contained a rare 'biconical' macehead (Garstang 1903: pl. XX,3).

Siltstone palettes, initially rectangular, began to appear in a great diversity of shapes, including elongated ovals, sometimes incised with depictions of animals but also very often zoomorphic in form. The artists were able to incorporate the distinctive features of the animals into the overall shape, emphasizing certain details by means of incisions. This 'bestiary' included fish, turtles and crocodiles as well as birds, hippopotami and elephants. Palettes in the form of the human figure, however, were rare. One particular palette type, which Petrie named 'Pelta' (because of its similarity to Amazon shields), takes the form of a curved boat from the centre of which a rectangular shape protruded, perhaps representing a cabin. The two ends of the boat (stern and prow?) developed into birds' heads, making a link between boat and bird in a similar way to the depictions painted on Gerzean (Naqada II) pottery vessels.

These palettes were occasionally accompanied by small pebbles of jasper, still retaining in places the traces of the ochre or malachite pigments that had been ground up. They were deposited near the deceased as part of the necessary equipment for bodily adornment. The fact that they almost always have what is described as a 'suspension' hole suggests that they might originally have been physically tied to the body.

This development of stone carving did not have the effect of diminishing the production of bone and ivory objects; on the contrary these also flourished. The carving of such artefacts as punches, needles, awls, long-toothed combs with decoratd handles, hair pins, bracelets and rings, and small ivory vessels (in similar shapes to the stone vessels) both extended and elaborated the repertoire of the preceding Badarian culture.

Stone tools are comparatively rare in Naqada I graves, but they tend to have been worked to a very high standard. These delicate and long bifacially worked blades, some as much as 40 centimetres long, were finely and very regularly denticulated, and, most unusually, they had all been polished *before* the application of long, flat retouches, thus enabling the blades to gain a high degree of slenderness. This process was also used on the so-called 'fishtail lanceheads' with bifurcated blades, which are also delicately denticulated along the active part of the tool. The latter look ahead to the Old Kingdom forked instruments known as *peshes-kef*, which were used in the so-called 'opening of the mouth' funerary ceremony.

But the Amratian lithic industry was by no means restricted to such exceptional items as these. Taking into account the formerly and recently excavated living sites of the Naqada I people, Holmes (1989b) defined a flake industry, using a fine beige type of flint which was available from both the desert and the local wadis. The main types of artefact were burins (both simple and broken), endscrapers (rarely circular), denticulates and notches, perforators (including the 'large perforator', see Tixier 1963: no. 15), truncations, backed tools, rabots, and, above all, small bifacial axes, frequently sharpened with a 'tranchet blow' (a knapping method whereby a flake was removed from the end of a bifacial; see Holmes 1990). Arrowheads (generally pointed bifacials with hollow bases) are rare. Numerous elements of bifacial or blade-based sickles, with signs of sickle sheen on the denticulation, indicate the role played by plant foods in the Amratian food supply.

Glazed steatite – already known in the Badarian period – continued in use, but it was in the Naqada I phase that the first attempts at creating Egyptian faience took place. This technical process involved first the shaping of a nucleus of crushed quartz into the desired form and then the application of a coat of natron-based glaze coloured by metallic oxides. A small bird-shaped pendant from a tomb at Naqada (Petrie and Quibell 1896: pl. LX,19), dated to Naqada I by the associated red ware with white crossed decoration, is probably the earliest example of Egyptian 'faience' (Kaczmarczyk 1983: A71). The control of firing procedures, the mastery of temperature control and the chemical processes that are necessitated by such glaze-working all form the basis of developments in pyrotechnology that are indissociable from the working of metals. In terms of metalworking, however, there are few differences from the Badarian period. Copper continued to be hammered into shape, but the products were both more numerous and more varied, including pins, harpoons, beads, bracelets, anklets, points, and even a few fish-hooks, as well as the tips of bifurcated spears from a tomb in Mahasna, which are the earliest known copper imitations of worked-stone artefacts. The gradual development of links with the copper-working northern site of Maadi must also be mentioned here (see pp. 212–15 below).

Many pottery vessels were incised with signs known as 'pot-marks', usually after firing. The fact that the same signs are repeated on different pots within particular graves suggests that they might sometimes have been indications of the ownership of the vessels. There are a large number of different designs of pot mark, ranging from the figurative (e.g. humans, animals and boats) to the abstract (e.g. crescents, arrows and triangles). Petrie and Quibell (1896: pls. LI–LVII) recorded a wide variety of them, but there has not yet been any detailed study either of their chronological development or of the links that may be established with such comparable phenomena as the designs on vessels and numerous similar rock carvings.

Finally, it is worth mentioning a sherd of red-polished black-topped ware from an Amratian tomb at Naqada, the outer surface of which was modelled, before firing, into a shape closely resembling the Red Crown of Lower Egypt (figure 8a). This crown was also part of the regalia of the goddess Neith of Sais, who was one of the symbols of northern Egypt in terms of the dualism of Egyptian kingship. This representation, published by Geoffrey Wainwright (1923), has given rise to various theories attempting to explain the presence of this Delta symbol in Upper Egypt at such an early date. However, there is nothing in the current state of research to suggest either that a kingdom of Lower Egypt could already have existed in the first half of the fourth millennium BC, or that local Delta cults, such as that of Neith, could already have developed to such an extent that their influence reached as far as Upper Egypt.

On the other hand, it is noticeable that a similar type of headgear is worn by two chiefly figures whose forms are carved on the rocks at Wadi

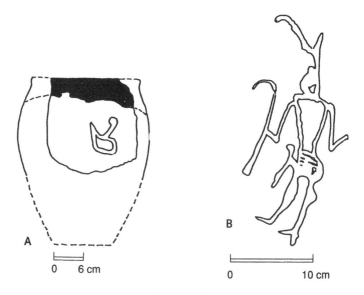

Figure 8   (a) Fragment of a black-topped red polished vessel, dating to the Naqada I period and bearing a relief decoration in the shape of the Red Crown (after Wainwright 1923: 32); (b) prehistoric rock carving in the Wadi Gash (after Winkler 1938: pl. XII1/2).

Gash in the Eastern Desert. One, dressed in a short loincloth and a penis-sheath is shown not only wearing a red crown but also holding a crook (figure 8b), which, in association with the flail or whip, was to become the principal sceptre held in the pharaoh's hand. The other, whose outfit is either less detailed or less visible, is shown holding a crook in the middle of a scene portraying the pursuit of great river beasts (rhinoceros and crocodiles), a type of hunt which usually took place in boats (Winkler 1938–9: I, pl. XIV). The presence of another figure with rounded upraised arms indicates the Naqada date of this last scene. It is not only the depiction of his apparel that makes him stand out (in a scene where the other individuals are rendered as rough sketches), but also the fact that he is positioned at the centre of the hunt, all of which suggests that he was a significant person – perhaps a chief, sorcerer or divinity – on whom the very success of the hunting may have depended.

Although the Red Crown eventually became a symbol of the Delta in the pharaonic period, there is nothing to indicate that this was originally the case, and in fact it might well have been simply adopted as such when Upper Egypt had come to dominate the north.

The first traces of Upper Egyptian settlements were found by Gertrude Caton-Thompson at Hemamia, taking the form of nine 'huts' – circular structures, varying from about 1 to 2.5 metres in diameter, partly dug out of a surface of beaten earth. Some of these can probably be regarded as human dwellings, on the basis that they included traces of hearths, but others, considering their smaller size, appear more likely to have been storage areas. The research undertaken by Fekri Hassan in the region of Khattara, since 1978, has, however, provided information allowing us to clarify our image of Amratian settlement strategies. About ten areas of occupation were located, in addition to the sites that Petrie had already identified along the low terraces overlooking the cultivated floodplain. These areas varied in size from a few thousand metres square to as much as three hectares, and the thickness of the deposits also varied considerably, ranging from a few centimetres to a full metre in depth. The ceramics and lithic material essentially conform to the Naqada I culture, although the presence of rippled potsherds meant that the remains were initially assigned to the Badarian (Hays 1984). No actual built structure has survived from this date, but the existence of numerous areas of earth rubble, as well as post-holes and hearths, suggests that mud-brick buildings were already being constructed.

Hassan's microstratigraphic analyses of thick deposits of animal dung (deriving from goats or sheep) suggest that there were up to five phases of occupation that were covered up and laterally displaced, demonstrating a phenomenon of successive phases of abandonment and reoccupation (Hassan 1988: 155). An average of 50 to 200 people seem to have occupied these sites over the course of about 200 years, at around 3750 BC, according to the average of the calibrated radiocarbon dates (Hassan 1985, 1988).

It is at Hierakonpolis, however, that the first indications of a truly new type of settlement have been found. When the American team (Hoffman 1980) excavated in a sector known as locality 29, they uncovered a set of remains comprising some type of oven or kiln and a rectangular house superimposed on the earlier traces of enclosures, dated by material relating to the Naqada I culture. The kiln, which was very damaged, measured about 5 × 6 metres and contained eight depressions, each 50–80 centimetres in diameter. In three of these depressions were found baked mud bricks which appear to have served as firedogs; in one depression, it was clear that these bricks had been placed in a triangular arrangement. A significant quantity of sherds deriving from large jars, which were found all around the oven suggest that pottery vessels of this type (the diameters of which varied from 50 to 100 centimetres) may have been placed on the firedogs and may themselves have contained many smaller vessels during the process of firing.

An unfortunate gust of wind had evidently caused the neighbouring house (perhaps the potter's) to catch fire. But this piece of bad luck for an Amratian inhabitant of Hierakonpolis worked to the advantage of the archaeologists who excavated the charred, solidified and preserved remains almost 6000 years later. These excavations revealed a rectangular, partly subterranean dwelling, measuring 4 × 3.5 metres (Hoffman 1982: figure VI,4). The walls of the substructure, reaching a depth of 40–80 centimetres, had been plastered with a mixture of mud and dung, as well as mud-brick rubble, the latter suggesting that such bricks were already in use. This mortar created a solid base for the eight posts (arranged in two rows of three and one of two), which must have supported the superstructure. On the basis of the height of the posts, indicated along the walls by accumulations of carbonized material, the overall height of the building is estimated to have been about 1.45 metres. On the northern and eastern sides of the house, small trenches show that there must once have been light outer walls of some kind, similar to modern enclosures. The entrance must also have been to the east. Inside the house were several fittings, including an oven, built on a mud platform which must have been created at the same time as the main building, a storage pot and a large upside-down vessel, all of which indicated cooking activities, suggesting to Hoffman that this structure might actually have been one specialized element of a more important complex.

The existence of well-built rectangular houses, firmly anchored into the ground, does not, however, rule out the presence of circular huts such as those at Hemamia, and the sense of a diversity of types of dwelling is echoed by our impression of economic and social variety at this date. The more ephemeral huts might correspond to temporary encampments during the seasonal exploitation of pastureland, whereas the more permanent Hierakonpolis house might be an indication of the emergence, during Naqada I, of more important centres which would soon be characterized by even more extensive development.

The faunal remains at Amratian settlements show that they were raising 'stock' comprising various domesticated species: goats, sheep, bovids and pigs, which even accompanied the deceased into the afterlife in the form of small clay figurines. The wildlife exploited by the Amratian people included gazelles and fish, remains of which are always present in large numbers. Barley and wheat were cultivated, perhaps alongside peas and vetch, as well as *nabk* berries from the Christ's-thorn bush (*Zizyphus spina-christi*) and a possible ancestor of the watermelon, all of which helped to expand the variety of available food sources.

When we consider the question of the origins and identity of the Naqada I people, we must accept the fact that there was no sudden cultural break between the people of the Badarian and Naqada periods, and in fact our most pressing problem now is to determine which cultural traits relate to each of these cultural entities.

The heartland of the Amratian culture is undoubtedly the Naqada-Mahasna region, for there we find not only the highest density of of Naqada I sites but also the the very earliest subphases of the Naqada culture, according to the ceramic analyses undertaken by Kaiser (1957; see also Appendices 1 and 2 of this volume). The Amratian culture expanded northwards into the territory traditionally associated with the Badarian, and also southwards, as far as Khor Bahan, 20 kilometres beyond the First Cataract; in this peripheral location there emerged a late form of the Naqada I culture that corresponds to the period just before the Amratian became absorbed into the emerging Gerzean (Naqada II) culture. The relationship between the Badarian and Amratian cultures therefore raises the question of their chronological order: which came first?

In the sub-breccia stratum at Hemamia, Kaiser (1956) noted that there were many Amratian-style potsherds that Caton-Thompson unhesitatingly described as Badarian, despite the fact that the site had even produced a virtually complete vessel bearing one of the pot-marks that are known only from the Naqada I phase. Conversely, Naqada I sites have sometimes included rippled sherds characteristic of the Badarian. Indeed, as we have already noted above, the presence of such sherds led Hays (1984) to mistakenly identify the el-Khattara occupations as Badarian, whereas a more thorough analysis of the whole set of artefacts resulted in their reattribution to the Naqada I culture or possibly even the early Naqada II.

It is partly for this reason that Diane Holmes (1989b: 182) wisely suggests that we should be cautious concerning Badarian-style sherds found at sites outside the Badarian heartland of Matmar-Mostagedda; she argues that we need to assess the full range of artefacts at such a site before identifying it as Badarian. The distinction between Badarian and Amratian appears to be a somewhat elastic boundary which should be expressed in vaguer terms, such as the presence of 'dominant traits', leaving to one side the question of their actual chronological succession. Indeed, the results of recent fieldwork in the Badari region (Holmes 1989a; Holmes and Friedman 1994) appear to be moving towards the same conclusion. Between the Badarian and the Gerzean, there is no Amratian phase representing the kind of intermediate stage that we might expect. Thus it seems as if the Amratian people were either never settled in the Matmar-Mostagedda region or were only present to a small extent; alternatively, it might be argued that their presence is simply not indicated by the same ceramic types as in Upper Egypt.

Although it still seems likely that the Badarian culture essentially emerged at an earlier date than the Amratian – given that the radiocarbon dates support this, and the stratified sequence discovered at Hierakonpolis (Hoffman 1989) certainly doesn't seem to contradict it. It also seems very probable that the Badarian heartland (the Matmar-Mostagedda region) was characterized by a local tradition that continued in existence alongside the upper Egytian Amratian sequence. Some trade must have taken place between these two regions, and this might explain the presence of sherds with rippled surfaces in the southern part of the Badarian region, which is the only instance of 'Amratianizing' in the Badarian zone. It is within this kind of regional perspective that we should view the Tasian culture, which Kaiser claims to have northern origins. Thus the Tasian might have functioned as a means by which the northern cultures were able to influence the early Naqada culture. This is an important element in the question of origins and identity which was posed above. We are currently experiencing difficulties in establishing a continuous cultural sequence from the Tarifian (our knowledge of which is still much too poor) to the Amratian, but the discovery in the late 1980s of very early levels at Hierakonpolis, dating back to the period before Naqada I – below the water table and therefore accessible only through the use of pumps – suggests that we should not reject the theory of a buried ancestral tradition, and it also emphasizes the degree to which our knowledge of these early cultures is dictated by the vagaries of Nile water levels. Perhaps we might even be entitled to feel that the whole destiny of the land is linked with that of its river.

The Gerzean (Naqada II)

The very northerly location of el-Gerza, the type site of the Gerzean culture, 5 kilometres to the northeast of the Meidum pyramid, immediately signals the fact that this second phase of the Naqada culture was essentially a phase of geographical expansion. The sites, consisting of both cemeteries and settlements, were no longer limited to the Naqada-Matmar (Luxor-Qena) section of the valley but were attested by three extensive cemeteries near the Faiyum region (el-Gerza, Haraga and Abusir el-Melek), the large group of graves recently found at Minshat Abu Omar (in the eastern Delta) and, in the south, a series of points of contact with the Nubian A Group.

There was already a growing tendency, in the Naqada I phase, for fewer and fewer individuals to be buried in tombs which were increasingly large, well-built and equipped with ever richer and more abundant grave goods. This trend began to accelerate in the Naqada II phase, ultimately creating a situation where the most colossal tomb ever constructed would be occupied by only one man: the pharaoh.

The Gerzean burials were generally simple pits containing single bodies. Sometimes an inhumation might include two bodies but there were rarely any more than this (the five bodies in grave T15 at Naqada being something of an exception). The corpse is usually found crouched in a foetal position, but the precise position of the body began to vary from one cemetery to another, with the Naqada I rules (laying it on its left side, with head to the south and face to the west) gradually becoming subject to more and more exceptions. The wrapping of the body in an animal skin – a custom that was unknown in the north – became much rarer, and instead mats or linen cloths began to be more widely used for this purpose. Children began to be buried in large pottery vessels (sometimes upturned), but the most significant development was the emergence of the coffin – initially made from basketry, then clay, and finally wood – which may have been the main reason why the shape of the graves belonging to 'richer' individuals became more rectangular. Certain funerary offerings began to be placed separately from the body, and these have been found in cubbyholes or compartments that were to make the structure of the tomb as a whole more and more elaborate, becoming more and more structural and compartmentalized with the use of earth, wood and mud bricks. Thus, only the offerings closely linked with the body itself (e.g. jewellery, weapons and cosmetic palettes) would presumably be at the immediate disposal of the deceased in the hereafter, scattered around the corpse according to a patterning system that is obscure to us now (special significance, for example, evidently being ascribed to objects that were placed directly by the face), whereas the other funerary goods (e.g. pottery and baskets) were placed separately from the corpse on benches, in compartments or in cubbyholes. The separation of the body from the grave goods was a phenomenon that became increasingly accentuated, constituting one of the basic principles of the Egyptian tomb.

The wide range of types of funerary arrangement in Gerzean cemeteries – small round pits with hardly any funerary equipment, burials inside pottery vessels, oval or rectangular pits with varying amounts of grave goods, different types of body wrappings and coffins, and varying numbers and quality of offerings – all reflect the growing complexity of the social structure, which was becoming both more diversified and more hierarchical.

In a study of artists and patrons in Predynastic Egypt, Whitney Davis (1983b) discussed the evidence provided by the main Naqada cemetery, consisting of nearly 3000 graves, among which the burials of artists and craftsmen were clearly differentiated by their distinctive grave goods. It appears that the same phenomenon was responsible for the inclusion among grave goods of fine flint knives (known as 'Predynastic knives', see Midant-Reynes 1987), since these do not appear in all graves but can sometimes indicate the 'richness' of particular burials.

This situation is the case with inhumations in cemeteries B, G and T at Naqada, each consisting of less than a hundred graves and all located at something of a remove from the main cemetery. Chronologically, they cover virtually the whole of the Gerzean period, but they differ from other graves at Naqada with regard to certain factors: their large size (T4 = 3.5 × 2 m, T5 = 4 × 2.8 m), a certain degree of wealth with regard to the quality of grave goods, and finally their evidence of unusual funerary rites. Grave T5 is of particular interest in that it was found intact (according to Petrie) and contained human remains piled along the walls, indicating the presence of secondary burials. Five crania had been carefully arranged, with the one in the centre placed on top of a brick, but it was impossible to determine whether these, along with the post-cranial bones, amounted to the full skeletons of five individuals. Petrie hypothesized that teeth marks and breaks on the long bones constituted evidence of cannibalism, but this theory has been criticized firstly by Hoffman (1980b: 116), who points out that none of these bones show any signs of burning (although he notes that human sacrifice is still a possibility), and secondly by Davis (1983a: 27), who argues that none of the five individuals appears to have suffered a violent death and that the marks on the bones could have been made posthumously, especially given that these were simply secondary inhumations.

Whatever the explanation, cemetery T at Naqada was distinguished by this combination of unusual features which suggest that it was connected with an elite group – princes perhaps (Kaiser and Dreyer 1982), or a 'definite class' (Davis 1983a) – and the same no doubt applies to cemeteries B and G, although the degree of grave robbing has been detrimental to any attempts at interpretation. The Gerzean material culture, resting on a Badarian/Amratian basis, was replete with technical innovations, technological refinements and new methods.

Two new types of pottery appeared: firstly the so-called 'rough' ware (Petrie's R-ware), which is considered to be an indication of influence from outside, and secondly a marly type of pottery made from calcareous clay (Petrie's L-ware), which is regarded as a sign of better knowledge of the environment. The rough ware, which emerged at the beginning of the Naqada II phase, according to Kaiser, seems to have appeared earlier in settlements, but its beginnings are still somewhat vague in terms of chronology. It was fashioned partly from Nile silt, tempered with straw and plant remains, and when lightly fired, it acquired a brownish-red colour. It was never polished but simply burnished, and was decorated with unusual incised motifs. The shapes, whether open or closed, very often had rounded or pointed bases, and these forms were then 'passed on' to the red-polished black-topped vessels. Towards the end of the phase, this trend was reversed, with rough ware vessels beginning to have flat bases.

The L-ware was made from clay obtained from the mouths of certain wadis; it contained no organic material, and the clay tempered with sand produced a pale pink colour when it was fired at low temperatures, and a greyish-green colour when it was exposed to greater heat. Its texture was hard and smooth, and its method of production has led to the suggestion that slow turntables may already have been in use, in the form of simple mats which the potter would have turned manually. Since this ware was burnished rather than polished, it belongs to Kaiser's subphase Naqada IIb. Out of the L-ware developed two of Petrie's other categories: 'decorated' (D-ware) and 'wavy-handled' (W-ware), on which he based his well-known sequence dating system (see Appendix 1).

The decorated Gerzean pottery was characterized by blackish-brown motifs painted on a cream background and was produced in large quantities as a replacement for red Amratian pottery with white-painted decoration. However, the survival of the latter into the early Gerzean period, and the coexistence of the two decorated types resulted in the production of Amratian pottery bearing Gerzean-style decoration, as well as cream Gerzean-style vessels bearing brown-painted Amratian-style motifs (Vandier 1952: 330–2).

The motifs decorating Gerzean pottery are of two basic types: firstly non-figurative (e.g. marks imitating stone, spirals, serpentine lines, waves and checker-patterns) and secondly scenes (figure 9), which have been

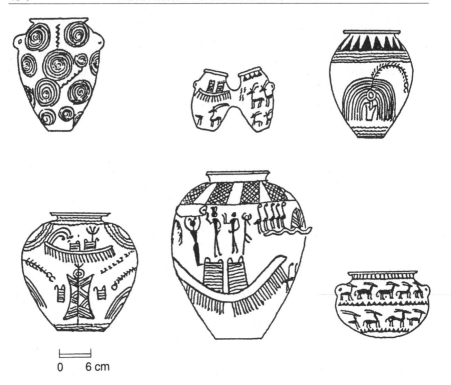

0   6 cm

Figure 9   Gerzean (Naqada II) pottery vessels (after Petrie 1953: pls. XXXIII/ 35N, 36H, 41U, pl. XXXIV 46D, 47M, 49F).

the source of some debate (see Vandier 1952: 336–9; Midant-Reynes 1987: 205, n. 47). Generally speaking, the repertoire of decoration on Gerzean vessels is limited to about ten elements which were depicted either in isolation or combined together according to a system that has never been elucidated. As already noted above (Midant-Reynes 1987: 207), these themes express the basic elements of the Egyptian world, such as water, which was indicated by the frequent depiction of boats (their scale often making them the centre-pieces of scenes), obviously playing a crucial role in a land that was entirely dependent on its river. The boats with rounded bottoms, their prows occasionally decorated with branches or horned animals, have one or two cabins and sometimes large numbers of oars, symbolizing rapid movement, which emphasizes the river's role as an artery of communication.

   These boats were usually surrounded by various images organized across a space which was not yet given any concrete form; these often included animals, some of which were characteristic of the Nile environment, including such birds as flamingoes, while others were part of the desert ecology, such as gazelles and antelopes. The motifs around the boats also featured schematic indications of brown and white land (perhaps interpretable as the two opposite poles of valley and desert) as well as trees, some probably representing aloes, willows, palms and a wild banana tree, recalling the basic element of nourishing vegetation. A recent study on this subject (Brack and Zoller 1989) discusses the specific botanical and morphological criteria for identifying wild banana trees (*Ensete ventricosum*) among these motifs, although Karl Butzer had already refuted this identification on the ecological basis that this species grows in Central Africa at an altitude of 2500 metres above sea level. Although, as Brack and Zoller suggest, climatic conditions were different in the Predynastic period, it is nevertheless the case that no pollen analysis of the Naqada region (Wetterstrom 1980, 1996; Emery-Barbier 1990) has yet located any *Ensete ventricosum*.

The human figure is never the dominant image in these scenes, appearing instead as a fairly minor element in the overall scheme. Women, identifiable on the basis of their steatopygy, with their arms raised above their heads in a curved fashion, seem to occupy a privileged position, judging from their relatively large size, although this impression is tempered by the almost constant presence of their male acolytes. More frequently, however, the occupants of the boats are asexual, each simply comprising a round ball placed on top of an inverted triangle, but it seems unlikely that these were mummies or statues, as F. el-Yakhi (1981) suggests. Brunner-Traut (1975) interprets the scenes as depictions of waterborne funeral cortèges like those that travelled up and down the Nile in pharaonic times, but it seems that we must be suspicious of such overt Egyptological references and be careful not to force the well-structured elements of the pharaonic repertoire onto a cultural scenario which was still in its early stages. Far from being pure descriptions, these scenes, according to Cauvin (1972: 11) 'refer to something pyschic, beyond their mere physical selves' and we will get nowhere unless we attempt to study them in terms of semiotics. In this sense our position is diametrically opposed to that of Jacques Vandier (1952: 330), who claims that 'the scenes depicted in the Naqada II phase do not generally signify anything, and their component parts are, with only a few exceptions, linked together in a way which is – or at least seems to us – totally arbitrary'.

From a chronological point of view, spiral decoration appeared from Kaiser's Naqada IIb onwards, followed by figurative scenes from IIc onwards; these decorated types gradually diminished in number until they vanished completely in the next phase, apart from the continuation of decorative schemes involving waves and checker patterns. It is not unusual for these vessels to have wavy handles modelled in relief, representing their 'degeneration' from functional handles to decorative motifs, which formed one of the basic premises of Petrie's intuitively derived sequence dating system (see Appendix 1).

The wavy-handled vessels are made in the same marl ware as the decorated pots. According to Kaiser, they first appeared in the middle of the Naqada II phase; they are contemporary with the jars with handles found at Maadi, which derived from Palestine and were used to transport oils. Contrary to the situation in Upper Egypt (where wavy-handled vases appeared out of the blue), the Palestinian vessels with handles have a long history of development, stretching back to the early Chalcolithic levels of stratum VII at Jericho and stratum XVIII at Beth Shan (Kantor 1965: 7–10). This area of cultural overlap between Upper Egypt and Palestine is all the more significant because the first wavy-handled vessels in Egypt were not local copies but actual imports (Amiran and Glass 1979). Maadi can thus be viewed as an actual staging post between Sinai and Upper Egypt, the first Egyptian site with a commercial role, breaking the comparative silence between the south and north in the Amratian period.

This pottery type develops in the way that Petrie deduced, from globular forms with pronounced handles to cylindrical forms on which the handles had become mere decoration, sometimes only painted on. The cylindrical jar with a painted wavy line around the middle thus became the most characteristic ceramic type of the Naqada III phase, judging particularly from the fragment found in tomb B7 at Abydos, dated to the reign of Ka (Petrie 1902: 3), who ruled just before the beginning of the 1st Dynasty.

In the other direction, towards Nubia, contacts are indicated by the existence of so-called 'Nubian' pottery, characterized by a silty fabric tempered either with animal dung or with an ashy mixture, fired at a low temperature which gives it a more porous and lighter texture than Egyptian pottery. Cups or open vessels with rounded or pointed bases, their exteriors lightly polished and bearing incised decoration (originally filled with white pigment) and/or somewhat blackened rims. This pottery is the diagnostic feature of a group of people whom we will discuss later in this chapter: the 'A Group'.

During the Naqada II period, there was considerable development in techniques of stoneworking: various different colours of limestone, calcites, marbles, serpentine, basalt, breccia, gneiss, diorite, gabbro and granites were naturally available all the way along the Nile Valley, and in the ancient formations of the Eastern Desert, particularly the Wadi Hammamat (see Klemm and Klemm 1981). The increasing production of jars with carved bases and handles, imitating pottery forms (especially the wavy handles), demonstrates the precocious mastery of hard stones, skills which foreshadowed the great achievements of pharaonic stone architecture.

As Rizkana and Seeher (1988: 56) have suggested, stone vessels, unlike pottery, could not have been used for everyday domestic purposes, but were instead restricted to luxurious functions as receptacles for high-quality products. In their imitation of stone vessels in clay they were replacing an object made from rarer material (perhaps even monopolized by a certain social class) with the cheapest and most easily obtained of all materials. There can be little doubt that the stoneworkers (like the potters, flint-knappers and metalworkers) were thus already operating as specialized workshops. We will return later to the socio-economic changes which effectively 'released' these non-productive social groups.

The production of zoomorphic cosmetic palettes, carved from schist, had been one of the salient characteristics of the Naqada I period, but these now became fewer in number, evolving towards simple rhomboidal shapes, often surmounted by two confronting animal heads. At the same time, however, they began to be decorated with reliefs, starting a line of development towards the narrative-style decorated palettes of the Naqada III period. The Manchester Palette (figure 10a), for example, is decorated with a relief carving of a row of three ostriches followed by a man clearly wearing a bird's head (perhaps a mask) which replicates the birds' heads at the top of the palette, separated by five crests perhaps indicating wings. A similar palette from a tomb at el-Amra bears a relief carving evidently representing the hieroglyphic sign *men*, which could be used to designate the god Min (figure 10b). Another palette, carved in a shortened oval shape, has one of its faces totally filled by a cow's head with stars perched at the ends of the horns, by each ear and above the crown of the head, thus evidently comprising a celestial cow which prefigures the goddess Hathor of the historical period (figure 10c).

The disc-shaped macehead of the Amratian period was replaced by the pear-shaped type, examples of which had already appeared at an earlier date in the settlement of Merimda Beni Salama. Mystery still surrounds the mechanisms by which the pear-shaped mace was adopted by the people of the Gerzean culture; the fact is that it became a symbol of power which was so vibrant that it lasted into the pharaonic period. The pear-shaped mace was to become the archetypal weapon with which the pharaoh massacred his enemies, from the Narmer Palette to the scenes on the pylons of New Kingdom temples. The well-known mace found in the wealthy tomb of an A-Group chief at Sayala in Nubia (figure 11), with its handle covered in gold foil and bearing repoussé depictions of 10 animals, speaks eloquently enough of the degree of power that would have been invested in the possessor of such an object. A second example of this type of mace, found in the same tomb, is decorated with horizon-

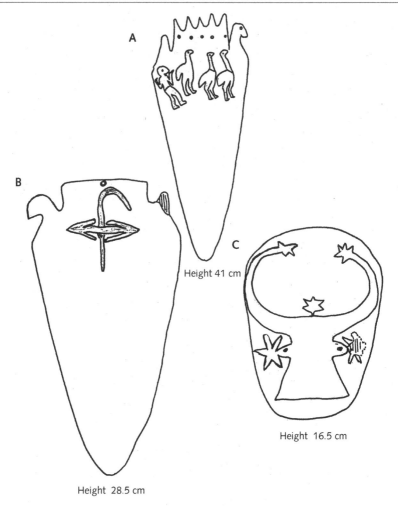

Height 41 cm

Height 28.5 cm

Height 16.5 cm

Figure 10   (a) The Manchester Palette (after Petrie 1953: pl. A2); (b) the Min Palette (after Petrie 1953: pl. A1); (c) the Hathor Palette (after Petrie 1953: pl. B.5).

tal ridges signifying the cord which would have been wrapped tightly around the handle (Firth 1927: 205–8). Like the disc-shaped mace, it became a hieroglyphic symbol, serving to write the phonogram *hedj* (bright/white).

It was also at this date that the copper industry began to flourish. Two copper axe-heads were discovered by Henri de Morgan at the site of Adaïma inside a pottery vessel that can be dated to the Naqada II phase (the specific corpus type being R.81). These axe blades, imitating pol-

Height = 27 cm

Figure 11   The Sayala mace (after Firth 1927: 205, fig. 8).

ished stone, had been cast in open moulds and finished off by hammering. Such copper artefacts as blades, bracelets and rings became much
more common, and the intensification of copper metallurgy took place
in tandem with the production of gold and silver. We know nothing
about the metalworkers themselves at this date, since the first representations of metalworking do not appear until the scenes on the walls of
some Old Kingdom *mastaba*-tombs showing furnaces heated up by tuyères
through which the air was blown by the workmen (as in the scenes in the
tombs of Ti and Mereruka). The ability to process metal ores in this way
is a likely indication of such factors as the ability to mobilize labour

forces and the creation of a group of 'non-producers', who would, moreover, have benefited from the prestige associated with precious metal. Indeed the desire to obtain these materials *at any cost* was ultimately to result in the greatest acts of malevolence that it would be possible for an Egyptian to imagine: tomb robbing. The careful excavation of cemeteries has constantly uncovered clear proof that it was in order to get hold of such finger rings, steal such anklets, and snatch such objects from chests that most of the graves were pillaged by the same people who had seen the funerals taking place, the same ones who, sometimes with astonishing precision, sought out these metal objects that they coveted beyond anything else.

A great deal of jewellery was produced, including beads made from bone, stone, ivory, shells, faience (replacing the glazed steatite) and lapis lazuli. The latter, a beautiful translucent blueish-green mineral came from the Badakshan region of northern Afghanistan, reaching Egypt, in the form of imported fragments, via indirect contacts with traders in Mesopotamia. Among the numerous pendant amulets, the 'bovid's head' (Petrie and Quibell 1896: pl. LXI,4) was reproduced in ivory, bone and a wide variety of stones. Rather than being primitive in style, the schematic nature of the lines shows a great mastery of the artistic image, the curve of the top of the skull is extended by down-turning horns which turn inwards below the eyes (two holes which were doubtless originally inlaid) and contrasts with the flat lower surface which gives a definite sense of the bovid's muzzle. The back is horizontally pierced to take a suspension cord, which would have held the object in a perfectly stable position. This small amulet, which is found in association with beaded necklaces, was undoubtedly worn for its magical properties, and the precision with which it was reproduced in such large numbers suggests that it was being produced by certain specialized workshops. Clearly we can assume a link with the 'celestial cow' depicted on the siltstone palette, but the reason for the amulet's inverted horns is probably purely technical: small horns that rose upwards from the surface of an ivory or stone object could have easily been broken off, which would have been detrimental to the amulet's purpose.

Long-toothed bone or ivory combs, surmounted by small animals, quickly declined in frequency. It has been suggested by Ludwig Keimer (1952: 64–77) that they might have been used to decorate men's hair, as is the case with nomads of the Eastern Desert, and the fact that some combs were decorated with a bearded head not only helps to corroborate Finkenstaedt's theory concerning symbols of masculinity but also supports the hypothesis proposed above whereby the heads of bearded men might have served as the essential symbols of a dominant social class.

Apart from the well-known bearded figures, which have already been discussed, the human body is most commonly represented in the Gerzean period by female statuettes with upraised arms, one of the finest examples of which (New York, Brooklyn; Needler 1984: 336, no. 267) was found in a tomb at Ma'marya in Upper Egypt; made out of terracotta coated with red slip, it has a 'bird face', a triangular upper torso and small breasts situated high on the body and slightly pendulous, their small scale contrasting with the swelling of the hips and buttocks. Her legs are indicated only by a slight groove in the compact, pointed mass of the lower body, which must have represented a dress, perhaps attested by traces of white paint. The arms, however, are raised up in two elegant curves stretching back a little to the rear of the head, which bears traces of resin, suggesting that hair (or a wig) must have been originally attached.

The question of the significance of these female figurines, which are the three-dimensional equivalents of the women painted on Gerzean vessels, is still some way from being resolved. The fact is that, like all of the Predynastic statuettes, they are not found in every grave, and, even if we took into account all of the pieces that have simply been bought rather than acquired by excavation, the total number of figurines would not even be close to the number of excavated tombs. Not everyone was provided with a female figurine. We might regard them, with considerable justification, as symbols of femininity linked with some kind of fertility ceremony, but it appears nevertheless that they particularized certain individuals within a cognitive system that is still totally obscure to us.

There are also many terracotta representations of animals, but it is often difficult to identify the type of animal being portrayed.

The image we have of the Egyptian economy at this date shows that the first stage of development of specialized workshops had been reached. The potters were producing vessels on a large scale, while at the same time painters were enriching this basic product, working within an organizational system that was already very strict. The rigidity of this system shows that the workshops were simultaneously functioning as the very places where sets of images and symbols were defined and taught; the limited number of themes is quite striking. The same can be deduced concerning the workshops of stoneworkers, whether producing vessels from hard stone or fine knives from flint, and metalworkers, whose activities, as we have shown above, were linked with the prestige of the metals.

Culturally speaking, Gerzean society had thus definitely crossed the threshold, although in a sense the real breakthrough had already been made in the preceding phase, in the form of the maintenance of groups of non-producers. It would, however, probably be premature to suggest that the Naqada I craftsmen were already subject to an overall ideology, as we assume was the case in the Naqada II phase. It seems virtually certain that, within a defined system, the Gerzean workmen followed a set of precise rules, formulated and prescribed by a group who had already achieved social dominance. It also seems extremely likely that a certain prestige was by now associated with these workers' vocations as craftsmen.

It is generally considered that each 'non-producing' craft-worker or official would have had to be supported by at least 50 agricultural 'producers', which would suggest that the total number of non-producers, in the large urban centres, would have been no more than a few hundred. Indeed, the high point of the Naqada II phase was the appearance of the first cities, residences of the elite, centres of cultural and commercial development, where the most skilful craftsmen were based.

Three principal centres arose in Upper Egypt: Naqada, Hierakonpolis (and perhaps later Elkab) and Abydos. The importance of the latter would become especially apparent at the end of the Predynastic and at the beginning of the pharaonic period, since it was here that the necropolis of the first pharaohs was to be located. Naqada, located at the mouth of the Wadi Hammamat (but on the west bank of the river), had already been the site of an Amratian settlement for about 500 years. Its continued importance during the Naqada II phase is therefore not surprising, and its pharaonic name, Nubt ('[town] of gold'), clearly indicates the importance of the settlement's links with the gold and copper mines of the Eastern Desert.

Two large residential zones were uncovered at Naqada by Petrie and Quibell (1896): the 'South Town' (in the central part of the site) and the 'North Town' (north of Naqada proper and immediately to the south of Ballas). The South Town, which undoubtedly corresponds to the site of Tukh visited by de Morgan (1896: 87–8, 1897: 39), incorporates a large rectangular mud-brick structure measuring 50 x 30 m, excavated by Petrie, which may possibly be the remains of a temple or a royal residence. To the south of this large structure, a group of rectangular houses and a 2-metre-thick enclosure wall can be made out on Petrie's plan (Petrie and Quibell 1896: pl. LXXXV). None of these walls, however, were relocated by the American team working at the site in the 1980s, who excavated several sondages in this very disturbed area of nearly 3 hectares in order both to examine the surviving traces and to assess the likelihood of obtaining radiocarbon dates. Although they had only limited success in terms of tracking down further traces of the settlement itself, they managed to obtain an average calibrated date of 3440 ± 70 BC from undisturbed deposits in a trench excavated in the northeastern section of the site. In addition, the analysis of surface material (Hassan and Matson 1989) revealed that the settlement had gradually moved, during the

Naqada II phase, from the southwest towards the northeast (the latter being the part of the site where Petrie's 'town' was located), in other words, from the desert towards the river. A similar phenomenon has been identified at Hierakonpolis (Hoffman 1984) and Adaïma (Midant-Reynes *et al.* 1990).

The North Town appears to be a limited area of man-made deposits, covering four hectares, where burials of very young children were excavated (Petrie and Quibell 1896: 1–2). A scientific surface survey (Hassan 1989) has revealed that the North Town, like the South, gradually moved during the Gerzean period, but in this case it was expanding both southwards and northwards, away from the centre of the region, at the same time as the South Town's late phase. No radiocarbon dates have yet been obtained from the North Town deposits.

Diane Holmes (1989b) has conducted a detailed study of the lithic material from the entire area of Naqada, emphasizing temporary variations within a very specific local industry. The tools were manufactured from nodules of good quality local flint deriving from the upper layers of the wadi environments. This is a flake-tool industry, in which the flakes were removed with a single platform; it evolved towards the greater production of standard blades of the type that have been found in the later parts of the North and South towns. The main categories of tools are represented by burins (some made by breaking, some by retouching an edge and others taking the form of dihedral burins), endscrapers, notches and retouched flakes, but the repertoire also includes perforators, truncations, backed tools, rabots (planes), chipped stone axe-heads and various bifacial implements. Parts of composite sickles are essentially found at the North and South towns. The assemblages of lithics found in Naqada graves consist of a funerary range of artefacts, which were initially assumed to be representative of the whole industry (until the domestic assemblages began to be studied). Beautiful blades and bladelets are the most common type, representing an unusual and specialized method of production whereby the flint was heated before being worked, thus increasing the sharpness of the tool and making it shinier and often much more aesthetically pleasing. Two remarkable finds are a flake and tool of obsidian, a material that is fundamentally foreign to the Nile valley (for further discussion of probable sources of obsidian, see pp. 236–7).

But it was the large bifacial blades of the Gerzean period that best exemplified the total mastery of the knapping of flint that had been achieved by this date. From great blocks of the finest quality flint, using a combination of percussion, pressure-flaking and polishing, they were able to produce very long and narrow blades, the forms of which developed from the elongated leaf shape to the classic knife blade, with one straight edge and the other gently convex, as well as an impressive point. They were also producing archaic-style fishtail lanceheads, the lines of which gradually evolved, accentuating the concave nature of the forked end in order to obtain an image of two opposing horns (Casini 1974). Ripple-bladed knives – such as the well-known Gebel el-Arak knife in the Louvre, with its decorated hippopotamus-ivory handle – are among the high points of the art of flint-working (Midant-Reynes 1987). Thus, like the stone vessels, metal artefacts and ceramics, these flint implements – masterpieces of worked stone – indicate the development of a group of specialized craftsmen, plying their trade alongside other workshops, according to precise standards. Both the workers' existence and the nature of their products were equally regarded as part of the responsibilities of society as a whole.

Naqada, despite its extensive cemeteries, was eclipsed at this date by Hierakonpolis (Nekhen), 17 kilometres to the northwest of Edfu, which was an urban centre recognized by the Egyptians themselves as a very ancient place, the heartland of the first pharaohs and capital of an early Upper Egyptian kingdom. Archaeological remains have survived in abundance at Hierakonpolis, and among the earliest is an immense area of Predynastic villages and cemeteries not only stretching for a distance of 2.5 kilometres along the floodplain (disappearing into the north), but also extending for about 3.5 kilometres into the so-called 'great wadi'. The earliest occupation at the site, however, stretches back to the final phase of the Palaeolithic, c.15,000 BP, judging from artefacts discovered in association with sediments dating to the end of the Pleistocene. No material has yet been found dating to the period between the late Palaeolithic and the Predynastic (the earliest traces of which go back at least as far as the Amratian).

Archaeological research at Hierakonpolis began at the very end of the nineteenth century, when James Quibell and Frederick Green (1902) unearthed the remains of an Early Dynastic religious precinct within which a temple had been founded in the Predynastic period and then reconstructed in the Early Dynastic period. The 'votive objects' belonging to the temple were found hidden in a cache: the famous 'main deposit', which contained some of the most important artefacts relating to the beginning of Egyptian history.

Among the poorly-published burials at Hierakonpolis is the famous Tomb 100 (the 'Painted Tomb'), which incorporated, partly preserved on its walls, the only funerary mural paintings that have so far been found from the Egyptian prehistoric period (see pp. 207–10 and figure 13).

After a very informative visit to the site by Kaiser (1961b), a more exhaustive study was undertaken by Barbara Adams (1974), and from

1978 onwards large-scale excavations were undertaken by an American team initially inspired by Walter Fairservis and directed by Michael Hoffman. These excavations were a multidisciplinary enterprise intended to place the site and its history in their palaeoecological context. In order to achieve this aim, a general survey was undertaken, followed by a series of sondages in various 'localities', over an immense area of the site; the results of the excavations at 'Locality 29' have already been mentioned above. The general image that has emerged concerning this long period of occupation (fixed by calibrated radiocarbon dates to *c.*3800–3100 BC) is of a movement of the population towards the river, characterized by an apparent concentration of Gerzean material near the modern cultivation (Locality 34b). According to Hoffman (1984: 239), several factors, probably operating in combination, can explain this topographical development of the settlement:

- the rapid degradation of the fragile desert ecosystem because of intensive exploitation of the vegetation, the pasturelands for livestock, the gathering of fuel for fires (particularly in connection with pottery kilns);
- general climatic change towards greater aridity;
- the defensive clustering of the community in the more important parts of the site, which were thus under greater threat from hostile forces;
- the development of a subsistence base that was more adapted to the annual flooding of the river plain;
- the attraction of the river, as the most important conduit for trade;
- finally, the fact that Hierakonpolis was an emerging religious centre, an important centre for power and prestige, and therefore an area where the social, political and ideological aspects of Egyptian culture were integrated.

In practical terms, there are two principal parts of Hierakonpolis that have been dated to the Amratian phase of occupation: Locality 29, covering an area of more than 200,000 m^2, stretches alongside the modern cultivation (which probably partially covers it), and Locality 11, a smaller area of 68,400 m^2, situated two kilometres into the desert at the point where the 'great wadi' leaves the high desert and broadens out into the floodplain. Beside Locality 11 there are also a few smaller areas of associated settlement. The excavations suggest that the main site (Locality 29) was more intensively occupied, while Locality 11 seems to have been a secondary centre connected with pasture-land and the distribution of pottery (given the presence of pottery kilns). The study of domestic fauna (sheep, goats, cattle, pigs and dogs; see McArdle 1982) reveals significant differences between the two sites; in particular, a greater proportion of sheep and goats at Locality 11, with an emphasis on the large number of young animals being slaughtered.

The Gerzean settlement was limited to a 300-metre strip along the edge of the modern cultivation; three sites cover an area of about 36,400 m², with the greatest density of population being at Locality 34b. In each case there is Amratian settlement immediately below the Gerzean remains.

A particular type of domestic structure is associated with this period: large rectangular rooms which are still visible because of their dry-stone foundations. The first rectangular houses, with mud walls, had already emerged in the Amratian period, but the characteristic appearance of the dwellings of the pharaonic period is already foreshadowed by the discovery, in a Gerzean tomb at el-Amra, of a small terracotta model house (British Museum EA35505; see figure 12a), which represents an important advance. Rectangular in shape, wider at the base than the top, its walls are slightly convex, suggesting a flexible structure of wattle and daub. Posts capable of supporting a roof made of plant materials can perhaps be discerned at the four corners, giving the tops of the walls a slightly concave appearance. The door, picked out in raised relief, is surmounted by a lintel (probably wooden in reality) which is much wider than the entrance. In the upper part of the door itself is a horizontal roll, probably representing a curtain or mat rolled up around a log. These two elements, the lintel and the roll, are such archetypal features of the Egyptian door that they feature in the 'false doors' that were a repeated motif in Egyptian art and architecture throughout the pharaonic period. Two double windows, located high up on the opposite side of the house to the door, are very small, in order to keep the room fresh, and both are surmounted by small wooden beams. On the basis of the height of the door (10 centimetres), Randall-MacIver and Mace suggested that the actual dimensions of the house as a whole would have been about 7.5 metres long and 5.5 metres wide.

An Amratian tomb from Abadiya has provided a strange clay model (Oxford, Ashmolean E.3202; figure 12b) representing the rounded corner of a crenellated wall, behind which two people are standing, the backs of their figures picked out in raised relief, only their bird-like heads protruding over the top of the wall. It is difficult to know whether these figures are intended to represent giant sentries or whether the wall itself is very low, but this is perhaps not important in terms of the model's overall significance. The important elements are the enclosure wall and the two look-out men, which indicate two important aspects of defence, thus recalling not only the tendency towards the clustering of populations from the Amratian period onwards (a factor which is archaeologically demonstrable) but also a more defensive mentality that is not otherwise indicated by the archaeological remains.

Towns surrounded by crenellated walls were very commonly depicted

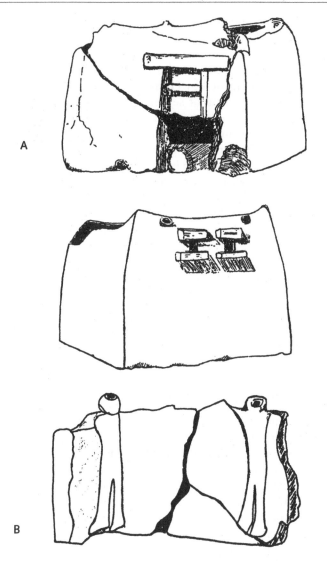

Figure 12   (a) Clay house model from el-Amra (after Capart 1904: fig. 142); (b) baked clay model from Abadiya, showing human figures standing behind a crenellated wall (after Capart 1904: fig. 143).

by the end of the Predynastic period, as we can see from the study of the ceremonial palettes at this date. They are thus an essential part of an ideological landscape that was evidently marked by a tendency towards violence, associated with the very image of the pharaoh.

At Hierakonpolis during the Gerzean period, the growth in specialized craftwork is expressed less in terms of finished products (as in the cemeteries of Naqada) and more in the occurrence of distinct patterns of activity, such as the numerous areas of pottery kilns or bifacial tool workshops, such as the site identified by Holmes (1989b) at Locality 29a. But it is especially in the clustering of settlement towards the river that the development of craftwork centres can be detected. Clearly environmental deterioration has contributed to this demographic move, but we should also note the important attraction exerted by the river as a means of communication that had become an important element in socio-economic strategy. Indeed the growth in contact with other groups is one of the main characteristics of the Gerzean period.

In the south, there were now firmly established links with the A-Group Nubians, and in the north, we have already mentioned the cemeteries near the Faiyum region. It was during the 1980s that a German team from Munich uncovered the large Predynastic cemetery of Minshat Abu Omar, at the eastern edge of the Delta, clearly a point of contact with Palestine (Kroeper and Wildung 1985). These contacts are known to have existed from the Badarian period onwards, loosely speaking, but they acquire a new intensity, in the Nile valley, with the arrival of wavy-handled vessels (probably as containers for oil and wine), which would quickly and decisively influence the development of Egyptian pottery. A number of other types of pottery at this date were also of Near Eastern origin, including footed, spouted and loop-handled vessels. This flood of goods passed through the trading settlements of northern Egypt, thus exposing them simultaneously to influences from the Naqada culture. Trade in copper, with Maadi evidently functioning as the main entrepot, took on a particular importance. Although the lightweight domestic buildings were still largely constructed from locally available organic materials (reeds, palm-leaves, acacia and tamarisk wood), the development of flat-bottomed boats, clearly made from wood, must have led to more long-distance trade in timber. The presence of beads of gold, Egyptian alabaster and faience, just as in the case of the bovid's head mentioned above, in EBAI levels at Asawir in Palestine, as well as 'Gebel el-Arak-style' blades in EBAI levels at Hazor suggest that there was a complex exchange system in operation, whereby manufactured products were traded for raw materials (for a recent discussion of relations between Egypt and Palestine, see de Miroschedji 1998). Contacts over even longer distances (with Sumer and Elam) had an especially significant effect on the final phase of the Predynastic; rough fragments of lapis lazuli and obsidian were reaching Egyptian craftsmen from at least as early as the Gerzean period (on the question of lapis lazuli see Bavay 1997) by a series of indirect links eventually developed into more direct trade routes.

The site of Elkab, which is close to Hierakonpolis but on the opposite (eastern) side of the river, was the local capital presided over by the vulture-goddess Nekhbet, who emerged from the royal crown alongside the snake-goddess Wadjyt (the goddess of Buto, a site at the northern end of the Delta). The two cities thus form part of a reference system that draws on the most fundamental sources of pharaonic duality. Few traces of this Buto/Elkab duality, however, have survived from the Predynastic period. Stan Hendrickx (1984) excavated a Naqada III cemetery within the enclosure wall of the pharaonic-period town of Elkab, and suggested, on this basis, that the Predynastic settlement might have been located nearer the bank of the river, under the silts of the modern floodplain.

Abydos, on the other hand, is situated further away from the river, therefore the remains of both Naqada-period cemeteries and settlements have survived, although the latter consisted only of small villages at the desert edge. Two zones of cereal kilns/ovens in particular were uncovered by Eric Peet (1914: 1–4) and carefully described by Jacques Vandier (1952: 503–8). By the beginning of the 1st Dynasty, an actual mud-brick town had been constructed at Abydos, at the same time that the rulers of the newly unified land of Egypt were building their tombs in western Abydos, at the site of Umm el-Qa'ab (the Arabic name meaning 'mother of pots', because of the huge quantities of sherds covering the surface). The ruling class at this site, who had now become truly autocratic in their powers, caused the centre of gravity of Egypt to move northwards. By founding their capital at This (no remains of which have yet been discovered) and establishing their royal cemetery at Abydos, the first kings of Egypt deprived both Hierakonpolis and Naqada of their roles as Upper Egyptian capitals.

At this time, c.3200 BC, Upper Egypt was a narrow valley scattered with villages: Mahasna, Abydos, el-Amra, Hu, Abadiya, Matmar, Naqada, Ballas, Armant, Gebelein, Adaïma, Hierakonpolis, Elkab, Elephantine. Remains of Predynastic huts have been found at Elephantine, for instance, by a team from the German Institute of Archaeology (see Werner *et al.* 1988). Since the Amratian, c.3800, the mode of subsistence largely comprised an economy based on the agricultural exploitation of land fertilized by the annual flood (wheat, barley and flax) and the use of pastureland in the area surrounding the valley, which was still wooded, defined by intermittently active wadis. The practice of fishing and especially of hunting in the desert were initially means of providing precious (sometimes indispensable) sources of protein in the diet, but it was not long before these activities became 'socialized', taking on new significance as the ritualistic actions of the elite, from which they tended to emerge as victors, with their powers to some extent invigorated.

In the second half of the fourth millennium BC, as the process of change

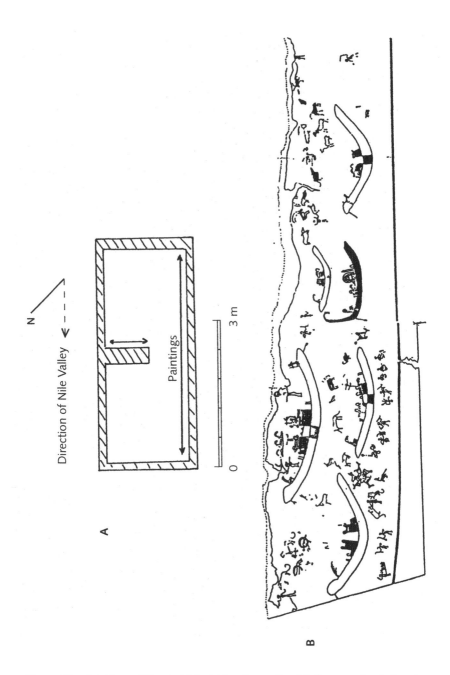

Figure 13 (a) Plan of Tomb 100 at Hierakonpolis; (b) the mural painting in Tomb 100 (after Quibell and Green 1902: pl. LXXV).

at Hierakonpolis, Naqada and Adaïma suggests, human activities tended to move away from the marginal areas that had become too arid, heading instead towards the floodplain, the favoured axis for trade. Two great centres then dominated a mosaic of villages: Naqada, at the western end of the gold-mining route through the Eastern Desert, and Hierakonpolis, at the southern frontier, which was a key site in terms of the gold, copper and ivory trade with the regions to the south. Both of these towns doubtless developed under the influence of the first kinglets, who gradually strengthened their grip over the comings and goings of raw materials and finished products, developing the production of exotic objects to their own benefit. There were thus more and more groups of 'non-producers' within the population, placing increasing pressure on the modes of production and forcing the agriculturalists to cast their eyes ever further beyond the existing areas of cultivated land and pasture. It was then, as Krzyzaniak (1977: 127ff) suggests, that the first attempts at local artificial irrigation systems began to be made, in the form of small basins, canals and dykes. This process of irrigation involved the control of meandering streams of water, the expansion of the regions under cultivation (thus enabling increased production and better control over it), and adaptation to new soils which were more difficult to cultivate, thus doubtless necessitating the use of hoes, and blazing a trail towards the invention of the ox-drawn plough.

At the same time as these new social and economic structures were evolving, an ideological system was being created, and the paintings in Tomb 100 at Hierakonpolis (figure 13) constitute an astonishing visual demonstration of this. Discovered by Quibell and Green in the early 1900s, Tomb 100 consists of a rectangle measuring 5.85 × 2.85 metres in area, with a depth of about 1.5 metres. The walls were lined with mud brick and there was also one free-standing brick wall that emerged halfway along the east wall and also stretched about halfway across the width of the tomb. Contrary to the initial opinion expressed in Green's notebook, it was not covered by a vaulted roof (as an apparent slight change of angle at the top of the walls had suggested, see Kemp 1973: 38). A layer of plaster covered the walls, enlivened on the west and partly also on the east by Gerzean-style figurative representations. However, on the basis of the originality and elaborateness of the paintings, it has been dated to the last phase of the Predynastic period: Dynasty 0 (Baumgartel 1960: 126). Brunton (1932) argued that, since there was no skeleton in the tomb, there might be some doubt as to whether it was a funerary structure; he thus suggested that it might instead have been some kind of chapel. This interpretation, however, was refuted by Helene Kantor (1944) who not only believed it to be a burial but also considered it to be Gerzean in date. There is no doubt that, as Kaiser (1958) has suggested, Tomb

100 consists of architecture comparable with the tombs in cemetery T at Naqada, but the numerous objects found inside it (Kaiser 1958; Case and Payne 1962; Payne 1973) date to Naqada IIc rather than the Protodynastic. From this point of view, the presence of the paintings is simply a reflection of the 'princely' nature of the tomb rather than an indication of its date.

The range of black, red and white images across an ochre background in Tomb 100 has been the subject of numerous discussions (e.g. Avi-Yonah 1985). No one yet appears to have come up with a satisfactory interpretation of the way in which these images should be read. This interpretive problem has already been noted above, in connection with the decorated vessels of the Gerzean period. Rather than assuming that the pictures are intended to be understood in a literal sense, it seems certain that these representations should be regarded as existing within their own specific set of spatial and temporal conventions. As Roland Tefnin (1979: 224) explains, 'the modern viewer tends to devote more attention to what the image might be saying as an account of actual events, rather than what it is clearly saying simply as an image. In other words, the analyses attempt to perceive the elements of the picture that are compatible with the restoration of a figurative order that is regarded as necessary, rather than expressing the real order of representation of the things being depicted, which is the only objective order that we can actually see in it'. Although this is not necessarily the right time to elaborate a strategy for approaching visual evidence of this kind, it seems extremely unlikely – here as elsewhere – that the images are portraying a particular historical event.

In the midst of a group of six immense boats (which dominate and, in a sense, punctuate the space), some small scenes are organized, without any ground lines or separate registers, dealing with the themes of hunting and warfare. The troubling aspect of these compositions is the fact that they include not only the world depicted on the Gerzean vessels, with their curved boats, but also the later images portrayed on the decorated ceremonial palettes of Dynasty 0. This is also doubtless one of the reasons why the tomb is usually assumed to have been protodynastic in date. It is not possible to look at the male figure standing between two animals (perhaps lions), and the pairs of warriors engaged in single combat to his left, without recalling the decoration on the Gebel el-Arak knife-handle. The imagery of ivory handles is also suggested by the depiction of a gazelle caught by a lassoo, with its head turning back, and the dogs pursuing oryxes. There is also the figure using a mace to strike three enemies (tied up perhaps) who are linked to him by some kind of rope – this is the embryonic form of the supreme triumphal image that emerges about 200 years later on the Narmer Palette, the constant symbol of royal power for many centuries.

Compared with the atmosphere of the images on the pottery vessels, the paintings in Tomb 100 begin to cast a shadow over these peaceful landscapes. We have already detected the emergence of violence, on the basis of the enclosure-wall model in the Ashmolean Museum and the evidence for humans' tendency to cluster together at this date, but these phenomena are expressed on the tomb walls with something of the 'freedom' of the earlier rock carvings. Here, as on the rocks, the background is able to unfold over a large area, allowing the execution of a more complex series of images than was ever possible on the vessels. The restriction on the images shown on vessels is not so much because of their physical shape or size but because of the overall meaning of the images, for there is no physical limitation that actually prevents the decorated vessels from bearing scenes of fighting between the boats' hulls and the bases of the pots; it is only tradition that stops this from happening. The Tomb 100 paintings are characterized by a certain freedom of expression. The image of violence – present but not omnipotent – gradually wormed its way into scenes that were dominated by boats, their curved hulls echoing the bases of the vessels (whereas flat-bottomed boats are more familiar in the rock-carvings). What is the significance of these boats? Are they intended to be funerary barks carrying the body of the deceased, foreshadowing the funerary rituals of the pharaonic period? This is perhaps so, but we might also interpret them as replicas of the boats which the deceased must surely have owned as a living person. In the end there are no written captions to inform us on this question. Certainly the sheer scale of the boats is an indication of their importance. It is the act of sailing that is thus being emphasized, and around it emerged scenes of hunting and war.

As well as the necessary acts of hunting for food (i.e. the pursuit of herbivores), there was also a more dangerous, status-enhancing kind of hunting: the lion hunt. Then the animal became man, and thus ensued the scenes of fighting from which the human victor could emerge endowed with the power of the animals. We have thus come full circle. From hunting to warfare, from hunting-mask to victorious bull-king, lion-king or falcon-king, impressive scenes of this type are sketched out on the Vultures Palette and the Lion Palette, and we should not forget the animal's tail attached to the loincloth of Narmer and that of all later kings. But before these symbols could reach a synthesis as powerful as the underlying ideology, they were broken up and scattered by a very strong image – sailing – around which everything is organized, everything is linked together, and everything appears and disappears.

It is hardly likely that Tomb 100 at Hierakonpolis was the only grave of this type, just as the painted fragments of cloth found in the Predynastic cemetery at Gebelein (now in the Museo Egizio, Turin; see Galassi 1955) were no doubt not unique, but its comparative rarity is hardly in doubt. It expresses, through its architecture and its paintings, the existence of a ruling class, an elite group, the rise of which – encapsulated by images of strength, physical vigour and therefore violence – is linked with the increasing importance of the river.

Lower Egypt: Maadi and Wadi Digla, Heliopolis, Buto and other Maadian sites

The Maadian cultural complex of about a dozen sites only became apparent as a result of research undertaken since the 1980s. These sites are essentially defined by the large cemetery and settlement complex excavated at Maadi itself: hence the term 'Maadian'. Apart from the eponymous site (and the neighbouring cemetery of Wadi Digla), Heliopolis and Buto were two other important centres that were particularly significant in the development of this culture.

Maadi and Wadi Digla

In a southern suburb of Cairo, the Predynastic settlement of Maadi occupies one edge of the Pleistocene terrace that overlooks the alluvial plain between the mouths of the wadis el-Tih and Digla, near the fertile land but raised above the level of the annual flood.

Excavated in 1930–53 by the University of Cairo, firstly under the direction of M. Amer and O. Menghin, and then, from 1933 to 1948, by M. Amer and I. Rizkana, the site covers about 18 hectares. It comprises an area of settlement, 40,000 m² of which have been excavated, as well as a cemetery, at the foot of the terrace. A second cemetery was discovered in 1948 at Wadi Digla, a kilometre further to the south, and this was investigated in 1948–53. Between 1977 and 1987, 200 m² in the eastern part of the settlement were excavated by a team from the University of Rome (Caneva et al. 1987), and since 1984 the complete documentary study of the site was undertaken and completed by I. Rizkana and J. Seeher, under the auspices of the German Institute of Archaeology in Cairo (Rizkana and Seeher 1987, 1988, 1989, 1990). The archaeological deposits, which were often as much as two metres in depth, consisted of an *in situ* layer at the bottom on which were found a succession of heaps of refuse accumulated by the inhabitants themselves in the course of different occupation phases or by *sebakhin* (local peasants in more recent times looking for fertile soil). This complicated system of interrelations between the different levels hinders any attempt to determine the stratigraphy.

The excavated structures show that there were three types of settlement remains. The first of these is unique in an Egyptian context, involving subterranean houses excavated from the rock in the form of large ovals measuring 3 × 5 metres in area and up to 3 metres in depth, each of which was entered via an excavated passageway; the walls of one of these subterranean houses were faced with stone and dried Nile-silt mud bricks – the only known instance of the use of mud brick at Maadi. A succession of post-holes along the walls suggest that there was also a wooden superstructure which would have given these vast buildings a truly monumental appearance. Some scholars, indeed, have interpreted them as ceremonial structures with no practical purpose, while Jacques Vandier (1952: 516), on the other hand, has suggested that they were simply storerooms. The presence of hearths, half-buried jars and domestic debris at the bases of the structures suggests that these were genuine permanent habitations, similar to those at Beersheba in southern Palestine (Perrot 1984).

The two other types of domestic structures at Maadi are both well-attested elsewhere in Egypt: firstly a form of oval hut accompanied by external stone-lined hearths and partly buried storage jars, and secondly a rectangular style of building comprising narrow trenches indicating the shape of enclosures made from the stalks of plants and probably used to shelter animals; the trenches would have helped to give these light walls a better grip in the soil to prevent them from being swept over by northerly winds (especially the *khamsin* that blows in the spring).

Here, as elsewhere, the pottery and the lithics constitute the most important remains of human occupation. The pots were made from Nile silt, hand-thrown apart from the rims, which may perhaps have been finished on a slow turntable. The surface of the vessels was smooth and coloured with various shades from reddish brown to black, often marked with darker areas indicating the use of an open kiln and an uncertain control over the firing procedures.

In general, the typical Maadian pottery vessel is globular with a flat base, a more or less narrow neck and a flared rim, but there were also bottle shapes, narow goblets, 'lemon' pots (with pointed bases) gradually developing towards flat bases, as well as bowls and cups with flat or rounded bottoms.

As far as surface treatment is concerned, Maadian vessels are rarely decorated, except sometimes with incised marks applied after firing. Such incised motifs include birds and the *serekh* frames enclosing the first Horus-names. Some painted decoration, brown on a clear background, is evocative of plant forms, and, in one case, there is the silhouette of a male figure – provided with a phallic curl – all of which is reminiscent of the painted decoration on Amratian vessels. There are more definite links with Upper Egypt, on the other hand, in the form of sherds from high-quality imported vessels of black-topped, red-polished ware, which the admiring Maadian potters were unable to resist copying. Indeed there are 'black-topped' red vessels that have clearly been *made* in Maadi, judging form the fact that the top of the vessel is coloured an uneven greyish brown on a reddish background, whereas the true black-topped ware has a deep black edge caused by the deep penetration of carbon into the fabric. The Maadian version of black-topped ware must presumably have been fired twice: the pot would have first been placed in a normal oxydizing kiln, and then, after it had cooled back down, its rim would have been exposed to black smoke in order to create the superficial effect of a darkened top. A Maadian imitation of a Gerzean vessel has also been found (Rizkana and Seeher 1987: pl. 43, 1–4 and 67, 6), identified as such through the use of local clay.

Conversely, the commercial links with Palestine account for the presence of distinctive footed ceramics, with neck, mouth, and handles decorated *en mamelons*, made from a calcareous clay fabric, which probably contained imported products (oils, wines, resins). These ceramics had a significant impact on Egyptian pottery in the form of the wavy-handled style.

Just like the pottery, Maadian flint working took the form of an original cultural tradition, which, however, was subject to influences from two major civilizations: Upper Egypt and Palestine. The Maadian lithics essentially comprised blades knapped from large nodules brought into the site, which were then worked further to transform them into scrapers, burins and perforators. There were also large circular endscrapers fashioned from wide flakes struck from pebbles and local nodules, while others derived from wide nodules with particularly polished surfaces, of a type known in Palestine and throughout the Near East. Also originating in Palestine were the exceptional edged blades with rectilinear ribbing, known as 'Canaanite blades', that appeared in the Nile valley; these were to develop into the pharaonic-period 'razors' (actually double scrapers) which were included among the funerary equipment of the earliest kings until the end of the Old Kingdom, sometimes polished and sometimes reproduced in copper and even gold.

The few bifacial tools include projectile points, daggers and sickle blades. The latter were gradually replaced by examples that were mounted on a blade (which might sometimes be a 'Canaanite blade'), thus the local tradition (i.e. the bifacial sickle attested at the Faiyum and at Merimda Beni Salama) was replaced slowly but surely by a foreign one (the Near Eastern style of sickle mounted on a blade). On the other hand, the large rippled blades are typically Egyptian, as well as a unique imitation taking the form of a forked implement known as a 'fishtail lancehead' which was fashioned from a large blade; it has retouches only on the upper face, the lower face being left unworked.

The stone vessels carved locally are made from soft stones (limestone and Egyptian alabaster), while the examples carved form hard stones (essentially basalt and diorite but also including a few rare items in marble, granite and conglomerate) are imported. The bowls and footed vessels (barrel-shaped or cylindrical) often furnished with tubular handles, were found alongside receptacles described as 'incense burners' which were always of limestone, open in form, very shallow and thick-walled; in several cases, their contents have been analysed, revealing a greasy vegetable material in a resinous matrix. These analyses suggest that the vessels are incense burners rather than lamps, on the grounds that a mass of oil and resin would no doubt be left as a residue after the perfume had been burnt off. Since the resin did not derive from Egypt, this presumably represents another instance of a product being imported from the Levant. Also found at Maadi is the top-hat-shaped style of stone vessel, almost always in basalt, the Badarian origins of which have been mentioned above.

Another class of imported artefact is the rhomboidal schist palette, the origins of which in the Naqada culture are virtually certain. Its status as a luxury product is indicated both by its comparative rareness and by the presence of many well-worn limestone palettes that were evidently used for more mundane purposes. Maceheads carved both from hard stones (granite and diorite) and from Egyptian alabaster are of the disc-shaped type characteristic of the Amratian and early Gerzean cultures. Many pestles and mortars made out of tough limestone were found, suggesting that various materials were being ground up. There were also many polishing stones and hammer-stones. A number of stones with gouges have been interpreted, on the basis of ethnographic parallels, as 'stick straighteners', while pierced limestone discs are assumed to have been spindle whorls.

Apart from several combs imported from Upper Egypt, objects in polished bone and ivory include the traditional repertoire of needles, punches and awls. It is by no means unlikely that the first spine of the pectoral and dorsal fins of catfishes may have served as arrow heads. These fishbone points appear to have been traded with Palestine, judging from the fact that they have also been found at the Palestinian site of Wadi Gazza (Rizkana and Seeher 1988: 33) and they were kept in jars at Maadi, clearly in preparation for export. They were therefore evidently among the products being exchanged for imported materials.

From this perspective, the role of copper at Maadi takes on a particular significance. Compared with their near absence at other Egyptian sites, metallic objects seem to have been particularly common here. Not only are there needles, fish-hooks and rings, but also rods, spatulas and axes, which take on a fresh appearance in the absence of polished stone. The stone versions of such artefacts had characterized the Faiyum and Merimda cultures, but now they were being recreated in metal. Such a technological development could not have taken place overnight, which suggests that there must have been some intermediate 'pre-Maadian' stage between the two. It is to this stage that we can perhaps assign the pottery vessels found in isolated storage pits at the site of Haraga, at the entrance to the Faiyum region (see Engelbach 1923: pls. XXX and LV). No traces of such vessels have been found within the area dominated by the Maadian culture. At the same period in Palestine, the total disappearance of pol-ished stone axes, and their replacement by metallic types (albeit with stylistic differences from the implements found at Maadi) cannot be the result of pure chance, but must have been the outcome of a definite proc-ess of technological change and must also be a reflection of genuine sym-biosis between the two regions (Lower Egypt and Palestine). Large quantities of copper ore have also been found at Maadi, which under analysis reveal a probable provenance in the region of Timna or Fenan, both of which are copper mining sites in Wadi Araba, at the southeastern corner of the Sinai peninsula. Far from being evidence for the processing of ore at Maadi itself, the copper ore appears to have been a trade prod-uct, essentially used for processing into cosmetics, and the initial ore processing must have been undertaken near the actual places of extrac-tion.

On the basis of this evidence, Maadi is regarded as something of a commercial centre, although the suggestion that its inhabitants were all merchant-venturers (Hoffman 1980b: 200–14) is probably rather exces-sive. Certainly trade routes opened up with the south, with the import of palettes, maceheads, a few fine black-topped vessels, and raw materials such as ivory and hard stones, while basalt vessels, ceramic styles and copper flowed southwards, as in the particular case of a fine copper axe, clearly Maadian in origin, which was found in a tomb at the Upper Egyp-tian site of Matmar, dating to Naqada II (Brunton 1948: 21, pls. 16, 47). It is surprising, however, that the contacts between Upper and Lower Egypt were not more intense (considering the incomparable nature of the Nile as a communication route) and that they were expressed mainly in imitations rather than actual imports and exports. We must also, of course, consider the problem of the 250 kilometres of cramped Nile valley in Middle Egypt, between Asyut and the entrance to the Faiyum, all empty of any traces of Predynastic occupation. Kaiser (1985) draws attention to the discovery of sites linked with the Maadian culture at Haraga and Sedment, thus suggesting that the Maadian may have actually extended much further to the south but the evidence has perhaps been destroyed by processes of erosion and sedimentation. It is also possible, as Jürgen Seeher (1990: 51) suggests, that a more or less independent Middle Egyptian cultural group (perhaps influenced by Maadi) played the role of a buffer between the 'two lands', allowing only certain artefactual types to filter through during the first phase of the Naqada period, but that the pressure of Gerzean expansionism would eventually have burst through this zone in the later phase of the Naqada.

The relations between the Maadian culture and the Levant were more straightforward, and the list of the Near Eastern products arriving in Maadi was a long one. Seeher (1990) describes the first stage in this process: ceramics, basalt vessels and rings, copper, large flint nodules and 'Canaanite blades', certain large circular scrapers, Red Sea shells, pigments, resins, oils, cedar wood and asphalt, the latter suggesting links with the Dead Sea to the northeast. In the final stages of the Predynastic and in the Early Dynastic, Eliezer Oren (1973, 1987) has reconstructed a trade-route passing through north Sinai and linking Egypt and Canaan together. The discovery of domesticated donkeys at Maadi (Bökönyi 1985) suggests that, as at el-Omari and also more commonly at later sites, the land-transport of commodities was undertaken with the use of such beasts of burden.

The people of the Maadian culture, involved as they were in a network of contacts with the marginal regions of the Near East, with Upper Egypt and with the Delta, were above all sedentary in their lifestyle, as their settlements indicate. There are few traces of wild fauna to counterbalance the enormous quantity of domesticated animals (Bökönyi 1985, Boessneck 1988), including cattle, sheep, goats and pigs, which, apart from the dog, comprised the basic meat supply of the community. This diet was supplemented by fish, which made up 10 per cent of the fauna – a small proportion compared with the Merimda and Faiyum cultures, where fish remains outnumbered those of animals. The Maadian people fished *Synodontis* for their 'darts' (used for artefacts) and *Lates niloticus* purely as a food source. They were not only herders and hunters but also totally agricultural. Kilos of grain found in jars and in storage pits include wheat and barley (*Triticum monococcum, Triticum dicoccum, Triticum aestivum, Triticum spelta, Hordeum vulgare*) as well as pulses such as lentils and peas.

There is a clear separation between Maadian settlements and cemeteries, but the presence of human bones in the disturbed remains of the Maadi settlement, as well as the discovery of an unburnt human skull in a hearth, suggests that there may have been certain aspects of their funerary practices that we do not yet fully understand. The burial of still-born babies within the settlement, sometimes in a pottery vessel, is, on the other hand, a more well-known phenomenon.

Generally speaking, the Maadian grave consisted of an oval pit measuring about 90 × 70 centimetres, in which the deceased was placed in a foetal position, wrapped in a mat or cloth. The spatial distribution of the graves on the little elevation that made up the cemetery of Wadi Digla allowed two phases of use to be distinguished. It turns out that, in the earliest period, the placement of the body with the head to the south was the only preference with regard to orientation, whereas the traditions seem to become more fixed in the next phase, with the head to the south, facing towards the east (i.e. the opposite of the situation in Upper Egypt, where the head usually faces west). The biggest difference, however, is the 'poverty' of the funerary equipment. One vessel, or sometimes two, accompanied the deceased, while palettes and flint tools were rare, and the appearance of an ivory comb in one tomb at Wadi Digla and a stone vessel in another seem to have been exceptions to this general tendency. More common, on the other hand, are the valves of *Aspatharia rubens*, a type of large Nile mussel which was often used as a spoon. No copper artefacts have been found, but the mineral is nevertheless found in the form of cosmetic pigment. Although animal bones may represent funerary offerings, there are nevertheless some graves in which dogs and goats or sheep are buried with the same care that was usually reserved for humans. These are to be found clustered together in the earliest part of the cemetery.

Finally, we cannot leave the cognitive world of the people of Maadi without noting the discovery of a distinctive human face modelled in clay, found in the settlement. It has a pointed skull, a prominent nose (effectively an extension of the forehead in a simple, gentle convex shape), a nutcracker chin, perhaps indicating a beard, two indentations for eyes and another for the mouth (Rizkana and Seeher 1989: pl. I.5).

Heliopolis

This Predynastic cemetery was discovered in 1950, when building work was taking place in modern Heliopolis, and it was excavated by Fernand Debono between 1950 and 1953. There were two preliminary reports on this work, but the final report was published 35 years later by the German Institute of Archaeology (Debono and Mortensen 1988).

Situated in the desert plain adjacent to Gebel Ahmar and the Mukkatam, 63 graves were uncovered, representing 45 human burials (36 adults, 2 adolescents and 7 children) and 11 animal burials (six goats and five dogs), as well as seven caches of pottery vessels without an accompanying traces of bones. The graves were simple oval pits (of uncertain depth due to the levelling of the ground by the modern builders), with traces of mats surviving along their walls, and the remains of wood perhaps indicating roofs of some kind. The human bodies were each in a foetal position – sometimes extremely tightly contracted – generally being placed on the right side, with head to the south and face to the east. According to the age of the bodies and the way that they were treated, four different types of burial can be distinguished: (1) those of adults who had not been wrapped in a mat or animal skin, buried with either few funerary offerings or none at all; (2) those of adults who were wrapped in a mat or skin or even protected by a wooden roof, with only a few offerings; (3) those of adults who were not only wrapped up but also surrounded by many offerings; and (4) those of children, sometimes provided with offerings but never wrapped in a skin or mat. In all four cases, pots were placed near the deceased, taking the form either of single examples or of groups of two, three, five, seven, nine and ten.

The goats' graves followed the same pattern as those of humans – they were small and not particularly deep, and the animal was placed in a contracted position on its right side, with the head to the south and its face to the east, wrapped in a mat or animal skin and provided with pottery vessels. The dogs' tombs were very small and close to the surface, with no apparent special treatment of the bodies.

Although the tombs excavated at Heliopolis represent only a part of the cemetery as a whole, thus making it difficult to draw general conclusions, the patterning of the graves appears to include some sectors where bodies were placed without any offerings, some where the dogs' graves (and also most of the goats') were concentrated, and others where children were buried. Surviving hearths in various locations suggest that funerary meals were perhaps cooked at various points in the site. The absence of still-born babies is probably due to the fact that they were traditionally buried within the settlement. The pottery shows close links with that of Maadi and Wadi Digla. Hand-made from Nile silt, with plant or mineral temper, the vessels' surfaces were smoothed or lightly polished, and grey-brown (or occasionally reddish) in colour. The jars were more or less ovoid in shape, with flat or slightly rounded bases and flaring rims. In some cases, the pot was distinguished by the presence of a conical foot and/or a narrow neck topped by a flaring or horizontal rim. Seven pots bear vertical lines or simple plant motifs incised before firing, which resemble the potters' marks appearing in Upper Egypt from the Amratian onwards. An interesting example is represented by a jar with a conical spout and foot, which incorporated a filter at its mouth (Debono and Mortensen 1990: figure 15/7). Finally, three vessels seem to be Palestinian imports, judging from their shape (only the photographs have survived), one being an ovoid jar with a wide flat base, a straight neck and a straight rim (Debono and Mortensen 1990: pl. 8).

A slightly ovoid basalt vessel with a conical foot and small ear-shaped handles represents a Palestinian form that is well attested both at Maadi and in Upper Egypt from the beginning of Naqada I onwards. Another stone vessel, carved from limestone, has a flat base, a pronounced shoulder and two holes which must have allowed a handle (perhaps metallic) to be fixed onto it.

The cosmetic palettes that have been found in the graves at Heliopolis are of a fairly basic type, fashioned from simple flat nodules of flint, sometimes still stained with ochre or malachite. Fragments of pigments have also been found on several occasions.

Two valves of *Unio*, Nile shells, were probably used as spoons, and in one instance the shell was placed against the mouth of the deceased. *Ancillaria*, marine gastropods from the Red Sea coast, appear to have been the only items of jewellery worn by the ancient Heliopolitans, and two translucent flint blades are the only surviving traces of flint-knapping at the site.

Buto

The sacred city of Buto, ancient Pe and Dep, seat of the uraeus-goddess Wadjyt, is the third centre in the north where the influence of the Maadian culture is attested. Situated at the northern end of the Delta, this city which the texts describe as the capital of an early Lower Egyptian kingdom, comparable with Hierakonpolis in the south, has been excavated by the German Institute of Archaeology since 1985, under the direction of Thomas von der Way (1997). Using a clever system of water-pumping, a series of trenches were dug below the water level, thus revealing the early phases of the site's occupation, rich in ceramic and lithic material comparable with that of Maadi, Wadi Digla and Heliopolis. The tendency towards local imitations of Naqada-culture forms is also in evidence at Buto, in the form of sherds deriving from local versions of Upper Egyptian wavy-handled vessels made from a local calcareous clay that have been found alongside authentic vessels of the same type made from Upper Egyptian clay. There are also fragments of beige vessels painted with brown motifs imitating Gerzean vessels. No examples of black-topped vessels have yet been excavated, suggesting that the earliest phase at Buto corresponds to the Naqada II phase, and, more precisely, to phases IIc–d in Kaiser's chronology, with the later stratigraphy stretching on, without a break, through the late Predynastic and Early Dynastic to the Old Kingdom (see von der Way 1989: figure 2).

Like all Maadian sites, Buto is at the frontier between two traditions:

the 'African' culture of Upper Egypt and the oriental culture of Palestine. Indeed it is the only place in Egypt, apart from Maadi, where it is possible to find the large tabular flint scrapers that are so typical of Palestinian culture at this date. However, the Maadian population of Buto had not only established links with the Levant but were also in direct contact with the Sumerians of Uruk VII–VI in southern Mesopotamia, judging from the discovery of fired clay cones with bases painted black, white or red, that were used to create a mosaic-style decoration on the walls of Sumerian temples. It may seem a little premature to suggest that this Sumerian architectural style was adopted at Buto, alongside the basic wattle structures associated with the site's marshy environment, but if this evidence turns out to be reliable then it may tie in with Thomas von der Way's theory that architectural styles are not exported in the same way as objects but by means of a system of diffusion of ideas and adoption of new concepts, thus indicating a closer relationship between the cultures involved. In contemplating this possibility, we should also bear in mind both the expansionism of the Sumerians between 3400 and 3100 BC (see Bower 1990) and the maritime nature of Buto.

As von der Way points out, Maadi is a riverine settlement, linked by a land route and donkey-train with Palestine, whereas it is possible that Buto constitutes one of the first ports from which more distant links may have been established with northern Syria, a region where the Sumerians might well have been encountered. Thus Buto, unlike Maadi, has yielded sherds of a pottery type decorated with spiral white bands (von der Way 1986: figure 3/1–4) similar to those from phase F at Amuq, a site located to the north of Antioch, which was itself related to the Uruk ceramics.

Other Maadian sites

Apart from these four sites (Maadi, Wadi Digla, Heliopolis and Buto), individual finds of Maadian material were made at Tura station, two kilometres south of Maadi (Junker 1912), at Giza (during the construction of a tramway), at Merimda Beni Salama, in a series of Predynastic tombs within the area of a Neolithic settlement (Badawy 1980), and finally, further to the south, at es-Saff (Habachi and Kaiser 1985), Sedment (Williams 1982) and Haraga (Engelbach 1923). More recently, pottery and lithics identical to those in the earliest strata at Buto have been found at Ezbet el-Qerdahi, two kilometres south of Buto, at a depth of more than two metres (Wunderlich et al. 1989).

As far as Maadian chronology is concerned, three phases have been distinguished among the material from Maadi, Wadi Digla and Heliopolis, on the basis of the material imported from Upper Egypt and Palestine. These three phases have been defined more in terms of changing frequencies of different types of artefact than as radical modifications in the nature of the assemblage as a whole, and they will no doubt be clarified or even altered in accordance with current and future research.

The earliest phase, according to Seeher (1990), generally coincides with the last two subphases of Naqada I and it is represented by the material from Maadi itself, this huge settlement and cemetery excavated in the Cairo suburb. Two phases have been identified in the Wadi Digla necropolis, the first of which is linked with the early Maadian, whereas the second is, like the remains at Heliopolis, an intermediate sequence in which Maadi is only a weak component but during which the earliest level defined at Buto emerges (i.e. between Naqada IIab and IIcd). The final Maadian phase is represented only at Buto – this was an extremely important time of transition, eventually merging with the homogenized culture of the protodynastic period. At the turning point of Naqada IIc/d, the material appeared at el-Gerza, Haraga, Abusir el-Melek and Minshat Abu Omar, all totally devoid of Maadian elements.

The Maadian culture, which probably emerged out of a local Neolithic tradition at about the time of el-Omari, seems to have simply been absorbed by the expanding culture of Upper Egypt (see chapter 8 for further discussion).

Lower Nubia: the A Group

During the second half of the fourth millennium BC, there emerged in Lower Nubia a new cultural group that was influenced both by the Nubian 'Cataract Tradition' and by the first Predynastic cultures in Egypt. It was first brought to light by the work of Reisner (1910), who called it the 'A Group', a form of terminology that indicates uncertainty concerning their origins and their sudden disappearance after the 1st Dynasty. Compared with the 'Khartoum Variant' and especially with the Abkan culture (with which it is partly contemporary, see Nordström 1972), the A Group is marked out by rich graves (comparable with those of Egypt) and several types of settlement, established on eroded silts or platforms at the edge of the river. It is mainly thanks to the offerings placed in the graves that it has proved possible to create a chronology dividing the development of the A Group into three phases, indicating a gradual movement of its settlements from north to south.

The first phase was contemporary with Naqada 1c/IIa–d, and occupied the region between Kubbaniya, in the north, and Dakka-Sayala in the south. The second phase flourished during the Naqada III period (see chapter 8 below), and the final phase corresponded to the so-called 'unification period' in Egypt and the beginning of the 1st Dynasty. The southward progression of the A Group eventually reached the Batn el-Hagar as far as Melik en-Nasir, about 50 kilometres to the north of the Dal Cataract. Some time later, it disappeared and was eventually replaced in this region by the C Group, several hundred years later, at about the time of the 6th Dynasty (c.2300 BC).

The earliest site relating to the A Group is Khor Bahan, to the south of Aswan. It consists of the cemetery of a small agricultural community established on the alluvial plain at the mouths of the wadis, beside which pasturage could be found. According to Bruce Trigger (1976), Khor Bahan is the prototype for the communities that swarm along the river as far south as the Batn el-Hagar, thus enabling them to 'absorb' the earlier 'Cataract Traditions'. The graves were provided with red-polished, black-topped pottery, fine bifacial flint tools, stone bowls, diamond-shaped schist palettes and conical maceheads, all of which indicate the influence of the Amratian culture. It is also at this date that copper artefacts first appear in Lower Nubia. It should be noted, however, that the presence of local Nubian pottery and certain Abkan-style aspects of the lithic industry all suggest that it was an indigenous population, with its own distinctive traditions, that was adopting these aspects of Egyptian culture. Indeed, alongside ceramics imported from Egypt there flourished a local style that had developed during the Abkan and was still in use at the time of the C Group. In particular, this local pottery included a series of red-polished, black-topped bowls with pointed bases and faint ripples across the outer surface, which is just as likely to have derived from the Abkan culture as to have been passed on from the Naqada people. The final phase of the A Group was characterized by unparalleled types of fine-walled vessels, known as 'eggshell' ware, the thin bases of which were decorated with an attractive combination of dark red geometrical motifs. The lithic industry was to some extent 'impoverished' compared with the earlier 'Cataract-Tradition' assemblages. As in the Abkan, there are many perforators and denticulate tools, as well as the fine bifacial techniques adopted from the Egyptian Predynastic.

In a general sense, the Nubian tombs were very similar to their Egyptian prototypes (see Hofmann 1967: 78): in an oval or sub-rectangular pit, the body was placed in a foetal position, on its left side, with the head to the south, wrapped up in matting; large Naqada pots were arranged alongside such artefacts as quartzite or limestone palettes, carved into simple shapes and often stained by pigments (ochre, apparently an important material used in funerary rites, was often painted over the body of the deceased). Schist zoomorphic palettes, comparatively rare in the south, are well attested in the more northerly cemeteries nearer to the Naqada culture from which they derived. Bodily adornment was accorded great significance, including beads and pendants made from bone, ivory, stone, metal (gold) and faience, as well as cloth capes decorated with ostrich feathers. The mica plaques found in these graves have been interpreted as mirrors.

Multiple burials appear to be more common than in Egypt. Two seated female figurines seem to be equivalent to those found in Naqada-period tombs. At Tungala West (Afia), cemetery 268, discovered by H. S. Smith (1962), has provided a series of tombs with circular stone structures, one of which – dated by ceramics to the final A-Group phase – consists of a pit (containing three bodies) roofed with stone slabs. Should we consider this arrangement as an exceptional one at Afia (see Nordström 1972) and therefore simply restrict ourselves to pondering on the possible unique reasons for this occurrence, or should we accept the suggestion made by Trigger (1976: 36) that these stone circles may have been relatively common elsewhere but have invariably been destroyed by erosion? Whatever the solution to this question may be, there is no doubt that the A-Group funerary practices were very much the heirs of Naqada traditions.

So far as we can tell, the way of life followed by the A Group remained semi-nomadic. The settlements take the form of human occupation layers with no traces of well-defined structures. We can reasonably assume that they were living in simple huts, the traces of which have been eroded away. Rock-shelters were sometimes used, as at Sayala, where the occupation lies alongside rock-paintings of great interest (Bietak and Engelmayer 1963). Few bones have been identified in the settlements to provide any definite evidence for the existence of domesticated species or fowl and animals. Such species are, however, attested in the tombs, in the form of bones and skins of goats and cattle, as well as the skeletons of domesticated dogs. Strangely enough, it is the local pottery that indirectly provides evidence for the proximity of domestic herds. This particular type of pottery has a similar surface treatment to an Abkan ceramic type, but its fabric is different; thin sections indicate that it is ashy rather than sandy, and includes a high proportion of cattle dung. It is not very likely that this dung is from wild herds, especially given the fact that the people of the Naqada culture, who represent such a strong influence on A-Group culture, were cattle farmers. The same situation applies to agriculture, which probably comes from Egypt, and which only seems to be fully developed in the final A-Group phase: carbonized grains of barley have been found in the settlement sites, as well as pulses (peas and lentils), but it is impossible to assess the exact role that was played by these agricultural products in the diet of the A Group. Fresh-water oysters and fish seem to have been fairly important in terms of the provision of protein. The continued importance of the hunting of wild animals and birds is indicated not by surviving bones but by the scenes painted on pottery vessels (including elephants, giraffes, gazelle and antelopes). Finally, beers and wines imported from Egypt in large wavy-handled jars seem to have been enjoyed by the A-Group elite.

Following the example of the Naqada culture, A-Group society appears to have undergone a process of 'hierarchization', judging from certain sites and tombs, such as the well-built domestic structures discovered by Smith at Afia in 1961, the rich tombs of cemetery 137 at Sayala, and those of cemetery L at Qustul, published by Bruce Williams (1986). Traces of huge stone-built houses incorporating two to six rooms were therefore discovered at site A5 in Afia, dating to the final A-Group phase. These were rectangular structures, entered from the north by several doorways, and the internal and external walls were built without the use of any mortar, the space between the two being filled with sand and silt. The wider outer corners were slightly rounded, and finally the ground had been covered with a layer of silt. Although no part of the published report can give any sense of the precise role played by these constructions, Trigger (1965: 77) suggests that we should regard them as the residences of local chiefs enriched by their commercial contact with Egypt. The 'princely' tomb in cemetery 137 at Sayala is significant in this respect.

Dated, like the Afia structures, to the last phase of the A Group, the Sayala tombs comprise rectangular shafts cut into the alluvium and roofed, as at Tungala West, by large sandstone slabs that cover several individual graves. The richest of these graves (Firth 1927: 201) contained, alongside stone vessels, copper axes, ingots and chisels, two immense palettes with a double bird's head, a lion's head made from green glazed rose quartz, a mica plaque (mirror?) and two piriform maces with gold-plated handles, one of which was decorated in repoussé with five pairs of animals (see figure 11) stylistically similar to the sculpted ivories of the Naqada period. This mace, which was unfortunately stripped of the gold decoration after it had arrived at the Cairo museum, is one of the masterpieces of Naqada art and also a good instance of the type of luxury product that the Predynastic Egyptians were trading with their contemporaries in Lower Nubia.

There can be no doubt that the A Group was a product of the Naqada-culture explosion. The development of commerce along the Nile and the consequent emergence of high quality craftsmanship led to the creation of anchorage points – 'trading posts' – the purpose of which was to ensure that the Naqada potentates were able to transfer raw materials from the south to the north, and this transferal at first took place in terms of reciprocity, but later, under the first rulers of dynastic Egypt, became more radically aggressive.

The site of Khor Daud, on the east bank of the river, is best understood in terms of such trading posts. There is no trace of permanent settlement, but there are 578 silos – simple shafts dug into the ground – containing a considerable number of Naqada artefacts. These artefacts, dating from the beginning of the Gerzean to the final phase of the Predynastic, comprise jars made from a calcareous fabric, both with and without wavy handles, and pottery vessels either with black tops or with red-polished surfaces, all of which seem to have been used to transport beer, wine, oil and perhaps also cheese. Khor Daud was therefore a site concerned with the exchange and redistribution of goods, but its location – in a region dominated by the great plain of Dakka and at the mouth of the Wadi Allaqi – also allowed it to serve as a point of contact with the pastoral nomads of the Eastern Desert and thus to act as a veritable commercial nerve-centre from which the A Group were able to draw considerable benefit as middle-men (see Piotrovski 1967; Nordström 1972: 26).

When the Naqada people exported the finished products created by their workshops, as well as food and drink, they gained in return essential raw materials: ivory, ebony, incense, vegetable oils, the skins of wild cats, deriving from southern regions, the shipment of which was in the hands of the men of the A Group. It is perhaps this period of commerce that is recorded in the many rock carvings of boats that are to be found along the Nile, from Upper Egypt down to the edge of the Batn el-Hagar.

The A Group, whose subsistence pattern was at first pastoralist and later agriculturally-based, owed its uniqueness (as well as its wealth) to a system of exchange and distribution with which its whole social and economic structure was integrated. However, it was this very *dependence* on the exchange system that was to prove its ruin. Indeed the flow of Egyptian imports suddenly stopped at the beginning of the 1st Dynasty, at about the same time that the indigenous products vanished. Fruitless investigations have been made, in search of the kind of climatic modifications that could have caused such a sudden disappearance, just at the very moment when the A Group was at its height. But it seems that the key to the problem is actually to be found not in Nubia itself but in profound changes that took place in the Egyptian section of the Nile valley, at the end of the Naqada period. It is possible to characterize this crucial period in a few words as the final stages of a process of accumulation of resources and monopolization of energies to the profit of a 'caste' of local 'dynasts' whose raison d'être was an ideology that linked their personal power with the need for stability in the world: this was already the idea of Maat, the foundation myth of the Egyptian state (see Assmann 1989, 1990).

But, in the network of relationships that united the Egyptians and the A Group, it was the latter who occupied a fragile position, not integrated into the complex social structure developing in Egypt, from which the image of the 'pharaoh' was emerging. Most probably the Naqada people would by this time have acquired a particular perception of the 'Land of the Bow' (ta-seti) – the Egyptian name for the territory occupied by the A Group, which first appeared in the 1st Dynasty – viewing it essentially as a land of 'foreigners' (Valbelle 1990). The establishment of a unique king, reigning over the entire land, indicates a system which was perhaps more rigid in terms of the redistribution of goods within Egypt itself, and the demand for raw materials would no doubt have increased, with disastrous consequences for the hitherto pampered middlemen. Trade was henceforth to be controlled by the Egyptian royal armies, whose numbers included the Nubians themselves, as mercenaries. Is this the new development that the Jebel Sheikh Suleiman rock carving was recording?

The Jebel Sheikh Suleiman carving (figure 14), published by Arkell (1950), consists of the figure of a Nubian captive, if we assume that he is to be identified by the bow – seti – which he holds in his hands tied behind his back. Behind this captive is the Horus-name of a 1st-Dynasty ruler (perhaps king Djer, although opinions differ on this, see Murnane 1987), and facing the royal name and captive are two circular town ideograms, one of which is surmounted by a falcon. On the right-hand side of the scene is a boat with a prisoner tied to its prow, perhaps with bodies of the dead floating below. After a number of visits to the site of the rock carving, Needler (1967) reported the existence of several other carvings in the immediate vicinity, which show scorpions holding captives and may therefore depict Egyptian raids prior to the 1st Dynasty.

Thus the Egyptians were at first the source of prosperity for the A Group but eventually they were also its nemesis. Was Egypt the only reason for the A Group's disappearance? In the absence of any other explanation, it is perhaps best to assume so.

The late Neolithic of Khartoum and the surrounding area (including el-Kadada)

It was long thought that the Khartoum Neolithic had died out by the beginning of the fourth millennium BC, without being followed by any known culture, leaving a gap of 3000 years until the emergence of the Napatan state in the eighth century BC. Arkell (1949) had detected, at Omdurman and Shaheinab, graves of a later type, which he considered to be protodynastic. But it was comparatively recently, in the late 1970s, that the existence of a late Neolithic culture, chronologically contemporary with the Nubian A Group, was brought to light by François Geus at the site of el-Kadada (Geus 1977, 1983, 1984, 1986, Reinold 1982, 1987).

Situated 200 kilometres to the north of Khartoum, on the right-hand

Figure 14 Rock carving and inscriptions at Jebel Sheikh Suliman (after Arkell 1975: fig. 24).

bank of the Nile, el-Kadada, which emerged on a piece of fossil terrace and the branch of a khor (water-course) fossilized since the Neolithic, comprises areas of settlement and a cemetery excavated over the course of nine seasons between 1977 and 1986. It was the establishment of a pumping system designed to provide water for the land situated between el-Kadada and Kabushiya near ancient Meroe which enabled French archaeologists to explore this area. As with the majority of the sites along the Nile, the study of el-Kadada was a long and laborious rescue operation. The 'villages' of el-Kadada, in common with all the settlement remains in this region (Reinold 1986), apart from the hearths of Shaheinab, comprised a substantial man-made layer sometimes as thick as two metres, without any stratigraphy or traces of domestic structures. The presence of potsherds, decorated with wavy lines, dotted lines and ripples of the type that Arkell had found at Omdurman, immediately suggested the possibility of a long period of exploitation at el-Kadada. Hundreds of tombs disrupted many of the settlement areas, some of these being Neolithic (including 300 excavated examples) and others stretching from Napatan times to the Islamic period.

Four different sectors have been distinguished for the Neolithic period, comprising, as far as excavated tombs are concerned, 73 individuals in cemetery A, 11 in cemetery B, 211 in cemetery C and 5 in cemetery D. The differences between these cemeteries and within cemetery C itself all attest to an evolution in funerary practices over the course of a relatively brief period.

As a general rule, each burial at el-Kadada took the form of a pit cut into open ground, the body being placed in a contracted or flexed position without any preference in terms of its orientation. In certain cases, the distinct curvature of the cervical vertebrae suggests the use of ligatures or bags to fix the bodies into a contracted position. Most remarkable of all are the burials of very young children in pottery vessels (Reinold 1985), the occasional presence of a dog near the deceased, and the practice of human sacrifice, brought to light by Reinold (1982, 1987). The use of such sacrificial acts has been suggested at sites throughout the length of the Nile, including the cemeteries of the Naqada culture and the A-Group graves, but no tangible piece of evidence has yet been found to provide definite proof.

At el-Kadada the practice of human sacrifice may be deduced from the relatively common occurrence of multiple inhumations, ranging from two to four bodies. There are no traces of the redigging of the pit either to add secondary burials or to retrieve the earlier body, as we might expect if this were a case of successive (rather than simultaneous) burials. The observations emerging from the excavation suggest, on the contrary, that there was usually one main body placed in a flexed position in the centre

of the pit, accompanied by funerary offerings deposited in separate locations and including a second human body probably buried in a bag (judging from the extreme contraction of the body). The close stratigraphic
relationship between the main body and the secondary one is sometimes
emphasized by the presence of a bucranium linking them together. Occasionally, in the southern part of cemetery C, the secondary body is that
of a child. These child-burials are placed in outstretched positions at the
edge of the pits, undoubtedly linking up with the funerary material in
which they have been placed. In the case of the triple burials, the last
body of the three, placed vertically precisely above the main body, perhaps indicates the redigging of the tomb.

It would seem, therefore, that each of the important individuals was
buried in a flexed position in the centre of the pit, then an individual was
sacrificed during the funeral ceremony and placed among the funerary
offerings. The latter was usually an adult enclosed in a bag, in the northwest section of cemetery C, but took the form of a child or adolescent in
an oustretched position in the more southerly part of the cemetery. Finally, at a later time, a further cadaver – perhaps a member of the same
family or clan – was given a burial just above the principal body.

In the case of the double burials, a dog takes the place of the 'sacrificial
victim'. Was there a gradual change from human to animal sacrifice, or
vice versa? Human sacrifices are attested in the Sudan in the Middle
Kerma period (c.1700–1600 BC) at the same time that whole sheep, and
sometimes dogs, were being buried alive in the tombs. We can see that
the originality of el-Kadada, and the Neolithic tradition that can at present
be linked with it, derives from the new importance accorded to the funerary
world.

The grave goods placed in the tombs correspond well to the objects
found in the settlement area. Since the many objects from the settlement
– amounting to tons of material according to Reinold (1987: 17) – have
not yet been studied and published, we must at present use the data from
the cemeteries to gain an understanding of the material culture of these
late Neolithic peoples in the Middle Nile valley.

The funerary offerings include pottery, tools carved from quartzite
(mainly not retouched), objects made from polished hard stones (e.g.
axes, pierced discs, palettes and pestles associated with the crushing of
pigments which one finds in the form of fragments of ferruginous sandstone and malachite, astonishing deposits of broken pebbles, millstones
and grinders, lip-ornaments, bone artefacts – sometimes the remains of
animal butchery placed in tombs – mollusc shells (*Aspatharia rubens*),
bracelets made from ivory or shells from the Red Sea, ostrich eggs used
as vessels or in the form of undecorated fragments, and finally mats and
animal hides serving to cover the burial. Many beads carved from vari-

ous stones, ivory, bone and shells were used for body decoration (necklaces and bracelets) – more than 200 of them, for instance, were found in grave KDD 86/16. Several burials included fired clay female figurines bearing incised decoration, some of which were characterized by bases rounded into a ball shape.

The pottery comprises vessels of very different sizes and a great variety of forms: goblets, bowls, circular and elliptical plates, hemispherical and chalice-like vessels, without any handles. One particular type, characterized by a kind of flared rim, was described as a 'ladle vessel' by Arkell. The hand-made el-Kadada pottery was generally decorated with incised geometrical motifs, punched holes either arranged in lines or scattered, sometimes inlaid with white pigment. Finally, certain surfaces were combed to produce the kind of rippled effect which is well-known from Badarian and A-Group pottery. The microscopic and chemical study of the pottery (De Paepe 1986) has enabled two principal groups of vessels to be distinguished: one set of local origin and the rest deriving from elsewhere, probably from the south, between Khartoum and Wad Ben Naga (see De Paepe and Geus 1987: 45). It would seem, however, that the most typical el-Kadada pottery vessels, including those decorated with ripple marks and those with chalice shapes, were all made by local potters. This indicates that the population were generally producing their own pottery, using the locally available clay.

The material culture of el-Kadada owed a great deal to the Khartoum Neolithic, particularly in its denticulate bivalves (*Aspatharia rubens*), amazonite beads, lip-ornaments, barbed harpoon points and fish-hooks made from shells. There are undoubted similarities between the el-Kadada culture and that of the A Group: the rippled effect on the surface of pottery vessels, certain methods of incised decoration, the discs and palettes of hard polished stone, the millstones of sandstone, and the baked clay figurines. Finally, in both cases, the gouges – which are so typical of the Shaheinab culture – are absent.

The people of el-Kadada were far more inclined than the Khartoum Neolithic populations to engage in a mixed economy within which the prime place was occupied by pastoralism (Gautier 1986). The small ovicaprid livestock (*Ovis ammon* and *Capra aegragus*) appear to have been more important than the larger animals (bovids: *Bos primigenius*), which suggests a catchment area that was less open to the great areas of pastureland, taking into account the context of the site and the behaviour of the river, without excluding the possible phenomena of ecological degradation due to over-pasturing. The wild mammals included monkeys (*Cercopithecus aethiops*), hares, various rodents, felines (wild cats, Persian lynxes and panthers), and to a lesser degree, elephants, warthogs, hippopotami, black rhinoceros, giraffes, koudou antelopes, topi and hartebeest,

Buffon's kob and various gazelles. All of these types suggest that the landscape basically comprised dry savanna, characteristic of the Sudano-Sahelian zone. However, the relative proportions of each of these animals (see Gautier 1986: table 5) tend to emphasize the semi-disappearance of the Buffon's kob, compared with the situation at the site of Saggai, and the importance of the hare, sign of increasing aridity as a result of a decline both in rainfall and in Nile floods. More pastoralists than hunters, the people of el-Kadada nevertheless collected and ate large numbers of molluscs (*Pila, Lanistes, Aspatharia*), and captured deep-water fish, large reptiles, birds and small mammals.

It is difficult, given the state of the settlements, to determine the degree of sedentism practised by the people of el-Kadada, but they were probably not agriculturalists (Stemler 1990) and, as Achilles Gautier (1986) remarks, the importance they appear to have given to stock-raising suggests transhumant movements synchronized with the rains and the Nile floods. Certainly they were pastoralists but the degree of elaboration on their artefacts suggests a certain refinement, their funerary customs denote a high degree of social complexity, and the presence of Red Sea shells indicate more distant contacts with the outside world. This culture has also been found further to the south at Khartoum (Omdurman) in those tombs which Arkell described as 'protodynastic', Saggai (Caneva 1983: 24–8), Geili (Caneva 1988), nearby at the site of el-Ghaba, and finally also in the north in the region of Kadruka (Reinold 1987).

From a chronological point of view, the el-Kadada culture lies at the end of Arkell's succession, at precisely the point when the Khartoum Neolithic seems to be disappearing. The radiocarbon dates, *c.*3599–2700 BC (Hassan 1986a), confirm el-Kadada's partial contemporaneity with the Lower Nubian A Group and the Egyptian Naqada culture. Although they were thus in potential contact with the Predynastic cultures via the A Group, the populations of the Middle Nile nevertheless seem to have retained a fierce individuality, in that no specifically Egyptian object – and certainly no copper artefacts – reached them.

With the late Neolithic we are thus able to fill a gap stretching up to the end of the fourth millennium BC. There are nevertheless still 2000 years of silence from then until the appearance of the Napatan culture. Some data at el-Kadada, and other sites in the same region, allow us a certain optimism that this gap too may eventually be partially filled (see Lenoble 1987).

8

The first pharaohs and the unification of the Two Lands

The last phase of the Naqada period was characterized by deep-seated social changes. Although ecological modifications were probably not the causes of these changes, they may well have been associated with the first emergence of social change, which was well attested by new artistic developments.

This transitional phase between Naqada II and the 1st Dynasty was identified by Flinders Petrie (1939), who named it 'Semainean' after the archaeological site by the village of Semaina, about 25 kilometres west of Esna. As far as Petrie was concerned, the end of the Naqada period was marked by a complete break which took the form of an invasion by people from the east, and it was from these invaders – a dynastic 'race' which Derry (1956) claimed to have identified anthropologically – that the pharaonic dynasties originally emerged. The theory of the 'invaders from the east' was supported by Hans Winkler (1938–9) when he discovered rock carvings in the Eastern Desert depicting flat-bottomed boats with vertical prows and sterns which were evidently Mesopotamian types of vessel, each containing human figures wearing feathers. Contrasting these oriental boats with the rounded, sickle-shaped boats portrayed on Gerzean pottery vessels, Winkler regarded these carvings as proof of an invasion through the Wadi Hammamat which would have reached the Naqada bend of the Nile and instilled into the Gerzean culture the necessary means by which it achieved the level of a true civilization.

In 1944, Helen Kantor dealt a severe blow to the concept of the Semainean, arguing that its particular characteristics were simply continuations of features of the previous Predynastic periods. Werner Kaiser (1957), however, included it in his chronology (although without assuming that it necessarily corresponded to a foreign invasion), and we recognize it today as the final burst of acceleration which propelled the whole of Egypt into a centralized state. It is at this point in time that there are clear indications of Mesopotamian influences which we have already mentioned in connection with Buto.

Kaiser (1957) divided Naqada III into two subphases. Naqada IIIa was a very late form of the Gerzean, during which processes of change were expressed more in terms of transformations of the toolkit than in territorial expansion. Naqada IIIb, on the other hand, was the final breath of the Predynastic, already looking ahead to the beginnings of the historical period. This phase was accompanied by the rulers' emergence from anonymity with the writing of the earliest royal names inside *serekh*s (rectangles sometimes surmounted by a Horus-falcon, see figure 15). These first 'Horuses' – the rulers of 'Dynasty 0' – gained control of the Memphite region (including the sites of Tura, Tarkhan, Helwan and Abu Rawash) and then extended their power southwards, down to the Second Cataract, building their royal tombs at Abydos (Kaiser and Dreyer 1982; Dreyer 1990, 1991).

From an ecological point of view, the final stages of the Predynastic were characterized by the gradual movement of human settlements from the deserts towards the river valley; this phenonomen, which had been well underway as early as the Naqada II phase, was greatly exacerbated, bringing with it the relative abandonment of pastoralism, and the adoption of intensified agriculture, backed up by increasingly systematic artificial irrigation. The macehead of King Scorpion (Oxford, Ashmolean E.3632; figure 16) may be the earliest evidence for artificial irrigation, showing the king using a hoe to open a canal in a great ceremonial act (on this problem, see Gautier and Midant-Reynes 1995; *contra* Cialowicz 1997). Hierakonpolis, moreover, is the site that has provided the majority of the data relevant to the Naqada III phase, and this is not by chance, since the brilliant development of the early city at Hierakonpolis cast a shadow over Naqada, its neighbour (and rival) before it was in its turn eventually eclipsed by Elkab, This and its necropolis Abydos, once the country had become unified.

The studies undertaken in the ancient city of the falcon by a team of American archaeologists, led in the 1980s by Michael Hoffman, showed that the growing Hierakonpolitan population was gradually squeezed into the confines of the alluvial plain, abandoning the desertified wadis, for the ecological reasons described above. Here, as at Elkab, the alluvial deposits of the 'Nekhen formation' came to an end in around 3200 BC (see Hoffman *et al.* 1986), at the same time as the last local phase of the Holocene pluvial. In the abandoned desert region, a carbonated level shows precisely when these last periods of rain fell, but paradoxically this precipitation could not bring about the reoccupation of the area in question; doubtless the reasons for this failure to reoccupy the desert may lie in the fact that the rainfall was too sporadic to allow long-term

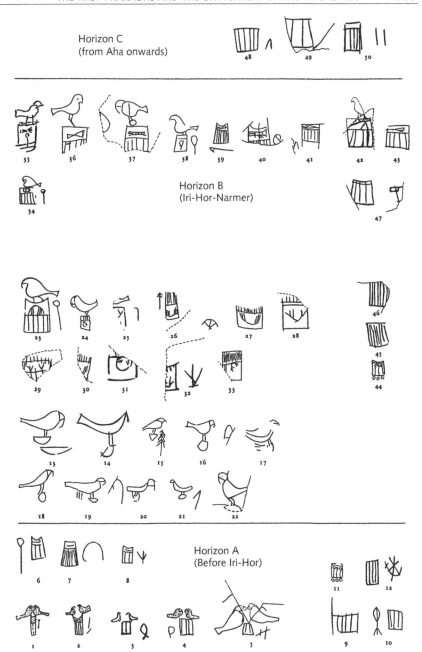

Figure 15   Examples of early Kings' names, Horus birds and *serekh* frames (after Kaiser and Dreyer 1982: Abb. 14).

Height = 25 cm

Figure 16   The scenes depicted on the Scorpion Macehead (after Gaballa 1976: fig. 1b).

exploitation, but we should also consider the possibility that population pressure was too great for the fragile ecosystems of these wadis, and finally we should also bear in mind the growing impact of 'royal' authority which may well have deliberately encouraged intensive agriculture supported by artificial irrigation.

Undoubtedly the population of Naqada III were concentrated in and around the fortified city of Nekhen, at the junction of the mouth of the Great Wadi and an ancient sand-dune, a high point which remained dry at the peak of the annual floods. The first traces of monumental architecture date to this period (Hoffman 1971–2), particularly the platform of the Early Dynastic temple and the large tombs in the cemetery known as 'Locality 6' (Hoffman 1982). Hoffman suggested that one of these graves, the brick-lined Tomb 1, measuring 6.5 × 3.5 × 2, might have belonged to King Scorpion himself.

Everywhere else in the valley, this final phase simply took the form of a continuation of the cultural traits that had developed during the Naqada II phase. It was in Naqada III that 'rich' tombs incorporating mud bricks appeared, and distinctions between different tombs were accentuated by variations in the quantity and quality of grave goods; important individuals were buried in wooden or clay coffins in these tombs. Clustering around Elkab (Hendrickx 1984) and Hierakonpolis (Locality 6: Hoffman 1982), these graves very often appeared within cemeteries of earlier date (e.g. T5 in cemetery T at Naqada, B201 and B217 at Abadiya) and did not generally exceed the tombs of Naqada IId in terms of size. Kaiser (1957) calculated that the average size was 150 × 110 × 125 in the Naqada IIIa1 subphase, 175 × 105 × 135 in the IIIa2 phase, 180 × 110 × 165 in IIId1 and 165 × 105 × 145 in IIId2. Multiple inhumations were not uncommon at this date, and the bodies were generally placed on their left sides, with their heads to the south and their faces towards the west.

The grave goods provided the clearest indications of the new spirit which influenced the end of the Naqada period, providing its main impetus. It was because they presented such a clear contrast with those of Naqada I and II that scholars initially believed them to be part of a radically new culture. What is the evidence?

- Theriomorphic palettes disappear almost entirely, being replaced by simple geometric forms (mainly rectangles and rhomboids) decorated with relief carved scenes which we will discuss below.
- Relief sculpture, which had begun to be used on pottery vessels and Gerzean palettes, underwent further development, reaching a very high quality on ivory artefacts and stone palettes.
- Painted pottery vessels became much less common, and their decoration was largely restricted to non-figurative forms of depiction such as waves, checker patterns and curved strokes. Eventually painted pottery died out almost entirely, at the same time that stone vessels were beginning to appear in larger numbers and of higher quality. Some unusual pottery vessels, however, were painted with motifs similar to those on the ivories and decorated palettes; this Naqada III style of painted pottery occurs particularly in the Nubian cemetery of Qustul and forms the subject of a monograph by Bruce Williams (1988).
- The black-topped, red ware was clearly no longer so significant, but red-polished vessels diversified in the form of large jars with pointed bases, made from calcareous clay, with the earliest Horus names carved on their shoulders.
- Copper continued to be used for more and more purposes, and there was a general increase in the numbers of amulets and items of jewellery made from gold, silver, obsidian, lapis lazuli and other gemstones.
- The production of faience was given fresh impetus.
- Finally, glyptics – the art of seal-making – emerged, including genuinely oriental elements of style – and spread like wildfire (Boehmer 1974).

To the cultural traits reviewed above, we might add the appearance of 'palace-façade' architecture (comprising a series of recessed niches) which may also have come from the east, and which appears to be reflected in the decoration of an ivory box found in a grave at Minshat Abu Omar (Leclant 1987: figure14).

From the outset, it appears that the search for raw materials became more and more important, given the need to equip the elite graves of Upper Egypt with exotic products in keeping with their high social ranking. Gold and ivory came from the south, stone vessels and copper from the Near East, and both lapis lazuli and obsidian come from more distant places. Small beads and simple slivers of obsidian were found here and there in Gerzean graves; a small retouched obsidian blade at Naqada (Petrie 1920: 43, pl. XLV/46) was pierced in order to be worn as a pendant, thus giving us a good indication of the great value ascribed to this rare material. Several unprovenanced obsidian 'fishtail lanceheads' are in the collections of the Louvre and the Berlin, Cairo and Brooklyn museums, and these have been dated, on the basis of their shape to the third and final phase of the Naqada period, where they represent an interesting transition from a type of prehistoric weapon to the instrument used in the 'opening of the mouth' ceremony (see Casini 1974; Needler 1984: no. 171). The strong symbolic 'charge' of the fishtail lancehead in the Naqada period is indicated by those examples which have decorated gold handles, one of which bears the name of the 1st-Dynasty ruler Djer (Needler 1956; Aksamit 1989). Little is currently known concerning the origins of the obsidian: there are sources in the south (among the massifs of Ethiopia) and in the north (in eastern Anatolia, near Lake Van, in central Anatolia, not far from the site of Çatalhöyük, and in the Aegean, particularly on the island of Melos). Trade in Anatolian obsidian began very early in the Levant and the Zagros mountains (Renfrew *et al.* 1966). Some flakes have been found at the Natufian sites of Mallaha and Mureybet, dating to *c.*10,000–8300 BC, and in the Pre-Pottery Neolithic A phase (*c.*8300–7600 BC) at Jericho, obsidian already represented 2.7 per cent of the lithics. However, towards the end of the sixth millennium in the Levant, the uses of this beautiful black volcanic stone, which was doubtless competing with copper, were restricted to luxury items such as beads, pendants, daggers, vessels and inlaid eyes in relief representations. In Egypt it was used for similar purposes. Too far away from the primary sources of the material (at least in the case of the northern sources), the Naqada heartland initially obtained this fine material only when it was accidentally brought by a few travellers (e.g. the pendant blade at Naqada), but once the culture had expanded across the whole country, and particularly Lower Egypt as far as the eastern edge of the Delta, obsidian filtered in bit by bit from the Near East where it represented only a medium for the making of certain luxury items. It gradually acquired symbolic characteristics in Egypt, as in the case of the fishtail lanceheads. In the pharaonic period, it was often used as inlay in the eyes of relief figures or statues. The Ethiopian sources of obsidian seem less likely to have provided the Egyptians with their obsidian because they do not appear to have lain at the heart of such early and systematic trade networks as the Anatolian quarries. Until it has proved possible to analyse enough Egyptian objects to gain a better sense of their provenances, the Anatolian sources would appear to be the most likely (for further discussion see Zarins 1989; Tykot 1996; and André et al. forthcoming). Thus, for instance, it was a 12th-Dynasty Egyptian tomb at Byblos that yielded an obsidian perfume vessel set in gold (Naville 1922).

The emergence of an elite in the great Upper Egyptian centres (particularly Hierakonpolis), who controlled the trade in raw materials and organized their transformation into profitable luxury items, went hand in hand with the appearance of a class of skilled workers who were attracted by the elevated status that could be conferred on such 'master craftsmen' by the early pharaohs. More and more non-productive members of a growing population were grouped together in the agricultural regions of the flood plain, exerting demographic pressure which would provide a decisive impetus to the eventual process of Naqada expansion. While the push southwards was essentially a form of colonization (see the discussion of the A Group in chapter 7), the northward expansion brought the people of the Naqada culture into contact with the Maadian agriculturalists in the north, who formed a buffer zone between Egypt and the Oriental trade networks. We have already discussed above the possible nature of the role played by Middle Egypt in these South–North relations. The fact is that no Maadian site (apart from Buto) seems to have been able to resist the final push by which the Naqada culture swept across the whole of Egypt.

The problem which must still be examined is by no means insignificant. Was the Naqada expansion a matter of purely cultural diffusion or was it an aggressive military process, and at what level, at what mysterious point in time should we assume that the whole land was unified under the rule of a king of both south and north? In other words, precisely how and when did Egypt pass from prehistory to history?

Was the process peaceful or warlike? The Narmer Palette – one of the first pieces of written information concerning Egyptian history – certainly implies a military process, apparently showing the southern king conquering the north. Indeed, this air of violence, which constantly appears in the protodynastic evidence, had already made a discrete appearance even earlier, in the so-called Painted Tomb at Hierakonpolis. However, there is no archaeological evidence to support this theory. Dieter Wildung (1984) notes that the grave goods in the cemetery of Minshat Abu Omar are much more evocative of a peaceful trading community than a group of warriors. The unification seems to have been not so much an act of conquest as a process of continouous change. Thus the transitional phase at Buto must, from this point of view, be examined with the greatest care.

Egypt, as we have seen, was *culturally* unified from the Naqada II phase onwards, well before its political unification was attested by written evidence. There was no apparent need, therefore, to resort to violence. However, even if aggression were not the sole characteristic of the unification process, it seems hardly likely that the chiefs of Hierakonpolis exerted pressure entirely without the use of violence. It would be surprising if their expansion had not met with some resistance, and, as Kaiser (1987a) points out, the lack of weapons in the graves at Minshat Abu Omar cannot in itself prove that there was no military invasion of Lower Egypt. With regard to this situation, the results of the analysis of carved decoration on ivories and palettes is incontrovertible. Before we move on, we must clarify one aspect of the interpretation of these pieces of evidence, which have long been considered to commemorate 'real' anecdotal or historical events. We have already expressed an opinion on this subject, *vis à vis* the painted images on pottery vessels and on the wall of Tomb 100 at Hierakonpolis.

The knife-handles, the earliest examples of which date to around Naqada IId (Midant-Reynes 1987: 220), form a representative group of decorated ivories. They are generally carved with depictions of rows of real animals, and the calmness, regularity and symmetry of the processions on both sides of the handle suggest an animal world which did not inspire terror but formed an integral and harmonious part of the Naqada universe. Alongside these ideas, the origins of which cannot be dissociated from Mesopotamian glyptics, new themes appeared: the image of two intertwined serpents, which one finds for example on the Gebel Tarif knife-handle (figure 17) or the depiction of lines of serpents under the feet of elephants (e.g. on the ivory comb, New York, Metropolitan 30.8.224; see also Keimer 1947). In the same way, on the palettes, imaginary creatures appear here and there accompanying scenes in which lions hunt down gazelles.

The very unusual Gebel el-Arak knife-handle, the authenticity of which has been questioned by some (see Godron 1961, and see also Boehmer 1991 for an alternative viewpoint), is decorated with a series of scenes oriented widthways (unlike the decoration on most handles which is usually arranged in rows along the length of the handle). On the boss side of the handle, two lions with flowing manes are separated by an individual whose feet are in the form of talons of a bird of prey, a kind of 'master of animals' whose appearance is very similar to a Sumerian depiction of

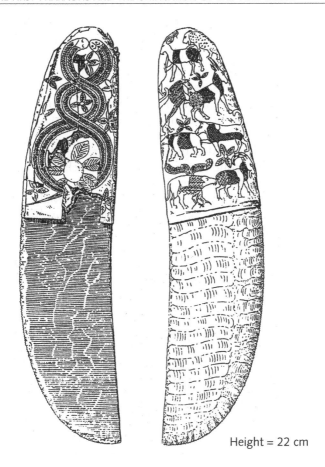

Height = 22 cm

Figure 17   The Gebel Tarif knife (after de Morgan 1896: 115).

Uruk date (Mode 1984), as well as the figure portrayed in the Painted Tomb at Hierakonpolis (in this case, in form rather than style). The four other scenes show the world of the hunt according to an artistic style similar to that of the palettes, with animals chasing, confronting and pursuing one another, depending on the species depicted. The Hierakonpolis tomb also appears to provide the inspiration for the opposite side of the handle which is decorated with battle scenes ranging from hand-to-hand combat to naval conflict, the latter including the same two types of boat as we have already seen dominating the painted wall in Tomb 100 with their immense silhouettes.

The number of decorated ceremonial palettes, including known fragments, amounts to about twenty. While this quantity can hardly be representative of the actual number of such palettes produced at this time, this at least gives us some idea of their restricted numbers, compared with the thousands of surviving potsherds from painted vessels. About a dozen of these palettes, including the famous Narmer one, are interpretable as sources of information since they have survived either totally or mostly complete.

Herman Ranke divided these intact palettes into two chronological groups. The first group comprised images which were all at roughly the same scale and scattered over the whole of the space available, without any use of registers or the appearance of any hieroglyphic signs. In palettes of the second type, the space was divided up by horizontal lines, and a hierarchy of different scales of image was created, accompanied by some of the earliest hieroglyphs, which represented a prelude to the emergence of true writing in Egypt.

The images representing east and west (or nomes 14 and 3 in the Delta) on the Hunters' Palette (British Museum EA 20790) might be regarded as hieroglyphic signs, but in other respects it would seem to be part of the earlier group of palettes. Two lines of hunters (whose orientation corresponds to an axis running from top to bottom of the shield-shaped artefact rather than from side to side) head towards a group of animals including a lion pierced by arrows and a gazelle trapped by a lassoo; on the other side of the scooped-out bowl in the middle of the palette are a line of gazelles and an ostrich, all pursued by dogs. Finally, in the bottom right-hand section of the palette, a lion pierced by arrows lies by itself with its head on the ground. Roland Tefnin (1979) argues that the general image of the hunt as a concept is represented here, rather than simply one specific hunting expedition. It is not necessary here to recount his theory in full, since we are simply trying to place this palette in the overall chronological sequence. It is worth stressing, however, that, quite apart from the style of the piece, it is full of the typical Naqada iconography, developing to some degree the theme which is apparent on the so-called Manchester Palette: the depiction of the wildlife associated with the hunt. The Hunter's Palette incorporates the pursuit of a lion (a dangerous and empowering act which gradually became the symbol of the victorious pharaoh, as in the Hierakonpolis Painted Tomb), and this scene serves as a kind of counterpart to the hunting of a gazelle on the Manchester Palette.

The decoration on the Hierakonpolis (or 'Two-dog') Palette (Ashmolean E.3924; figure 18) is framed on both sides by wolf-like animals, between which is a melée of wild beasts chasing and attacking one another. Although these animals clearly include dogs, gazelle, ibex, mouflons, lions

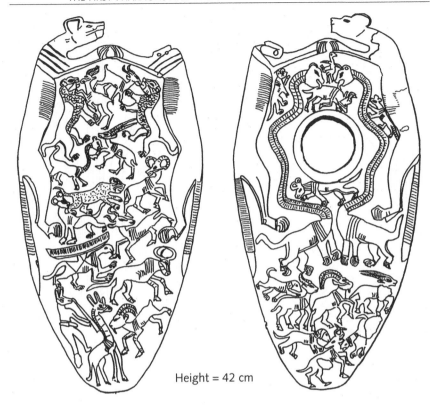

Height = 42 cm

Figure 18   The Hierakonpolis Palette (after Petrie 1953: pl. F).

and a giraffe, there are also a number of fantastic creatures which are more difficult to identify, such as bird-headed animals and lions with snake-like necks, not to mention the strange figure wearing a giraffe-head mask, apparently engaged in an attempt to charm the adjacent giraffe by some kind of magic.

The Metropolitan Palette (Fischer 1958) is framed in a similar way to the Hierakonpolis Palette, but the images are more similar to those on the Louvre Palette, i.e. wolf-like creatures and a long-necked animal; the former are females, each suckling three young (as in the case of a fragment from Munagat, see Fischer 1958: figure 11), while a *serekh*-style Horus-falcon is perched on the central depression of the palette, surrounded by the coils of a serpent, as on the ivory handle of the Gebel Tarif knife (figure 17). The main elements of decoration on the Louvre Palette (figure 19) are essentially a variation on the design of the Hierakonpolis Palette, except that the verso features less aggressive im-

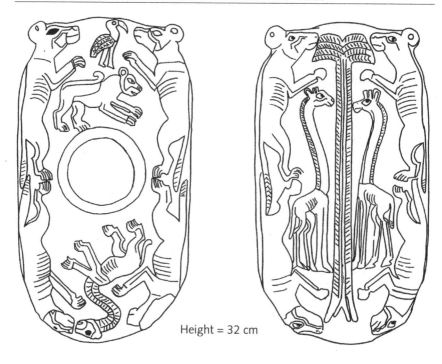

Height = 32 cm

Figure 19   The Louvre Palette (after Petrie 1953: pls. B8 and C9).

ages of giraffes facing one another on either side of a palm tree, which forms the central axis of the piece. On the recto, on the other hand, is another monstrous serpent-headed lion.

The same motif of a palm tree between two confronted giraffes can be found on the verso of the Vultures (or 'Battlefield') Palette, although in this case depicted in greater detail and rather more elaborately (British Museum EA 20791; figure 20). On the recto of this palette, on the other hand, is a very violent scene, foreshadowing the images on the Narmer Palette with its prisoners – hands tied behind their backs – being dragged along by standards held by hands. The triumphant figure on this palette is a lion with a luxuriant mane, depicted on a larger scale and trampling on foreigners, while dead bodies float around in the pictorial space, forming the prey of vultures. The Bull Palette (Louvre E 11255; Petrie 1953: pl. 6) is similar to the Vultures one, featuring a bull in the role of conqueror goring an enemy, under the representation of two superimposed towns with crenellated ramparts. On the other side of the palette, stand-

Height = 33 cm

Figure 20   The Vultures (or Battlefield) Palette (after Petrie 1953: pls. D, E).

ards with their bases ending in hands hold on to a rope attached to a defeated enemy.

On the Libyan (or 'Towns') Palette (Cairo JE 27434; figure 21), the images are organized in rows processing along actual lines – the first use of genuine 'registers' in Egyptian art. Various creatures wielding hoes are depicted surmounting the crenellated walls of seven towns, each containing ideograms presumably indicating their toponyms (although opinions differ as to their translation). Of the seven hoe-wielding creatures, only four are visible: a falcon, a pair of falcons on standards, a scorpion and a lion, each perfectly signifying the image of conquering kings. But there is a major problem in the interpretation of the scene: are the creatures ritually founding cities, or are they destroying them? The other side of the palette is decorated with peaceful rows of bovids, donkeys and the well-known sheep with twisted horns. Below these are a set of trees accompanied by the throw-stick ideogram *tjehenu*, which may designate the Libyans.

The famous Narmer Palette (Cairo JE 32169; figure 22), the first artefact of this type to bear the name of a king inscribed in a *serekh* frame, presents, within a space organized into several registers, the first evidence for the unification of the two lands. On the verso, the king, wearing the white crown of Upper Egypt, uses a pear-shaped mace to smite a kneeling enemy near whom is a hieroglyphic inscription reading 'the

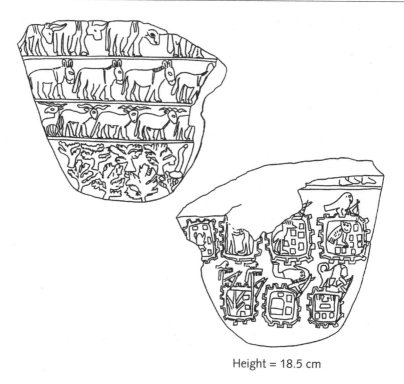

Height = 18.5 cm

Figure 21   The Libyan (or 'Towns') Palette (after Petrie 1953: pls. G19 and G20).

domain of the harpoon', which is known from later texts to be the sixth Lower Egyptian nome. Above this scene the Delta is again symbolized, this time by an oval shape (the 'land' ideogram) with the head of a vanquished enemy at the end facing the pharaoh; there is also a thicket of six papyrus fronds emerging from the top of the oval, which in turn is surmounted by a falcon holding in one of its talons (transformed into a hand) a length of rope, the other end of which is attached, perhaps by a ring, to the prisoner's nose. The message is crystal clear: 'the king has defeated the Delta enemy' (regardless of how we choose to interpret the phrase 'domain of the harpoon', see Kaiser 1964: 89) and 'Horus takes him prisoner'. The scene is dominated by two depictions of the head of a cow-goddess (Hathor or Bat?) on either side of a *serekh* containing the king's Horus-name. The 'heavenly' positions of the cow-goddesses and the king's name tend to suggest a certain degree of similarity to the so-called Hathor palette (figure 10c), while below the level of the pharaoh, at the bottom of the palette, are two floating figures (whose origins are

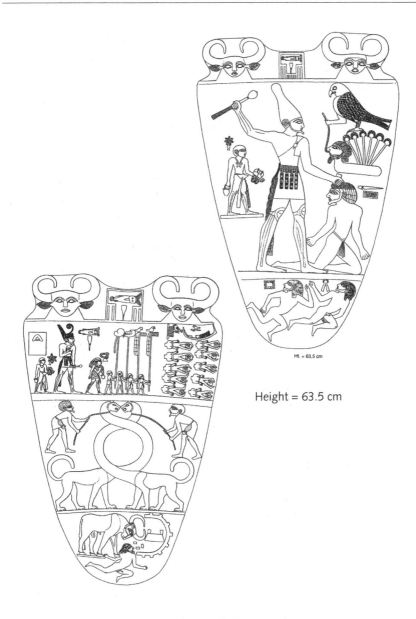

Ht. = 63.5 cm

Height = 63.5 cm

Figure 22   The Narmer Palette (after Quibell 1898: pl. XII).

presumably identified by the two mysterious accompanying ideograms), their presence evidently stressing the triumphant nature of the striding figure of the king. Finally, behind the king is the royal sandal-bearer, a much smaller human figure placed on his own register and holding a ewer, presumably with a view to a purification ritual. Generally speaking, the most striking aspect of this group of images is the fact that they are already depicted in what might be described as the 'classic' Egyptian artistic style. A major difference between the more chaotic earlier depictions, such as the melée of images on the Hierakonpolis Palette, and the carefully separated scenes on the Narmer Palette is the appearance of the hieroglyphic sign expressing phonetic (as opposed to visual or symbolic) values. This interplay between image and sound spatially organizes Egyptian figurative images according to one principal criterion: readability, moving away from the oriental forms of winged monsters and establishing a fixed iconographic repertoire. From this point of view, it appears that the recto of the Narmer Palette, with its long-necked serpopards (beasts resembling serpent-necked leopards) intertwining to form the central receptacle, belongs more with the style of the earlier palettes. In the upper register, the king, wearing the red crown and holding the ceremonial flail across his chest, walks forward towards a group of signs which might be read as the 'great gate of Horus, the harpooner' (perhaps designating the Delta town of Buto), with his scribe and standard-bearers marching in front of him. At the right-hand side, below the group of signs, two rows of five outstretched decapitated human bodies lie with their heads between their legs, signifying the abject nature of their defeat.

Thus the imagery of the last phase of Naqada sculpture includes both Asiatic sources of inspiration (see Boehmer 1974; Mode 1984) and a general break from the past, taking the form of a gradual increase in violence (hunted animals, monsters and scenes of fighting) which no doubt reflect changes in the real world. While Egyptian society was being transformed by the rise of an elite group controlling resources and trade-goods, there was also a pyschological change taking place, involving a kind of celebration of violence which, far from being a simple product of actual events, constituted a sublimation of strength and power, demonstrating the emergence of a new ideology and shaping the image of the pharaoh.

If we reintroduce the idea of the unification of Egypt into this hypothesis, then it seems less like political conquest and more like a phenomenon in which the north was culturally assimilated into the south. War was just one of the elements in this process, but because it was a means of aggrandizing the triumphant party, it was always likely to be accorded greater prominence than other factors, such as the creation of alliances and diplomatic marriages.

From this perspective, the Egyptian sense of dualism did not derive from an actual political division of the country into two separate king-doms, each ruled by its own powerful and bellicose chief, but instead resulted from an Upper Egyptian ideological principle which was then applied to the entire state, encouraging the proliferation of new symbols capable of explaining the 'conquest' of the north (see Otto 1938, Bonhême and Forgeau 1988: 101ff). But how did the actual process of political unification fit into this hypothesis, and who was the first ruler of a united Egypt?

It is traditionally suggested that history began with King Menes and that the Narmer Palette constitutes the first piece of written evidence for a southern ruler's conquest of the north. Can we therefore correlate Menes, Narmer and the first ruler of a unified Egyptian state? Kaiser argues that there must have been a kind of oral historical tradition before historians began to trace the course of events. The analysis of the sources from which Egyptian and Classical accounts derive, compared with the documents which were produced at the very time that the process of unification was happening, leaves us with little doubt that there were several generations of kings before the 1st Dynasty.

By means of the Palermo Stone, the Turin Canon, the king-lists of the New Kingdom and the surviving excerpts from Manetho's history of Egypt, we can deduce part of the succession of the Egyptian kings, in-cluding Menes who is mentioned in several instances as the first ruler. There are, however, clearly historical events which took place before Menes, according to the Turin Canon and Manetho: a series of semi-divine rulers who filled the gap between the reigns of the gods and the emergence of Menes. These semi-divine rulers can be equated with the 'followers of Horus' who appear on the Palermo Stone and also in much later texts (von Beckerath 1956, Kaiser 1959; 1960; 1961; 1964), prob-ably constituting distant echoes of prehistoric oral traditions.

Let us consider the evidence which has survived from the actual period of the unification. The *serekh*s, rectangles hatched in the palace-façade style, were used to frame the king's 'Horus-name' (the first known ele-ment of the royal titulary) since at least as early as the time of a ruler named Ka. However, these *serekh* names, whether incised or painted, appear on certain specific types of pottery vessel from the beginning of Naqada IIIb onwards. Some of the *serekh*s were left empty, while others were inscribed with as yet untranslatable words possibly indicating the pot's owner or provenance. The typological classification of these ceramics, from the types closest to the Naqada period to those that were only found in the following phase, allowed Kaiser (1964) to place the serekhs (and therefore the king's names) in chronological order (see figure 15). Three horizons have been distinguished: horizon A consists of *serekh*s without any inscriptions but often surmounted by double falcons; horizon B features the appearance of a ruler called Iry-Hor (see Kaiser and Dreyer 1982), followed by Ka and Narmer; and finally horizon C begins with King Aha. This sequence of rulers (Iry-Hor, Ka, Narmer, Aha) seems to be corroborated by the architectural evolution of the tombs in Cemetery B at Abydos (Kaiser and Dreyer 1982; Dreyer 1990), which includes a tomb for each of these individuals (apart from Iry-Hor, who is not definitely known to have existed as a ruler).

Where is Menes in all this? The research seeking to correlate the ceramic and architectural sources of evidence has led to the suggestion of a number of different possibilities. Menes may be identified with Narmer or Scorpion (the king associated with the macehead from Hierakonpolis), or perhaps with both, thus forming a single ruler called Menes-Narmer-Scorpion. However, the reading of the hieroglyphic sign *mn* on several ivory tablets belonging to King Aha (Kaiser and Dreyer 1982: pl. 57c), and on a fragment of a plate (de Cenival 1981: 13) has prompted speculation that Menes = Aha. The story would end there if it were not for the fact that some scholars have been reluctant to accept that the *mn* ideogram is necessarily a writing of the name Menes. Since this ideogram is written on a number of different documents/artefacts, we would have to posit the existence of several kings called Menes, according to Vikentief (1942). Even more radically, Philippe Derchain (1966) goes so far as to deny the existence of Menes on the grounds that the *mn* sign was actually an expression used to designate any individual on whose behalf ritual ceremonies were undertaken (i.e. the equivalent of our expression 'so-and-so' or 'Mr X'). Incapable of reading the names figuring in the ancient lists, the New Kingdom scribes might have replaced these illegible names with the *mn* ideogram (i.e. 'someone') which then became fixed in the form Meni and which can be found in the New Kingdom king-lists.

In an equally radical theory, Jean Vercoutter (1990) discusses numerous small objects dedicated to Amun, which were found in an 18th-Dynasty temple (c.1580–1314 BC) on the island of Saï in Sudan. These objects were inscribed with the name Meni, which in this context might be assumed to be a version of the name of the god Amun. Is it not possible that the 18th-Dynasty pharaohs might have conceived of Amun, their most favoured deity, as the first of all the pharaohs, referring to him cryptographically as Meni? Vercoutter concludes: 'Whether this was a scribal interpretation or a creation of the New Kingdom, it seems likely that Menes never existed, so that it would be pointless to try to find his name on the monuments of the 1st Dynasty'. However, neither Dietrich Wildung (1969) nor David Lorton (1987) agree with Vercoutter's suggestion.

Whether Menes was a mythical figure or whether he concealed his identity behind some other designation, we still have the problem of knowing which of the early kings known to us by their Horus names established his capital at This and founded Memphis, as Menes is traditionally said to have done, and can thus be regarded as the first ruler of the 1st Dynasty. Ka, Narmer and Aha satisfy both of these propositions in that they each have a grave at Abydos and their names are all inscribed on material deriving from cemeteries in the Memphite region, at Tura, Tarkhan and Helwan. But it was under Aha (whose name means 'the fighter') that the first tombs were built in the cemetery at Saqqara, and finally it is he who was evidently the first to date the years of his reign by the occurrence of outstanding events. The introduction of this first 'sense of history' (assuming that it did not exist previously), combined with the establishment of the great Memphite necropolis and the existence of the term *mn* on the Aha labels, all serve to explain the presence of this king at the head of the currently surviving lists (see Vercoutter 1992).

This, however, raises a new question: what about the unification of the 'two lands', which is not implied in the definition of the first king of the 1st Dynasty? Tradition describes Menes as the first of the human rulers and the founder of Memphis, but does not identify him as the one who united the two lands. This proposal had, however, begun to be construed as an actual fact, since the foundation of Memphis took place in the context of a conquest of the north. On the other hand, according to the hypothesis whereby Aha was the first king of the 1st Dynasty, it appears that he nevertheless had at least four predecessors: Narmer, Ka, Iry-Hor and Scorpion. It is clear beyond any doubt that Narmer reigned over a unified country. As for King Scorpion, the analysis of his well-known (but unfortunately incomplete) macehead (figure 16) can hardly be interpreted in any other way than as a dualist expression of the monarchy. The triumphant king appears, indeed, depicted according to a hierarchical canon of proportions that was already well-established, adorned with the traditional royal attributes, at the edge of a canal, with a hoe in his hand and facing two servants, one carrying a basket and the other a sheaf of some kind of cereal. In front of him several standard-bearers are marching forwards, while behind him, but still connected with him, are two fan-bearers. In front of his face are two hieroglyphic signs: the rosette and the scorpion; these have been read as 'King Scorpion', but it is worth noting that all of the recent German discoveries at Abydos tend to suggest that the term 'scorpion' is a title rather than a name. The depictions behind this group include the characteristic plants of Lower Egypt, a group of dancers (?) and individuals being carried along in chairs, followed by a man with a stick heading towards the other side of the macehead, where the decoration has been destroyed but probably originally comprised an image of the king wearing the red crown. Above the scene of the king in the white crown are *rekhyt*-birds, representing conquered peoples (but not always symbolic of Lower Egypt, see Kaiser 1964: 91, n. 3), hanging from a row of standards. Below the king, a fragmentary register shows a canal branch, along which are depicted three human figures, one holding a hoe, a palm-tree behind a fence (or, more likely, at the edge of an irrigated field), the bows of a boat, and a building with a curved roof, similar to the one depicted on the Hunters' Palette, which has been interpreted as a sanctuary, perhaps the Lower Egyptian 'per-nu chapel'. Drawing on the primordial theme of the victorious pharaoh, the act depicted, in its religious and ceremonial context, might here be that of irrigation. Yet, whatever type of act is portrayed – whether smiting a captive, irrigating the fields or celebrating the royal jubilee ceremony, as on the Narmer Macehead (Helck 1987; Millet 1990) – in every instance, the scene was part of the general concept of victory, judging from the fact that certain essential aspects of the imagery appear to remain constant from one object to another.

Does this mean that Scorpion was the first king to rule over a united Egypt? On the basis of his carefully re-examination of the traditional sources, Kaiser proposed that we should interpret the 'Followers of Horus' on the Turin Canon as Predynastic rulers remembered in a form of oral history, distant memories of which were eventually preserved in the textual record. He argued that their rule over the whole country was confirmed by the homogeneity of the Naqada culture, which had by then spread over both Lower and Upper Egypt. Bruce Trigger (1987), however, qualifies this theory, suggesting that prior to the first monumental tombs at the end of the Naqada III phase there is no evidence to allow us to posit the existence of actual kings. If truth be told, without denying the importance of this debate, the event can only be assessed in terms of its repercussions. From the second half of Naqada II onwards, it is possible that fairly powerful kinglets were occasionally able to bring together the population under their control. But we can be sure that there were rulers – founders of the Egyptian system of kingship – who enjoyed sufficient power and charisma in themselves to bring together all of the symbols necessary for them to be regarded as guarantors of order in the world.

From this point of view, the Narmer Palette illustrates a cultural scenario which by this stage was already well advanced; it therefore should perhaps be regarded as a monument commemorating an already achieved state of unity rather than depicting the process of unification itself. Like the inscription on one of the statues of Khasekhemwy, two centuries later, it provides evidence of the 'smiting of Lower Egypt'. In other words, it is simply the earliest known example of a violent means of expressing a process which had already taken place in much earlier times: the assimilation of the people of the north into the southern Naqada culture.

Conclusion

More than ever before, the modern study of Predynastic Egypt is subject to rapid developments in the nature of research. Above all, the discoveries of the last 30 years or so have had the effect of obliging researchers to reassess many aspects of the subject and to identify gaps in our knowledge.

From the time when the adaptation to a Nilotic way of life was first taking place to the time of the emergence of the first pharaohs, the Egyptians' gradual adoption of a 'production economy' was equalled only by the extraordinary acceleration of the fourth millennium BC. We are still some way from being able to comprehend the various facets and the twists and turns of these great periods in all their complexity.

Even as this book is going to press, laboratories will be providing new dates, and the researches of one or other of the institutions engaged in fieldwork will be revealing new sets of data which may confirm, qualify or refute the evidence with which we have been dealing. At the same time, however, intellectual and conceptual advances will also modify the views of researchers in a variety of ways. None of us can escape from our own historical contingencies.

The study of Egyptian prehistory began in the nineteenth century, dominated by migrationist theories in which the whole idea of 'race' was treated in a way that modern researchers would no longer accept. At that time, any important cultural change or disruption of the material culture tended to be interpreted anthropologically, as in the case of Derry's 'Dynastic Race', the existence of which was based solely on the study of skull types.

This brings us to the consideration of the problem of physical anthropology, a subject upon which we have been very unforthcoming throughout this book. There is still a great deal left to do in a crucial and meaningful area which has provoked – and still provokes, even now – considerable passions. Jean Vercoutter (1978) has provided a synthesis of the various theories concerning the 'peopling' of Egypt.

From the very origins of the discipline of Egyptian prehistory, thousands of excavated skeletons (forming the basis of Petrie's discoveries) were subjected to morphometrical studies. All these analyses tended to work on the assumption that samples of human populations (deriving from cemeteries) incorporated constant physical types by means of which their 'race' could be determined – a concept which is now considered to be controversial. After all, such an approach to the human remains is based on two premises:

- that the sample is representative of the entire population under consideration
- that the nature of the typological physical characteristics regarded as distinguishing features would have continued unchanged over vast periods of time, remaining exactly the same today as they were in the past.

The results of recent research tends to suggest, on the contrary, that all funerary practices tend to create a bias in relation to the initial population being sampled (Crubezy 1992). They also pose the question: do morphological affinities reflect genetic affinities (Greene 1981)? Can we be sure that there really are such things as typological descriptions corresponding to variations among populations, and that these are actually diagnostic of race? The evidence shows that observed typological differences are the result of complex polygenetic processes in which the environment interacts with the genotype to influence the growth and development of individuals. In the geographical areas under consideration here, human groups evolved in a similar manner, so that they may appear to share physical characteristics allowing them to be categorized as a 'race' (although they might actually be more the product of the environment). The term 'race' is ultimately something of an abstraction, and the problem would actually be better approached in terms of the study of 'biological identity', thus opening up investigative possibilities in the area of biochemical research.

As far as the surviving human remains are concerned, if we reject the idea of a racial stereotype, the approach becomes a purely inductive one, and the sets of bones can then be considered not so much as the focus of research in themselves but as the central elements in funerary practices. E. Crubezy, H. Duday and T. Janin (1992: 22) note that,

> All studies of tombs must therefore begin with a dynamic approach (i.e. field anthropology) the dominant feature of which is the reconstruction of the funerary practices, studying post-depositional distortions and taphonomic factors (the whole set of processes that influence the way in which

the burial is preserved) in order to determine the original appearance of the tomb. When the rest of the archaeological data are then taken into account, it is possible to discuss the whole set of funerary practices and their significance as reflections of the ideology and socio-economic structure of the group (Duday and Sellier 1990). The next stage is an anthropological analysis, taking into account the demographic data, then the research into family links between the various individuals, and finally the palaeopathological data examined from an epidemiological point of view, which will allow the demographic make-up of the site (or the excavated areas) to be clarified. It is only at this point in the investigations that it will be possible to set out a palaeoethnological interpretation (as Leroi-Gourhan puts it) and suggestions can then be made in terms of comparisons between different human populations.

It was precisely this kind of perspective that Podzorski (1990) adopted in her remarkable study of human remains in the Predynastic cemetery at Naga ed-Der.

Tucked away in the northeast corner of the African continent, the Nile valley has, since its origins, simply been one section of an immense cultural entity. Contrary to Edmond Vignard's opinion (that Egyptian prehistory was a time of cultural stagnation), Egypt is part of the dynamics of global cultural processes, but it has stamped its distinctive nature on the people who settled there as a result of climatic change. Its unique hydrological situation favoured one particular agricultural lifestyle, an exploitation of the environment that was tied in with the maintenance of an ecological equilibrium: in other words, the Nilotic adaptation (see chapter 4). Thus we see groups of hunter-fisher-gatherers, initiated into the wonders of a lighter and more efficient toolkit consisting of microliths, settling in smaller groups at the mouths of wadis and at the edges of lakes (nowadays fossilized but at that time periodically flooded) where they could exploit the rich biotope. They practised deep-water fishing during the inundation months, and when the waters retreated they searched for marshland fishes, gathered plants and hunted the species of big game that were beginning to venture onto the alluvial plain. We can detect in this scenario of early Nilotic adaptation the distant origins of the Egyptians' three seasons: the inundation (*akhet*), the retreat of the waters (*peret*) and the heat of summer (*shemu*). Moving within the confines of a deliberately restricted area, these groups developed a set of common practices and a kind of communal spirit which can be perceived both in their regular return to certain regions and the nature of their utilization of the available resources. In this 'idyllic' context, the adoption of a more efficient 'production economy' was slow to arrive. But the forces of nature were poised to overturn this favoured state of equilibrium.

A period of aridity around 7000–6000 BP forced the pottery-using populations of the Western and Eastern Deserts in towards the Nile valley. We know little of events in the Nile valley at this time, but in northern Sudan we can see, emerging out of the Epipalaeolithic 'Cataract Traditions', certain new technological aspects of the working of stone, as well as the first pottery in the region, without the development of sedentism or the domestication of plants or animals. This Neolithization of the Nile valley appeared from the eighth millennium BC onwards, further to the south, in the region of Khartoum, where the earliest pottery vessels were fashioned among the barely sedentary fisher-hunter-gatherer populations. We have to wait for the fifth millennium BC before the first visible traces of Neolithic sites appear in the Egyptian section of the Nile valley: the Faiyum and Merimda cultures each integrate domesticated and cultivated species.

But it was in the south, in Upper Egypt, doubtless from the end of the fifth millennium BC, that there came into being something which, if not the basis of pharaonic civilization, was at least one of its most important elements. With the Badarian/Amratian phase of the Predynastic the techniques of metalworking and the culture of 'death' both appeared. These pastoralist agriculturalists, still very much involved in a broad-spectrum economy whereby fishing and hunting played a crucial role, were able to exploit a large part of their ecosystem, extending from those parts of the wadis that were still regularly humid to the sometimes crowded banks of the river. Graves and funerary offerings convey the image of a society which, after some 500 years of existence, was diversifying (with specific types of objects appearing in specific individuals' tombs) and becoming more hierarchical (with accumulations of grave goods in the larger tombs). These two trends were to become more prominent in the next major cultural phase: the 'expansionist' Gerzean period.

Throughout the Badarian/Amaratian phase, in the more open landscape of Lower Egypt, true sedentary cultures were developing, consisting of pastoralist agriculturalists with direct links to the Near East. Maadi and Buto have the air of key sites through which Asiatic goods were filtering into Upper Egypt. It may have been a case of gradual contact during Naqada I, but foreign relations became considerably more apparent in the following period, and the Maadian culture presumably played some part in this. Although the Gerzean (Naqada II) culture developed out of the African-influenced Badarian/Amratian culture, its generally flat-based pots, its wavy handles and its original styles of decoration suggest that it was turning more towards the north than the south. Life in Upper Egypt was concentrated around the banks of the Nile. Abandoning the edges of the wadis, which had become inhospitable as a result of ecological change, the populations gathered together in the more limited area of the floodplain. The economy was transformed from one based on

pastoralism to one that was entirely agriculturally based, and the hitherto scattered groups of people began to cluster together much more
closely. This demographic concentration was not merely a physical phenomenon but also indicates the emergence of a dominant social class
who were the consumers of luxury goods and therefore directed their
energies into the control of raw materials. Once a class of specialized
craftsmen had also emerged, the Naqada society was increasingly dominated by 'non-producers' within a restricted territory, more and more
dependent on those who were still farming the land. For the first time,
the Egyptians were beginning to attempt to control the river, interfering
with the equilibrium of the Nilotic adaptation that had existed for a
millennium: they were going to irrigate the land. With the symbolic act
portrayed on the Scorpion Macehead, this hydrological intervention became part of a growing obsession with 'power'.

This wave of Naqada II culture was eventually to spread over the entire country. In the north it probably came into contact with the people
of Middle Egypt, who were part of the Maadian sphere of influence and
who constituted a kind of buffer-zone between the so-called 'Two Egypts'
or 'Two Lands'. This spread of the Naqada culture, the ultimate aim of
which was presumably the control of raw materials, must have been accompanied by a certain degree of violence. There is, however, nothing
to prove that it was actually a military campaign of conquest; on the
contrary, we cannot exclude the use of alliances and marriages. In the far
south, on the other hand, the people of the Naqada II culture benefited
from their precious allies in Nubia: the A-Group. Indeed, throughout
their history (including the Kushites of the 25th Dynasty), these south-
erners were never regarded as complete foreigners in the area of the Nile
valley to the north of the First Cataract. A little later, however, during
the 1st Dynasty, the desire to gain direct access to the precious goods
would lead to the absorption of Lower Nubia and its transformation
into a hierarchical land dominated by the image of the victorious pharaoh. In the face of royal armies charged with ensuring the security of the
southern trade-routes, the A-Group people were evidently wiped out.

If it was once believed that pharaonic Egypt simply burst out of the
sands at the very beginning of the third millennium BC, Petrie's discoveries quickly demonstrated that a process of gradual cultural maturation
had taken place, the precise length of which has proved difficult to assess. Despite this, we still tend to balk at the idea of these Neolithic peoples living along the banks of the Nile being the ancestors of their
celebrated historical successors. The Asiatic route opened onto a more
glorious past ... but Egyptian civilization was essentially based on the
Naqada culture. It is possible to look beyond even the immediate past,
and to see the origins of the pharaonic culture, in a sense, even in those

Palaeolithic hunter-fisher-gatherers, who – 20,000 years before the hydraulic activities of King Scorpion – had developed the essential patterns
of a communal life based on adaptation to the flooding and receding
waters of the river. They created the framework within which the various elements of Neolithization appeared, and then the Neolithic itself, a
production economy adapted to the particular regime of the Nile valley.
Finally, in the fourth millennium BC, there emerged the social and ideological apparatus that was to bring into being the pharaonic civilization,
with all its excavated monuments, images and texts.

Appendix 1: Relative chronology and the traditional dating systems

Flinders Petrie's system of 'sequence dates' was the first attempt to create a chronological framework for the Predynastic period. Based on 900 graves in the cemeteries of Hu and Abadiya, the method consisted of assigning the different types of material to a corpus and then arranging them according to a system of seriation (Petrie 1901: 4–12). Nine types of pottery were defined, partly according to the shape and decoration of the vessels. Petrie formulated the intuitive hypothesis that wavy-handled pots evolved gradually from globular vessels with clearly moulded functional handles toward cylindrical forms on which the handles were merely decorative. The 'sequence dating' chronology was thus initially organized around this concept of evolution in wavy-handled design.

A table of 50 sequence dates resulted, numbered from 30 onwards, in order to leave space for earlier cultures which had not yet been discovered. This turned out to be a wise precaution, given that Guy Brunton's excavations at el-Badari would later result in the identification of the Badarian period (see chapter 6). The lengths of the individual phases represented by each of these sequence dates were variable, and the only link with any absolute date was that between SD79–80 and the accession of King Menes in about 3100 BC.

Three great cultural changes were distinguished and these were assumed to correspond to three chronological phases:

- The Amratian (or Naqada I), comprising SD30–8, which corresponds to the maximum development of the black-topped, red ware (Petrie's 'type B') and vessels with painted white decorative motifs on a red body (type C).
- The Gerzean (or Naqada II), comprising SD39–60 and characterized by the appearance of pottery with wavy handles (type W), the so-

called coarse ware (type R) and decorations comprising brown paint on a cream background (type D).

- Finally there was Naqada III (corresponding to Petrie's so-called Semainean period), which was SD61–79/80, during which Petrie's 'late' (or type L) pottery appeared, so-called because its forms already suggested the pottery of the Dynastic period. According to Petrie, it was during the Naqada III phase that an Asiatic 'New Race' arrived in Egypt, sparking off the pharaonic civilization.

It is obvious that the validity of a system of this type depends on the reliability of the ceramic corpus on which it is based as well as on the coherence of the different procedures (18 in all) which allowed it to be used. On the other hand, since it was based on material from the Naqada region it was not necessarily applicable to the cemeteries in northern Egypt or Nubia, and it was for this reason that Junker, Scharff, Firth and Reisner refused to use it. Despite its obvious flaws, the system formed the sole means of organizing the Predynastic into cultural phases until Werner Kaiser devised his so-called 'Stufen' in 1957.

In 1942, however, the sequence dating ceramic corpus was seriously questioned by Walter Federn, a Viennese exile to the USA. While classifying the vessels from de Morgan's collection in the Brooklyn Museum, he was obliged to revise Petrie's types, although it is true that his work did not lead to any publication before Winifred Needler mentioned it in the *Journal of the Society for the Study of Egyptian Antiquities* in 1981. Based not only on the shape and decoration of the vessels but also on the different types of fabric used to make them, Federn's revised corpus removed Petrie's types L and F (i.e. his so-called 'fantastic' and 'late' types) and also qualified and completed the other types.

The essential work of revision, however, was undertaken by Kaiser, who, in the course of his doctoral thesis at Munich University, devoted himself to a crucial re-examination of the material forming the basis for the sequence dates. It emerged from his analysis that the W1 and W3 sub-types (i.e. the globular vessels with wavy handles) were problematic. Some examples will suffice here to demonstrate this point – thus, W1, fixed at SD40, refers only to a purchased vessel rather than an excavated one (as Elise Baumgartel noted elsewhere), while W1g, dated to SD58, actually covered SD58–70 (as grave b224 at el-Amra indicates), and the grave corresponding to W2a is unpublished.

Generally speaking, it appears that the 17 globular ceramics making up W1 and W3, Petrie's first eight sequences, are revealed by the analysis to be later, appearing only in SD46. Thus the famous wavy-handled pottery is no longer the guiding principle of Naqada II but simply a feature that happens to appear in the course of the development of this phase, as one particular aspect of its evolution.

There was therefore a perceived urgency to devise a new chronology. Kaiser did so using material from cemetery 14/1500 at Armant, excavated in the 1930s by Robert Mond and Oliver Myers. At once it became apparent that the horizontal patterning of the 170 published graves corresponded to a process of chronological evolution. The black-topped red ware was relatively common in the southern part of the cemetery, while the 'late' forms were concentrated towards the northern end. A detailed analysis of the classification, still based on Petrie's corpus, allowed Kaiser to correct and fine-tune the sequence dating system, which was by then about 60 years old. Three major phases of the Naqada period were thus confirmed, but refined by subdividing them into 11 *Stufen* from Ia to IIIb. In 1989, Stan Hendrickx's doctoral thesis allowed Kaiser's system to be applied to all of the Naqada-culture sites in Egypt. This resulted in slight modifications, particularly to the transitional subphases between Naqada I and II.

Finally, we should also mention the work of Barry Kemp (1982), who proposed new methods for an old problem, using mathematical seriation in place of Petrie's more subjective approach. His analysis also confirmed the delineation of three major groups, corresponding to the Amratian and Gerzean phases, as well as a final phase combining the final stages of the Predynastic with the early part of the Dynastic period.

Appendix 2: 'Absolute dates'

Both Petrie's sequence dates and Kaiser's *Stufen* can only be used as relative dating systems and strictly speaking only applied to sites in the Naqada bend of the river. It is clear that each site develops its own internal chronological sequence, as the recent excavations at the Delta-site of Buto have demonstrated.

However, the necessary links to an absolute chronology were made possible in the second half of the twentieth century by the development of methods of dating based on the analysis of physical and chemical phenomena, including thermoluminescence (TL) and radiocarbon (C-14) dating.

We know that Willard Libby tested the accuracy of the radiocarbon-dating system on material from the Faiyum region. From that point onwards, material from the whole of ancient Egypt – and particularly Predynastic Egypt – became the preferred focus of fieldwork with regard to the new dating technique because it was possible to compare the radiometric results with an existing chronological framework. This frenzy however led to a certain amount of misconception (see Säve-Söderbergh and Olsson 1970), given the complexity of the phenomena under consideration and the margins of uncertainty that they implied.

The basic principle of radiocarbon dating is the constant rate at which the amount of radioactive carbon diminishes once an organism (whether vegetable, animal or human) has died. Libby obtained a period of 5570 ± 30 for the so-called half-life of the ^{14}C isotope (i.e. the time taken for an amount of the isotope to be reduced by half). This is another way of saying that there was a 68.5 per cent chance of this half-life being between 5540 and 5600 years BP (before present), the 'present' being fixed at 1950, so that the latter had to be subtracted from the BP date in order to obtain a BC one.

All of this was originally based on the assumption that (1) the earth's atmosphere has always contained the same amount of radiocarbon as today, (2) the exchange with the biosphere is a rapid process, and (3) that the concentration of of radiocarbon in this biosphere is constant. However, we now know that there have been variations in the amount of radiocarbon in the atmosphere over the course of time, due to such factors as changes in the earth's magnetic field, climate changes, and, most recently, nuclear explosions. We also know that the system of exchange with the biosphere is not constant (more so in the case of wood than shells or bone), and the risks of contamination by other sources of radiocarbon (e.g. humus and limestone dissolved in water) are significant. Finally, it was determined in 1962 that the half-life of radiocarbon was not 5570 ± 30 but 5730 ± 30.

It therefore began to be regarded as essential to calibrate radiocarbon dates with the use of other dating methods. In the 1960s, the work of Suess on the Californian bristlecone pine (*Pinus aristata*), a tree which could live for up to 1000 years, allowed the first calibration tables to be created, whereby the radiocarbon years could be corrected and converted into calendar years by means of dendrochronology. There are now several such tables, allowing dates as early as 7000 BP to be calibrated.

It is therefore clear that the utilization of radiocarbon dating is not an easy task, in that various factors must be taken into account if it is to be used properly, such as assessment of the quality of the sample (removing from consideration those that have clearly been stored for a long time or subjected to contamination), the need for a multiplicity of dates (a few isolated dated samples count for little), and finally critical analysis of the results (rejecting those which are clearly aberrant) and careful statistical analysis of the data, as Fekri Hassan has done for the Predynastic (Hassan 1985) and the Sudan (Hassan 1986a). For the Predynastic period, our references to absolute dates are reliant on Hassan's work, and it is for this reason that I have chosen to cite BP (i.e. uncalibrated) dates for the immense period preceding 7000 BP, while I have used BC (calibrated BC) for the calibrated dates collected by Hassan from 7000 BP onwards.

Chart 3 (after Hassan 1985) synthesizes the calibrated radiocarbon dates, while chart 4 (after Kaiser 1985) integrates Kaiser's data into the overall system. Comparing the two, it is clear that there is a difference in terms of the respective positions of the Merimda and Faiyum cultures.

Charts and Maps

TYPE OF DEPOSIT	GEOLOGICAL FORMATION	INDUSTRY/SITE	CLIMATIC PHASE
	> 40,000 BP (C-14), 60,000 BP (TL)		
	Dibeira-Jer (Masmas?) ——?——	Early Sebilian? Khormusan	HYPER-ARID
	Korosko ——?——	Makhadma 6 Beit Allam	INCREASING ARIDITY
	c.100,000 BP	Nazlet Khater 2, 3 Nazlet Khater 1	
	5-metre Nile flood (Sohag region)		
	Unspecified	Acheulean sites at Nag el-Khalif	MORE HUMID
	c.300,000 BP		
	Dendera		HYPER-ARID Crisis at Dendera
	c.400,000 BP		
	Unspecified		GREATEST HUMIDITY

(Vertical labels spanning rows: Palaeolithic — Middle Palaeolithic — Lower Palaeolithic)

☐ Fine deposits   ○ Gravel deposits

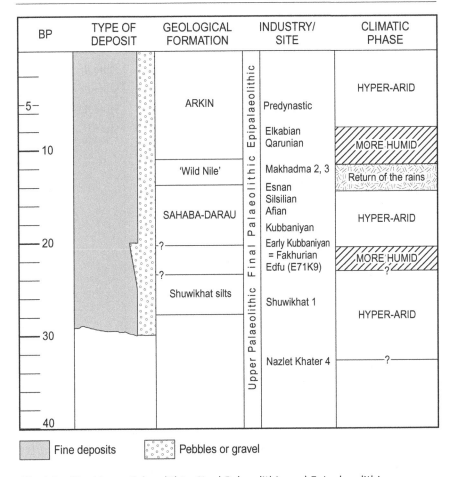

BP	TYPE OF DEPOSIT	GEOLOGICAL FORMATION	INDUSTRY/ SITE	CLIMATIC PHASE
			Epipalaeolithic	

Fine deposits   Pebbles or gravel

Chart 2   The Upper Palaeolithic, Final Palaeolithic and Epipalaeolithic industries of Egypt in their palaeoclimatic context, c.40,000–5,000 BP.

Opposite:
Chart 1   The Lower and Middle Palaeolithic industries of Egypt in their palaeoclimatic context, from 400,000 to 40,000 BP.

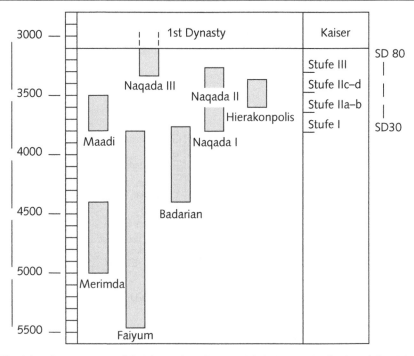

Chart 3 Comparison of Predynastic cultures with Kaiser's 'Stufen' and Petrie's 'sequence dates' (after Hassan 1985: fig. 2).

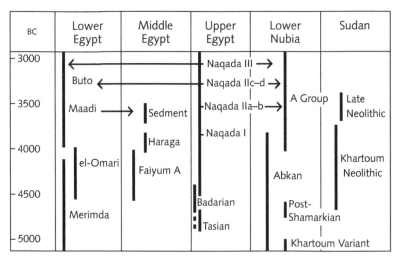

Chart 4 Radiocarbon-dated prehistoric phases in Egypt, Lower Nubia and Sudan (after Kaiser 1985: Abb. 10).

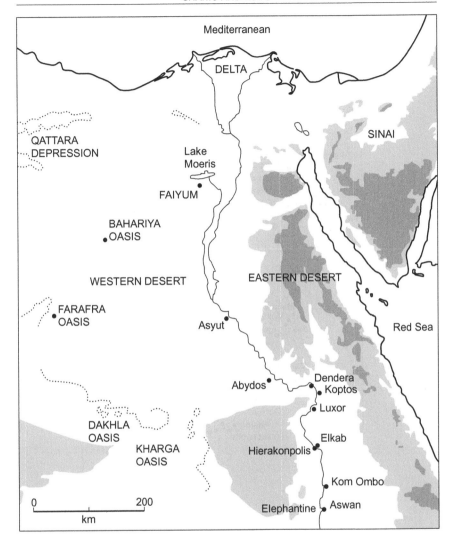

Map 1   The Nile valley and the surrounding deserts: the three great regions.

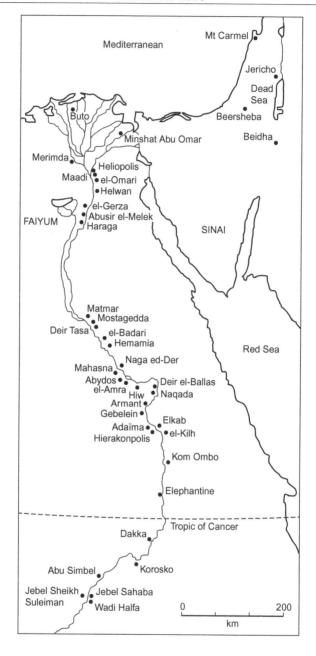

Map 2   The Nile valley from the Delta down to Wadi Halfa, showing the locations of prehistoric sites mentioned in the text.

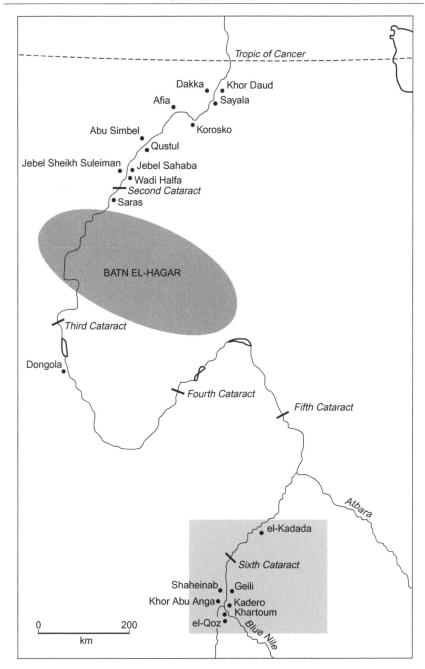

Map 3 The Sudanese section of the Nile valley, from the Tropic of Cancer down to the Blue Nile, showing the locations of prehistoric sites mentioned in the text.

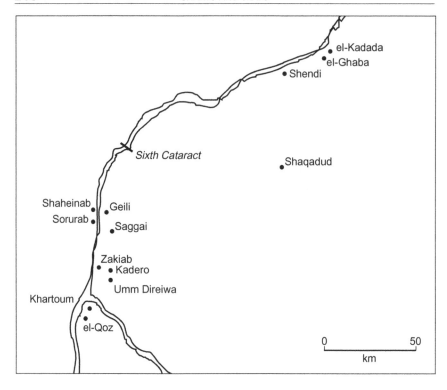

Map 4 The Sixth-Cataract region of the Nile valley, showing the locations of Khartoum Mesolithic and Khartoum Neolithic sites.

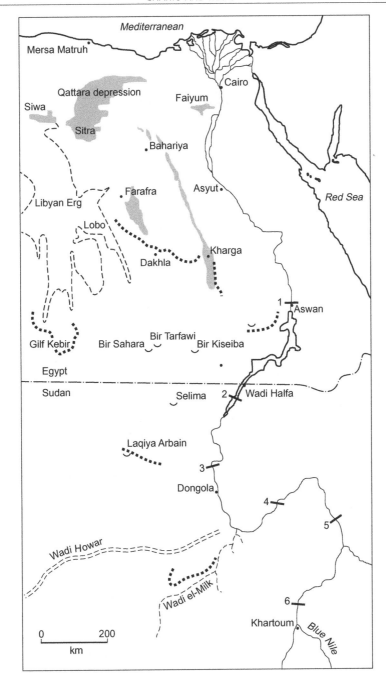

Map 5   The Western Desert.

Glossary

Acheulean Stone tool industry, characterized by roughly symmetrical bifacial handaxes and cleavers, which is linked with the appearance of *Homo erectus* and also early *Homo sapiens*.

angle burin Type of burin (see below) in which the facet meets an edge trimmed by chipping.

Aterian Palaeolithic industry (named after the site of Bir el-Ater in eastern Algeria) which was characterized by a distinctive type of tanged stone point (implying the use of hafting).

backed blade(let) Type of blade first produced in the early Upper Palaeolithic; when a blade or bladelet is 'backed', at least one edge is blunted by secondary retouch, thus allowing the tool to be handled more comfortably.

bulb of percussion Convex bump on the inside surface of a struck stone flake, immediately below the point of impact.

burin Multi-purpose blade tool (usually fashioned from flint) which is a typical Upper Palaeolithic artefact; its gouging or chisel-like working edge is formed by the removal of a distinctive flake or 'burin spall'. Burins are thought to have been used for graving or chiselling.

Cataracts, Nile The six rocky areas of rapids in the middle Nile valley between Aswan and Khartoum.

colluvium Type of unlithified deposit that can result from such natural processes as rock slides, soil erosion and solifluction. Colluvia (often located on hillslopes or at the bases of hills and cliffs) sometimes cover or displace archaeological deposits.

Cretaceous Last period of the Secondary geological era, divided into upper and lower Cretaceous and lasting from 130,000,000 to 65,000,000 BP. The period derives its name from the Latin word for chalk (*creta*), which is the dominant feature of its geological formations.

denticulate Flake or blade tool which has had a number of notches removed from its working edge, thus creating a kind of toothed effect.

endscraper Type of flake tool with a rounded retouched end, often made on a blade.

Epipalaeolithic Chronological term usually applied to the last phase of the Palaeolithic period in north Africa and the Ancient Near East. The Egyptian and Lower Nubian Epipalaeolithic (*c.*10,000–5500 BC) is characterized mainly by its innovative lithic technology (microlithic flake tools) and its chronological position between the Nilotic Upper Palaeolithic and Neolithic.

faience Glazed non-clay ceramic material widely used in Egypt for the production of such items as jewellery, *shabti*s and vessels.

Fakhurian Microlithic industry of the Late Palaeolithic, which flourished between about 16,000 and 15,600 BC. The blades are frequently less than 3 centimetres in length.

flake tool Sliver of stone removed from a core, which may either be used as a simple unmodified tool, or retouched to transform it into a specific type of artefact, such as an endscraper (see above).

Halfan Late Palaeolithic industry, found principally at encampments of hunters and fishers along the Nile valley in Sudan and Egypt, between about 18,000 and 15,000 BC. The assemblages include small Levallois-style tools used to produce harpoons and arrows.

hieroglyphics (Greek: 'sacred carved (letters)') Script consisting of pictograms, ideograms and phonograms arranged in horizontal and vertical lines, that was in use from the late Gerzean period (*c.*3200 BC) to the late fourth century AD.

Holocene The last part of the Quaternary geological era, beginning around 12,000 BP and continuing up to the present day. The beginning of the Holocene coincides with the appearance of the earliest Neolithic cultures of the Near East and Middle East.

Horus name The first royal name in the sequence of five names making up the Egyptian royal titulary, usually written inside a *serekh* (see below).

inselberg Steep-sided hill rising up out of a flat plain, characteristic of semi-arid regions.

el-Khiam point Type of point (named after a site in Paalestine) consisting of a truncated and symmetrically notched bladelet, sharpened at the end by marginal retouch.

Levallois technique Method of producing large standardized flake tools from specially prepared flint cores (sometimes described as 'tortoise cores', because of their regular faceted appearance), usually dating to the Middle Palaeolithic (*c.*100,000–35,000 BP), but also occasionally occurring in both Lower and Upper Palaeolithic industries. The technique – closely associated with early *Homo sapiens* and Neanderthals – is named after Levallois-Peret, a site in the Seine valley, France.

mastaba (Arabic: 'bench') Type of Egyptian tomb, the rectangular superstructure of which resembles the low mud-brick benches outside Egyptian houses. It was used for both royal and private burials in the Early Dynastic Period but only for private burials from the Old Kingdom onwards.

microburin Although microburins have the appearance of small burins (see above), they are actually not tools at all but simply waste chips produced when microliths are made by the so-called 'microburin method', whereby a blade is notched and then has a small portion snapped off. It is this snapped-off portion of the blade which has been given the somewhat confusing name of microburin.

microlith Type of stone tool, comprising a small blade or fraction of blade, usually less than 5 mm long and 4 mm thick, which is regarded as the archetypal tool of the Mesolithic period, although it is now also recognized in some Palaeolithic industries. Single microliths were sometimes used as the tip of an implement, weapon or arrow, while multiple examples were evidently hafted together to form composite cutting edges on tools.

Mousterian One of the key stone tool industries of the Middle Palaeolithic, based on flakes produced from carefully prepared cores using the Levallois technique, which gradually replaced the heavier handaxes of the Acheulean industry (see above).

nome, nome symbols Greek term used to refer to the 42 traditional provinces of Egypt, which the ancient Egyptians themselves called *sepat*. For most of the dynastic period, there were 22 Upper Egyptian and 20 Lower Egyptian nomes.

Oligocene Part of the Tertiary geological era which lasted from *c*.30,000,000 to 25,000,000 BP.

Opening of the Mouth ceremony Funerary ritual by which the body of the deceased and/or his funerary statuary were brought to life.

opposed-platform core Core with striking platforms on two opposite sides, enabling two sets of flakes to be removed.

Ouchtata retouch Process by which a blade is 'backed' (i.e. one edge dulled by controlled flaking), leaving behind minute flake scars, thus allowing the artefact to be held in the hand or more efficiently hafted into a compound tool.

palace-façade Architectural style comprising a sequence of recessed niches, which was particularly characteristic of the external walls of Early Dynastic funerary buildings at Abydos and Saqqara.

platform (striking platform) Term used in the description of methods of stone tool production. It refers to the part of a core which is struck in order to create a flake. In the course of this act of striking, the platform itself becomes partially detached from the core, along with the flake. In some cases, the platform may be 'prepared' before striking, in order to facilitate the production of narrower, longer flakes.

playa Plain characterized by a hard clayey surface and intermittently submerged beneath a shallow lake.

Pleistocene The earlier part of the Quaternary geological era, which was itself divided into the 'lower', 'middle' and 'upper' Pleistocene. Lasting from about 1.8 million to 12,000 years ago, it followed the Pliocene and preceded the Holocene (see above). During the Pleistocene period, Palaeolithic cultures flourished throughout the world.

Pliocene Stratigraphic division from the end of the Tertiary geological era, lasting from about 5 million to 1.8 million years ago. It followed the Miocene and preceded the Pleistocene.

Pyramid Texts The earliest Egyptian funerary texts, comprising some 800 spells or 'utterances' written in columns on the walls of the corridors and burial chambers of nine pyramids of the late Old Kingdom and First Intermediate Period.

Quaternary Geological entity corresponding to the most recent period of the Cenozoic era. The Quaternary is made up of two phases: the Pleistocene (extending from 1.8 million years to 12,000 years ago) and the Holocene (from

12,000 years ago to the present).

rekhyt-bird   Egyptian term for the lapwing (*Vanellus vanellus*), a type of plover with a characteristic crested head, often used as a symbol for foreigners or subject peoples.

royal titulary   Classic sequence of names and titles held by each of the pharaohs consisting of five names (the so-called 'fivefold titulary'), which was not fully established until the Middle Kingdom. It consisted of the Horus name, the Golden Horus name, the Two Ladies name (*nebty*), the birth name (nomen; *sa-Ra*) and the throne-name (prenomen; *nesu-bit*)

scalene triangles   Type of geometric microlithic tool, also known as a 'microtriangle', characteristic of Epipalaeolithic industries such as the Afian and the Silsilian. Groups of geometrics of this type were designed to be mounted as boring and cutting tools.

Sebilian   Upper Palaeolithic industry occurring at sites in Upper Egypt (*c.*13,000–10,000 BC). It was first identified in 1923 by Edmond Vignard, who suggested that it evolved gradually from the use of the Levallois technique to the production of microblades, although more recent research suggests that this chronological explanation is less likely. It seems to have been roughly contemporary with the Sebekian and Silsilian industries, although it is not clear whether these three industries correspond to different ethnic groups.

sed-festival   (*heb-sed*; royal jubilee) Royal ritual of renewal and regeneration, which was intended to be celebrated by the Egyptian king only after a reign of thirty years had elapsed.

sequence dating   Method of 'occurrence seriation' developed by Flinders Petrie (initially on the basis of pottery from Diospolis Parva) as a means of assigning relative dates to unstratified prehistoric material from Predynastic cemeteries. He was able to discern changing patterns in material culture by observing the presence or absence of particular artefacts and styles. (See Appendix 1.)

serekh   Rectangular panel (perhaps representing a palace gateway) surmounted by the Horus falcon, within which the king's 'Horus name' was written.

sidescraper   Flake tool with a retouched working edge along its length.

Silsilian   Sophisticated Upper Palaeolithic blade and microblade industry, using flint and chalcedony to make truncated blades, backed bladelets, notches, denticulates and occasional burins.

single-platform core   Core with only one striking platform.

striking platform   See *platform*.

technocomplex   Group of cultures each of which produces assemblages comprising some types of artefacts from a general 'family', but none of which contains the whole repertoire. All of the cultures in the technocomplex tend to be similar to one another in terms of their economic, technological and ecological adaptations.

tuff   Type of rock formed by the consolidation of volcanic ash.

Abbreviations

AAR	*The African Archaeological Review*
AN	*Archéo-Nil*
ANM	*Archéologie du Nil Moyen*
ASAE	*Annales du Service des Antiquités de l'Egypte, Cairo*
BAIEPE	*Bulletin de l'Association Internationale pour l'Etude de la Préhistoire Egyptienne, Paris*
BAR (IS)	British Archaeological Reports (International Series)
BCE	*Bulletin de Liaison du Groupe International d'Etude de la Céramique Egyptienne*
BIE	*Bulletin de l'Institut de l'Egypte*
BIFAO	*Bulletin de l'Institut Français d'Archéologie Orientale, Cairo*
BiOr	*Bibliotheca Orientalia, Leiden*
BSAE	*British School of Archaeology in Egypt*
BSAP	*Bulletin de la Societé d'Anthropologie de Paris*
BSFE	*Bulletin de la Société Française d'Egyptologie, Paris*
BSGE	*Bulletin de la Société de la Géographie de l'Egypte*
BSGF	*Bulletin de la Société de Géologie de France*
BSPF	*Bulletin de la Société Préhistorique Française, Paris*
CA	*Current Anthropology*
CdE	*Chronique d'Egypte*
DE	*Discussions in Egytology, Oxford*
IEJ	*Israel Exploration Journal*
JAH	*Journal of African History*
JAOS	*Journal of the American Oriental Society, New Haven CT*
JARCE	*Journal of the American Research Center in Egypt, Princeton NJ*
JAS	*Journal of Archaeological Science*
JASt	*Journal of African Studies*
JbRGZM	*Jahrbuch des römisch-germanische Zentralmuseen, Mainz*

JEA	*Journal of Egyptian Archaeology, London*
JFA	*Journal of Field Archaeology*
JHE	*Journal of Human Evolution*
JNES	*Journal of Near Eastern Studies, Chicago IL*
JPOS	*Journal of the Palestine Oriental Society*
JRAI	*Journal of the Royal Anthropological Institute*
JSSEA	*Journal of the Society for the Study of Egyptian Antiquities, Toronto*
JWP	*Journal of World Prehistory*
LÄ	*Lexikon der Ägyptologie. Wiesbaden*
MCRAPE	*Mémoires du Centre des Recherches: Anthropologie, Préhistoire et Ethnographie, Paris*
MDAIK	*Mitteilungen des Deutschen Archäologischen Instituts, Abteilung Kairo, Wiesbaden*
NA	*Nyame Akuma*
NAR	*Norwegian Archaeological Review*
PPS	*Proceedings of the Prehistoric Society*
RdE	*Revue d'Egyptologie, Paris*
SAK	*Studien zur Altägyptischen Kultur, Hamburg*
VA	*Varia Aegyptiaca*
ZÄS	*Zeitschrift der für ägyptische Sprache und Altertumskunde, Berlin*

Bibliography

Adams, B. 1974. *Ancient Hierakonpolis (and Supplement)*. Warminster.

Adamson, D.A. 1982. The integrated Nile. In M.A.J. Williams and D.A. Adamson (eds), *A Land Between Two Niles*. Rotterdam, pp. 221–34.

Aksamit, J. 1989. The gold handle of a fishtail dagger from Gebelein (Upper Egypt). In L. Krzyzaniak and M. Kobusiewicz (eds), *Late Prehistory of the Nile Basin and the Sahara*. Poznan, pp. 325–32.

Albright, W.F. 1935. Palestine in the earliest historical periods. *JPOS* 15.

Ambrose, S.H. 1984. The introduction of pastoral adaptations to the highlands of East Africa. In J.D. Clark and S.A. Brandt (eds), *From Hunters to Farmers: The Causes and Consequences of Food Production in Africa*. Berkeley, pp. 212–39.

Amiran, R. 1974. An Egyptian jar fragment with the name of Narmer from Arad. *IEJ* 24: 4–12.

—— and Glass, 1979. An archaeological-petrographical study of 15 W-Ware pots in the Ashmolean Museum. *Tel Aviv* 6: 54–9.

André, L., Navez, J., De Putter, Th. and Bavay, L., forthcoming. *In situ* trace element determination by laser ablation inductively coupled plasma spectrometry: an application to Syrian and Egyptian obsidian artefacts.

Arkell, A.J. 1949. *Early Khartoum*. Oxford.

—— 1950. Varia Sudanica. *JEA* 36: 24–40.

—— 1953a. *Shaheinab*. Oxford.

—— 1953b. The Sudan origin of Predynastic 'Black Incised' pottery. *JEA* 39: 76–9.

—— 1955. *A History of the Sudan from the Earliest Times to 1821*. London.

—— 1960. The origin of the black-red pottery. *JEA* 46: 105–6.

—— 1975. *The Prehistory of the Nile Valley*. Handbuch der Orientalistik 1. Leiden.

—— and Ucko, P.J. 1965. Reviews of Predynastic development in the Nile Valley. *CA* 6: 145–66.

Asselbergh, H. 1961. *Chaos en Beheersing. Documenten uit aeneolitisch Egypte*. Leiden.

Assman, J. 1989. *Maat, l'Egypte pharaonique et l'idée de justice sociale*. Paris.

—— 1990. *Ma'at: Gerechtigkeit und Unsterblichkeit im Alten Ägypten*. Munich.

Atzler, M. 1981. *Untersuchungen zur Herausbildung von Herrschaftsformen in Agypten*. Hildesheimer Ägyptologische Beiträge 16. Hildesheim.

Aurenche, O., Cauvin, J., Cauvin, M-C., Copeland, L., Hours, E., Salanville, P. 1981. Chronologie et organisation de l'espace dans le Proche-Orient de 12000 à 5600 avant J.-C. (14000 à 12000 BP). In *Préhistoire du Levant: chronologie et organisation de l'espace depuis les origines jusqu'au VI millénaire*, Lyon, Colloques internationaux du CNRS no 598, Paris, Maison de l'Orient méditerraneéen, pp. 571–601.

Avi-Yonah, E. 1985. To see the God . . . reflections on the iconography of the decorated chamber in ancient Hierakonpolis. In S. Groll (ed.), *Papers for Discussion Presented by the Department of Egyptology, Jerusalem, The Hebrew University* II. Jerusalem, pp. 7–82.

Ayrton, E.R. and Loat, W.L. 1911. *Predynastic Cemetery at El Mahasna*. London.

Badawi, A. 1978. Die Grabung der ägyptischen Altertümerverwaltung in Merimde Benisalame im Oktober/November 1976. *MDAIK* 34: 43–51.

—— 1980. Beigabengräber aus Merimde. *MDAIK* 36: 70–76.

Baines, J. 1988. Literacy, social organization, and the archaeological record : the case of early Egypt. In J. Gledhill, B. Bender and M.T. Larsen (eds), *State and Society. The Emergence and Development of Social Hierarchy and Political Centralisation*. London, pp. 192–214.

Ball, J. 1939. *Contributions to the geography of Egypt*. Cairo.

Balout, L. 1955. *Préhistoire de l'Afrique du Nord*. Paris.

Banks, K.M. 1982. Late Paleolithic and Neolithic grinding implements in Egypt. *Lithic Technology* 60/1: 12–20.

Bar Josef, O. and Philips, J. 1977. *Prehistoric Investigations in Gebel Maghara, Northern Sinai*, Qedem 7, Monographs of the Institute of Archaeology, The Hebrew University of Jerusalem. Jerusalem.

Bard, K. 1987. The geography of excavated Predynastic sites and the rise of complex society. *JARCE* 24: 81–93.

Barich, B. 1978. La seria stratigrafica de l'Uadi Ti-n-Torha (Acacus, Libia). Per una interpretazione della facies a ceramica saharosudanesi. *Origini* 8: 7–184.

—— 1984. The Epipaeolithic-ceramic groups of Libyan Sahara: notes for an economic model of the cultural development in the West-Central Africa. In L. Krzyzaniak and M. Kobusiewicz (eds), *Origin and Early Development of Food-Producing Cultures in North-Eastern Africa* . Poznan, pp. 399–410.

—— 1989. Uan Muhuggiag rock shelter (Tadrart Acacus) and the late prehistory of the Libyan Sahara. In L. Krzyzaniak and M. Kobusiewicz (eds), *Late Prehistory of the Nile Basin and the Sahara*. Poznan, pp. 499–505.

—— and Hassan, F. 1987. The Farafra Oasis archaeological project. *NA* 29: 16–21.

Barocas, C., Fattovich, R. and Tosi, M. 1989. The Oriental Institute of Naples expedition to Petrie's South Town (Upper Egypt), 1977–1983 : an interim report. In L. Krzyzaniak and M. Kobusiewicz (eds), *Late Prehistory of the Nile Basin and the Sahara*, Poznan, pp. 295–302.

Baumgartel, E. 1955. *The Cultures of Prehistoric Egypt* I. 2nd edn. (1st edn. 1947), London.

—— 1960. *The Cultures of Prehistoric Egypt* II. London.

—— 1970. *Petrie's Nagada Excavations : A Supplement.* London.

Bavay, L. 1997. Matière première et commerce à longue distance: le lapis-lazuli et l'Egypte prédynastique. *AN* 7: 79–100.

Beadnell, H. J. L. 1905. *The Topography and Geology of the Fayum Province of Egypt. Geological Survey of Egypt.* Cairo.

von Beckerath, J. 1956. *Šmsj-Hr* in der ägyptischen Vor-und Frühzeit. *MDAIK* 14: 1–10.

Beit-Arieh, I. 1980. A Chalcolithic site near Serabit el-Khadim. *Tel Aviv* 7: 45–64.

Besançon, J. 1957. *L'Homme et le Nil.* Paris.

Beyries, S. and Inizan, M.L. 1982. Typologie, ocre, fonction. *Studia Praehistorica Belgica* 2: 313–22.

Bietak M. and Engelmayer, R. 1963. *Eine frühdynastische Abri-Siedlung mit Felsmalereien.* Vienna.

Boeda, E. 1982. Etude experimentale de la technologie des pointes levallois. *Studia Praehistorica Belgica* 2: 23–56.

Boehmer, R.M. 1974. Das Rollsiegel im prädynastischen Ägypten. *Archäologische Anzeiger* 4: 495–514.

—— 1991. Gebel el-Arak und Gebel el-Tarif-Griff: keine Falschungen. *MDAIK* 47: 51–60.

Boessneck, J. 1988. *Die Tierwelt des Alten Ägypten.* Munich.

Bökönyi, S. 1985. The animal remains of Maadi, Egypt: a preliminary report. In M. Liverani, A. Palmieri and R. Peroni (eds), *Studi di Paletnologia in onore di Salvatore M. Puglisi.* Rome, pp. 495–9.

Bomann, A. 1995. Fieldwork 1994–5: Wadi Abu Had-Wadi Dib, Eastern Desert. *JEA* 81: 14–17.

—— and Young, R. 1994. Preliminary survey in the Wadi Abu Had Eastern Desert, 1992. *JEA* 80: 23–44.

Bonhême M.A. and Forgeau, A. 1988. *Pharaon. Les secrets du pouvoir.* Paris.

Bower, B. 1990. Civilization and its discontents. Why did the world's first civilization cut a swathe across the Near East? *Science News* 137: 136–9.

Brack A. and Zoller, H. 1989. Die Pflanze auf der dekorierten Naqada II-Keramik: Aloe oder Wildbanane (Ensete?). *MDAIK* 45: 33–53.

Brewer, D.J. 1987. Seasonality in the prehistoric Fayum based on the incremental growth structures of the Nile catfish (Pisces: Clarias). *JAS* 14: 459–72.

—— 1989a. A model for resource exploitation in the prehistoric Fayum. In L. Krzyzaniak and M. Kobusiewicz (eds), *Late Prehistory of the Nile Basin and the Sahara.* Poznan, pp. 127–38.

—— 1989b. *Fishermen, Hunters and Herders, Zooarchaeology in the Fayum (ca.8000–5000 BP),* BAR IS 478. Oxford.

Brezillon, M. 1971. *La dénomination des objets de pierre taillée: matériaux pour un vocabulaire des préhistoriens de langue française.* Paris [supplement of *Gallia Préhistoire*].

Brünner-Traut, E. 1975. Drei altägyptische Totenboote und vorgeschichtliche Bestattungsgefässe. *RdE* 27: 41–55.

Brunton, G. 1932. The Predynastic town-site at Hierakonpolis. In *Studies Pre-*

sented to F. Ll. Griffith. London, pp. 272–6.

—— 1937. *Mostagedda and the Tasian Culture*. London.

—— 1948. *Matmar*. London.

Brunton G. and Caton-Thompson, G. 1928. *The Badarian Civilisation*. London.

Butler, B.H. 1974. Skeletal remains from a Late Paleolithic site near Esna, Egypt. In D. Lubell (ed.), *The Fakhurian, a Late Paleolithic Industry from Upper Egypt*. Cairo, pp. 176–83.

Butzer, K.W.1959. Environment and human ecology in Egypt during Predynastic and Early Dynastic times. *BSGE* 32: 51–9.

—— 1976. *Early Hydraulic Civilisation in Egypt*. Chicago.

—— 1980. Pleistocene history of the Nile Valley in Egypt and Lower Nubia. In M.A.J. Williams and H. Faure (eds), *The Sahara and the Nile*. Rotterdam, pp. 253–80.

—— and Hansen, C.L. 1968. *Desert and River in Nubia: Geomorphology and Prehistoric Environments at the Aswan Reservoir*. Madison.

Camps, G. 1968. *Amekni, néolithique ancien du Hoggar*. Paris.

—— 1974. *Les civilisations préhistoriques de l'Afrique du Nord et du Sahara*. Paris.

Camps-Faber, H. 1966. *Matière et art mobilier dans la préhistoire nord-Africaine et saharienne*. Paris.

Caneva, I. (ed.) 1983. Pottery using gatherers and hunters at Saggai (Sudan): preconditions for food-production. *Origini* 12: 7–278.

—— 1988. *El Geili: The History of a Middle Nile Environment, 7000 BC–AD 1500*. BAR IS 424. Oxford.

—— and Marks, A. 1990. More on the Shaqadud pottery : evidence for Sahara-Nilotic connections during the 6th–4th millennium BC *ANM* 4: 11–35.

—— and Zarattini, I. 1983. Microlithism and functionality in the Saggai 1 industry. *Origini* 12: 209–33.

——, Frangipane, M. and Palmieri, A.M. 1987. Predynastic Egypt: new data from Maadi. *AAR* 5: 105–14.

——, —— and —— 1989. Recent excavations at Maadi. In L. Krzyzaniak and M. Kobusiewicz (eds), *Late Prehistory of the Nile Basin and the Sahara*, Poznan, pp. 287–94.

Capart, J. 1904. *Les débuts de l'art en Egypte*. Brussels.

Carlson, R.L. and Sigstad, J.S. 1973. Paleolithic and late Neolithic sites excavated by the Fourth Colorado Expedition. *Kush* 15: 51–8.

Case, H. and Payne, J.C. 1962. Tomb 100 : the Decorated Tomb at Hierakonpolis. *JEA* 48: 5–18.

Casini, M. 1974. Manufatti litici Egiziani a Coda di Pesce. *Origini* 8: 203–28.

Castillos, J.J. 1982. *A Reappraisal of the Published Evidence on Egyptian Predynastic and Early Dynastic Cemeteries*. Toronto.

Caton-Thompson, G. 1952. *Kharga Oasis in Prehistory*. London.

—— and Gardner, E.W. 1934. *The Desert Fayum*. London.

—— and Whittle, E.H. 1975. Thermoluminescence dating of the Badarian. *Antiquity* 49: 89–97.

Cauvin, J. 1994. *Naissance des divinités. Naissance de l'agriculture. La révolution des symbóles au Néolithique*. Paris.

—— and M.C. 1985. Néolithisation. In *Encyclopedia Universalis*. Supplement, pp. 1073–9.

Cauvin, M.C. 1974. Hâches à encoches de Syrie: essai d'interpretation culturelle. *Paléorient* 2/2: 311–22.

de Cenival, J.L. 1981. *Un siècle de fouilles françaises en Egypte, 1880–1980*. Paris, IFAO/Musée du Louvre, p. 13 [no.7: fragment of a plate bearing the name of King Aha-Menes].

Chmielewski, W. 1968. Early and Middle Paleolithic sites near Arkin, Sudan. In F. Wendorf (ed.), *Prehistory of Nubia* I. Dallas, pp. 110–93.

Churcher, C.S. and Smith, P.E.L. 1972. Kom Ombo: preliminary report on late Paleolithic sites in Upper Egypt. *Science* 177: 1069–76.

Cialowicz, K.M. 1987. *Les têtes de massues des periodes prédynastique et archaique dans la vallée du Nil*. Warsaw and Cracow.

—— 1997. Remarques sur la tête de massue du roi Scorpion. In J. Sliwa (ed.), *Studies in Ancient Art and Civilization 8*. Cracow, pp. 11–27.

Clark, J.D. 1970. *The Prehistory of Africa*. London.

—— 1978. The microlithic industries of Africa : their antiquity and possible economic implications. In V.N. Misra and P. Bellwood (eds), *Recent Advances in Indo-Pacific Prehistory*, pp. 95–103.

—— 1989. Shabona: an Early Khartoum settlement on the White Nile. In L. Krzyzaniak and M. Kobusiewicz (eds), *Late Prehistory of the Nile Basin and the Sahara*. Poznan, pp. 387–410.

—— and Brandt, S.A. (eds) 1984. *From Hunters to Farmers: the Causes and Consequences of Food Production in Africa*. Berkeley, Los Angeles, London.

Close, A.E. (ed.) 1986. *The Wadi Kubbaniya Skeleton: a Late Paleolithic burial in Southern Egypt*. Dallas.

—— 1987. *Prehistory of Arid North Africa: Essays in Honour of Fred Wendorf*. Dallas.

Connor, R.D. and Marks, A. 1986. The Terminal Pleistocene on the Nile: the final Nilotic adjustment. In L.G. Strauss (ed.), *The End of the Paleolithic in the Old World*, BAR IS 284, pp. 171–99.

Crowfoot-Payne, J. 1993. *Catalogue of the Predynastic Egyptian Collection in the Ashmolean Museum*. Oxford.

Crubezy, E. 1991. *Caractères discrets et évolution: exemple d'une population nubienne Missiminia (Soudan)*. Unpublished PhD thesis. Bordeaux.

—— 1992. De l'anthropologie physique à la paléo-ethnologie funéraire et à la paléobiologie. *AN* 2: 7–19.

—— Duday, H. and Janin, T. 1992. L'Anthropologie de terrain: le particularisme égyptien. *AN* 2: 21–36.

Czielsa, E. 1989. Sitra and related sites at the western border of Egypt. In L. Krzyzaniak and M. Kobusiewicz (eds), *Late Prehistory of the Nile Basin and the Sahara*. Poznan, pp. 205–14.

Davis, W. 1976. The origin of register composition in Predynastic Egyptian art. *JAOS* 96/3: 404–8.

—— 1981. The foreign relations of Predynastic Egypt, 1: Egypt and Palestine in the Predynastic period. *JSSEA* 11/1: 21–7.

—— 1983a. Cemetery T at Nagada. *MDAIK* 39: 17–28.

—— 1983b. Artists and patrons in Predynastic and Early Dynastic Egypt. *SAK* 10: 119–39.

De Paepe, P. 1986. Etude mineralogique et chimique de la céramique néolithique d'El Kadada et ses implications archéologiques. *ANM* 1: 113–37.

—— and Geus, F. 1987. Recent research of Sudanese ceramics. *BCE* 12: 41–6.

Debono, F. 1948. Le Paléolithique final et le Mésolithique à Helouan. *ASAE* 48: 629–37.

—— 1950. Désert oriental: mission archéologique royale 1949. *CdE* 25: 237–40.

—— 1951. Expedition archéologique royale du désert oriental. *ASAE* 51/1: 59–91.

—— 1970. Un site negadien: les trouvailles prédynastiques de Deir el-Médineh. In *Deir el-Medineh 1970*. Cairo: IFAO, p. 15.

—— and Mortensen, B. 1988. *The Predynastic Cemetery of Heliopolis*. Mainz am Rhein.

—— and —— 1990. *El Omari: a Neolithic Settlement and other Sites in the Vicinity of Wadi Hof Helwan*. Mainz am Rhein.

Derchain, R. 1966. Menès, le roi 'quelqu'un'. *RdE* 18: 31–6.

Derry, D.E. 1956. The Dynastic Race. *JEA* 42: 80–5.

Devroey, E.J. 1950. Les sources du Nil au Congo belge et au Ruanda-Urundi. *Bulletin de l'Institut Royal Colonial Belge* 21: 248–79.

Dollfus, G. 1989. Les processus de néolithisation en Iran: bilan des connaissances. In O. Aurenche and J. Cauvin (eds), *Néolithisations: Proche-Orientale, Méditerranée orientale, Nord de l'Afrique, Europe méridionale, Chine, Amerique du Sud*. BAR IS 516, pp. 37–64.

Dreyer, G. 1990. Umm el-Qaab, Nachuntersuchungen im frühzeitlichen Königsfriedhof. 3/4 Vorbericht. *MDAIK* 46: 53–89.

—— 1991. Zur Rekonstruktion der Oberbauten der Königsgräber der 1. Dynastie in Abydos. *MDAIK* 47: 93–104.

—— Hartung, V., Hikade, T., Köhler, C., Müller, V. and Pumpenmeier, F. 1998. Umm el-Qaab, Nachuntersuchungen im frühzeitlichen Königsfriedhof 9/1/ Vorbericht. *MDAIK* 54: 79–165.

Duday, H. and Sellier, P. 1990. L'archéologie des gestes funeraires et la taphonomie. *Nouvelles de l'Archéologie* 40: 12–14.

Dutour, O. 1989. *Hommes fossiles du Sahara: peuplements Holocènes du Mali septentrional*. Paris.

Edward, I. and Hope, C.A. 1989. A note on the Neolithic ceramics from the Dakhleh Oasis (Egypt). In L. Krzyzaniak and M. Kobusiewicz (eds), *Late Prehistory of the Nile Basin and the Sahara*. Poznan, pp. 233–42.

Eiwanger, J. 1978. Erster Vorbericht über die Wiederaufnahme der Grabungen in der neolithischen Siedlung Merimde-Benisaläme. *MDAIK* 34: 33–42.

—— 1979a. Zweiter Vorbericht über die Wiederaufnahme der Grabungen in der neolithischen Siedlung Merimde-Benisaläme. *MDAIK* 35: 23–57.

—— 1979b. Geschoßspitzen aus Merimde. *JbRGZM* 26: 61–74.

—— 1980. Dritter Vorbericht über die Wiederaufnahme der Grabungen in der neolithischen Siedlung Merimde-Benisaläme. *MDAIK* 36: 61–76.

—— 1982. Die neolithische Siedlung von Merimde-Benisalame. *MDAIK* 38: 67–82.

—— 1983. Die Entwicklung der Vorgeschichtlichen Kultur in Ägypten. In J. Assmann and G. Burkard, *5000 Jahre Ägypten. Genese und Permanenz pharaonischer Kunst*. Heidelberg, pp. 61–74.

—— 1984. *Merimde-Benisaläme I: Die Funde der Urschicht*, Archäologische Veröffentlichungen 47, Mainz am Rhein.

—— 1987. Die Archäologie der späten Vorgeschichte: Bestand und Perspektiven. In J. Assmann, G. Burkard and W.V. Davies (eds), *Problems and Priorities in Egyptian Archaeology*. London and New York, pp. 81–104.

—— 1988. *Merimde-Benisalame II: Die Funde der mittleren Merimdekultur*, Archäologische Veröffentlichungen 51, Mainz am Rhein.

—— 1992. *Merinde Benisalame III. Die funde der jüngeren Merindekultur*, Archäologische Veröffentlichungen 47, Mainz am Rhein.

El-Baz, E. 1984. *The Geology of Egypt: An Annotated Bibliography*. Leiden.

El-Hadidi, N. 1980. Vegetation of the Nubian Desert (Nabta Region). In F. Wendorf (ed.), *Prehistory of Eastern Sahara*. New York, pp. 345–51.

El-Yakhi, E. 1981. Remarks on the armless human figures represented on Gerzean boats. *JSSEA* 11/2: 77–83.

Emery, W.B. 1961. *Archaic Egypt*. Harmondsworth.

Emery-Barbier, A. 1990. L'homme et l'environnement en Egypte durant la période prédynastique. In S. Bottema, G. Entjes-Nieborg and W. van Zeist (eds), *Man's Role in the Shaping of the Eastern Mediterranean Landscape*. Rotterdam.

Engelbach, R. 1923. *Harageh*. London.

Fattovich, R. 1989. The late prehistory of the Gash Delta (Eastern Sudan). In L. Krzyzaniak and M. Kobusiewicz (eds), *Late Prehistory of the Nile Basin and the Sahara*. Poznan, pp. 481–98.

Finkenstaedt, E. 1976. The chronology of Egyptian Predynastic black-topped ware. *ZÄS* 103: 5–8.

—— 1979. Egyptian ivory tusks and tubes. *ZÄS* 106: 51–9.

—— 1980. Regional style painting in prehistoric Egypt. *ZÄS* 107: 116–20.

—— 1981. The location of styles in paintings: white cross-lined ware at Nagada. *JARCE* 8: 7–10.

—— 1983. Beads at Badari. *ZÄS* 110: 27–9.

—— 1984. Violence and kingship: the evidence of the palettes. *ZÄS* 111: 107–10.

Firth, G.M. 1912. *Archaeological Survey of Nubia: Report for 1908–1909*. Cairo.

—— 1927. *Archaeological Survey of Nubia: Report for 1910–1911*. Cairo.

Fischer, H.G. 1958. A fragment of Late Predynastic Egyptian relief from the Eastern Delta. *Artibus Asiae* 21/1: 64–88.

Gaballa, G.A. 1976. *Narrative in Egyptian Art*. Mainz.

Gabra, S. 1930. Fouilles du Service des Antiquités à Deir Tasa. *ASAE* 30: 147–58.

Gabriel, B. 1976. Neolitische Steinplätze und Palaeoökologie in den Ebeneti der östlichen Zentralsahara. *Palaeoecology of Africa* 9: 25–40.

—— 1977. *Zum ökölogischen Wandel im Neolithikum den östlichen Zentralsahara*. Berlin.

—— 1984. Great plains and mountainous areas as habitats for the Neolithic man in the Sahara. In L. Krzyzaniak and M. Kobusiewicz (eds), *Origins and*

Early Development of Food-Producing Cultures in North Africa. Poznan, pp. 391–8.

Galassi, G. 1955. *L'arte del piu' antico egitto nel museo di Torino*. Rome.

Gardiner, A. 1969. *Egyptian Grammar: Being an Introduction to the Study of Hieroglyphs*. 3rd edn. London.

Garrod, D. 1932. A New Mesolithic Industry: the Natufian of Palestine. *JRAI* 62: 257–69.

—— 1937. *The Stone Age of Mount Carmel*. Oxford.

Garstang, J. 1903. *Mahasna and Bet Khallaf*. London.

Gautier, A. 1978. La faune de vertébrés des sites épipaléolithiques d'Elkab. In P. Vermeersch (ed.), *Elkab II. L'Elkabien, Epipaléolithique de la vallée du Nil égyptien*. Brussels and Leuven, pp. 103–14.

—— 1984. Archaeozoology of the Bir Kiseiba region, Eastern Sahara. In F. Wendorf, R. Schild and A. Close (eds), *Cattle-Keepers of the Eastern Sahara*. Dallas, pp. 49–72.

—— 1986. La faune de l'occupation néolithique d'El Kadada (Secteurs 12–22–32) au Soudan central. *ANM* 1: 59–105.

—— 1988. Notes on the animal bone assemblages from the Early Neolithic at Geili. In I. Caneva (ed.) *El Geili: The History of a Middle Nile Environment, 7000 BC–AD 1500*. BAR 424. Oxford, pp. 57–63.

—— 1989. A general review of the known prehistoric fauna of the Central Sudanese Nile Valley. In L. Krzyzaniak and M. Kobusiewicz (eds), *Late Prehistory of the Nile Basin and the Sahara*. Poznan, pp. 353–8.

—— 1990. *La domestication. Et l'homme crea ses animaux*. Paris.

—— and Midant-Reynes, B. 1995. La tête de massue du roi Scorpion. *AN* 5: 87–127.

Geus, F. 1977. Découvertes récentes au Soudan: la fouille d'el-Kadada. *BSFE* 79: 7–21.

—— 1983. *Direction générale des antiquités et des musées nationaux du Soudan. Section française de recherche archéologique: rapport annuel d'activité 1980–1982*. Khartoum.

—— 1984. *Rescuing Sudan Ancient Cultures*. Khartoum.

—— 1986. La section française de la direction des antiquités du Soudan: travaux de terrain et de laboratoire en 1982–1983. *ANM* 1: 13–41.

Ginter, B. and Kozlowski, J. 1979. Excavation report on the prehistoric and Predynastic settlement in el-Tarif during 1978. *MDAIK* 35: 87–102.

—— and —— 1984. The Tarifian and the origin of the Naqadian. In L. Krzyzaniak and M. Kobusiewicz (eds), *Origin and Early Development of Food-Producing Cultures in North-Eastern Africa*. Poznan, pp. 247–60.

——, —— and Drobniewicz, B. 1979. *Silexindustrien von El Tarif*. Mainz am Rhein.

——, ——, Pawlikowski, M. and Sliwa, J. 1982. El Tarif und Qasr el-Sagha. Forschungen zur Siedlungsgeschichte des Neolithikums, der Frühdynaztischen Epoche und des Mittleren Reiches. *MDAIK* 38: 97–129.

Godron, G. 1963. Compte rendu de Assemberghs (1961). *BiOr* 20: 254–61.

Goedicke, H. 1988. Zum Königskonzept der Thinitenzeit. *SAK* 15: 123–41.

Greene, D.L. 1981. A critique of methods used to reconstruct racial and population affinity in the Nile Valley. *BSAP* 8: 357–65.

Grove, A.T. 1980. Geomorphic evolution of the Sahara and the Nile. In M.A.J. Williams and H. Faure (eds), *The Sahara and the Nile: Quaternary Environment and Prehistoric Occupation in Northern Africa.* Rotterdam, pp. 7–16.

Guichard, J. and Guichard, G. 1965. The early and middle Paleolithic of Nubia: a preliminary report. In F. Wendorf (ed.), *Contribution to the Prehistory of Nubia.* Dallas, pp. 57–166.

—— and —— 1968. Contribution to the study of the early and middle Paleolithic of Nubia. In F. Wendorf (ed.), *Prehistory of Nubia* I. Dallas, pp. 148–93.

Haaland, R. 1981. Migratory herdsmen and cultivating women: the structure of Neolithic seasonal adaptation in the Khartoum Nile environment. Bergen.

—— 1987. *Problems in the Mesolithic and Neolithic culture-history in the central Nile Valley.* In T. Hägg (ed.), *Nubian Culture, Past and Present.* Stockholm, pp. 47–74.

—— 1989. The late Neolithic culture-historical sequence in the Central Sudan. In L. Krzyzaniak and M. Kobusiewicz (eds), *Late Prehistory in the Nile Basin and the Sahara.* Poznan, pp. 359–68.

Habachi, L. and Kaiser, W. 1985. Ein Friedhof der Maadikultur bei es-Saff. *MDAIK* 41: 43–6.

Hakem, A.M.A. and Khabir, A.M. 1989. Saroubad 2 : a new contribution to the Early Khartoum tradition from Bauda site. In L. Krzyzaniak and M. Kobusiewicz (eds), *Late Prehistory of the Nile Basin and the Sahara.* Poznan, pp. 381–6.

Hassan, F. 1972. Note on a Sebilian Site from Dishna Plain. *CdE* 47: 11–16.

—— 1974a. A Sebilian assemblage from El Kilh (Upper-Egypt). *CdE* 49: 211–21.

—— 1974b. *The Archaeology of the Dishna Plain, Egypt: A Study of a Late Palaeolithic Settlement.* Cairo.

—— 1976. Prehistoric Studies of the Siwa Region, Northwestern Egypt. *NA* 9: 13–34.

—— 1978. Archaeological Exploration of Siwa Oasis. *CA* 19: 146–8.

—— 1979. Archaeological explorations at Baharia and the West Delta. *CA* 20: 806.

—— 1980. Prehistoric settlement along the main Nile. In M.A.J. Williams and H. Faure (eds), *The Sahara and the Nile: Quaternary Environment and Prehistoric Occupation in Northern Africa.* Rotterdam, pp. 421–50.

—— 1985. Radiocarbon chronology of Neolithic and Predynastic sites in Upper Egypt and the Delta. *AAR* 3: 95–116.

—— 1986a. Chronology of the Khartoum 'Mesolithic and Neolithic' and related sites in the Sudan: statistical analysis and comparisons with Egypt. *AAR* 4: 83–102.

—— 1986b. Desert environment and the origins of agriculture in Egypt. *NAR* 19: 63–76.

—— 1987. Desert environment and origins of agriculture in Egypt. In T. Hägg (ed.), *Nubian Culture, Past and Present.* Stockholm, pp. 17–32.

—— 1988a. Desertification and the beginning of the Egyptian agriculture. In S. Schoske (ed.), *Akten des vierten internationalen Ägyptologen Kongresses,*

München 1985. Band 2, *SAK* Beiheft 2: 325–31.

—— 1988b. The Predynastic of Egypt. *JWP* 2/2: 135–85.

—— and Holmes, D. 1985. *The Archaeology of the Umm el-Dabadid Area, Kharga Oasis, Egypt*. Cairo.

—— and Matson, R.G. 1989. Seriation of Predynastic potsherds from the Nagada region (Upper Egypt). In L. Krzyzaniak and M. Kobusiewicz (eds), *Late Prehistory of the Nile Basin and the Sahara*. Poznan, pp. 303–16.

Hayes, W.C. 1964. Most ancient Egypt. *JNES* 23: 74–114.

—— 1965. *Most Ancient Egypt*. Chicago.

Hays, T.R. 1984. A reappraisal of the Egyptian Predynastic. In J.D. Clark and S.A. Brandt (eds), *From Hunters to Farmers*. Berkeley, pp. 65–73.

—— and Hassan, F. 1974. Mineralogical analysis of Sudanese Neolithic ceramics. *Archaeometry* 16: 71–9.

Heinzelin de Braucourt, J. de 1957. *La fouille d'Ishango*. Brussels.

—— and Paepe, R. 1965. The geological history of the Nile valley in Sudanese Nubia: preliminary results. In F. Wendorf (ed.), *Contributions to the Prehistory of Nubia*. Dallas, pp. 29–56.

Helck, W. 1987. *Untersuchungen zur Thinitenzeit*. Wiesbaden.

Hendrickx, S. 1984. The late Predynastic cemetery at Elkab (Upper Egypt). In L. Krzyzaniak and M. Kobusiewicz (eds), *Origins and Early Development of Food-Producing Cultures in North-Eastern Africa*. Poznan, pp. 225–30.

—— 1989. *De grafvelden der Naqada-cultuur in Zuid-Egypte, met bijzondere aandacht voor het Nagada III grafveld te Elkab. Interne chronologie en sociale differentiatie*. Unpublished PhD thesis, Catholic University of Leuven.

Henneberg, M., Kobusiewicz, M., Schild, R. and Wendorf, F. 1989. The Early Neolithic, Quarunian burial from the Northern Fayum Desert (Egypt). In L. Krzyzaniak and M. Kobusiewicz (eds), *Late Prehistory of the Nile Basin and the Sahara*. Poznan, pp. 181–96.

Henry, D.O. 1974. The utilization of the microburin technique in the Levant. *Paléorient* 2/2: 389–98.

Hoffman, M.A. 1971–2. Occupational features at the Kom el Ahmar. *JARCE* 9: 35–47.

—— 1980a. A rectangular Amratian house from Hierakonpolis and its significance for Predynastic research. *JNES* 39: 119–37.

—— 1980b. *Egypt Before the Pharaohs: The Prehistoric Foundations of Egyptian Civilization*. London.

—— 1982. *The Predynastic of Hierakonpolis: An Interim Report*. Egyptian Studies Association, Publication no. 1, Cairo University Herbarium, Faculty of Science, Giza, Egypt, and the Department of Sociology and Anthropology, Western llinois University, Macomb, Illinois.

—— 1984. Predynastic cultural ecology and patterns of settlement in Upper Egypt as viewed from Hierakonpolis. In L. Krzyzaniak and M. Kobusiewicz (eds), *Origins and Early Development of Food-Producing Cultures in North-Eastern Africa*. Poznan, pp. 235–46.

—— 1989. A stratified Predynastic sequence from Hierakonpolis (Upper Egypt). In L. Krzyzaniak and M. Kobusiewicz (eds), *Late Prehistory of the Nile Basin and the Sahara*. Poznan, pp. 317–24.

—— Hamroush, H., and Allen, R. 1986. A model of urban development for the Hierakonpolis region from Predynastic through Old Kingdom times. *JARCE* 23: 175–87.

Hofmann I. 1967. *Die Kulturen des Niltals von Aswan bis Sennar, vom Mesolithikum bis zum Ende der christlichen Epoche.* Hamburg.

Holmes, D. 1989a. The Badari region revisited. *NA* 3: 15–18.

—— 1989b. *The Predynastic Lithic Industries of Upper Egypt: A Comparative Study of the Lithic Traditions of Badari, Nagada and Hierakonpolis.* BAR (15) 469. 2 vols. Oxford.

—— 1990. The flint axes of Nagada, Egypt: analysis and assessment of a distinctive Predynastic tool type. *Paléorient* 16/1: 1–21.

—— 1993. Rise of the Nile Delta. *Nature* 363: 402–3.

—— and Friedman, R. 1994. Survey and test excavations in the Badari region. *PPS* 60: 105–42.

Huard, P. and Leclant, J. (with collaboration of L. Allard-Huard) 1980. *La culture des chasseurs du Nil et du Sahara.* Algeria.

—— and Massip, J.M. 1964. Harpons en os et céramique à décor en vague (Wavy Line) au Sahara Tchadien. *BSPF* 66/1: 105–23.

Hurst, H.E. 1952. *The Nile: A General Account of the River and the Utilisation of Its Waters.* London.

Inizan, M.-L., Reduron, M., Roche, H., Tixier, J. 1995. *Technologie de la pierre taillée.* Préhistoire de la pierre tailée 4. Meudon.

Junker, H. 1912. *Bericht über die Grabungen der Kaiserlichen Akademie der Wissenschaften in Wien auf dem Friedhof in Turah, Winter 1909–1910.* Denkschriften der Kaiserlichen Akademie der Wissenschaften in Wien, Philosophisch-historische Klasse, Vienna.

—— 1928. *Vorläufiger Bericht über die Grabung der Akademie der Wissenschaften in Wien nach dem Westdelta entsendete Expedition (20 Dezember 1927 bis 25 Februar 1928).* Denkschriften der Kaiserlichen Akademie der Wissenschaften in Wien, Philosophisch-historische Klasse, Vienna.

—— 1929–40. Vorläufiger Bericht über die Grabung der Akademie der Wissenschaften in Wien auf der neolithischen Siedlung von Merimde Benisalame (Westdelta). *Anzeiger der Akademie der Wissenschaften in Wien, Philosophisch-historische Klasse* 1929/XVI–XVIII: 156–250; 1930/V–XIII: 21–83; 1932/I–IV: 36–97; 1933/XVI–XXVII: 54–97; 1934/X: 118–132; 1940/I–IV: 3–25.

Kaczmarczyk, A. and Hedges, R.M.E. 1983. *Ancient Egyptian Faience: An Analytical Survey of the Egyptian Faience from Predynastic to Roman Times.* Warminster.

Kaiser, W. 1956. Stand und Problem der ägyptischen Vorgeschichtsforschung. *ZÄS* 81: 87–109.

—— 1957. Zur Inneren Chronologie der Naqadakultur. *Archaeologia Geographica* 6: 69–77.

—— 1958. Zur vorgeschichtlichen Bedeutung von Hierakonpolis. *MDAIK* 16: 183–92.

—— 1959. Einige Bemerkungen zur ägyptischen Frühzeit. I. Zu den šmsw-Hr. *ZÄS* 84: 119–32.

—— 1960. Einige Bemerkurgen zur ägyptischen Frühzeit. I. Zu den šmsw-Hr.

(forts.). *ZÄS* 85: 118–37.

—— 1961a. Einige Bemerkungen zur ägyptischen Frühzeit II. Zur Frage einer über Menes hinausreichenden ägyptischen Geschichtsüberlieferung. *ZÄS* 86: 39–61.

—— 1961b. Bericht über eine archäologisch-geologische Felduntersuchung in Ober- und Mittelägypten. *MDAIK* 17: 1–53.

—— 1964. Einige Bemerkungen zur ägyptischen Fühzeit III. Die Reicheinigung. *ZÄS* 91: 86–125.

—— 1969. Zu den königlichen Talbezirken der 1. und 2. Dynastie in Abydos und zur Baugeschichte des Djoser-Grabmals. *MDAIK* 25: 1–21.

—— 1981. Zu den Königsgräbern der 1. Dynastie in Umm-el-Qaab. *MDAIK* 37: 247–54.

—— 1985. Zur Südausdehnung der vorgeschichtlichen Deltakulturen und zur frühen Entwicklung Oberägyptens. *MDAIK* 41: 61–87.

—— 1986. Vor- und Frühgeschichte. *LÄ* VI: 1069–76.

—— 1987a. Zum Friedhof der Naqadakultur von Minshat Abu Omar. *ASAE* 71: 119–26.

—— 1987b. Vier vorgeschichtliche Gefässe von Haraga. *MDAIK* 43: 121–2.

—— 1988. Zum Fundplatz der Maadi-Kultur bei Tura. *MDAIK* 44: 121–4.

—— and Dreyer, G. 1982. Umm el Qaab: Nachuntersuchungen im frühzeitlichen Königsfriedhof. *MDAIK* 38: 211–69.

Kantor, H. 1942. The early relations of Egypt with Asia. *JNES* 1: 174–213.

—— 1944. The final phase of Predynastic culture: Gerzean or Semainean? *JNES* 3: 110–36.

—— 1965. The relative chronologies of Egypt and its foreign correlations before the Late Bronze Age. In R.W. Ehrich (ed.), *Chronologies in Old World Archaeology*. Chicago.

Keimer, L. 1947. *Histoires de serpents dans l'Egypte ancienne et moderne*. Cairo.

—— 1948. *Remarques sur le tatouage dans l'Egypte ancienne*. Cairo.

—— 1952. Notes prises chez les Bisarin et les Nubiens d'Assouan, IIe partie. *BIE* 33: 43–84.

Kemp, B.J. 1968. Merimda and the theory of house burial in prehistoric Egypt. *CdE* 85: 22–33.

—— 1973. Photographs of the Decorated Tomb at Hierakonpolis. *JEA* 59: 36–43.

—— 1982. Automatic analysis of Predynastic cemeteries: a new method for an old problem. *JEA* 68: 5–15.

—— 1989. *Ancient Egypt: Anatomy of a Civilization*. London.

Khabir, A.R. 1985. A Neolithic site in the Sarurab area. *NA* 26: 40.

Klees, F. 1989. Lobo: a contribution to the prehistory of the eastern Sand Sea and the Egyptian oases. In L. Krzyzaniak and M. Kobusiewicz (eds), *Late Prehistory of the Nile Basin and the Sahara*. Poznan, pp. 223–32.

Klemm, R. and Klemm, D. 1981. *Die Steine der Pharaonen*. Munich.

Kozlowski, J. (ed.) 1983. *Qasr el-Sagha 1980*. Warsaw and Cracow.

—— and Ginter, B. 1989. The Fayum Neolithic in the light of new discoveries. In L. Krzyzaniak and M. Kobusiewicz (eds), *Late Prehistory of the Nile Basin and Sahara*. Poznan, pp. 157–79.

Kroeper, K. and Wildung, D. 1985. *Minshat Abu Omar, Münchner Ost-Delta Expedition, Vorbericht 1978–1984*. Munich.

Krzyzaniak, L. 1977. *Early Farming Cultures of the Lower Nile: The Predynastic Period in Egypt*. Warsaw.

—— 1982. Radiocarbon measurements for the Neolithic settlement at Kadero. *NA* 21: 21.

—— 1984. The Neolithic habitation at Kadero. In L. Krzyzaniak and M. Kobusiewicz (eds), *Origins and Early Development of Food-Producing Cultures in North-Eastern Africa*. Poznan, pp. 309–16.

—— 1986. Recent results of excavations on the Neolithic settlement at Kadero (Central Sudan). In M. Krause (ed.), *Nubische Studien. Tagungsakten der 5. Internationalen Konferenz der International Society for Nubian Studies. Heidelberg 22–25 September 1982*. Mainz am Rhein.

—— 1989. Recent archaeological evidence on the earliest settlement in the eastern Nile Delta. In L. Krzyzaniak and M. Kobusiewicz (eds), *Late Prehistory of the Nile Basin and the Sahara*. Poznan, pp. 267–86.

—— and Kobusiewicz, M. (eds) 1984. *Origin and Early Development of Food-Producing Cultures in North-Eastern Africa*. Poznan.

—— and —— 1989. *Late Prehistory of the Nile Basin and the Sahara*. Poznan.

Kuper, R. 1981. Untersuchungen der Besiedlungsgeschichte der östlichen Sahara. Vorbericht über die Expedition 1980. *Beiträge zur allgemeinen und vergleichenden Archälogie* 3: 215–75.

—— 1989a. The Eastern Sahara from North to South: data and dates from the B.O.S Project. In L. Krzyzaniak and M. Kobusiewicz (eds), *Late Prehistory of the Nile Basin and the Sahara*. Poznan, pp. 197–204.

—— (ed.) 1989b. *Forschungen zur Umweltgeschichte der Ostshara*. Cologne.

Larsen, H. 1962. Die Merimdekeramik im Mittelmeersmuseum Stockholms. *Orientalia Suecana* 11: 4–89.

Leakey, L.S.B. 1931. *The Stone Age Cultures of Kenya Colony*. Cambridge.

Leclant, J. 1973. Une province nouvelle de l'art saharien: les gravures rupestres de Nubie. In *Maghreb et Sahara, études géographiques offertes à Jean Despois*. Paris, pp. 239–46.

—— 1987. Fouilles et travaux en Egypte et au Soudan: Minshat Abu Omar. *Orientalia* 56/3: figure 3.

—— 1990. Egypte, Sahara, Afrique. *AN* 0: 5–9.

Lecointe, Y. 1987. Le site néolithique d'El Ghaba: deux années d'activité (1985–1986). *ANM* 2: 69–87.

Le Mière, M. 1979. La céramique préhistorique de Tell Assouad, Djezireh, Syrie. *Cahiers de l'Euphrate* 2: 5–76.

Lenoble, P. 1987. Quatre tumulus sur mille du Djebel Makbor A.M.S. NE–36-0/3-X-1. *ANM* 2: 207–47.

Lenormant, F. 1870. *Notes sur un voyage en Egypte*. Paris.

Leroi-Gourhan, A. (ed.) 1988. *Dictionnaire de la Préhistoire*. Paris.

Lorton, D. 1987. Why 'Menes'? *VA* 3: 33–8.

Lubell, D. 1971. *The Fakhurian: A Late Palaeolithic Industry from Upper Egypt and Its Place in Nilotic Prehistory*. Cairo.

Lucas, A. 1962. *Ancient Egyptian Materials and Industries*. 4th edn, rev. J.R.

Harris. London.

McArdle, J. 1982. Preliminary report on the Predynastic fauna of the Hierakonpolis Project. In M. Hoffman (ed.), *The Predynastic of Hierakonpolis: An Interim Report*, pp. 110–15.

McBurney, C.B.M. 1967. *The Haua Fteah (Cyrenaica) and the Stone Age of the South East Mediterranean*. Cambridge.

McDonald, M. 1985. Dakhleh Oasis Project, Holocene prehistory: interim report on the 1984 and 1986 seasons. *JSSEA* 15: 126–35.

McHugh, W.P. 1975. Some archaeological results of the Bagnold-Mond expedition to the Gilf Kebir and Gebel Uweinat, Southern Libyan Desert. *JNES* 34/1: 31–62.

Magid, A. 1989. Exploitation of plants in the Eastern Sahel (Sudan), 5,000–2,000 BC In L. Krzyzaniak and M. Kobusiewicz (eds), *Late Prehistory of the Nile Basin and the Sahara*. Poznan, pp. 459–68.

Maitre, J.P. 1971. Contribution à la préhistoire de l'Ahaggar 1 (Tédéfest centrale). Paris.

Maley, J. 1969. Le Nil: données nouvelles et essai de synthèse de son histoire géologique. *Bulletin Ass. Sénégal et Quatern. Ouest africain* 21: 40–8.

Marks, A. 1968a. The Mousterian industries of Nubia. In F. Wendorf (ed.), *The Prehistory of Nubia* I. Dallas, pp. 194–314.

—— 1968b. The Khormusan: an Upper Pleistocene industry in Sudanese Nubia. In F. Wendorf (ed.), *The Prehistory of Nubia* I. Dallas, pp. 315–91.

—— 1968c. The Halfan industry. In F. Wendorf (ed.), *The Prehistory of Nubia* I. Dallas, pp. 392–460.

—— 1968d. The Sebilian industry of the Second Cataract. In F. Wendorf (ed.), *The Prehistory of Nubia* I. Dallas, pp. 461–531.

—— 1976. *Prehistory and Paleoenvironments in the Central Nequev, Israel* I. Dallas.

—— 1977. *Prehistory and Paleoenvironments in the Central Nequev, Israel* II. Dallas.

—— 1983a. *Prehistory and Paleoenvironments in the Central Nequev, Israel* III. Dallas.

—— 1983b. The Middle to Upper Palaeolithic transition in the Levant. In F. Wendorf and A. Close (eds), *Advances in World Archaeology* 2. New York, pp. 51–98.

—— 1989. The later prehistory of the Central Nile Valley: a view from its eastern hinterlands. In L. Krzyzaniak and M. Kobusiewicz, (eds), *Late Prehistory of the Nile Basin and the Sahara*. Poznan, pp. 443–50.

—— and Fattovich, R. 1989. The later prehistory of the Eastern Sudan: a preliminary view. In L. Krzyzaniak and M. Kobusiewicz (eds), *Late Prehistory of the Nile Basin and the Sahara*, Poznan, pp. 451–8.

——, Peters, J. and Van Neer, W. 1987. Late Pleistocene and early Holocene occupations in the Upper Atbara river valley, Sudan. In A. Close (ed.), *Prehistory of Arid North Africa*. Dallas, pp. 137–61.

Massoulard, E. 1949. *Préhistoire et protohistoire d'Egypte*. Paris.

Mazuel, J. 1935. À la recherche des sources du Nil. *Bulletin of the Faculty of Arts* 3/1: 8–18.

Midant-Reynes, B. 1987. Contribution a l'étude de la societé prédynastique: le cas du couteau 'Ripple-Flake'. *SAK* 14: 185–224.

——, Buchez, N., Hesse, A. and Lechevalier, T. 1990. Le site prédynastique d'Adaïma. Rapport préliminaire de la campagne de fouille 1989. *BIFAO* 90: 247–58.

——, B., Buchez, N., Crubezy, E. and Janin, T. 1991. Le site prédynastique d'Adaïma. Rapport préliminaire de la 2ᵉ campagne de fouille. *BIFAO* 91: 231–47.

Millet, N.B. 1990. The Narmer Macehead and related objects. *JARCE* 27: 53–9.

Miroschedji, P. de 1998. Les Egyptiens au Sinaï du nord et en Palestine au Bronze ancièn. In D. Valbelle and C. Bonnet (eds), *Le Sinaï durant L'Antiquité et le Moyen-Age: 4000 Ans d'Historie pour un Désert*. Paris.

Mode, M. 1984. Frühes Vorderasien und frühes Ägypten, Motivgeschichtliche Berührungspunkte in der Kunst. *Beiträge zur Orientwissenschaften* 6: 11–35.

Mohammed Ali, A.S.A. 1982. *The Neolithic Period in the Sudan, c.6000–2500 BC*. BAR (IS) 139. Oxford.

—— 1987. The Neolithic of Central Sudan: a reconsideration. In A. Close (ed.), *Prehistory of Arid North Africa*. Dallas, pp. 123–36.

—— and Jaeger, S.J. 1989. The early ceramics of the Eastern Butana (Sudan). In L. Krzyzaniak and M. Kobusiewicz, (eds), *Late Prehistory of the Nile Basin and the Sahara*. Poznan, pp. 473–80.

Mond, R. and Myers, O.H. 1937. *Cemeteries of Armant*. 2 vols. London.

Montenat, C. 1986. Un aperçu des industries préhistoriques du Golfe de Suez et du littoral égyptien de la Mer Rouge. *BIFAO* 86: 239–55.

de Morgan, J. 1896. *Recherches sur les origines de l'Egypte I: L'age de la pierre et des metaux*. Paris.

—— 1897. *Recherches sur les origines de l'Egypte II: Ethnographie préhistorique et tombeau royal de Negadah*. Paris.

Mori, F. 1965. *Tadrart Acacus. Arte rupestre del Sahara preistorico*. Turin.

Murnane, W.J. 1987. The Gebel Sheikh Suleiman monument: epigraphic remarks. In B.B. Williams and T.J. Logan: The Metropolitan Museum knife handle and aspects of pharaonic imagery before Narmer. *JNES* 46: 94–5.

Mussi, M. 1976. The Natufian of Palestine: the beginnings of agriculture in a paleo-ethnological perspective. *Origini* 10: 89–170.

——, Caneva, I. and Zarattini, A. 1984. More on the terminal Palaeolithic of the Fayum Depression. In L. Krzyzaniak and M. Kobusiewicz (eds), *Origins and Early Development of Food-Producing Cultures in North-Eastern Africa*. Poznan, pp. 185–91.

Muzzolini, A. 1983. *L'art rupestre du Sahara central. Classification et chronologie. Le boeuf dans la préhistoire saharienne*. 2 vols. Unpublished PhD thesis, Université Aix-en-Provence.

—— 1986a. *L'art rupestre préhistorique des massifs centraux sahariens*. BAR (IS) 318. Oxford.

—— 1986b. L'intensité des 'humides' holocènes sahariens: estimations maximalistes et estimations modérées. In *Archéologie Africaine et Sciences appliqués à l'Archéologie, 1er Symposium International de Bordeaux 1983*. Bordeaux, pp. 53–65.

—— 1987. Les premiers moutons sahariens d'après les figurations rupestres. *Archeozoologia* 1/2: 129–48.

—— 1989. La 'Néolithisation' du Nord de l'Afrique et ses causes. In O. Aurenche and J. Cauvin (eds), *Néolithisations. Proche et Moyen Orient, Méditerranée orientale, Nord de l'Afrique, Europe meridionale, Chine, Amérique du Sud.* BAR (IS) 516. Lyon, pp. 145–86.

Myers, O. 1958. Abka re-excavated. *Kush* 6: 131–41.

—— 1960. Abka again. *Kush* 8: 174–81.

Naville, E. 1922. Le vase à parfum de Byblos. *Syria* 3: 291.

Needler, W. 1956. A flint knife of King Djer. *JEA* 42: 41–4.

—— 1966. Six Predynastic human figures in the Royal Ontario Museum. *JARCE* 5: 11–17.

—— 1967. A rock-drawing on Gebel Sheikh Suliman (near Wadi Halfa) showing a scorpion and human figures. *JARCE* 6: 87–91.

—— 1981. Federn's revision of Petrie's Predynastic pottery classification. *JSSEA* 11/2: 69–74.

—— 1984. *The Predynastic and Archaic Egypt in the Brooklyn Museum.* New York.

Neumann, K. 1989. Holocene vegetation of the Eastern Sahara : charcoal from prehistoric sites. *AAR* 7: 97–116.

Neuville, R. 1951. *Le Paléolithique et le Mésolithique du desert de Judée.* Paris.

—— 1952. Station acheuléenne du Sinai septentrional: Djebel el Faleq. *BSPF* 49: 77–80.

Nordström, H. 1972. *Neolithic and A-Group Sites.* The Scandinavian Joint Expedition to Sudanese Nubia. Uppsala.

Oren, E.D. 1973. The overland route between Egypt and Canaan in the Early Bronze Age. *IEJ* 23: 198–205.

1987. The 'Ways of Horus' in North Sinai. In A.E. Rainey (ed.), *Egypt, Israel, Sinai: Archaeological and Historical Relationships in the Biblical Period.* Tel Aviv, pp. 69–120.

Otto, E. 1938. Die Lehre von den beiden Ländern Ägyptens in der ägyptischen Religiongeschichte. *Analecta Orientalia* 17: 10–35.

Otto, K.H. 1963. Shaqadud: a new Khartoum Neolithic site outside the Nile Valley. *Kush* 11: 108–15.

Paulissen, E. and Vermeersch, P. 1987. Earth, man and climate in the Egyptian Nile Valley during the Pleistocene. In A. Close (ed.), *Prehistory of Arid North Africa.* Dallas, pp. 29–67.

—— and —— 1989. Le comportement des grands fleuves allogènes: l'exemple du Nil saharien au Quaternaire supérieur. *BSGF* 8/5: 73–83.

——, —— and Van Neer, W. 1985. Progress report on the Late Palaeolithic Shuwikhat sites (Qena, Upper Egypt). *NA* 26: 7–14.

Payne, J.C. 1973. Tomb 100: the Decorated Tomb at Hierakonpolis confirmed. *JEA* 59: 31–5.

Peet, T.E. 1914. *The Cemeteries of Abydos* II. London.

Perrot, J. 1984. Structures d'habitat, mode de vie et environnement. Les villages des pasteurs de Beersheva, dans le Sud d'Israel, au IVe millénaire avant l'ère chrétienne. *Paléorient* 10: 75–96.

Peters, J. 1986. A revision of the faunal remains from two Central Sudanese Sites: Khartoum Hospital and Esh Shaheinab. *Archeozoologia* 5: 11–35.
—— 1989. The faunal remains from several sites at Jebel Shaqadud (Central Sudan): a preliminary report. In L. Krzyzaniak and M. Kobusiewicz (eds), *Late Prehistory of the Nile Basin and the Sahara*. Poznan, pp. 469–72.
Petrie, W.M.F. 1901. *Diospolis Parva*. London.
—— 1902. *Abydos*. London.
—— 1920. *Prehistoric Egypt*. London.
—— 1921. *Corpus of Prehistoric Pottery and Palettes*. London.
—— 1939. *The Making of Egypt*. London.
—— 1953. *Ceremonial Slate Palettes*. London.
—— and Quibell, J. 1896. *Nagada and Ballas*. London.
——, Wainwright, G.A. and Mackay, E. 1912. *The Labyrinth, Gerzeh and Mazguneh*. London.
Phillips, J. 1987. Sinai during the Paleolithic: the early periods. In A. Close (ed.), *Prehistory of Arid North Africa*. Dallas, pp. 105–21.
—— and Butzer, K. 1973. A Silsilian occupation site (GS2B-II) of the Kom Ombo Plain, Upper Egypt: geology, archeology and paleoecology. *Quaternaria* 17: 343_86.
Piotrovski, B. 1967. The Early Dynastic settlement of Khor-Daoud and Wadi Allaki. The ancient route to the gold mines. In *Fouilles en Nubie (1961–1963)*: 127–40.
Podzorski, P.V. 1990. *Their Bones Shall Not Perish. An Examination of Predynastic Human Skeletal Remains from Naqa ed-Der*. Whitstable.
Quibell, J.E. 1898. Slate palette from Hierakonpolis. *ZÄS* 36: 81–4.
—— 1900. *Hierakonpolis* I. London.
—— 1905. *Archaic Objects*. Cairo.
—— and Green, F.W. 1902. *Hierakonpolis* II. London.
Randall-Maciver, D. and Mace, A.C. 1902. *El Amrah and Abydos*. London.
Reinold, J. 1982. *Le site préhistorique d'el Kadada (Soudan central). La nécropole.* Unpublished PhD thesis, University de Lille III.
—— 1985. La necropole néolithique d'El Kadada au Soudan central: les inhumations d'enfants en vase. In F. Geus and F. Thill (eds), *Mélanges offerts à Jean Vercoutter*. Paris, pp. 279–89.
—— 1987. Les fouilles pré- et proto-historiques de la section française de la Direction des Antiquités du Soudan: les campagnes 1984–5 et 1985–6. *ANM* 2: 17–56.
Reisner, G.A. 1910. The Archaeological Survey of Nubia. Report for 1907–1908. Cairo.
—— 1966. Black-topped pottery. *JEA* 5: 7–10.
Renfrew, C., Dixon, J.E. and Cann, J.R. 1966. Obsidian and early cultural contacts in the Near East. *PPS* 32: 30–72.
Richter, J. 1989. Neolithic sites in the Wadi Howar (Western Sudan). In L. Krzyzaniak and M. Kobusiewicz (eds) *Late Prehistory of the Nile Basin and the Sahara*. Poznan, pp. 431–42.
Rizkana, I. and Seeher, J. 1987. *Maadi I: The Pottery of the Predynastic Settlement*. Mainz am Rhein.

—— and ——1988. *Maadi II: The Lithic Industries of the Predynastic Settlement*. Mainz am Rhein.

—— and ——1989. *Maadi III: The Non-Lithic Small Finds and the Structural Remains of the Predynastic Settlement*. Mainz am Rhein.

—— and ——1990. *Maadi IV: The Predynastic Cemeteries of Maadi and Wadi Digla*. Mainz am Rhein.

Rognon, P. 1960. L'évolution de la vallée du Nil d'après les études recentes. *Institut des Recherches Sahariennes* 19: 151–6.

Roset, J.P. 1983. Nouvelles données sur le problème de la neolithisation du Sahara méridional: Air et Teneré, au Niger. *Cahier ORSTOM, sér. 'Géologie'* 13/2: 119–42.

—— 1985. Les plus vieilles céramiques du Sahara (Préhistoire du Niger). *Archéologia* 183: 43–50.

—— 1987. Paleoclimatic and cultural conditions of Neolithic development in the early Holocene of Northern Niger (Air and Tenere). In A. Close (ed.), *Prehistory of Arid North Africa*. Dallas, pp. 211–34.

Roubet, C. and El-Hadidi, N. 1981. 20000 ans d'environnement préhistorique dans la vallée du Nil et le désert égyptien. *L'Anthropologie* 85: 3–57.

Said, R. 1962. *The Geology of Egypt*. 1st edn. Amsterdam and New York.

—— 1975. The geological evolution of the River Nile. In F. Wendorf and A.E. Marks (eds), *Problems in Prehistory: North Africa and the Levant*. Dallas, pp. 7–44.

—— (ed.) 1990. *The Geology of Egypt*. 2nd edn. Rotterdam.

——, Wendorf, F. and Schild, R. 1970. The Geology and prehistory of the Nile Valley in Upper Egypt. *Archeologia Polona* 12: 43–60.

Sandford, K.S. and Arkell, W.J. 1928. *First Report of the Prehistoric Survey Expedition*. Chicago.

—— and —— 1929. *Prehistoric Survey of Egypt and Western Asia, Palaeolithic Man and the Nile Fayum Divide*. Chicago.

—— and —— 1933. *Prehistoric Survey of Egypt and Western Asia, Palaeolithic Man and the Nile Valley in Nubia and Upper Egypt*. Chicago.

—— and —— 1939. *Prehistoric Survey of Egypt and Western Asia. Lower Egypt*. Chicago.

Sauneron, S. 1968. *L'Egyptologie*. Que Sais-Je? series. Paris.

Säve-Söderbergh, T. and Olsson, I.U. 1970. C14 dating and Egyptian chronology. In I.U. Olsson (ed.), *Radiocarbon Variations and Absolute Chronology*. Stockholm, pp. 35–55.

Scharff, A. 1928. Some prehistoric vases in the British Museum and remarks on Egyptian prehistory. *JEA* 14: 261–76.

Schenkel, W. 1978. *Die Bewasserungsrevolution im alten Ägypten*. Mainz am Rhein.

Schild, R. 1987. Unchanging contrast? The Late Pleistocene Nile and Eastern Sahara. In A. Close (ed.), *Prehistory of Arid North Africa*. Dallas, pp. 13–27.

——, Chmielewska, M. and Wieckowska, H. 1968. The Arkinian and Shamarkian industries. In F. Wendorf (ed.), *The Prehistory of Nubia* II. Dallas, pp. 651–767.

Schmidt, K. 1980. Paläolithische Funde aus Merimde-Benisalame. *MDAIK* 36:

411–36.

Schön, W. 1989. New results from two playa-sites from Gilf Kebir (Egypt). In L. Krzyzaniak and M. Kobusiewicz (eds), *Late Prehistory of the Nile Basin and the Sahara*. Poznan, pp. 215–22.

Schuck, W. 1989. From lake to wells : 5,000 years of settlement in Wadi Shaw (Northern Sudan). In L. Krzyzaniak and M. Kobusiewicz (eds), *Late Prehistory of the Nile Basin and the Sahara*. Poznan, pp. 421–30.

Seeher, J. 1990. Maadi eine prädynastische Kulturgruppe zwischen Oberägypten und Palästina. *Prähistorische Zeitschrift* 65/2: 123_56.

—— 1991. Gedanken zur Rolle Unterägyptens bei der Herausbildung des Pharaonenreiches. *MDAIK* 47: 313–8.

Sethe, K. 1930. *Urgeschichte und älteste Religion der Ägypter*. Leipzig.

Shiner, J. 1968a. The Cataract Tradition. In F. Wendorf (ed.), *The Prehistory of Nubia II*. Dallas, pp. 535–629.

—— 1968b. Miscellaneous sites. In F. Wendorf (ed.), *The Prehistory of Nubia II*. Dallas, pp. 630–50

—— 1968c. The Khartoum Variant. In F. Wendorf (ed.), *The Prehistory of Nubia II*. Dallas, pp. 768–90.

Small, M.F. 1981. The Nubian Mesolithic: a consideration of the Wadi Halfa remains. *JHE* 10: 159–62.

Smith, H.S. 1962. *Preliminary Report of the Egypt Exploration Society's Nubian Survey*. Cairo.

Smith, P.E.L. 1966. New prehistoric investigations at Kom Ombo. *Zephyrus* 17: 31–45.

—— 1967a. New investigations in the late Pleistocene archaeology of the Kom Ombo Plain (Upper Egypt). *Quaternaria* 9: 141–52.

—— 1967b. A preliminary report on the recent prehistoric investigations near Kom Ombo, Upper Egypt. *Fouilles en Nubie 1961–1963*: 195–208.

—— 1968. A revised view of the Later Palaeolithic of Egypt. In F. Bordes and D. de Sonneville-Bordes (eds), *La Préhistoire, problèmes et tendances*. Paris, pp. 391–9.

Speke, J.H. 1863. *Journal of the Discovery of the Source of the Nile*. London.

Spencer, A.J. 1993. *Early Egypt*. London.

Stadelmann, R. 1991. Das Dreikammersystem der Königsgraber der Frühzeit und des Alten Reiches. *MDAIK* 47: 373–88.

Stemler, A. 1990. A scanning electron microscopic analysis of plant impressions in pottery from the sites of Kadero, El Zakiab, Um Direiwa and El Kadada. *ANM* 4: 87–105.

Sutton, J. 1974. The aquatic civilization of Middle Africa. *JAH* 15/4: 527–46.

Tefnin, R. 1979. Image et histoire. Réflexions sur l'usage documentaire de l'image égyptienne. *CdE* 54/108: 218–44.

Testart, A. 1977. Ethnologie de l'Australie et préhistoire de l'Asie du Sud-Est: évolution technique et milieu naturel. *Journal de la Societé des Océanistes* 33: 77–85.

—— 1982. *Les chasseurs-cueilleurs ou l'origine des inégalités*. Paris.

Thoma, A. 1984. Morphology and affinities of the Nazlet Khater Man. *JHE* 13: 287–96.

Tigani el Mahi, A. 1988. *Zooarchaeology in the Middle Nile Valley: A Study of Four Neolithic Sites Near Khartoum*. BAR (IS) 418. Oxford.

Tillier, A.M. 1992. Les hommes du Paléolithique moyen et la question de l'ancienneté de l'homme moderne en Afrique. *AN* 2: 59–69.

Tixier, J. 1958–9. Les pièces pédonculées de l'Atérien. *Libyca* 6–7: 127–58.

—— 1962. Le Ténéréen de l'Adrar Bous III. *Mission Berliet-Ténéré-Tchad. Documents scientifiques*. Paris, pp. 353–62.

—— 1963. *Typologie de l'Epipaléolithique du Maghreb*. Paris.

—— 1972. Les apports de la stratigraphie et de la typologie au probleme des origines de l'homme moderne. *Origine de l'Homme moderne*. *Actes du Colloques de Paris*. UNESCO, pp. 121–7.

Tixier, J. and Inizan, M.L. 1981. Ksar Akil: stratigraphie et ensembles lithiques dans le Paléolithique supérieur. Fouilles 1971–1975. In *Préhistoire du Levant. Chronologie et organisation de l'espace depuis des origines jusqu'au VIe millénaire*. Maison de l'Orient méditerranéen, 10–14 juin. Paris, Colloques internationaux du CNRS, no. 598. Paris, pp. 353–67.

——, Inizan, M.L. and Roche, H. 1980. *Préhistoire de la pierre taillé I: Terminologie et technologie*. Valbonne.

Trigger, B. 1965. *History and Settlement in Lower Nubia*. New Haven.

—— 1976. *Nubia under the Pharaohs*, London.

—— 1987. Egypt: a fledgling nation. *JSSEA* 17: 58–66.

Tutundzic, S.R. 1989. The problem of foreign north-eastern relations of Upper Egypt, particularly in Badarian period: an aspect. In L. Krzyzaniak and M. Kobusiewicz (eds), *Late Prehistory of the Nile Basin and the Sahara*. Poznan, pp. 255–60.

Tykot, R.H. 1996. The geological source of an obsidian ear (04.9941) from the Museum of Fine Arts Boston. *RdE*: 47: 177–9.

Ucko, P.J. 1968. *Anthropomorphic Figurines of Predynastic Egypt and Neolithic Crete with Comparative Material from the Prehistoric Near East and Mainland Greece*. London.

Vala, F. 1975. *Le Natoufien, une culture préhistorique en Palestine*. Paris.

Valbelle, D. 1990. *Les Neuf Arcs: l'égyptien et les étrangers de la préhistoire à la conquête d'Alexandre*. Paris.

van den Brink, E.C.M. (ed.) 1988. *The Archaeology of the Nile Delta. Problems and Priorities*. Amsterdam.

—— 1989. A transitional late Predynastic – Early Dynastic settlement site in the northeastern Nile Delta, Egypt. *MDAIK* 45: 55–108.

Vandermeersch, B. 1981. *Les hommes fossiles de Qafzeh (Israël)*. Paris.

Vandier, J. 1952. *Manuel d'archéologie égyptienne. Les époques de formation 1/ 1*. Paris.

Van Neer, W. 1986. Some notes on the fish remains from Wadi Kubbaniya (Upper Egypt; Late Palaeolithic). In D.C. Brinkhuizen and A.T. Clason (eds), *Fish and Archaeology: Studies in Osteometry, Taphonomy, Seasonality and Fishing Methods*. Oxford, pp. 101–13.

—— 1989. Fishing along the prehistoric Nile. In L. Krzyzaniak and M. Kobusiewicz (eds), *Late Prehistory of the Nile Basin and Sahara*. Poznan, pp. 49–56.

Van Peer, P. 1986. Présence de la technique nubienne dans l'Atérien. *L'Anthropologie* 90/2: 321–4.

Vercoutter, J. 1978. Le peuplement de l'Egypte ancienne et le déchiffrement de l'écriture méroitique. In UNESCO (ed.), *Histoire générale de l'Afrique*. Paris, pp. 15–36.

—— 1990. A propos des Mni = Menes. In S. Israelit-Groll (ed.), *Mélanges Lichtheim: Studies in Egyptology* II. Jerusalem, pp. 1025–32.

—— 1992. *L'Egypte et la vallée du Nil. Des origines à la fin de l'Ancien Empire*. Paris.

Vermeersch, P. 1978. *L'Elkabien, Epipaléolithique de la vallée du Nil égyptien*. Leuven and Brussels.

—— 1981. Contribution of Belgian prehistoric research to the knowledge of the Egyptian Paleolithic. *BIE* 63: 85–108.

—— 1992. The Upper and late Palaeolithic of Northern and Eastern Africa. In F. Klees and R. Kuper (eds), *New Light on the Northeast African Past*. Cologne, pp. 99–154.

—— 1994. Sodmein Cave Site, Red Sea Mountains (Egypt). *Sahara* 6: 31–40.

——, Paulissen, E. and Van Neer, W. 1989. The Late Palaeolithic Makhadma sites (Egypt): environment and subsistence. In L. Krzyzaniak and M. Kobusiewicz, (eds), *Late Prehistory of the Nile Basin and the Sahara*. Poznan, pp. 87–116.

——, —— and Van Peer, P. 1990a. Le Paléolithique de la vallée du Nil égyptien. *L'Anthropologie* 94: 435–58.

——, —— and —— 1990b. Palaeolithic chert exploitation in the limestone stretch of the Egyptian Nile Valley. *AAR* 8: 77–102.

——, —— and —— 1991. Vallée du Nil. In *Sahara. Paléomilieux et peuplement préhistorique au pleistocene supérieur. Colloque Solignac*, pp. 1–19.

——, Paulissen, E., Otte, M., Gijselings, G. and Drappier, D. 1980. Acheulean in Middle Egypt. In R.E. Leakey and B.A. Ogot (eds), *Proceedings of the 8th Panafrican Congress of Prehistory and Quaternary Studies, Nairobi 1977*. Nairobi, pp. 218–21.

——, Huyge, D., Paulissen, E., Gisjelings, G. and Lauwers, R. 1985. An Epipaleolithic industry at Arab el Sahaba, Middle Egypt: a preliminary report. In M. Liverani, A. Palmieri and R. Peroni (eds), *Studi di Paletnologia in onore di Salvatore M. Puglisi*. Rome, pp. 383–93.

——, Paulissen, E., Gijselings, G., Otte, M., Thoma A. and Charlier, C. 1984. Une minière de silex et un squelette du Paléolithique supérieur ancien à Nazlet Khater, Haute-Egypte. *L'Anthropologie* 88: 231–44.

——, Paulissen, E., Stokes, S., Charhier, C., Van Peer, Stringer, C. and Lindsay, W. 1998. A Middle Palaeolithic burial of a modern human at Taramsa Hill, Egypt. *Antiquity* 72: 475–84.

Vignard, E. 1923. Une nouvelle industrie lithique : le Sebilien. *BIFAO* 22: 1–76.

Vikentief, V. 1942. Les monuments archaïques. La tablette en ivoire de Naqâda. *ASAE* 41: 277–94.

von den Driesch, A. and Boessneck, J. 1985. *Die Tierknochenfunde aus der neolithischen Siedlung von Merimde Benisalâme am westlichen Nildelta*. Munich.

von der Way, T. 1986. Tell el-Fara'in-Bouto. 1. Bericht. *MDAIK* 42: 191–212.
—— 1987. Tell el-Fara'in-Bouto. 2. Bericht. *MDAIK* 43: 241–57.
—— 1988. Tell el-Fara'in-Bouto. 3. Bericht. *MDAIK* 44: 283–306.
—— 1989. Tell el-Fara'in-Bouto. 4. Bericht. *MDAIK* 42: 275–307.
—— 1991. Die Grabungen in Buto und die Reichseinigung. *MDAIK* 47: 419–24.
—— 1997. *Tell el-Fara'in-Buto I. Ergebnisse zum frühen Kontext Kampagnen der Jahre 1983–1989*, Archäologische Veröffentlichungen 83, Mainz am Rhein.
Wainwright, G.A. 1923. The red crown in early prehistoric times. *JEA* 9: 26–33.
Wendorf, F.W. (ed.) 1965. *Contributions to the Prehistory of Nubia*. Dallas.
—— 1968. *The Prehistory of Nubia*. 2 vols. Dallas.
—— and Hassan, F. 1980. Holocene ecology and prehistory of the Egyptian Nile. In M.A.J. Williams and H. Faure (eds), *The Sahara and the Nile: Quaternary Environment and Prehistoric Occupation in Northern Africa*, Rotterdam, pp. 407–19.
—— and Schild, R. (eds) 1976. *Prehistory of the Nile Valley*. New York.
—— and —— 1980. *Prehistory of Eastern Sahara*. New York.
——, —— and Close, A.E. (eds) 1980. *Loaves and Fishes: the Prehistory of Wadi Kubbaniya*. Dallas.
——, —— and —— (eds) 1984. *Cattle Keepers of the Eastern Sahara. The Neolithic of Bir Kiseiba*, Dallas.
——, —— and —— (eds) 1989. *The Prehistory of Wadi Kubbaniya, III: Late Palaeolithic Archaeology*. Dallas.
——, —— and Haas, H. 1979. A new radiocarbon chronology for prehistoric sites in Nubia. *JFA* 6/2: 219–23.
Wenke, R. and Casini, M. 1989. The Epipalaeolithic-Neolithic transition in Egypt's Fayum depression. In L. Krzyzaniak and M. Kobusiewicz (eds), *Late Prehistory of the Nile Basin and the Sahara*. Poznan, pp. 139–56.
Werner, W., Dreyer, G., Jaritz, H., Krekeler, A., Lindeman, J., Pilgrim, C., Seidlmayer, S. and Ziermann, M. 1988. Stadt und Tempel Elephantine. *MDAIK* 44: 135–82.
Wetterstrom, W. 1980. Early agriculture in Upper Egypt: a note on palaeoethnobotanical studies at Predynastic sites in the Naqada area. *BAIEPE* 2: 20–32.
—— 1996. L'apparition de l'agriculture en Egypte. *AN* 6: 53–77.
Wildung, D. 1969. *Die Rolle ägyptischer Könige im Bewusstsein ihrer Nachwelt*. Berlin.
—— 1984. Terminal prehistory of the Nile delta: theses. In L. Krzyzaniak and M. Kobusiewicz (eds), *Origins and Early Development of Food-Producing Cultures in North-Eastern Africa*. Poznan, pp. 265–9.
Williams, B. 1982. Notes on prehistoric cache fields of Lower Egyptian tradition at Sedment. *JNES* 41/3: 213–21.
—— 1986. *The A-Group Royal Cemetery at Qustul: Cemetery L*. Chicago.
—— 1988. *Decorated Pottery and the Art of Naqada III*. Munich.
Williams, M.A.J. and Adamson, D.A. (eds) 1982. *A Land Between Two Niles, Quaternary Geology and Biology of the Central Sudan*. Rotterdam.
—— and Faure, H. (eds) 1980. *The Sahara and the Nile: Quaternary Environ-*

ment and Prehistoric Occupation in Northern Africa. Rotterdam.

Winkler, H. 1938–9. *Rock Drawings of Southern Upper Egypt*. 2 vols. London.

Wright, G.E. 1937. *The Pottery of Palestine from the Earliest Times to the End of the Bronze Age*. New Haven.

Wunderlich, J., von der Way, T. and Schmidt, K. 1989. Neue Fundstellen der ButoMaadi-Kultur bei Ezbet el-Qerdahi. *MDAIK* 45: 309–18.

Yoyotte, J. and Chuvin, P. 1983. Le Delta du Nil au temps des Pharaons. *L'Histoire* 54: 52–62.

Zarattini, I. 1983. The hypothesis of the Saharian-Sudanese unity. *Origini* 12: 252–71.

Zarins, J. 1989. Ancient Egypt and the Red Sea trade: the case for obsidian in the Predynastic and archaic periods. In A. Leonard Jr. and B. Beyer (eds), *Essays in Ancient Civilization Presented to Helen J. Kantor*. Chicago, pp. 339–68.

Index

Tushka, 56, 65, 89
Tutundzic, S., 161
Two-dog Palette, 240–1
Tykot, R.H., 237
typologies, age of, 7

Ucko, Peter, 81, 175, 176
Uganda, 33
Umm el-Dadadib, 91
Umm Direiwa, 129, 133
Umm el-Qa'ab, 205
UNESCO, 6
unification process, xiii, 5–6, 9–10,
    237–8, 246–7, 249
Unio shells, 52, 55, 218
Upper Capsian, 66
Upper Palaeolithic, 4, 44–66
    blade industries, 42–3, 44–7, 59–60
    grains at Wadi Kubbaniya, 29, 35
    Nazlet Khater 4, 42
    el-Tarif, 124
urbanization, 118, 198
*Urgeschichte und älteste Religion der
    Ägypter*, 5
Urschicht, 109–11, 112, 113, 118
Uruk, 219, 239
Uweinat Oasis, 20, 151

Vala, F., 84
Valbelle, D., 225
Van Neer, W., 53, 58, 99
Van Peer, P., 39, 42, 46, 51, 55, 57
Vandier, Jacques, 104, 114, 116, 171,
    179, 189, 190, 191, 205, 211
vases, 84, 121
Vercoutter, Jean, 248, 249, 251
Vermeersch, Pierre, 8, 25, 32, 36, 39
    Arab el-Sahaba, 55
    earliest human skeleton, 37
    Elkab, 80, 81
    Halfan transition, 45
    Idfuan sites, 46, 51
    Makhadma sites, 57
    Mechtoid, 66
    Nag Ahmed el-Kalif, 26, 30
    Nazlet Khater 4, 42
    Nubian Middle Palaeolithic, 39
    Shuwikhat, 45
    Silsilian, 55
    Sodmein cave, 99
    Wadi Kubbaniya, 52
vetch, 185
Victoria Lake, 16
Vienna West Delta Expedition, 108
Vignard, E., 4, 7, 48, 49, 50, 56, 253

Vikentief, V., 248
von den Driesch, Angela, 111
von der Way, Thomas, 218
Vultures Palette, 209, 242, 243

el-Wad points, 61
Wadi Abu Had, 163
Wadi Akarit, 41
Wadi el-Akhdar, 149
Wadi Arabah, 161, 214
Wadi Bakht, 148–9
Wadi Digla, 210, 216, 220
Wadi Feinan, 161
Wadi Gash, 182–3
Wadi Gazza, 213
Wadi Gulan, 162
Wadi Halfa, 26, 33, 44, 47–8, 50, 55–6,
    63, 98, 142–4
Wadi Hammamat, 21, 152, 163, 192
Wadi Hellal, 80, 81
Wadi Howar, 147, 150
Wadi Kubbaniya, 35–6, 51–4, 148
    Afian, 55
    Amratian, 170
    Aterian, 38
    food storage, 53–4, 59
    fossilized skeleton, 65
    grain species, 29
    thermoluminescence dating, 40, 41
Wadi Mushabi, 62
Wadi Quderat, 27
Wadi Shait, 54
Wadi Shaw, 150
Wadi T'mila, 37
Wadjyt, 205, 218
Wainwright, Geoffrey, 182
warthogs
    Acheulean, 28
    Bir Sahara-Bir Tarfawi, 40
    el-Kadada, 229
    Khartoum Mesolithic, 92
    Saggai, 94
    Shabona, 97
Way, Thomas von der, 8
weaving, 115
wedge-core, 48
wells, Nabta Playa, 76
Wendorf, Fred, 7, 25, 29, 32, 151
    Acheulean, 27
    Afian, 55
    Ballana region, 50, 54
    el-Beid, 73
    Bir Kiseiba, 74, 75
    Dibeira West, 77, 79
    Esna-Edfu, 45, 54, 55

Lightning Source UK Ltd.
Milton Keynes UK
UKOW06f1417060315

247391UK00002B/75/P